Fighting at Sea in the Eighteenth Century

The Art of Sailing Warfare

Fighting at Sea in the Eighteenth Century

The Art of Sailing Warfare

Sam Willis

THE BOYDELL PRESS

First published 2008
The Boydell Press, Woodbridge
Reprinted 2009, 2010, 2011, 2012, 2013

ISBN 978-1-84383-367-3

The Boydell Press is an imprint of Boydell & Brewer Ltd
PO Box 9, Woodbridge, Suffolk IP12 3DF, UK
and of Boydell & Brewer Inc.
668 Mt Hope Avenue, Rochester, NY 14620, USA
website: www.boydellandbrewer.com

A CIP record for this book is available
from the British Library

This publication is printed on acid-free paper

Designed and typeset in ITC Bodoni Twelve and Seventy Two by
David Roberts, Pershore, Worcestershire

Printed in Great Britain by
CPI (Group) UK Ltd, Croydon CR0 4YY

Contents

Illustrations

Still for Tors

Preface

Some years ago now the challenge of writing a history of sailing warfare that was faithful to the practical realities of life at sea in the eighteenth century was brought to my attention; the subsequent research, which started at sea before moving to the archives and museums, has resulted in this series of essays. They are designed to provide a thematic interpretation of fighting at sea, and they follow a very rough chronological narrative of two ships or fleets meeting, through chase and escape, and their manœuvring for position to engagement, and so on to the aftermath of battle. This book is not a narrative of any one action or even a series of battles. Quite to the contrary and quite deliberately, it has abandoned the cosiness of such a conservative approach for one which allows a greater penetration of the subject matter. The subject of fighting at sea in the age of sail has long lain dormant, and I hope that by providing fresh perspectives and alternative narratives this book will generate new discussion. Areas of investigation that have been closed must be reopened; new subjects must be explored; new approaches considered. Debate of the nature and development of fighting tactics must, once again, flourish.

There has been much to cover, and certain subjects do not feature in this book. I do not, for example, cover the practicalities of the immediate aftermath of battle in which seamanship skills were tested in a different way from in the heat of battle, nor have I been able to cover certain specifics, like fighting at anchor. The book is also focused on the experience of the Royal Navy, at the expense of others.

The thematic approach certainly raises its own problems, not least the frequent need to refer to a number of naval battles that took place throughout the century. To ease the reader through such references, the general background detail to the most important actions is presented in an appendix. A major purpose of this book is to open up a previously closed world to a wider readership; this inevitably requires the use of many technical terms. These are explained in a glossary.

Maritime historians are all too aware of the difficulties and rewards of their profession, and there is a healthy network of support for those seeking to enter it; we are, after all, in the same boat. The man responsible for bringing my attention to this subject was Professor Nicholas Rodger, who has guided me with a generous and steady hand throughout. Dr Michael Duffy has also been there from the start. Many others have made an important impact on my work for their general support, detailed advice, raised eyebrows, impatient coughs and selective deafness. I must thank in particular Professor Roger Knight, Dr Colin White, Mr Peter Sowden, Mr Andrew Bond, my grandfather Commander Derek

Willis, who read this through numerous times in draft, and the staff of the NMM, British Library and National Archives. The Phillip Nicholas Trust was very generous at an early stage in my career. Mr Roger Brien and Mr James Turner were indispensable for providing entertainment (of sorts) in the long days of writing. Jamie Whyte is the artist responsible for the beautiful illustrations and maps; I owe him a great debt. Last in this list but first in my heart is Torsy, whom I must thank for everything; without her this book could never have been written.

It would be impossible to write such a complex book without making a number of mistakes. Some of those have come to light already, and many others no doubt will do so in the course of this book's life. All of those mistakes are my own.

Sam Willis
Trafalgar Place, July 2007

Abbreviations

Add. Ins.	Additional Instructions
BL	British Library
Ins.	Instructions
MM	*Mariner's Mirror*
NMM	National Maritime Museum
NRS	Navy Records Society
TNA	The National Archives

Maps

All the maps were drawn by Jamie Whyte.

THE ATLANTIC

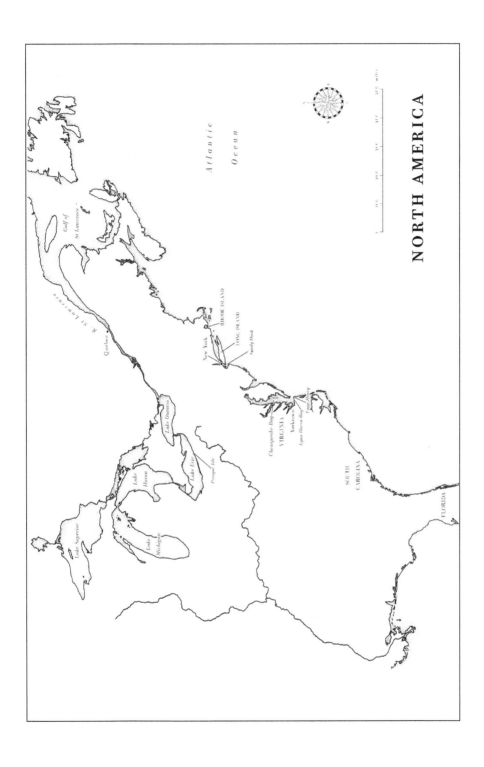

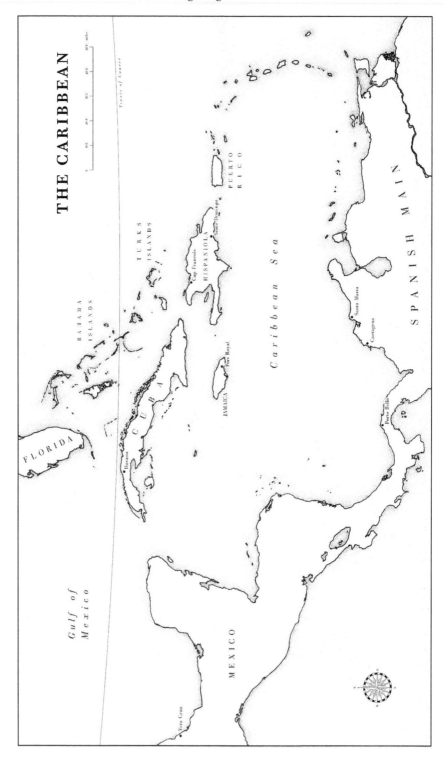

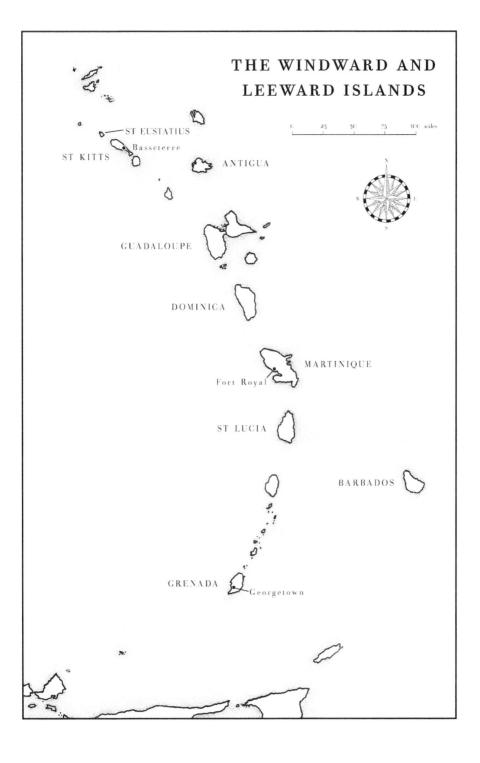

THE WINDWARD AND
LEEWARD ISLANDS

ST EUSTATIUS
Basseterre
ST KITTS
ANTIGUA

GUADALOUPE

DOMINICA

MARTINIQUE
Fort Royal

ST LUCIA

BARBADOS

GRENADA
Georgetown

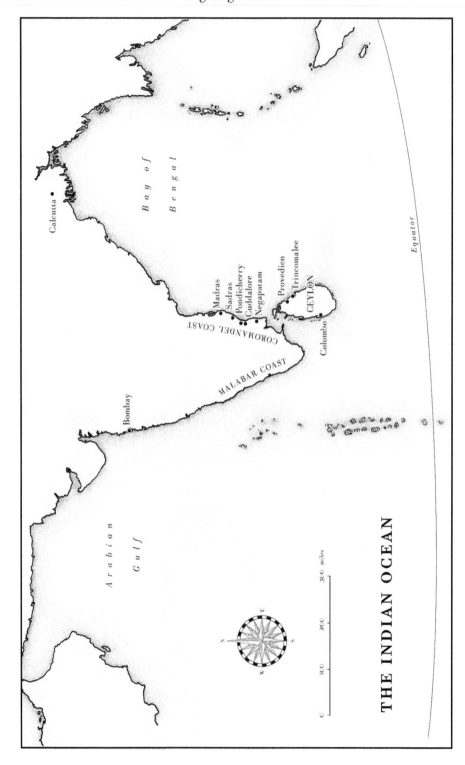

THE INDIAN OCEAN

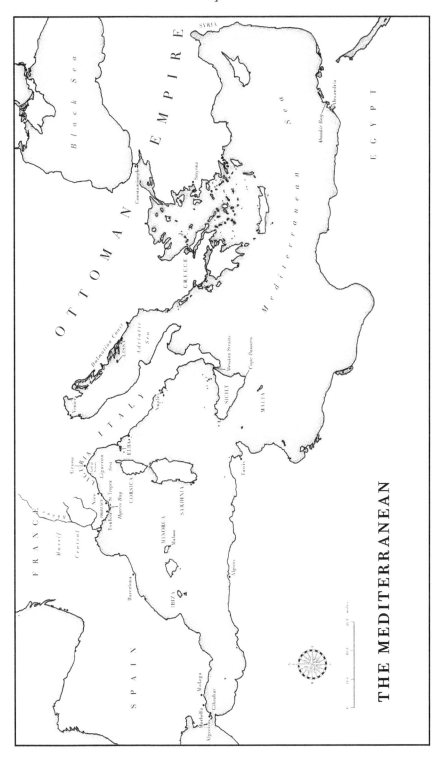

THE MEDITERRANEAN

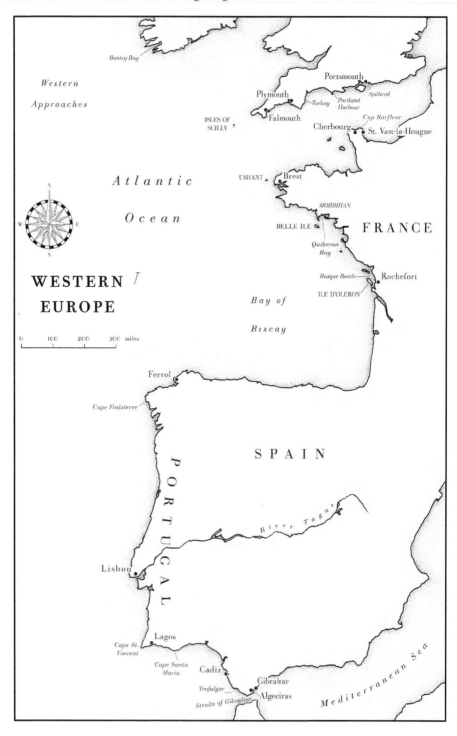

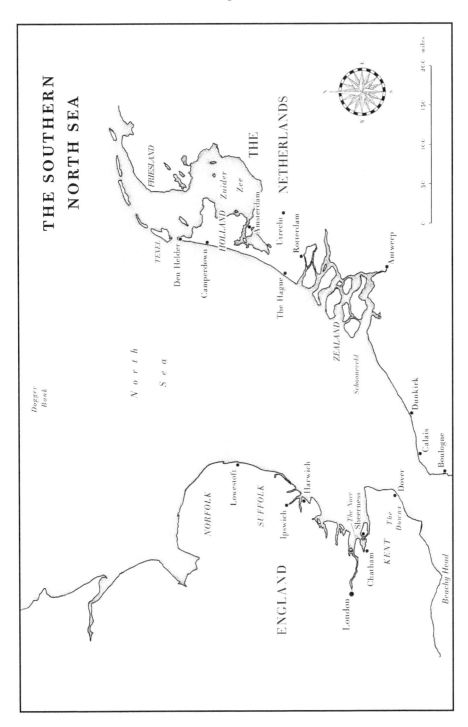

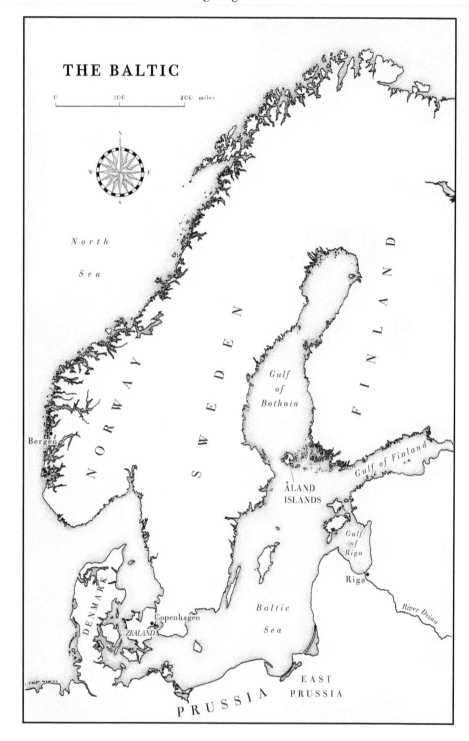

THE BALTIC

0   100   200 miles

North

Sea

N O R W A Y

S W E D E N

F I N L A N D

Gulf
of
Bothnia

Gulf of Finland

Bergen

ÅLAND
ISLANDS

Gulf
of
Riga

DENMARK

ZEALAND

Copenhagen

Baltic

Sea

Riga

River Dvina

P R U S S I A

EAST
PRUSSIA

Introduction

In *The Tempest* William Shakespeare was responsible for the greatest stage direction ever penned: 'Enter mariners, wet.' Shakespeare's audience was discerning. They expected authenticity and accuracy in the portrayal of the maritime world, and would not be insulted by anything as improbable as a dry mariner in a storm. Very little has changed since, and an ever-increasing body of fine scholarly literature portrays our maritime past with an impressive degree of accuracy. For those who like more flesh on the bones of their story, a fine and continuing tradition of naval fiction exists which has translated well to television and film. Many of these authors of fiction are familiar with much of the scholarly historiography, and all of them owe a great deal to the grandfather of naval fiction, Frederick Marryatt, who served in the navy for twenty-four years between 1806 and 1830. Although his works are fictional, there is little reason to doubt their technical detail and it is immediately obvious to any reader that the strength of his stories lies in his intimate knowledge of the ships and men about which he writes. The best modern authors of naval fiction have learned that lesson.

For those who seek to experience their subject in more than books or film, a handful of ships from that era survive in varying conditions, and in maritime museums throughout the world lie important collections of artefacts that relate to men of war. Maritime archaeologists continue to discover more, and conservators are becoming increasingly skilled at the preservation of these ships and their material culture. In most cases public and private support somehow match the daunting financial challenge posed by its preservation, and these important collections will only grow for future generations to enjoy.

With such an established tradition of scholarly research backed, and in many respects driven, by public and commercial interests in sailing warfare, one may be forgiven for thinking that we know more about how sailing warships of the eighteenth century were fought and how battles were won or lost than we actually do, but the reality of the situation is far less encouraging. There is indeed much that we do not know, and much of what we do know is unsafe. This is a bold claim, and it is not designed in any way to denigrate those historians who have laid the foundation for this work. No one can begin to investigate sailing warfare without being immediately and profoundly impressed by the depth and width of the extant scholarship. There are reference works on ship construction, guns and gun founding, rigging, shiphandling, signals and instructions, tactics, command, the infrastructure and development of contemporary navies which have made this work possible.

The numerous issues tackled in this book can be reduced to a deceptively simple problem. Sailing warfare is a practical subject, and to retain any accuracy the historian must think about it in a practical way: his work must reflect the kinetic, bruising, and unpredictable nature of warfare at sea in the eighteenth century. This is the challenge that historians of sailing warfare have always been faced with, and there has been a growing acknowledgement that it must be met.[1] The extent to which it has been remains limited, however, and there are two main reasons for this.

The first is that to write about sailing warfare, one must first master its language. One must know a spritsail from a studdingsail, a topsail from topgallant sail, and a bowsprit from a jib-boom. But this is far from easy. In his memoirs Commander James Gardner recalled an anecdote concerning an eccentric seaman named Billy Culmer of the *Barfleur*. Culmer travelled to London for his lieutenant's exam in 1790, and when brought in front of the Navy Board he cheekily asked the commissioners the meaning of the word 'azimuth', telling them that 'he could never find any *wa wa* that knew a word about it.'[2] It appears that Gardner found this anecdote amusing for its tongue-in-cheek honesty: Culmer used the formal condition of interview to feign or confess ignorance of a peculiar-looking and -sounding word, but one that was central to the skill of the very profession for which he was being examined. It is a clear reminder that then, as now, the art of the sailor was at once protected and defined by its own language, and then, as now, the complexity of that language was often baffling, even a source of amusement to the sailors themselves. It is enough to send a shiver up any historian's spine. What hope have we as alien observers of this distant culture that could puzzle those even at its heart?

The second reason for our inability to understand the practical reality of fighting at sea is the continued use of contemporary sources that are not themselves rooted in those practical realities. There are two main culprits here: contemporary treatises on naval tactics and the Fighting Instructions. In both examples, many specimens survive. They are often lavishly illustrated, beautifully presented and many are well preserved. Somewhat inevitably historians have been drawn to them like moths to a flame. All works on fighting at sea are heavily influenced by both these sources, and some rely entirely on one or the other.[3] To understand their flaws, it is necessary to consider each separately.

THE FIGHTING INSTRUCTIONS

The Fighting Instructions are well named. They are lists of instructions from an admiral to his fleet captains that explain what is meant by a particular signal made in battle. Thus, the very first instruction in Edward Russell's Fighting Instructions of 1691 reads:

I. When the Admiral would have the fleet draw into a line of battle, one ship ahead of another (according to the method given to each captain) he will hoist a union flag at the mizzen peak, and fire a gun; and every flagship in the fleet is to make the same signal.[4]

A focus on the Fighting Instructions and signal books has necessarily led to a concentration by historians of eighteenth-century sailing warfare on the nature and development of the command system, and for years there was a tendency to over-emphasise the rigidity of that system. Primarily responsible were those early historians of the navy who wrote in the late nineteenth and early twentieth centuries with an agenda of studying the past to illustrate strategic, tactical and command principles for their contemporary navies, and to stimulate discussion on aspects of contemporary professional interest.[5] With such an agenda, a certain degree of bias was influential in their writing. The most prominent concerning command and command efficiency was a fear of restrictive dogma. Such a fear is common to all armed forces.[6] It is born of an inherent conflict: tactical systems must be rooted in experience, but they must also look to the future. The concern of being caught unprepared, whether by a magnificent new weapon or a new tactic, ensures that armed forces must continually strive for innovation. For the earliest historians of the eighteenth-century Navy, this led directly to a witch-hunt for restrictive dogma in all aspects of fleet operations. Disasters had to be attributed to it, and successes to reaction against it, and there was a good deal of evidence to flatter their prejudices.[7]

Such severe interpretations have gradually been eased,[8] but there still remain a number of problems with our understanding of command in practice as it stems almost entirely from the Fighting Instructions. They have, for example, never been put into any sort of context regarding other methods of communication between a commander and his subordinates or notions of professionalism and duty: we have been led to believe that subordinates acted unthinkingly in relation to the receipt of signals or instructions, and nothing else. This is certainly unrealistic. In practice, contemporary courts martial for conduct in battle judged innocence or guilt according to a broader concept of duty, and obedience to specific instruction constituted only a fraction of the evidence used at those trials.[9] To retain any accuracy, therefore, our approach needs to mirror that of the contemporaries we study; we need to consider the signals and Fighting Instructions as just one ingredient of that body of knowledge that influenced subordinate behaviour, and not as the whole embodiment of it.

CONTEMPORARY TREATISES

The other main focus of modern historians has been on contemporary treatises on naval tactics. From the late seventeenth century the study of fighting tactics established itself as a significant intellectual tradition. Père Paul Hoste set the precedent with his widely acclaimed *L'Art des armées navales* (Lyon, 1697), which was followed in the second half of the eighteenth century by a spate of similar works: Bigot de Morogues's *Tactique navale* (Paris, 1763); Bourdé de Villehuet's *Le Manœuvrier* (Paris, 1769); le vicomte de Grenier's *L'Art de la guerre sur mer* (Paris, 1787); and the Scotsman John Clerk's *An Essay on Naval Tactics* (London, 1797).[10]

It has, however, been made quite clear recently that there was a wide gulf between tactical theory and tactical practice.[11] Hoste, for example, the author upon whose work all later authors heavily rely, had spent nearly twelve years at sea with the admirals le comte d'Estrées and le comte de Tourville, and the Général des Galères le duc de Vivonne et Montmarte. He had also witnessed fleet battle at first hand, being present at the battles of Beachy Head (1690) and Cape Barfleur (1692). Crucially, however, he was not a professional naval officer but a chaplain. His primary interests were in science, mathematics and astrology, and he died aged only forty-seven as Professor of Mathematics at the Royal Seminary at Toulon.[12] Most significantly, he died in 1700, three years after publishing his work on naval tactics. His experience of sailing warfare was restricted to the cumbersome ships and fleets of the last quarter of the seventeenth century, when the line of battle itself was a relatively new concept. The eighteenth century brought with it much improvement in ship and fleet capability through design improvements in hull and rig, not least the replacement of the whipstaff with the wheel, deeper understanding of the practical problems of fleet performance and capability, and a greater sophistication of both practical skill and theoretical philosophy: Hoste knew a different age from that which modern writers have used his writings to illustrate and explain.

The motive of Hoste's writing was also far removed from modern standards of historical observation and research. His intention was to write a text to promote the intellectual study of sailing tactics. As a man with the intellectual aspirations and principles of the Enlightenment, his goal was to analyse and describe the natural world according to precise scientific method.[13] He believed that without knowledge and without order, everything depended on caprice and chance,[14] and he sought to apply this philosophy to naval warfare. Through detailed but speculative argument demonstrated through complex geometrical patterns and shapes, Hoste explained how naval warfare could be understood and explained. In doing so, he was always careful to promote the numerous tactical ideas of his patron, Admiral Tourville.

To act as a solid foundation for his highly theoretical arguments, Hoste, much like modern historians of naval warfare, needed a formulaic 'key' of easily digestible facts regarding ship and fleet sailing capability from which he could logically expand. Without such a key, his arguments would neither make sense, nor be easily explained according to clear and demonstrable principles. This would be quite contrary to his avowed intention of creating a system of naval evolutions that were '... so simple, and that without presuming any knowledge of geometry, that a little application, with practice, will suffice to render their use familiar to the dullest comprehension'.[15]

The haphazard reality of tactics in practice and the relative variation in ship and fleet capability that characterised actual performance could have no place in such a work, and would have made his theorising all but impossible. He settled, therefore, on a simple and uncompromising understanding of sailing capability that bore little relation to reality, and, crucially for modern historians, his approach was mirrored – and in many instances copied verbatim – in the works of those who followed him. Indeed, in his introduction to *L'Art de la guerre sur mer* (Paris, 1787), the viscomte de Grenier is explicit that his tactics should never be practised, and he further adds that the works of Hoste, Bigot de Morogues and the chevalier du Pavillon's *Tactique navale* (Versailles, 1773) 'are of no service than to teach the manner of ranging the ships for battle'.[16] These sources must not be used blindly to illustrate naval tactics, therefore, as they bore little relation to reality. Because they cover a subject that so few understand in any depth, however, many historians have done just that, mistaking confident for accurate prose.

UNCONSIDERED QUESTIONS

With historians of sailing warfare concentrating so hard on the Fighting Instructions and contemporary treatises as the only two major bodies of evidence available to them, subjects highly significant to battle which are not mentioned in these sources have been consistently overlooked. We do not know, for example, how two or more ships recognised each other as friend or foe upon initial contact. How did a captain decide if he was to fight or to flee? What, moreover, were the tactics used in chase and escape? How did the signalling system actually work in battle? How did ships maintain station in a fleet? How did position in relation to the wind really affect tactics? What impact did certain types of damage have on a ship's or fleet's capability, and how did they influence tactics and the outcome of battle?

In the absence of a consideration of such questions, the intricate three-dimensional business of fighting at sea has been reduced to a sterile one-dimensional narrative cleansed of its complexity. If, as one anonymous contemporary commented, 'the way of making war at different ages is as much a fashion as that of our apparel',[17] one could say that we currently know a little about the hat and the overcoat, but nothing of what was worn underneath, and still less of the process of dressing. The problem is best summed up by the most frequently quoted of contemporary theoretical writers on naval tactics, John Clerk. It was Clerk, a civilian with no formal connection with the navy, or, indeed, with anything maritime, who roundly declared in his 1797 *Essay on Naval Tactics*:

> That the face of the ocean, considering it as a field for military operations, but more particularly as a field for immediate engagement, the hostile fleets opposed, having neither rivers, ravines, banks, woods, or mountains, to stop progress, or interrupt the fight, so that ambuscades or stratagems can be formed, and while each are extended in line of battle, where every individual ship, and the line into which she belongs, is operated upon by the same wind, at the same time, and by the laws of mechanism, confined to movements in every respect consonant in relation to each other, should not every occurrence, every transaction, for these reasons, and in such circumstances, be the more easily conceived, understood, and explained, than even in military operations on land?[18]

Clerk poses a rhetorical question, but the answer must surely be 'no'. In fact the whole point about the inadequacy of our understanding of sailing warfare is that it is *not* easily conceived, understood or explained. Indeed, Clerk's argument raised the ire of Captain Graham Moore, a frigate captain with an excellent reputation, who declared Clerk's belief that command of a fleet required inferior talents to those which were requisite for the general of an army 'was an argument not worth entering'.[19] The future Rear-Admiral Leake asked himself a similar rhetorical question after the Battle of Malaga in 1704, but with a lifetime of experience of the sea and a poetic capacity for understatement, he remarked 'there is surely some skill in sea as well as land actions'.[20] There certainly was, and in a series of thematic chapters, starting with initial contact and ending with the impact of damage, this book will set out to explain how and why.

CHAPTER I

Contact

If e'er I saw wood and canvas put together before in the shape of a ship, that there is one of John Bull's bellowing calves of the ocean, and not less than a forty-four gunner.[1]

Any sea fight necessarily began with the meeting of two ships or fleets. It was a critical time: it tested the seamanship and decision-making skills of the officers, dictated the tactics that would be most effective, and provided opportunities for tactical advantage to be won or lost. It was also a particularly delicate situation for the captains concerned. A captain needed to exercise prudence to prevent a potential enemy from taking advantage of any inaction on his part, and also to avoid assaulting friends and countrymen. Hundreds of lives, great wealth, and personal and professional reputations were all at stake. To compound matters, it is equally clear that the identification of friend or foe was not straightforward. To be good at it required experience and skill, intuition and judgement. One contemporary with considerable personal experience of the navy and of combat believed that there was in fact 'no situation perhaps more difficult and demanding so much caution as the occasional meeting with a doubtful ship.'[2]

NATIONALITY

The physical characteristics of a ship could offer important clues to her nationality, and their interpretation became a science in its own right. Upon initial contact this job fell to the signalman. The lookouts would report a sighting, and the signalman would climb aloft, armed with a looking glass.[3]

Hull form was a common tell-tale. Thomas Pasley, then captain of the *Glasgow* escorting a fleet of merchantmen back from Jamaica in the summer of 1778, professed to be able to identify every one of the forty-seven ships in his charge if he was only near enough to see their hulls, though unsurprisingly such an ability was achieved 'through unwearied attention ... and at the expense of my eyes'.[4] There were a number of generations of each class of ship designed and built by each shipbuilding nation, each with their own distinguishing features, but as a general rule British warships were shorter than their French equivalents, which in consequence had more guns per tier. The British warships, being shorter, tended to have more freeboard. Those of the 1780s were well known for carrying more and larger gun ports along their upperworks to house the carronades, a short-range cannon adopted by the British in 1779 and unique to the Royal Navy for more than twenty years. Very large eighty-gun

two-deckers were characteristically French, whereas Dutch warships were traditionally small for their class. Height of the poop, shape of the head and design
of the bowsprit were other distinguishing features. Spanish ships in particular
were known for their foreshortened beak-heads.[5]

The shape and decoration of the stern and quarter galleries was also important. The horseshoe shape, for example, was characteristically French, and
Spanish ships were known for their almost vertical sterns. One of the most
obvious differences between national styles was the form taken by the lower
finishing (sometimes called the 'drop') of the quarter gallery. On French and
Spanish ships this took the form of a forward sweeping volute (Fig. 1), but in
English vessels the design was conical (Fig. 2). Even the fashion in which the
ship's name was displayed was significant. The French preferred to place it in
small letters, inside a decorative framework or cartouche, while in British ships
of the 1770–80s the name was painted in large letters across the upper counter.
Later on in the century British warships would often remove their names altogether for security reasons.[6]

There were also national characteristics associated with rig construction
and style. Towards the end of the century an equality in the height of the fore
and main topgallant masts suggested a Frenchman, and it was characteristic of
small French brigs to set the channels below the gun ports.[7] The shape of the
sails was another tell-tale. Unfortunately, little information survives regarding
the actual detail of this, but at the court martial which enquired into the loss of

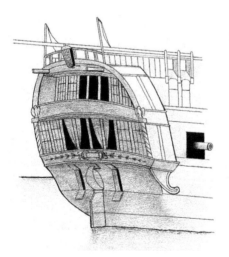
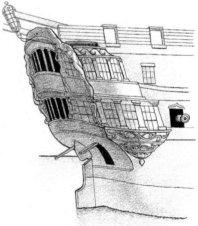

1 The stern of a French warship, with its typical
horseshoe shape. Notice, too, the forward-
sweeping volute at the bottom of the stern
decorations, also characteristic of Spanish
ships.

2 The stern of a British warship, showing
the conical finishing of the stern decoration
in place of the more Continental curled volute.

the *Ardent* in 1779, it was reported that the officers identified a strange fleet as English on the grounds that their sails were 'very square'.[8]

There were, therefore, a large number of distinguishing features, but their analysis was not a panacea in the identification of nationality. Owing to the constant international exchange of vessels through trade and warfare, even a combination of these identification techniques was an unreliable guide to a vessel's nationality. In the above example, the crew of the *Ardent*, once so confident in their identification of the strangers as English warships, were more than a little surprised to find themselves in the midst of the French fleet. In a similar incident, an unfortunate French officer mistook the British fleet for the French in 1782, and carried his dispatches to a rather surprised Rear-Admiral Hood instead of to their intended recipient, the comte de Grasse.[9] One contemporary, writing nearly a century earlier, suggests that this type of confusion had long been happening at sea: 'I have known that divers strange ships have passed through the very midst of a main fleet even at noon day, without any discovery made upon them, or scarce any notice taken of them, until it was too late.'[10]

In an attempt to counter this potential for confusion, private signals were always used, and it was an established custom that the private signal was to be made before a shot was fired.[11] These signals varied widely and were frequently elaborate. George Anson's 'Private Signals by Day' of 22 March 1752 required that:

> When any of the Fleet lose Company And meet again those to Windward shall brail up their Foresail and those to Leeward shall answer by brailing up their Main Sail, then he who made the first Signal, after being answered by the Sail of the other, shall hoist his Ensign, with the Cross downwards at the Mizzen Peak and the other shall answer by hoisting his Jack on the Ensign Staff.[12]

At night a combination of lights, false fires and voices were used. A set of private signals by night from December 1757 required:

> The ships to windward shall show three lights in a triangle at the mizzen peak and two lights of equal height in the mizzen shrouds. The other shall answer by showing three lights in the fore and three in the mizzen shrouds of equal height. Then the ship who made the signal first shall burn three false fires and the other shall answer by burning two. If within hail, he who hails first shall ask: *What ship's that?* The other shall answer: *God Save the King.* The other shall reply: *Halifax.*[13]

Yet the effectiveness of these private signals for the identification of friend or foe was restricted by the problems of visibility that attended any attempt to signal with flag, sail or lantern. A lack of response might indicate an ignorance of the correct response, but it might as easily be caused by the weather being too dark, misty, sunny or foggy for the colours of the signal to be seen, too dark for any signal to be seen at all, or by the canvas blanketing the signal, thus rendering it invisible. Nor was it safe to assume that ignorance of the correct response immediately identified a ship as a foreigner. Private signals were not standard service-wide but were issued to specific squadrons or fleets by the commanding officer and were constantly changed to reduce the likelihood of their discovery. They were also unknown to the entire merchant marine unless they had been specifically issued to a convoy under naval protection, when they would be peculiar only to that convoy and their escort.[14] Ignorance of a private signal therefore only made it more likely that the strange ship was a foreigner; it did not distinguish her as one.

FRIEND OR FOE?

So captains were faced with a formidable problem: there were certain techniques that might hint at the origin of a ship, but none that could be wholly relied upon. Far from creating certainty in the mind of the captain, the value of these techniques lay in creating uncertainty, in encouraging caution. For each captain a fundamental question remained to be answered: Was the stranger welcoming or hostile? Was he friend or foe?

It was a critical but complex question. Not only was nationality hard to ascertain with confidence, but it was also frequently of little help in distinguishing friend from foe. Contact with pirates was always tricky, for then nationality was irrelevant, and on foreign stations it did not necessarily follow that a captain knew which nation he was at war with, or, indeed, if he was at war at all.

The situation in the West Indies in the winter of 1740 is a case in point. The British had been at war with the Spanish for over a year, and Edward Vernon had been appointed to the Jamaica command since July 1739. By November he had taken Porto Bello and razed the fortifications, a fearful blow to Spanish commerce. But the Spanish fleet remained a threat, and their fourteen warships – four more than the British – lay nearby at Havana. Meanwhile Vernon received the troubling news that the French, who had remained neutral in this conflict for some time, had set sail for the Caribbean with twenty-two ships of the line. He had no idea of their intentions and ordered his captains to be particularly on their guard should they meet any of these French ships. He wrote, 'We cannot certainly know the latitude of their orders, and have no reason to apprehend their being in any sort favourable to us.'[15] Vernon was right to be cautious: Vice-Admiral the marquis d'Antin had orders to unite with the Spanish fleet under Don Rodrigo de Torres and launch a surprise attack on Vernon at Jamaica. In such situations the ability to judge hostility was more important than the ability to judge nationality, and at times it was all that mattered. But how was it done?

Contemporary accounts of the preliminary stages of battle suggest that in some way the behaviour and appearance of the strange ship or ships was considered important. When describing in his journal a contact with a strange fleet in March 1797, Bartholomew James (the future rear-admiral) was particularly careful to explain how he was satisfied that they were enemies from their failure to answer the private signal 'as well as from every appearance and manœuvre.' He was right: the strangers were Spanish.[16] This is not a lone example. In the spring of 1805, while cruising between the Isle of Man and Carlisle, Captain Laforey came across two large frigates and a corvette. He wrote in his report back to the Admiralty, 'From their not answering the private signal and their manœuvring they were evidently French.'[17] In September 1806 Captain Larkins of the Indiaman *Warren Hastings* identified a strange sail as an enemy on the grounds of her 'manner of manœuvring, being sensible that an English man of war would not have acted as she did'.[18]

The above is testimony to the ability to identify a foe through appearance and behaviour. It hints at a level of subtlety and sophistication of battle-seamanship that is not traditionally allowed for in the pages of maritime history. It is clear that to the eyes of contemporaries, the way that a ship was sailed could reveal more information of immediate tactical and practical significance than the design of the hull, rig, sails and signals put together. In order to understand how and why this was so, we must first adjust our understanding of sailing warship capability and performance.

The sailing warship was a more flexible craft than we might assume. It had at least twenty sails, and could be sailed with one sail set, all sails set, or any number in between and in any combination (Fig. 3). Each individual sail could then be fully set or partially set, trimmed to catch the wind or trimmed to spill the wind. It could be sailed on twenty of a possible thirty-two points of the compass; only those six points either side of the eye wind were impossible (Fig. 4).

Taken together, this gave any captain a considerable degree of choice and control over how he sailed his ship in both course and speed. But to balance this adaptability was a certain quality of conservatism, stubbornness and rigidity associated with the sailing warship. In spite of its leviathan appearance, the sailing warship was a sensitive beast. To prevent damage and to maximise performance capability, the captain needed to control and manage her carefully. To perform specific manœuvres safely and successfully, certain sail plans were obligatory, certain patterns of behaviour inevitable. The result of this mixture of flexibility and constraint was a certain level of transparency in a ship's behaviour; it was often obvious what her captain was trying to do. The particular technique chosen could then be interpreted to provide an insight to the thought processes and mindset of that ship's captain, betraying a hostile, friendly, or cautious intent.

A change of course upon contact was often the first sign that something was

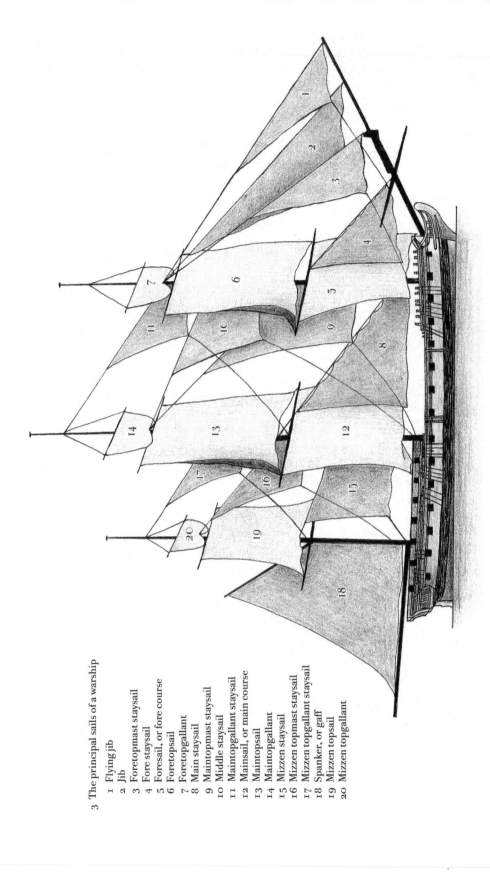

3 The principal sails of a warship

1 Flying jib
2 Jib
3 Foretopmast staysail
4 Fore staysail
5 Foresail, or fore course
6 Foretopsail
7 Foretopgallant
8 Main staysail
9 Maintopmast staysail
10 Middle staysail
11 Maintopgallant staysail
12 Mainsail, or main course
13 Maintopsail
14 Maintopgallant
15 Mizzen staysail
16 Mizzen topmast staysail
17 Mizzen topgallant staysail
18 Spanker, or gaff
19 Mizzen topsail
20 Mizzen topgallant

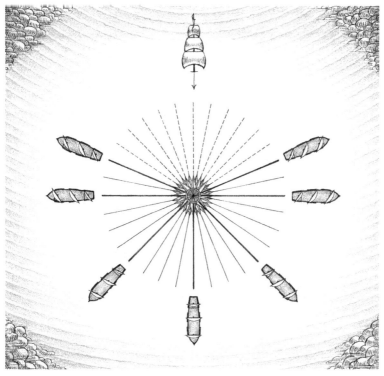

4 The sailing warship could not sail any closer than six points to the wind.

amiss, as it suggested a change in priority.[19] With a stranger in sight, escape might now take precedence over an intended destination, or a ship patrolling for prizes might now chase her quarry. To change course and make sail directly for a stranger was a clear indication of confidence and a warning of potential hostility. It suggested a captain who sought contact, one who was unafraid of combat. On the other hand, to change course but to continue away from the stranger was to suggest a captain intent on escape. Sailing warships each had their own best point of sailing – not necessarily the point at which they sailed fastest – but the point at which their performance was best in relation to other vessels. For example, a ship might sail fastest on a broad reach, but her ability to make ground to windward (albeit at a slower speed) might be her best attribute in comparison with the performance of other vessels. In a chase, this ship was more likely to escape from another if she sailed close-hauled than if she sailed on a broad reach. A ship intent on escape, therefore, would maximise her chances by changing course onto her best available point of sailing. A ship *not* changing course might also be interpreted in a number of ways. It might suggest a captain unaware of a strange vessel nearby or, more dangerously perhaps, a captain who was aware of a strange vessel, but who treated her with contempt.

5 A square sail neatly secured to its yard with gaskets.

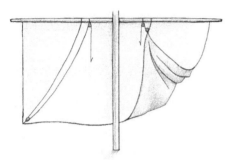

6 The clewline gathered the corner of the sail up towards the yard, near the mast.

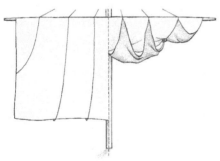

7 The buntlines hung vertically down the sail to its foot and gathered the sail up towards the yard horizontally. Leechlines gathered the edge of the sail – the leech – in towards the yard. The largest sails, the courses, were also rigged with martnets, not shown here.

Choice of sail plan was particularly significant, as the sails were far more than just the engine of the warship. Certain sail plans could be used to create significant advantages in manœuvrability and position while others could not. It was therefore possible to describe a ship as potentially hostile or submissive from her sail plan alone. For example, a captain could reduce the speed of his ship in a number of ways and the method chosen could be interpreted to reveal the aggressive or defensive mindset of that ship's commander.

A captain could reduce the way of his ship by bringing to and furling all her sails, tidily securing them to the yards by the gaskets (Fig. 5). To set sail from this situation would first require men to go aloft and free the gaskets before the sail could then be set from deck. This would be relatively time-consuming. Admiral Latouche-Tréville recorded with pride how his squadron made all sail in fourteen minutes when in chase of Nelson in the summer of 1804.[20] The length of time it would take a ship to get under way, let alone under full sail from this position would therefore suggest a good degree of security in the mindset of the captain: he did not expect to find himself in a situation that required a quick burst of acceleration or any degree of manœuvrability. A ship under this sail plan therefore was still vulnerable. In the words of Admiral Rodney, the only way for a ship to be on her guard was 'to be on easy sail, and ready to make more sail, bear away, or wear as occasion may require'.[21]

Alternatively, a captain could reduce the way of his ship by casting off the sheets and hauling on the clewlines, buntlines and leechlines – these were all ropes that brought the foot or side of the sail up towards the yard to make it easier to furl (Fig. 6 and 7). Thus secured, the sail was neither set nor stowed. It could remain like this for as long as necessary (though it might start to chafe in strong winds), and crucially it could be set quickly from deck without the inconvenience and loss of time incurred in sending people aloft to free the sails from the yards. The crew would simply release the clewlines and buntlines and haul on the sheets. This technique was particularly useful in battle, as it allowed captains to minimise the amount of canvas vulnerable to enemy shot whilst enabling them to set the sails at very short notice to provide bursts of power whenever required.[22] This sail plan therefore suggested a captain with a considerably more cautious mindset than one who had tightly secured his sails to the yards. However, it still required a degree of organisation to set the sails, and, if stationary, also required a certain amount of time to gather momentum to get back under way, regain manœuvrability and hold a course.

A still more cautious captain who wanted to slow down, but was not prepared to take in sail and thereby expose himself to potential disadvantage, would heave-to. A square-rigged ship had the peculiar advantage of being able to impart instantly an exact and opposite force astern to that which drove it ahead by backing the yards of one of the masts, while leaving the other mast with the sails full. Methods of heaving-to varied because either the foremast or the mainmast could be backed, but backing the mainmast seems to have been the commonest method for men of war (Fig. 8).[23] With the rig thus balanced, the backed mainmast forced the ship astern at the same time as the full foremast drove her ahead and the ship was in a state of equilibrium. A sailing ship hove-to was thus not simply in 'neutral' and adrift, but in a state of controlled immobility, a facility peculiar to the square-rigged ship and an advantage not lost on contemporaries.[24]

By heaving-to, therefore, headway could be reduced without the time and manpower required to take in sail, and likewise, no sail had to be set to increase headway from that position. Rather, the speed of the vessel was

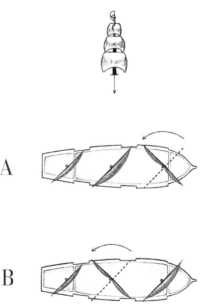

8 A ship could heave-to either by backing the square sails of the foremast (A) or the mainmast (B).

controlled using the braces to catch or spill the wind of the sails as required, the captain using the backed mast as a brake or accelerator pedal. A ship with her maintopsail to the mast still retained steerage way, and so by heaving-to, headway could be reduced in a controlled fashion without actually losing that all-important momentum, a most effective tool for station keeping in fleets and for combat.[25]

If a captain was not even prepared to back the sails on one mast, he could still radically reduce his speed by 'shivering' the sails of one or more masts (Fig. 9). This method of speed control could be practised with more sail set, for the force imparted astern was not as violent as when the sails were fully backed. Headway was reduced, but the ship would still retain a good deal of momentum, and the captain could impart maximum bursts of acceleration simply by bracing the yards around a few points to catch the wind. A ship thus poised in effect adopted a crouching position of controlled aggression from which it could react with power and manoeuvre with precision as the need arose: it was like a cat coiled to spring, ready to react in an instant to changing circumstances. It suggests a nervous or aggressive captain, poised to attack or escape as necessary, and is a far cry from a ship with her sails hanging in the clewlines and buntlines or even hove-to, indicating a secure or submissive mindset like a dog rolled onto its back.

It is also clear that the appearance of a sailing warship could be indicative of intention or mindset in other ways, particularly with regard to aggressive intent. Sir Kenelm Digby wrote of an encounter with a strange ship in the first half of the seventeenth century: 'When we were within a league of meeting, in warelike manner [she] fitted herself for fight.'[26] Over 130 years later, one of Howe's Additional Instructions, issued in the spring of 1762 when in command of a squadron monitoring the French fleet at Rochefort, carried with it the preamble: '... if the appearance of the enemy is deemed such that a general attack upon the squadron is to be apprehended ...'[27]

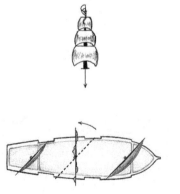

9 The mainmast is 'shivered', the yards aligned with the wind.

To run out the guns with the tompions out so that they showed 'like the teeth of the snarling wolf'[28] is perhaps the best known and most obvious indication of aggressive intent, but there were other lesser-known and equally significant procedures standard before fighting that affected the appearance of a ship. The ship approaching the expectant Digby 'furled up her maine saile [and] brought her spritsaile yard alongst shippes'.[29]

As Digby noted, one potential sign of aggressive intent – or at least the expectation of a fight – was a reduction in sail. The sail area was reduced for a number of reasons. Excessive speed was highly disadvantageous to accurate gunnery.[30] A heavy press of canvas would also cause the ship to heel, which might expose the lowest gun ports to flooding, while burning wads from guns might blow back and set fire to the sails. The courses, being the lowest sails, were the most vulnerable to fire, and it was time-honoured practice to stow them on coming to action, particularly for ships to leeward.[31] Sail was also reduced for ease of manœuvre. With the majority of hands stationed at the guns and a reduced crew working the ship itself, a reduction in the quantity of canvas set would make sail handling, and therefore manœuvre, easier in the heat of battle.[32] The loose-footed courses were stowed to prevent any further confusion on deck, as their large tack blocks, if not the foot of the sail itself, were often at head height when set. The spritsail would invariably be taken in prior to action. Although many captains found them useful for manœuvre, particularly for wearing, they were found frustrating in equal measure by obscuring the view ahead.[33] In a boarding attempt the bowsprit was often used as a makeshift bridge to be run over the enemy's bulwarks, which also required the spritsail to be taken in and the yard secured lengthways under the bowsprit.[34] Finally, to reduce sail was to minimise potential damage in action. Large sails set fore and aft posed a tempting target to a ship alongside, and square sails stood little chance of escaping damage from a raking fire.

Nevertheless, a captain had to keep some canvas set. It was needed to provide drive and manœuvrability, to control speed, and crucially in battle, to ease the roll of the ship. Roll was a major factor in battle because of its effect on gunnery. While it was accepted that a warship would never be motionless in a seaway, a captain could exercise a good degree of control over the type of motion a ship experienced. Ideally, roll would be smooth and slow, and therefore predictable in some measure. This would give the gunners the best chance of finding their target. An easy and controlled roll was also less likely to expose the hull below the waterline to the shot of the enemy. The key to controlling this motion at short notice was the canvas, which was used to dampen the oscillation of the masts, acting in effect as a brake. The equation was simple: the more canvas set, the more resistance there was aloft, and consequently the harder it was for the ship to force its rig through the air, and thus roll. With these requirements in mind, the topsails were always kept set in action. They were a superior choice to the large and cumbersome course sails, as they could be braced about and taken in more easily. For a ship thus working under topsails alone, a headsail (jib) was then necessary to keep her manageable, and was always kept set for action.[35]

To the trained eye there would also be a deal of conspicuous and particular activity on the deck and in the rig of a ship preparing for action. The boats would be hoisted overboard to reduce the likelihood of their being damaged by enemy fire, and to provide more room to fight the guns and to handle the sail. Hammocks, hawsers and even spare clothes were secured above the sides of the ship to provide added protection from bullets and grapeshot. Barricades might also be constructed to provide added protection to the quarterdeck, and often between the mainmast and the taffrail, where many ships were particularly open.[36] Any furniture, boxes or other cargo in the way of the guns was thrown overboard if time was short. In clearing for action before the Battle of Trafalgar the crew of the *Ajax* threw overboard six ladders, ten cot frames, a grinding stone, a set of screens that had formed the walls of cabins, four sails and 30 feet of the copper pipe that was used for the funnel of the galley stove.[37] Nets would be slung above deck level to provide protection from falling rigging and would be secured above the sides of the ship as an obstacle to boarders. Sailors would work quickly aloft to prepare the rig for action by doubling-up particularly important lines (Fig. 10).

THE *AMETHYST* AND THE *WOLVERENE*

The extent to which the behaviour and appearance of a sailing warship was a language or code that could be 'read' to reveal intention, and the subsequent role this had in determining tactics is best illustrated by a contemporary example.

In 1805 two British ships, the eighteen-gun brig-sloop *Wolverene* and the thirty-eight-gun frigate *Amethyst* became embroiled in a situation that tarnished the honour of both captains and of the Navy itself. 'An instance' wrote Captain Smyth of the *Wolverene*, 'I would were buried in oblivion'. They met, mistook each other for enemies and opened fire. Such instances of friendly fire are particularly distasteful and always provoke heated debate; this was no exception. The captains exchanged lengthy correspondence of allegation and self-justification, and explained to each other in detail their motives and reasoning. This dossier of letters offers a rare and colourful insight to the intricacies and subtleties of sea warfare under sail by illustrating how this system of visible intention and 'readable' action might have worked in practice, for the whole incident came about purely from the appearance and behaviour of each ship.

In late November of 1805 both ships were patrolling off the coast of Madeira. The frigate *Amethyst* was hunting for a French privateer, and the brig *Wolverene* had been dispatched from a squadron to search for a convoy. At just after eight in the evening, with variable westerly winds, sailors aboard the *Wolverene* stumbled across a strange sail passing in front of them on the opposite tack. Captain Smyth assumed she was the sternmost ship of the convoy he had been sent in search of, and fired two muskets to order her to bring-to. These were

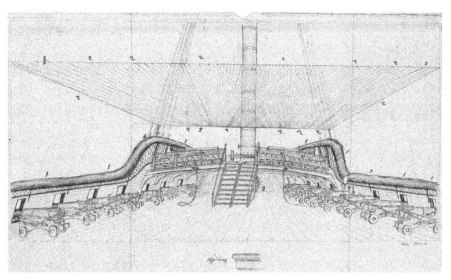

10 The quarterdeck and poop of HMS *Venerable* cleared for action. The temporary partitions dividing the Admiral's cabin into sections have been taken down, and one can now see right through to the windows at the stern. The furniture has also been removed, and all of the guns have been run out. A net has been stretched overhead to protect the men from falling rigging in the heat of battle. The poop ladders have been moved from the sides to the centre of the deck to avoid fouling the guns.

ignored by the stranger, and Smyth ordered two cannon to be fired across her bows.

The officers of the frigate *Amethyst*, meanwhile, were anxious to identify the strange brig on their lee beam. They in turn fired a shot ordering the other vessel to bring-to and made the private signal with a light. The shots were ignored and the signal not returned. The officers aboard the *Wolverene* certainly saw the light, but did not consider it to be a signal. Now close enough to hail, the officers of the *Wolverene* sought to clear up the confusion by word of mouth and repeatedly hailed the stranger. Those aboard the *Amethyst* now became increasingly nervous. To hail in a foreign language was an established deception and such behaviour could not be trusted.[38] There was no escaping that the strange brig had failed to reply to their private signal, and she was clearly a small, handy and fast ship; there was every possibility that this strange brig was the privateer they were hunting, so they hove-to under her lee to prevent any attempt at escape.

Smyth was equally suspicious of the behaviour of the larger ship that would not reply to his hailing and had now hove-to under his lee. He reacted accordingly. He slowed his ship to acknowledge the stranger, but did not allow all headway to be lost. Instead of fully backing the mainsail he kept it shivering to preserve momentum, steerage way and his advantageous position to windward. In this position the ship could be sufficiently slowed to acknowledge the presence of a larger ship, but at a moment's notice the maintopsail could be filled for a burst of acceleration that would give the *Wolverene* the head start she needed to escape her larger adversary. To further assist an escape she kept her topgallants and royals set to make the most of the light airs.

Lying to in this way, the *Wolverene* was coiled to spring, and all of this was clearly visible to Captain Spranger of the *Amethyst*, who was properly lying to with double-reefed topsails and topgallant sails to the mast and her royals furled. The *Wolverene*, with her royals set and maintopsail only shivering, was clear in her intent to take advantage of the hove-to *Amethyst* should she need to escape. This behaviour strongly suggested to Captain Spranger that the *Wolverene* was the privateer he had been hunting, as her behaviour was 'exactly what might have been expected from an enemy discovering her mistake in bearing up'.

In all of this confusion, it was the turn of the *Amethyst* to start acting suspiciously. On assuming that the *Wolverene* was a privateer, Captain Spranger of the *Amethyst*, carrying only low sail in such light airs, was anxious to keep his position to leeward of the *Wolverene* to prevent her escape should she run to leeward. As the *Wolverene* shivered her mainmast, threatening to put on a burst of speed to outmanœuvre the *Amethyst*, the *Amethyst* dropped away to leeward. Captain Smyth saw this move to leeward as hostile, assuming her movement to keep away was with a view to rake the *Wolverene*, and in response hauled up the fore course of the *Wolverene* (to prevent it catching fire) and presented her broadside – a clear act of aggression. The *Amethyst*, a larger and slower ship with less canvas set had no choice but to fire, both to protect herself and to prevent the escape of the *Wolverene*.[39]

TO FIGHT OR TO FLEE?

There were, therefore, numerous ways in which a captain might positively identify a stranger as friend or foe, or at the very least, by which he might gather sufficient information upon which to act. His next challenge was to decide how to act. If the stranger proved to be a friend he might heave-to and share a few words from quarterdeck to quarterdeck through a speaking trumpet, or, if time allowed, he might take a boat across to socialise in more comfort. But if faced with an enemy, a pivotal question remained to be answered: to fight or to flee?

To help make that decision a captain needed to consider the relative sailing and fighting capabilities of the enemy ship in relation to his own. Once again, this could be achieved in impressive detail through analysis of the strange ship's appearance and behaviour. In a contemporary treatise on seamanship, captains were advised to 'Act according to the circumstance and the condition you find yourselves in compared with the appearance of that of the enemy and their motions.'[40] Put into practice, Rear-Admiral Charles Knowles asserted at his court martial in 1748 that he was quite happy to attack a squadron of the enemy that consisted of seven ships (Knowles's squadron numbered five), but if there were any more he could give no answer until he had 'reconnoitred them well.' [41] This ability to 'read' an enemy ship was clearly of great importance: it was the ability to gain an insight to the strengths and weaknesses of the enemy, and such intelligence could be used to great advantage.[42]

The size and strength of an enemy was often magnified by the expectations or fears of the pursuers. To gain a realistic impression of the size and strength of the stranger, was therefore always a priority. For a general impression gained from a distance, mast height and spacing would suggest the size of a ship, as bigger ships could carry taller masts stepped at larger intervals. For a more detailed impression, it was possible to compare various parts of the enemy ship with those of your own. Nathaniel Boteler explains:

> By standing on the poop of your own ship and diligently observing the poop of your enemies ship ... if you can see the horizon circle over the poop of that ship, you may certainly conclude that your ship's poop is higher of board than theirs ... and in this manner you may understand of what height a ship is in any place and part of her by removing yourself from place to place in your own ship and observing the corresponding parts of your enemies ship.[43]

This was of immediate practical significance because of the tactic of boarding. In a fight that was likely to be decided by boarding, any information regarding relative size and proportion was used to plan for the positioning of the ships to maximise the ease of boarding or to minimise the threat of being boarded.[44] A high freeboard would also suggest more gun decks, and therefore more men and more guns.

As the strange ship came closer, gun ports could be counted, but only from a position with an unobstructed view of the stranger's broadside. Ships directly astern of their enemy would be unable to assess strength in this way, a particular problem for those in chase. There are also numerous examples of ships being 'pierced' for a certain number of guns but actually carrying fewer guns, and so the viewer had to remain cautious in his estimation of the enemy's strength.[45] To assess the weight of an enemy's broadside by waiting until the guns had actually been run out was therefore the more reliable, if more hazardous, method.

To assess the relative sailing qualities of the ships was the captain's next priority. The performance of a sailing ship was determined by many factors. Hull design, rig design, seamanship skill, wind, weather and sea conditions all played their part. An equality of performance between two ships was therefore unlikely, and the inevitable disparity in performance was always tactically significant. Large ships, for example, performed well in heavy weather; those with deeper hulls held their wind well; ships of lighter construction sailed fast in light airs; fine bow lines enhanced speed and manœuvre, though with a tendency to pitch into a head sea; fine stern lines made a ship responsive to the helm but vulnerable to being pooped;[46] shorter ships would always retain an advantage in battle over larger ships, being much quicker at tacking and wearing.[47] A ship riding high would sail better large (with the wind on her stern quarter) than on a wind, but a deeply loaded ship would sail better on a wind than large.[48] All of this was valuable information if the captain intended to chase the strange sail or escape from it, as he would gain a clearer idea of where his advantage or disadvantage in sailing performance might lie.

If both ships were on the same point of sail, the captain could then ascertain specific information about the two ships' relative performance on that point of sail by measuring the bearing between them and keeping it monitored. If it remained the same, the performance of both ships was judged to be equal. Otherwise, the rate of change in the bearing would indicate the relative superiority or inferiority of sailing. A fast rate of change would suggest a marked disparity in performance; a slow rate would indicate a near equality.[49]

The detail of a sailing ship's performance would also effectively reveal the skill, experience, training and even the morale of her crew. The observation of the French admiral the comte de Conflans's fleet in Brest Roads in 1759 prior to the Battle of Quiberon Bay is testament to the accuracy and significance of this. During the blockade of Brest in the Seven Years War, Edward Hawke created an inshore squadron commanded by Augustus Hervey. Hervey monitored all motions of the French and otherwise threatened and disrupted enemy shipping, while Hawke patrolled offshore with the main Channel Fleet. In the middle of July 1759 Hervey made a daring run under the guns of the Conquet fort and cut out four merchantmen who were waiting for the tide to allow them access to Brest harbour. While so close in, Hervey was able to see into the harbour itself. The enemy were exercising their crews at setting, furling and working the sails, which Hervey reported back to Hawke, 'they do surprisingly bad indeed'. The evident incompetence of the French convinced him that the rumours of a manning crisis in the French navy were accurate; and so they proved to be. The chevalier de Guébriant, one of Conflans's *chefs d'escadre*, later complained that he had not thirty men aboard the *Orient* 'who deserved the name of seamen', and when the fleet eventually sailed, Guébriant could only negotiate the Goulet by making his officers handle the sails.[50]

In contrast, the British fleet was manned by highly proficient seamen, their skills honed over endless months of blockade duty. Hawke knew that this superiority in seamanship would tell in a fight. On the morning of 20 November 1759, in heavy squalls, the French fleet was sighted inshore of the Belle Isle. It was not until late afternoon that the engagement began, and Hawke's decision to persevere with an attack on a dangerous lee shore, in volatile weather and with night rapidly approaching, was a shrewd and subtle tactical decision:

he put the inexperienced French sailors under extreme pressure, backing his more experienced blockade-hardened squadron to cope to a much greater degree with the appalling conditions. Hawke turned the battle into a seamanship contest that he knew he would win.

A similar confidence was gained prior to the Battle of St Vincent in 1797. The master of Rear-Admiral Parker's flagship the *Prince George* commented after the battle: 'On our closing up so fast with them they attempted to draw upon the larboard tack, I say attempted, because they formed the evolution so ill, that in viewing them with a seaman's eye it was sufficient to inspire us with a confidence of success in spite of the superiority of their numbers.'[51] The impression gained was accurate. De Cordoba's flagship, the *Santisíma Trinidad*, was reported to have only sixty experienced seamen out of a crew of 900.[52]

DECEPTION

An interesting by-product of this idiosyncrasy of sailing warship capability was a magnified emphasis on deception as a tactic. Deception and surprise has always gone hand in hand with any type of warfare, but the quantity and tactical significance of the information that could be gained from the appearance and behaviour of a ship in the age of sail made sea warfare in this period particularly fertile ground for trickery and cunning.

The most basic deception was to disguise the nationality of a vessel. By night a ship might hail a stranger in a foreign language; by day they might run up false colours. A frequently used and well-known deception, to fly false colours, was rarely enough to dupe an enemy, but it would often buy time in a pressure situation. In the summer of 1805 Captain Zachary Mudge identified a ship flying English colours as an impostor from the make and colour of the bunting of their flag, but otherwise it was very difficult to disprove the nationality of a vessel. If a ship persisted in flying a flag that was suspected of being false, the only recourse was to draw alongside and hail, or to send a boarding party to investigate further.[53] Those ships that were marked in their origin by hull or rig design were particularly suited to this work. Captain Maxwell thus used the *Arab* (22) (previously the French *Le Brave* captured in 1798) under American colours to entrap a privateer off Cape Verde in 1805 'being in her hull one of the greatest deceptions in the Navy'.[54]

To fake or otherwise disguise performance capability was another popular deception. Warships could sometimes be identified from their merchant sisters by their style of manœuvring, behaviour, or simply by their speed,[55] and this could be used to deceive. In his log of a journey to the Mediterranean in the first half of the seventeenth century, Sir Kenelm Digby illustrated what such cunning might consist of. After lunch on New Year's Day 1628, a strange sail was spotted running downwind towards them from the direction of Gibraltar. Digby was anxious to lure her on, hoping that she would make a valuable prize. To give the impression of flight, he immediately changed course and stood away from the stranger under all the sail that his ship could bear, but to hinder his way he attached to his stern 'coyled hawsers, a bight of a cable, two filled buttes, and other dragges'.[56]

There is also reason to believe that attempts were made to disguise the size or type of ships. In one instance a great deal of attention was paid to the size and 'neatness' of the rigging as well as the painting of the ships to make them look smaller than they really were. Smaller ships carried smaller masts, which in turn required smaller and fewer ropes to support them. To the casual observer, therefore, a reduction in the backstays would suggest a smaller ship, but it was not without danger. In the fifteen months that this deception was used aboard Sir William Dillon's ship the *Defence* (74), eighteen topmasts were sprung or carried away.[57]

The painting of warships was also distinctive. Before 1780 a warship's sides were protected by varnish but left unpainted, and only their topsides above the channel wales were painted, usually dark blue or red. This changed in 1780 with an order from the Admiralty that allowed captains to paint the sides of their ships.[58] There was no official style, but a yellow side with the topsides picked out in contrasting colours seems to have been preferred. In the early nineteenth century many of those who sailed with Nelson (and later many of those who didn't, and even some captains in foreign navies) painted their ships in his favourite style, the 'Nelson Chequer', with the lines between each gun deck and the lids of the gun ports picked out in black. Picking out the gun ports in this way allowed a single-deck ship to appear as a two-decker by painting on false gun ports.[59] In a similar vein, merchantmen could be painted with gun ports to make them appear larger and stronger than they were (Fig. 11).[60]

The painting of French warships tended to vary, but after the Revolution they favoured red, which was considered 'expressive of their determination to conquer or die in the cause in which they had engaged'.[61] As a general rule the flagships were more lavishly decorated, with rich colours – vermilion, ultramarine or gold leaf – while other ships were painted with colours that used cheap pigments – red ochre, yellow ochre, black and white lead.[62] The masts of ships, particularly line of battle ships, might also be distinguished between nations, as it was customary to paint the 'hoops' of each mast so that in battle, when the smoke obscured the hulls of the combatants, the masts, visible above the smoke might still indicate friend or foe. At the Battle of Trafalgar the French and Spanish ships had black hoops, and the British upon seeing this, painted theirs yellow.[63]

It was, therefore, relatively easy to disguise a warship by painting her in a style not traditionally associated with warships, a deception which Captain

11 The *Atlas*, an armed merchantman painted with extra gun ports to resemble a powerful two-decked line of battle ship.

Graham Moore used to great effect against French cruisers and privateers in the summer of 1799. He painted his frigate, the *Melampus*, entirely black to disguise her as a merchantman.[64] A few years later off the Mediterranean coast, Thomas Cochrane took this deception further, and painted his brig the *Speedy* in exact imitation of a locally known Danish brig, the *Clomer*. He acquired or possibly made some Danish colours, and even employed a Danish quarter-master – fitted out in a Danish officer's uniform – to complete the deception. It proved highly effective, and Cochrane escaped from the clutches of a Span-ish frigate.[65] If there was not sufficient time to paint the ship itself, a painted canvas could be hung over the side which might serve to deceive long enough for the ships to close to engaging distance. The timing of the removal of the painted canvas and the running out of the guns without spooking the 'prey' nevertheless remained problematic.[66]

If a captain was not prepared to disguise *what* he was, he might well dis-guise the condition of his ship or his crew. He might, for example, appear unprepared for battle: In 1779 Douglas had perfected a technique by which he could fire his cannon up to three points before or abaft the beam without run-ning them out, and thus without warning the enemy of his hostile intentions.[67] A captain might also make his ship appear disabled or damaged in some way to lure an enemy within range. A ship could be worked 'as if she were distressed, and lie like a wreck in the sea; she must cast dregs, hogsheads, and other things overboard to hinder her way; she must show no more than an ordinary gang, and haul in her ordnance, and shut her ports.'[68] She could appear short handed and ill disciplined by manœuvring slowly, handling sail inefficiently, or simply by hiding the majority of the crew in the hold.

With a little more preparation the opposite deception was also possible: a short-handed ship could give the impression of being manned by a large and highly disciplined crew. As a very rough deception, cut-out figures of men could be made and put on deck. Alternatively, the gaskets of the sails could be cast off and replaced by a temporary spiral of spunyarn. This yarn would keep the sails secured to the yards but was easily broken by hauling the sheets to set the sails. A ship could thus make sail very quickly without having to send men aloft. At anchor in Basque Roads in 1762, Howe, anticipating a flash attack from the French with fireships, included a specific instruction for his fleet to furl their sails with yarns 'in readiness for being set at the shortest warning'.[69] Cochrane was particularly fond of this technique as a deception and used it to great effect aboard the frigate *Pallas* in the spring of 1806. Short-handed and isolated in the face of three hostile and inquisitive ships, he set all of his sail instantly, suggesting the military precision of a first class and determined crew. The enemy ships fled.[70]

The potential value of deception was great, but there remained some contemporary concerns over the ability of the Englishman to act in such a way. It was advised that 'the Englishman's character, which disdains any thing that can be called foul play ... should, when opposed to an intelligent, cautious and in force generally superior enemy, be retrained by some circumspection.'[71] One can safely assume, however, that such dastardly activities were widely practised. Indeed, this brief survey of the curious relationship between two ships or fleets during the preliminary stages of battle reveals complex and colourful behaviour that was central to success in any sea fight, and to jump straight to the gunfire is to ignore the bristling of feathers, puffing of chests or the cunning disguise of first contact. An intricate dance performed by both parties, this was the time to guess intent and to gauge capability, to probe for weakness and to seek out advantage. The art of the fighting captain in the age of sail demanded analytical and decision-making skills that spliced together the dual strands of tactics and seamanship in a way that was peculiar to the era. The heavily fortified steam warships of a later generation were unreadable masked faces, but in the age of sail there was far more to the sailors' gaze than meets the eye.

CHAPTER 2

Chase and Escape I: Speed and Performance

Send the royal yards up – clear away the studding sails – keep her with the wind just two points abaft the beam, that's her favourite position; and I think we may give the slip to that old-country devil in the course of the night.[1]

Once two ships or fleets had made initial contact, one of two things would then happen: they would prepare to engage, or one would flee and the other would chase. It was rare indeed for two ships or fleets to meet and both be intent on action, and usually the aggressive party in some way had to force action on his enemy. The captains of both ships, therefore, now turned their minds to the question of speed.

As a general rule, the captains of single ships in chase did not need to concern themselves with station keeping or the principles of mutual support in a squadron or convoy, and would set as much sail as their ships could bear in the extant weather conditions. This could take some time. As a rough guide the French Admiral Latouche-Tréville recorded with great pride how his squadron, in chase of Nelson, made all sail in fourteen minutes.[2] It took a particularly long time to set studding sails. These were sails that were set outside the square sails, and required both a boom from which the sail was set, and the sail itself, to be sent aloft and then rigged before they could be set (Fig. 12). For this reason it was not uncommon in light airs for a chasing ship to rig a studding sail boom and prepare the sail for setting in case the chase changed course to one that allowed the studding sails to be set.[3] In light winds a captain could also increase the efficiency of the courses beyond their maximum by adding a bonnet or drabbler, a strip of canvas secured to the foot of the course, a technique which originated in the 1500s but carried through well into the eighteenth century.[4]

Once all sail had been set, extra rigging could be set up to provide the masts and yards with further support which would in turn allow the ship to carry more sail than she normally would in the extant conditions.[5] These extreme measures were only advisable in a steady breeze, however.

12 A warship with her studding sails set.

The rigging could support huge forces if applied steadily, but was not designed to cope with violent or jarring motion: the yards would quickly crack and the lighter spars would simply be carried away.[6]

With all possible sail set, the speed that a ship could attain was now dependent on a number of factors. Each ship had her own best point of sailing. Thus Admiral Pasley recorded with acute disappointment how his ship the *Jupiter* was out-sailed by the *Romney* with the wind right aft, but was prepared to 'answer with his life' that the *Jupiter* would outperform the *Romney* with the wind abeam.[7] A ship with a generally good sailing record might equally perform badly in very specific circumstances. In this way the *Victory* was renowned for carrying her helm a-lee in particular swell and wind conditions.[8] The condition of a ship's bottom was also critical. A ship overgrown with weed and barnacles would perform significantly worse than one that had been freshly scraped. In the same way, a ship with a copper bottom would outperform an uncoppered ship, and a newly coppered ship would outperform one whose copper was old and fouled. As a general rule a ship with a clean bottom would sail as much as 1½ knots faster than a fouled one.[9]

Less well-known factors in determining a ship's speed, but critical in the pressurised conditions of chase, were those techniques of seamanship that could be used by a captain and his crew to exert a measure of control over the speed of their ship. Sailing performance was determined to a large extent by the interdependent relationship between the rudder, sails, trim and stability of the ship. It did not necessarily follow, for example, that a ship with full sails was by definition sailing at her most efficient; nor would a ship necessarily sail faster by setting more sail.[10] The trim of the hull was a crucial factor in this equation. A ship out of trim would yaw excessively. If by the stern, she would tend to fall off; if by the head, continually point up and pitch. She would be hard to manœuvre, sluggish, leewardly, and roll heavily – in all senses she would keep the sea badly. Trim was of sufficient importance that from the 1750s details of stowage and trim were recorded by the dockyards whenever a ship went to sea, and during the American War recommended ballasting plans were drawn up.[11]

The difference between a ship being in trim and out of trim was often marginal; Pasley grumbled that the *Glasgow* was only 2 inches too deep for her proper sailing trim.[12] It was thus possible to affect significantly the performance of a ship through minimal and temporary alterations in stowage. Boscawen tested the performance of his ship to both extremes, from 18 inches by the head to 20 by the stern.[13] For an immediate impression of how changes in stowage would affect the steering and to allow for more immediate and greater subtlety in its calculation, Cochrane used the entire crew of the *Ajax* (74), a weight he estimated at 36 tons, moving them around on deck until the best possible trim was achieved.[14] A more unfortunate crew were made to move fore and aft by their captain with as many shot as they could all carry with them.[15]

In this way a captain could exercise a surprising degree of control over specific performance characteristics of his ship. A ship carrying lee helm could
be corrected by altering the ballast. Empty beer and water casks could be filled
with salt water as the ship became increasingly tender as the stores were con-
sumed.[16] If extreme weather was considered likely, the topmasts would be
struck, as removing weight from aloft lowered the centre of gravity and made
the vessel more stable. Even ships with inherent design flaws could be dealt
with temporarily until the ship could be docked and altered. In this way the *Vic-
tor* (18), notorious for plunging into head seas, was stowed heavily by the stern
until she could be docked and her foremast moved aft,[17] and the over-masted
Hampton Court (64) was made safer by adding extra ballast and reducing the
sails.[18]

In the pressure of chase such subtle alterations were impossible, but significant changes could nevertheless be made, usually by throwing things overboard. Anchors, the ship's launch, cannon, their carriages and shot, spare
masts and yards were all thrown overboard to significant effect.[19] A 32-pounder
gun with its carriage and shot weighed over 3 tons, more for the heavier French
cannon, and even if the cannon were smaller a significant number could be
removed. Rear-Admiral James recalled in his memoirs of March 1797 that being
chased in the little eighteen-gun brig *El Corso* by nine Spanish warships, he
ordered all but two of his eighteen guns and their associated carriages to be
thrown overboard.[20]

The relationship between rig and the rudder was also highly significant in
determining the performance of a sailing warship. Two forces act on a sailing
ship: the action of the wind upon the sails causes her to describe and shape
the course she is to steer, and the action of the water upon the rudder turns
her about, keeping her upon that course. A ship will sail to her best advantage
when these two factors work together in equilibrium, with neither one nor the
other bearing greater strain to keep the ship steady on her desired course. The
advantage of a balanced ship in chase should not be underestimated. An unbalanced ship carrying weather or lee helm posed a considerable practical problem because of the sheer size of the rudder. With the rudder pointing fore and
aft, drag through the water is minimised, allowing for maximum speed.[21] A
ship thus balanced could sail up to a knot faster than one carrying weather or
lee helm.[22] With an average speed of between four and six knots, a ship's speed
could therefore be increased by as much as a quarter through sail trim alone.

To have a balanced ship was also to have advantage in manœuvre. Keeping the rudder fore and aft maximised its efficiency when it was used for manœuvre. A ship carrying two turns of lee helm to maintain her course would
inevitably have a reduced arc of turn to windward. When turning in either
direction more helm was also needed to manœuvre an unbalanced ship, and
this had to be countered by an equal amount of opposite helm to steady the ship

on her way. This excessive helm and over-steering made a ship very hard to control, often causing her to yaw wildly and making her inefficient and imprecise in manœuvre. By contrast, a well-balanced ship could be brought to wind with only small helm, allowing for more control and maximum speed, which in turn made for efficient and effective manœuvre, all of which were critical in a chase.

All of these factors ultimately depended on the quality of the helmsman, however. Continual over-steering would cause a dramatic reduction in speed, and a ship would be likely to roll heavily. On the other hand, a poorly set-up ship could have a measure of control exerted over it by an experienced and alert helmsman. Wind does not blow steadily nor do waves come at regular intervals and sizes, so gusts of wind or larger waves could be pre-empted and reduced in their potency, if not completely countered, by a skilful helmsman.

Helming, however, is not easy, and is entirely different from steering. While the one only requires only sight and reason, the other involves both feeling and intuition. It is a skill that has variously been compared to riding a bicycle or playing the violin.[23] Because helmsmanship was at once both so difficult and so important, a 'good man' would always be sent to the helm in times of pressure such as chase, irrespective of his position on board.[24] Captain Ambrose of the *Rupert* believed his cook to be such a good steersman that he always had him at the helm when in any chase or when likely to come to an engagement.[25]

Sailing performance, therefore, was neither predetermined, uniform nor reliable: too much depended on the ability of each captain to sail his ship to its full potential in the prevailing conditions by what was described as 'artful management'.[26] Captains went to great lengths to realise the potential of their ship, which was both a test of their skill and experience. 'In my chace', wrote Sir Kenelm Digby, 'I tried all the wayes for advantage that I could imagine.'[27] Inevitably captains and crews took a great deal of pride in the sailing qualities and performance of their ships. At his court martial in 1750 Rear-Admiral Knowles was quizzed over the performance of Captain Innes's ship, the *Warwick*, and was particularly asked if he had often heard Captain Innes boast of his ship's sailing. He replied: 'I really don't remember; I have heard most of the captains boast of their ships.'[28] This pride and boasting reflects the significance of skill in determining performance and capability, for the performance of a ship directly reflected the ability of her captain and crew. In the words of Cochrane, the impact of steam 'equalised' seamanship to a great extent,[29] and in doing so changed for ever the nature of warfare at sea. With such a magnified emphasis on human input in sailing performance, diversity in speed was, perhaps, the defining characteristic of both ship and fleet capability in the age of sail.

All of these techniques relied on the presence of wind. In its absence the captain of a galley could turn to his oars. Large-oared warships survived in diminishing numbers until 1800, with France, Spain, Malta, Venice and the Ottoman

Empire maintaining large permanent flotillas in the Mediterranean; Russia and Sweden in the Baltic; and the Americans on the Great Lakes. All these galleys carried sails, but their reliance on muscle power retained their ascendancy over all other craft in calm weather.[30]

In a chase between two becalmed sailing ships both captains would still strive to make any headway they could. This could be done by launching the boats and towing, an exhausting process but one by which a ship might be able to make about a knot in the desired direction. It was also highly dangerous for the men in the boats of the chasing ship, as it would be them, and not the armed ship herself, who would first come within range of the escaping ship. In this scenario the aim of the chasing ship was not to get right up to the chase but to get within gunshot range.[31] If several boats were being used, the heaviest (being the best for towing), was placed closest to the ship, and the others positioned in diminishing order of size further away from the ship. If several boats were used, the crews might take it in turns to allow some rest and maintain a tow for longer periods. In August 1761 the British *Aquilon* (26) was chased in light airs by a French 74, but they escaped by rowing for 26 hours non-stop.[32] The ship being towed might keep all sail set in the hopes of catching any breath of wind, but such a configuration also increased the resistance against which the rowers had to pull.[33] One solution was to furl the sails, but to secure them to the yards by temporary seizings which could be broken from on deck.[34] Otherwise the ship's boats could be used to 'kedge' the ship and maintain some headway. This was extremely hard and slow work. One of the ship's boats would row out ahead of the ship with her anchor. The anchor would then be dropped, and the capstan on the ship hauled, thus dragging the ship forward against her anchor. In 1812 the USS *Constitution* used this method to get away from an English squadron off New York.[35]

SPEED IN FLEETS

Maximising speed in fleets was another matter entirely. The whole purpose of a fleet was to achieve strength in numbers, and that required a certain degree of cohesion. A fleet strung out over miles of ocean posed little collective threat offensively, and could offer little collective resistance defensively; a fleet in close formation, on the other hand, was a fearsome opponent. The basic problem for a fleet in chase, therefore, was that the building blocks of fleet performance, the performance of the individual ships themselves, was neither uniform nor reliable. The frustrations that this could cause are well illustrated by Sir Kenelm Digby:

> Before I did rather outsail my Viceadmirall then lose to her, the rest of
> the day she outsailed me somewhat, which wee attributed to the being

then a lesse wind then before, which hath most power upon least ships,
and that the tide was then against us which had more power upon my
shippe then upon the other, because it did draw four or five foote more
water.[36]

It was axiomatic that no fleet could make the best of each ship's individual
capability, for fear of faster sailers leaving the slower, which in their turn might
impede those further behind.[37] The only way to maintain prescribed intervals
was to sail at a speed which allowed all ships to work together as a unit. The
poor performance of a single ship, sailing 'like a haystack'[38] or a 'sad clog',[39]
could thus lead to the straggling of an entire squadron. The irregular disposi-
tion of Knowles's squadron prior to its engagement with a Spanish fleet in
October 1748 was attributed at the court martial to the bad sailing of the *Warwick* alone,[40] and in 1758 Pocock's fleet was unable to get to windward, specifically because of the poor sailing of the *Cumberland*.[41] In any fleet of sailing ships there would, moreover, always be a 'poorest' ship. Even if a fleet was
made up of ships all of the same class, and they had all been coppered at the
same time, and their copper had deteriorated at the same rate, their performance was still largely dependent on the skill of the crew and the peculiar sailing
characteristics of each ship.

The dilemma facing the fleet commander in chase, therefore, was to go at the
speed of the slowest performer or to sacrifice any hope of cohesion. Sacrificing
cohesion was highly risky: it opened the fleet up to attack and brought with it a
heightened risk of collision. If a fleet was committed to a general chase through
individual action, with each captain free to do exactly as he saw fit to bring
his ship up with the enemy as quickly as possible, the behaviour of each ship
immediately became unpredictable. In fair weather this could be problematic
enough, but if the weather turned foul, chaos was inevitable.

This is exactly what happened to the British fleet in the skirmishes preceding the Battle of the Glorious First of June 1794. On 28 May reconnoitring British frigates signalled to Howe that the French had been sighted. As the French
appeared to be taking avoiding action, Howe signalled a general chase, but the
British fleet was suddenly taken by a violent squall accompanied by thick mist
and rain. Once it had cleared, 'nothing but confusion was visible in our fleet
whilst the enemy's line was in perfect order' wrote William Dillon aboard the
Defence.[42] The difference between the two fleets was that the French, already
set upon a course, had only to continue upon it in the sure knowledge that their
colleagues' speed and direction were approximately conforming with their
own. The British, on the other hand, had no such comforting assurance, as
they were already committed to individual action. The squall threw them into
disarray, and it was lucky indeed for Howe that the French commander, Rear-
Admiral Villaret-Joyeuse, did not take this opportunity to attack.

In a general fleet chase it was also inevitable that the ships that made first contact with the enemy would sustain severe damage. Gunnery was hard and hot work, and the first few broadsides from any ship when the guns and the gunners were fresh were always the most effective. To make matters worse for the chasing fleet, it was important that the leading ship in chase did not stop and engage the rearmost ship of the enemy, but continued her progress up the enemy fleet to avoid congestion as the slower ships in the chasing fleet caught up.[43] The leading ships would therefore receive the first punishing broadsides from every enemy ship that they passed and ran the risk of being isolated and overwhelmed by the enemy fleet. At the First Battle of Finisterre (1747) the four leading ships of the British fleet were mauled by the closely packed French fleet as they overhauled their rear and were all engaged by two or more French ships. The *Centurion* (50) which led the British line was engaged by both the *Sérieux* (64) and the *Invincible* (74) together for nearly a quarter of an hour before she could receive any support from the British ships in her wake. By the time the French were ready to surrender, some of the slowest sailers in the British fleet were still to get into action.[44]

The same, of course, can be said for the sternmost ships of the fleet being attacked. As each ship of the chasing fleet sailed by, they received yet another fresh broadside fired by fresh and eager crews. At the Moonlight Battle in 1780 a Spanish fleet was overhauled from the rear in exactly this way. The battle started as the leading British ship, the *Edgar* (74), fired a murderous broadside into the sternmost of the Spaniards, the *Santo Domingo* (70). The *Edgar* then moved on up the Spanish line and was closely followed by the *Marlborough* (90) which fired a fresh broadside into the *Santo Domingo* as she passed. The *Marlborough* was in turn followed by the *Ajax* (74) and then again by the *Bienfaisant* (64). At 5 p.m., as the *Bienfaisant* prepared to give the *Santo Domingo* her broadside, the Spanish ship exploded in a sheet of flame and completely disappeared.[45]

Leading the fleet into battle thus required exceptional courage, and it is instructive that Captain Graham Moore, himself a frigate captain with a reputation for bravery, described it as the 'Post of honour and peril'.[46] He described in his diary with glowing praise the actions of Captain Thomas Troubridge prior to the Battle of St Vincent in 1797. Two days before the action the *Colossus* (74) collided with Troubridge's ship, the *Culloden* (74), leaving her badly damaged.[47] For a while it was thought impossible for her to be kept at sea, but Troubridge worked ceaselessly to repair her so that he might take his allocated position at the head of the British fleet in the coming battle. He went into action with the chain pumps working constantly to keep her afloat. He then fought with distinction, received heavy damage and reported his actions with characteristic modesty.[48]

The risk of isolation run by the leading ships and the inevitable loss of cohesion amongst the fleet also meant that this type of chase could not be used if the enemy fleet was a significant way away. The longer the chase, the more stretched out the chasing fleet would be and the more they would open themselves up to the possibility of defeat in detail. In practice, therefore, chase actions in which the fastest ships of the chasing fleet bore down on the enemy occurred over relatively short distances, and were usually made possible by the escaping fleet accidentally or intentionally allowing the chasing fleet to get too close. At the Battle of Cape Passaro, for example, the French fleet formed a line of battle before attempting to escape, and thus allowed Byng to close.[49] Similarly, at the First Battle of Finisterre in 1747 the marquis de La Jonquière first formed a line of battle to allow the convoy he was protecting extra time to escape. Only when he had given the convoy a head start did he run, and by then Anson was close enough to order a general chase.[50]

The only notable exception to this pattern is the Moonlight Battle of 17 January 1780. Early in the afternoon of the 16th, Rodney encountered a squadron under Admiral Don Juan de Lángara which immediately fled for Cadiz. The British chased through the night and caught up with the Spaniards, six of which were captured or wrecked in the battle. This chase was only made possible by the marked difference in performance between Rodney's fleet and the Spanish: Rodney's ships had been newly coppered.[51] At the same time the Royal Navy enjoyed a similar advantage in performance over the French, who were slower to appreciate the benefits of copper sheathing, lacked sufficient quantities of proper nails, and suffered from distribution problems with their matériel.[52] The ability of a coppered ship to outrun an uncoppered ship led to a high degree of optimism in these years. 'Copper bottoms need fear nothing', wrote Sandwich to Hood in November 1781.[53]

To undertake a general chase in a fleet was the ultimate test in battle seamanship. It could only be considered by a fleet commander who had a large degree of confidence in the courage, skill and ability of his subordinates – particularly those in the van of the fleet – to succeed in a mêlée. A powerful impact could shock those being attacked into a defensive mindset, but a weak initial contact could draw an aggressive response, and the leading ships of the attacking fleet might soon find themselves isolated and outnumbered. To reduce the likelihood of this happening it also required a commander to be able to judge the distance between the two fleets and their relative speeds accurately before committing his fastest ships to attack. He then had to be able to rely absolutely on the courage and sense of duty among the captains of the slower ships to go to the aid of those already engaged.

Nevertheless this type of chase was used by the British throughout the century, and it was used with success. The Battle of Cape Passaro (1718), the First and Second Battles of Finisterre (1747), the Battle of Lagos Bay (1759), the Battle of Quiberon Bay (1759) and the Moonlight Battle (1779) were all chase battles, and all were victories. These successes were both a symptom and a cause of British confidence, courage and seamanship. Success bred success, and there was nothing that motivated an English sailor more than the sight of a Frenchman or Spaniard trying to avoid battle. There were in fact few things that a well-trained crew in a well-maintained ship or fleet of any nationality enjoyed more than a good chase. An enemy that sought to escape from a stranger revealed his weakness in so doing: to flee was the sign of a ship or fleet that did not trust itself to prevail in battle or was under strict orders from a higher authority to avoid battle. In either case the challenge to the aggressor was to bring a reluctant enemy to battle. In overcoming this reluctance and forcing battle, the aggressor had the opportunity to demonstrate a personal and professional superiority perceived in the immediate circumstance of first contact when the enemy chose to run.

This perceived superiority was an important part of the psychology of warfare among the crew, and was usually expressed with a degree of nationalistic fervour and in a number of ways. In the early years of the French Revolutionary War, for example, it was believed that that the French officers 'gave their seamen spirits to excite them to fight'.[54] Such lower-deck rumours formed part of a widely held belief among British crews that they were more courageous than the French.[55] As a generalisation this was untrue of the French navy, whose behaviour was often marked by conspicuous bravery in the face of overwhelming firepower, but the important underlying belief for those British crews was that the rumours *were* true; that the French were reluctant to fight, and needed to boost their courage with alcohol. An appreciation and celebration of that reluctance allowed the British sailors to take professional pride in going 'coolly and steadily to work' in battle.[56]

A visibly fleeing ship encouraged the sailors of a chasing ship in exactly the same way as did lower-deck rumours of national cowardice, but with more immediacy: it was undeniable proof, visible to all, that the enemy did not want to fight. No other action could give such a significant psychological advantage so powerfully and so completely to the enemy. By contrast, the captain and the crew of the chasing ship welcomed battle by definition; their actions heralded their intent, their willingness and their confidence. For the crew of a ship being chased down, therefore, the slow but relentless progress of a faster ship was a visible manifestation of an unknown fate. A creeping sense of dread would infuse the crew of a ship attempting to flee as quickly and as thoroughly as a sense of self-belief would grow aboard the chasing ship. Even before battle had been joined, therefore, the psychology of chase had made its mark.

CHAPTER 3

Chase and Escape II: The Tactics of Chasing

Made all sail in chase of the Russian fleet ... ship all ready for action, ready to take any advantage a favourable slant might offer.[1]

It has been argued that once a chase had been established, with both ships sailing as fast as they could, the only chance of escape for a slower craft rested on 'shifts of wind, squally weather, or the blunders of the chaser'.[2] It is a statement that implies both a passive role for the captain of the escaping ship and a sense of inevitability in the outcome of the chase, both of which are unjust. The outcome of any chase, however ill matched the ships or fleets, was characterised by a marked unpredictability; it was an activity in which everything remained uncertain. Any attempted theorisation of 'chase' must include the daily cycle of light and dark, of tides, currents, and the vagaries of sea and weather conditions, because in practice these chases were fought over huge distances and over many hours. Shifts of wind and squally weather were only to be expected, and the success of a chase did not rest on the appearance of such phenomena, but on the relative ability of the captains to cope with them. Moreover, in chase the dominant outlines of the system which focused on the twin issues of speed and position in relation to the wind were in-filled with multiple tactics to aid chase or escape: the experienced captain of a ship in chase was not reduced to a passive role, but was ready to create and embrace any advantage, however slim.

DISTANCE

Once initial contact had been made, it was not uncommon for the chase to continue with both parties out of sight. Prior to the Battle of Malaga in 1704, the French fleet were out of sight but were chased by the sound of their signal guns.[3] Ideally, however, detailed intelligence of the chase's destination was required if a chase was to be carried out successfully with both parties out of sight of each other. Nelson's continued pursuit of Villeneuve in the first six months of 1805 is a case in point. Since September 1804 Napoleon's naval strategy had vacillated through eight separate plans before finally settling on the invasion of England. An important prerequisite of his invasion plan was to draw the Royal Navy away from its position in the Channel and Western Approaches, thus leaving him free to unite his dispersed naval forces, take command of the Channel and launch the invasion. With this in mind, Villeneuve escaped from Toulon in March 1805 and headed for the West Indies. Nelson came to know of Villeneuve's destination through a dislocated network of intelligence gathered from frigates and merchantmen, and set sail for the West Indies in pursuit of Villeneuve, arriving in Barbados twenty-four days later.[4] On discovering Nelson's arrival in the West Indies, the French fleet, now united with the Spanish under Admiral Federico Gravina, headed back to Europe. With no detailed intelligence of their destination, Nelson declared that there were 'as many opinions as there are persons'. He considered Havana, Cadiz, Toulon and Egypt all likely.[5]

In this case the variety of possible destinations meant a chase was no longer viable, and Nelson headed back to his station in Gibraltar. But if the destination of an escaping ship or fleet was not known, all was not necessarily lost. If two ships had met, entered a chase and then lost contact with each other, a predictable pattern of behaviour could ensue. In this instance, once an escaping ship had made it out of sight of her pursuer, her invisibility had to be maintained at all costs. A ship being chased could reasonably be expected, therefore, to continue on the point of sail at which she performed best, even when out of sight of an enemy. This was especially true if the chase had only just dropped over the horizon; a sudden calm, accident or variation in the wind or sea conditions could soon see the enemy in sight again.

Local geography might also provide a clue to the destination and possible course of a fleeing ship. Before the mid-eighteenth century the inability to calculate longitude with any accuracy made the whole business of approaching land extremely dangerous. One of the solutions was to get into the latitude of a good landfall. Ports such as Lisbon, which had deep water near land and were easily located at sea by a nearby prominent peak, were therefore popular. As a rule, islands were particularly difficult to find, but some, like St Helena, Madeira and Tenerife, were renowned for being an easy landfall: St Helena because it was relatively isolated but had a stationary cloud over the island which could usually be seen for up to 100 miles; Tenerife and Madeira because of their high peaks. All three were directly on or close to the usual transatlantic sailing routes. Easy, safe landfalls were well known and uncommon, and this made the path of ships in some degree predictable. In exactly this way, the likely path of ships entering the Caribbean from the Atlantic was well known, and French privateers took full advantage during the Seven Years War. By cruising 50–100 miles to windward in the latitude of Barbados they made easy pickings.[6]

For all these reasons, chases over long distances with neither ship in sight of the other were always possible, but even if the two ships or fleets stayed in sight of each other, the distances could still be considerable. One contemporary estimated that, in the right conditions, three-masted ships with their lofty sails set could be seen from each other's mast heads at 7 leagues (21 miles) distance.[7] If these two ships knew each other to be enemies at first sight, with the escaping ship travelling at 5 knots and the chasing ship at 5½ knots,[8] by the time they

were within gunshot, a full 40 hours would have passed, and nearly 200 miles
would have been logged. Even assuming a conservative estimate of 12 miles as
the distance at which the same two ships might have known or suspected each
other to be enemies, a full 24 hours would have passed, and the ships would
have covered nearly 125 miles. Chases lasting a number of days were not therefore uncommon,[9] and emphasise how even a minor advantage in sailing performance could play a major part in the outcome of a chase.

With chases being run over such huge distances, it was also likely that the
weather and sea conditions would change during their course, although this
depended to a certain extent on the location and season. Around the trade wind
latitudes the weather is often reliable, whereas the Bay of Biscay is particularly
vulnerable to the rapid onset of weather fronts that mature in mid-Atlantic.
It was perfectly possible, therefore, for a ship or fleet seeking to escape to lie
becalmed while the chasing ship bore down at the very edge of a weather front.
This is exactly what happened in the action between Vice-Admiral La Clue-
Sabran and Edward Boscawen off Lagos in 1759. Boscawen, chasing down La
Clue's squadron enjoyed a fine easterly breeze while the French had barely
enough wind to give them steerage way.[10] To see one vessel becalmed very
near another keeping steadily head on was particularly common in the West
Indies.[11]

The escaping or chasing ship, however outclassed, therefore always had a
chance of success, and it was in maximising such opportunity that the outcome lay. This in turn placed a magnified emphasis on the ability to 'read' the
weather, if no opportunity arising from localised weather conditions or whole-
sale changes to weather fronts was to be lost: in chase, weather prediction and
instant reaction to changing circumstance were as important as knowing how
to get the best speed out of your ship.

In a calm, lookouts would be stationed aloft to search for the tell-tale signs
of an approaching wind: a shadow on the surface of the sea; white horses on the
tops of waves; a change in the direction or strength of the swell. The colour of
the sky and the height, shape and movement of clouds were all traditional ways
of predicting changes in the weather. Even the metaphorical 'texture' of clouds
was considered important; 'soft' clouds were believed to presage a reduction
in wind with an increase in rain, but the more 'greasy, rolled, tufted or ragged'
the clouds were, the stronger the coming wind would be.[12] Squalls could easily
be seen, and it was an established maxim in a ship of war never to be overtaken
unprepared by one – as much as it was a maxim never to be surprised by an
enemy.[13] In fact so potentially dangerous were squalls that their identification
became a science in its own right. A storm cloud with soft diffuse edges was
considered less dangerous than one with well-defined but ragged edges; a squall
that could be seen through was less dangerous than an opaque black cloud. The
relationship of wind and rain was considered important in predicting strong

winds.[14] In certain parts of the world there were also particular phenomena that betokened poor weather: off the east coast of Africa a sudden calm with a tiny cloud on the horizon usually meant the rapid onset of a tornado, and off the Cape of Good Hope a whale spouting repeatedly before diving beneath troubled waters was a sign of poor weather to come.[15]

To be aware of potential weather changes was only half of the battle, however. The captain and crew had to be ready and able to take advantage of those changes, with the crew stationed at the sheets, halliards and braces to set or furl sail and to trim the yards as the wind shifted. If the crew were indeed ready, a considerable advantage could be gained. Whilst cruising off Tenerife in March 1797, Rear-Admiral Bartholomew James fell in with four Spanish sail of the line and five frigates. James's command, the eighteen-gun brig *El Corso*, was no match for the larger Spanish ships, and they closed fast, but just when any chance of escape seemed impossible, the little brig was overcome by a squall. Prepared for any such eventuality and with the crew at their stations, James clewed up and bore away. The squall threw the leading Spanish ship into some confusion, and she ran a considerable distance past before discovering she had lost her chase. James, meanwhile, had the pleasure of seeing the whole Spanish squadron then pass him by '... while the little *Corso* was lying to, under the heavy seas, as snug as the darkness made her secret; and so soon as I has fairly counted them all by their lights, I wore under an easy sail, and altering half a point every half hour, I bid the Dons an eternal farewell'.[16] To chase in such squally and unpredictable weather, making use of the windows of advantage that arose while maintaining the safety of the ship, was a mark of true seamanship.

VISIBILITY

Another prime concern of the captain of an escaping ship was visibility. To be to windward might help him disappear; it was believed by some that it was relatively harder to look to windward than to leeward, particularly if there was a glare.[17] A captain set on escape might also risk taking in sail to make his ship less visible.[18] Any ship being chased would welcome poor weather or the coming of night; it gave the escaping ship the chance to change course, to act unpredictably, to disappear. This was not an absolute advantage, however. The sails could often remain visible at night, as the white canvas reflected the moonlight. As the visibility of those sails rested on the angle at which the escaping ship was viewed in relation to the moon, it was often advisable for the chasing ship to sail a point or two either side of the established course to maximise the possibility of catching a glimpse of the escaping ship's sails in the moonlight.[19]

To improve their ability to see at night, those officers who could afford them used night telescopes. Invented about 1750, these had larger objective lenses than the normal daytime telescope, and channelled more light towards the eye-piece. Telescopes built for use during the day were also fitted with a number of internal 'erecting' lenses which corrected the inverted image created by the objective lens, but these caused light loss and were removed in the earliest night telescopes, resulting in a better quality picture but unfortunately one which was upside down, in which 'the ocean and every ship are turned topsy-turvy'.[20] The problem was soon solved, and a night-glass became an indispensable part of any officer's stores. The quality of all telescopes still varied widely, however, and a poor-quality lens was useless for detailed observation of the enemy's strength or behaviour.[21] The user also had to be aware that a common optical illusion when viewing objects in the moonlight was that they appeared considerably closer than they really were.[22]

With invisibility not guaranteed by the coming of night, poor weather or a densely clouded sky was required for an effective escape. A captain would also ensure that all lights aboard were extinguished, especially those in the stern cabin, and that the blinds were pulled down to cover the windows.[23] This raised serious practical problems for ships in company. Accurate station keeping in a fleet was impossible at night,[24] but lights were used more generally by the ships to keep in contact with each other and reduce the likelihood of collision. Certain colours or formations of lights could also be used to distinguish friendly ships from the enemy at night.[25] The extinction of a fleet's lights, therefore, could cause either a perceived or a real loss of cohesion, as the French Rear-Admiral La Clue-Sabran discovered to his cost in August 1759. La Clue was ordered from Toulon to the West Indies, where the British had recently taken Guadeloupe. He was sighted as he passed through the Straits of Gibraltar, where Boscawen lay with his fleet. La Clue knew that he would have to avoid Boscawen in his escape from the Mediterranean, and in case they met at night he had carefully included an instruction that required all ships in the fleet to extinguish all lights aboard their ships as soon as he did so.[26] At two in the morning he duly extinguished his lights. When he scanned the horizon at dawn three of his line of battle ships were nowhere to be seen. They had lost contact with the main body of the fleet in the night and chosen the safety of Cadiz over the possibility of isolation in the face of the British fleet.[27]

A further advantage for an escaping ship of keeping a stern lamp alight was the potential for deception. Aboard the frigate *Pallas* in March 1805 Cochrane was chased down by three French warships off the Azores. He well knew that his ship was no match for his pursuers, and so lowered a ballasted cask with a lantern attached to it, extinguishing that on his own ship at the same time. The cask bobbed off to leeward with the enemy hot in pursuit, while Cochrane kept steady on his course and escaped into the night.[28] Gardner recalled such a ploy working effectively for a merchant ship intent on escape in 1796,[29] but it did not always succeed. The stratagem was used by a strange ship as she was chased down by the forty-gun *Unité* in the summer of 1806 off Cartagena, but this time the deception was detected with the help of night-glasses.[30]

SILENCE

Silence was always important in such situations: a ship may not have been visible at night, but she was often audible. A crew, often consisting of more than 500 men and sometimes as many as 1,000, crammed into a relatively small space, created a permanent low murmur, and if roused had the potential to produce a cacophony. A relaxed crew was particularly noisy: the harsh bark of human laughter carried for miles at sea, as did the beat of drums and the high melodies of pipes and fiddles. Ships of the line were always noisier than frigates, as larger ships required more men to work in less space in proportion to smaller vessels. Moreover, when the masts, yards, ropes and sails were proportionally larger, more men were required to carry out the same task as on a smaller ship.[31] The bosun's call was used night and day, and was specifically designed to cut across the noise of wind, sea and human voice. It was a complex language in its own right, each call denoting a particular order, recognised by the pitch and duration of the call. Drums, the ship's bell or a trumpet might also be used to accompany orders.[32] The ship's bell, moreover, was rung at regular intervals to mark the passing of time, and the captain would sometimes ring a bell to summon the officer of the watch.[33] Orders themselves might be shouted, but officers knew that excessive noise was a potential source of confusion, and the best always kept noise to a minimum.[34]

To reduce the noise level involved in manœuvre, the captain alone might be allowed to speak,[35] but if absolute silence was required, orders could be passed by hand through a series of runners to all parts of the ship. Midshipmen were commonly used for this task, although William Rhodes, captain's clerk of Palliser's flagship, the *Formidable* was stationed in the gunroom at the trumpet from the wheel during the Battle of Ushant in 1778, to deliver orders from the quarterdeck to the lower deck.[36] A practised crew might even be able to manœuvre a ship under hand signals alone.[37] But even if the crew could achieve and then maintain a reasonable silence, the ship itself produced a distinctive sound. The bow surged and punched its way through the swell; the wind whistled through the rigging, the canvas strained with the force of the air behind it; the mast and yards creaked as they took the strain of the sails; the blocks and tackles whirred or screeched if they were not regularly lubricated with tallow. To pass another ship by unnoticed was difficult, but this meant that silence, if it could be achieved, was an effective tactic: a silent ship was simply unexpected. Indeed, ships in the night very rarely passed like ships in the night.

For that reason, a surprise attack by one squadron on another was always more likely to succeed than a surprise attack on a single ship. A single ship

would be acutely aware of any noise or movement that was not its own, but the
alertness of a crew of a ship in company was necessarily dulled by the accepted
presence of other ships. After the Battle of Malaga in 1704 Rear-Admiral
George Byng mistook the French admiral's flagship for his own, brought his
ship alongside and was pulled across in the longboat, entirely undetected and
oblivious to his mistake. He was finally hailed only as he was about to climb on
board. They pulled away very quickly.[38] Some turned this potential for confusion to their advantage in chase. In July 1801, when Sir James Saumarez chased
a combined French and Spanish squadron bound for Cadiz, he did so at night
with no lights or signals and in complete silence. Captain Richard Keats was
the first to get into action in the swift *Superbe*, and was convinced that they had
achieved total surprise: the Spaniard into whom they poured their first broadside failed to fire back immediately, and when she did it was into another Spanish ship.[39]

GEOGRAPHY, WIND AND TIDE

If it was impossible to clear the horizon or to hide under the cover of darkness,
a number of tactical options remained open to the captain of the fleeing ship.
A ship with shallow draught seeking to escape from a larger adversary might
find temporary protection in shoal water. Reefs and sandbanks could play to
the advantage of a captain who knew the local waters well. The intention in this
instance was 'to draw the enemy out of his knowledge'.[40] While the local sailor
could chart a course through the known channels between the sandbanks or
reefs, a strange ship would have no choice but to post a leadsman in the bows
and to creep forward as the soundings were taken.

The best-known example of an admiral using knowledge of local geography
and hydrography to guide his tactical decision making comes from the Battle
of Quiberon Bay in the winter of 1759. Hawke was heading from Torbay to his
blockading position off Ushant when the French fleet was sighted on the morning of 20 November. The British fleet was slightly larger, twenty-three sail to
the comte de Conflans's twenty-one, and Conflans had no intention of engaging a superior force. He headed for the safety of Quiberon Bay, the entrance
to which is guarded by large islands, rocks and shoals. He led his fleet through
the gap, only 6 miles wide, between the rocks known as Les Cardinaux and Le
Four shoal. Once through that gap, the bay further narrowed with only a 2-mile
gap between Dumet Island and La Recherche shoal. Beyond lay only the rocky
estuary of the Vilaine River. Conflans relied entirely on his local knowledge and
Hawke's ignorance of the waters. He never expected to be followed, and prepared to form a line of battle once past Les Cardinaux. Night was coming on
fast. The sea was heavy, the wind strong, and Hawke had neither reliable charts
nor local pilots aboard to guide him.[41] Nevertheless, Hawke reasoned that

where Conflans could go, he could also, and he followed the French into the troubled waters of Quiberon Bay. The wind then veered a full two points and threw the French into confusion. Hawke's fleet seized their opportunity, and by next morning one French ship had been taken and six were wrecked or sunk. Two British ships had also been wrecked, but their crews were saved.[42] To shelter in dangerous waters was to turn a battle into a test of seamanship, and in this instance the Royal Navy rose to the challenge, while the French collapsed. Conflans's tactical decision was sound, but it was executed, as one contemporary noted, with 'plenty of zeal but no ability'.[43]

Knowledge of local weather conditions, of the breezes or calms that characterise certain stretches of coastline, was also potentially significant in a chase.[44] In hot climates, for example, it was usual for an offshore breeze to blow at night, but during the day, as the land heated up, the wind would blow onshore. In the Mediterranean, the effect of these breezes could be felt up to 12 miles from the coast, and was highly significant for navigation as it allowed a vessel to navigate for a short time against the prevailing winds. The shape of the local coastline was also potentially significant, particularly where mountains fell straight into the sea. The *mistral* of Provence, for example, is an icy blast of cold air that rushes down to the coast from the Massif Central; similarly the *tramontana* of Liguria bursts off the coast direct from the Alps in spring or autumn, drawn into the local depression over the Gulf of Genoa through the Rhône Gap; and again, the *bora* is a similar phenomenon on the Dalmatian coast.[45] The proximity of high mountains to the coast could equally produce calms such as those frequently experienced off the coast of Dominica.[46]

The sea itself is not static, but moves according to the current and tide, often at considerable speeds. A current of half a knot was not considered strong,[47] but even this could create a significant advantage in chase. A really strong current could dictate the course a vessel might steer: a ship caught broadside on to a strong current would lose considerably more ground than if her bows were pointed into it. Current alone was often a factor in preventing ships from getting to windward, and certain places were renowned for it. Fleets in the St Lucia Channel trying to get to windward of Martinique often found themselves in difficulty because of the strong currents,[48] and the coast off Negapatam in India was notorious during the monsoon season.[49] In some areas tides even run in opposite directions. It was well known in the 1740s, for example, that between the Suffolk coast and that of Holland and Zealand, the flood tide set to the south off the Dutch coast, but the same tide set to the north off the English coast. In a chase in these waters, a prodigious advantage could therefore be taken by an experienced seaman.[50]

Harnessing the currents was far from straightforward, however. The purest form of navigating that used only the tides, a process known as 'drifting', was an art form in its own right, and the incorporation of tides and currents into navigation was a daily requirement that required considerable expertise.[51] The strength of a current was dependent on the contortions of the coast, the contours of the sea bottom and the lunar cycle, and had to be 'read' before advantage of it could be taken.[52] Some rules were generally applicable, however: it was believed, for example, that in most places the tides ran longer in the offing than close in with the shore, and that the in-draughts before rivers altered the true set of the tide. Harnessing that tide with confidence required detailed knowledge of its particular characteristics, however. How much was the tide altered by the in-draught of a river, and exactly where and when did the race appear? To what extent did the speed of the tide alter out to sea compared to close in shore? Did nearby headlands and reefs affect the set of the tide? Where did the tide run longest and strongest?[53]

To complicate matters still further, the effect of the tide on a ship was determined by the shape of the hull and the angle at which the hull met the current. This all had to be taken into consideration by the captain who wished to harness the current to aid his chase or escape. In 1807, for example, John Burnet, the Master of the *Uranie*, recorded how his ship, a renowned poor sailer, still closed fast on a chase through use of the local conditions. The enemy ran close inshore while the *Uranie* stayed a little further out, where there was more wind, and altered course to run across the tide while their enemy took it ahead.[54] The relationship between the force and angle of the current and the force and angle of the wind as separate factors determining a vessel's speed was also uncertain. For example, no fixed rules could be made to determine if a ship sailing with the wind and tide on her quarter, with all her sails full, sailed faster than a ship running directly before the tide, where she would enjoy the full strength of the tide's push but could only set a portion of her available canvas. In this, or indeed any situation, only experiment and experience would provide the answer.[55]

With the effect of the tide on the speed of a vessel dependent on such a variety of factors, any attempt to provide formulae dictating how to act in specific circumstances was necessarily doomed. Nevertheless, one contemporary commentator considered in detail nineteen separate scenarios, such as 'how to act with the wind and tide making an angle and the enemy to windward', with the 'wind making a right-angle with the tide, and the enemy to windward', and yet again, with 'the enemy in the wind's eye and a current setting to leeward'.[56] Although written with the commendable intention of providing inexperienced merchant captains with a guidebook of how to act in a chase situation, the result is confusing and inflexible: there is no index by which the numerous scenarios can be searched, and the unfortunate captain who was eventually able to find the scenario matching his predicament, or that which was least different from it, would no doubt find that the time to act decisively had long since past. Hidden within the text, however, are some sensible suggestions which negated any complex comparison of relative sailing performance. A ship escaping in a tideway, for example, could suddenly furl all sail and drop her anchor, leaving the unsuspecting and unprepared enemy to be carried away with the tide.[57]

COURSE

Chasing to windward posed its own problems and created its own debate. A sailing warship was unable to make progress directly into the wind. The closest she could sail to the wind was six points, as a square sail was restricted in its positioning in relation to the wind by the yard to which it was attached. With a northerly wind, therefore, the best course that could be sailed by a sailing warship was ENE or WNW (Fig. 4). With these practical restrictions, if a sailing warship was to make ground directly to windward she had to follow a zig-zag course which required a regular change of tack. She could change tack either by 'tacking' – putting the bows through the wind (Fig. 13) – or by 'wearing' – putting her stern through the wind in the equivalent of a jibe in a modern yacht (Fig. 14). Wearing ship was a more reliable manœuvre; it was less dangerous and much less could go wrong, but in the process of a wear significantly more ground would always be lost to leeward than if the ship tacked. In a pressurised situation such as chase, therefore, a ship would always choose to tack.[58] The tricky question remained of when to tack, and the timing of that manœuvre was much debated.

As a general rule the use of 'long boards' – long distances between tacks – by the chasing ship was ill-advised, as it could lead to the two ships being at some considerable distance from each other – a situation that the ship seeking to escape could easily profit from if there was a shift in wind direction.[59] Some proposed to tack whenever the chase bore abeam[60] but for others it depended very much on circumstance.[61] However it was done, there was always a strong emphasis on manœuvre in any chase to windward, and it was therefore characterised by a magnified impact of seamanship on the outcome: a chase to windward could quickly become a tacking contest, and tacking ship was not a straightforward process. All ships lost

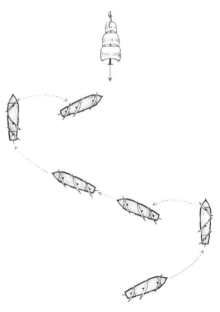

13 Changing tack by tacking: the bows go through the eye of the wind.

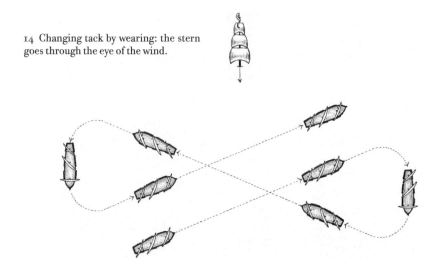

14 Changing tack by wearing: the stern goes through the eye of the wind.

ground to windward in the process of tacking, but the amount of ground lost depended entirely on the design of the ship and the skill of the crew.[62] A highly trained crew in a weatherly ship could overhaul a sluggish and leewardly ship with a poorly trained crew in an astonishingly short period of time. This is one of the principal reasons for British success against the Russian navy in 1808; chases in confined waterways such as the Gulf of Finland required regular and precise manœuvre, at which the British seamen excelled.[63]

Chasing downwind had its own difficulties, because it did not necessarily follow that steering directly for the enemy ship was the most efficient way of chasing. There were a number of reasons for this. In terms of sail plan and point of sail, the ship that was escaping had one highly significant advantage over her pursuer: her captain could choose the point of sail on which the race would be run. In races between differently rigged ships this was a significant advantage for the escaping ship. A two-masted vessel such as a brig being chased by a three-masted ship, for example, might alter course to run downwind. With the wind directly aft, the yards of both ships would be braced square. This would bring the three masts of the pursuing enemy into one, the fore and main masts being 'blanketed' by the mizzenmast. The potential advantage of the larger ship in being able to set more sails than her smaller adversary was therefore minimised. In this scenario, the tactic might be countered by the larger ship sailing on a broad-reach, with all her sails on all of her masts drawing, and zigzagging up to the enemy. Some believed that the added advantage gained in extra speed outweighed the extra distance that had to be travelled.[64]

If the two ships were not in each other's wake, a chasing ship with superior speed could plot a course to intercept the escaping enemy that would be significantly shorter than steering directly for her (Fig. 15).[65] To shape such a course was quite difficult, however, and required no little skill and patience. One

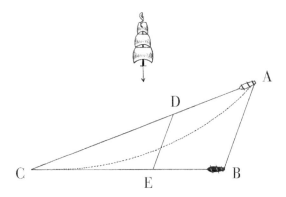

15 If the ship A steers directly for her enemy, ship B, she will describe an arc, illustrated by the dotted line. This will prove to be significantly longer than an intercepting course, ADC. To plot such a course, ship A must maintain ship B at a steady bearing, so when she is at D the enemy is at E.

contemporary cautioned that 'many a chase escapes through too much haste in the chaser'.[66]

The basic principle of interception was to take a bearing of the enemy and then to keep her steady on that bearing. This would inevitably lead to a point at which the two ships would meet.[67] To intercept a ship in this way also required the enemy to maintain a steady course and speed that would ultimately and obviously deliver her into the arms of her pursuer. In practice it was highly unlikely that an escaping ship would act like this; the captain would do his utmost to lengthen any pursuit, and one way to do this was to alter course as soon as it was clear that the chasing ship had settled on an intercepting course.[68] Nevertheless, that this method was used is certain.[69]

In an obviously outmatched chase in which the chasing ship was clearly and steadily gaining on the chase, the captain of the chase would steer on his own bearing from the chaser – the course that carried his ship directly away from the threat.[70] In this situation no such intercepting course existed; the chase would simply become a competition of speed on a single point of sail.

In all these scenarios the ability to take an accurate bearing of the enemy was critical; the relative speed of the enemy ship could then be ascertained and an appropriate tactic adopted for chase or escape. The ability to read this type of bearing required the skilful use of the azimuth compass, which allowed the observer to take accurate bearings of another vessel or a point of land for a visual fix (Fig. 16). An eighteenth-century steering compass did not have an azimuth ring, so an azimuth compass, if one was available, would have to be set up on a stable

16 An azimuth or bearing compass.

base; ideally a stand would be fitted at the binnacle, high enough to distinguish objects in the horizon over the hammocks.[71] This technique was accurate but complicated, and to chase in the wake of the escaping ship retained a distinct advantage. In this instance the chasing ship could keep exactly the same bearing as his enemy by keeping the masts of the chasing or escaping vessel 'in one'. It was a particularly accurate technique to ensure that one's course was the same as that of another ship, as her three masts worked as a sensitive transit.[72]

GUNNERY IN CHASE

At some point in an uneven chase the two ships would be within gunshot of each other and both crews could look to their guns to influence the outcome of the chase. The ability of a captain to estimate when this might happen was critical in his tactical decision making, and many lives could depend on the accuracy of his answer. It was worked out through a simple time/distance/speed equation informed through comparison of the relative sailing of the two ships and the range of the guns. Grapeshot would carry further than musket shot, perhaps more than a mile,[73] but the outer limit of a cannon's effective range was just over a mile.[74] Although a gunner would know roughly how far his cannon might fire in theory, distance was always difficult to judge at sea, and a ranging shot was necessary to see if the cannon would have any execution. If the experimental shot landed around or beyond the target, it was then up to the captain to decide how – or indeed if – he might chose to fire on his opponent. In chase, this was not the straightforward decision that we might assume it to be.

The idea in this situation was to target the rig of the enemy.[75] This was not a tactic that varied according to the chasing or escaping ship, to nationality or period. A chase by definition required one ship to be ahead of another, and so the hull of each ship was never viewed from the other broadside to broadside – when the enemy hull presented the largest target. Rather the hull of the enemy presented a target that became proportionally smaller as the ships moved into each other's wake. When viewed from directly bow-on or stern-on, the hull of another ship was less than a quarter of the size that it was when viewed broadside to broadside.[76] The rig of a ship, on the other hand, was a vast target. If viewed directly from the broadside with all thirty-seven sails set, the rig of a first-rate ship of the line filled in 6,510 square yards (5,468.4 square metres). The rig was also easier to damage; to split a crucial line or injure a spar required far less velocity from a shot than to inflict significant damage on the hull of another ship, which, if it was a warship, could be as much as 3 feet thick. A shot fired at distance that struck the hull might simply bounce off, with no material effect on ship or crew.

Success at this range, even when targeting the rig, was far from guaranteed, however. At the extremity of a cannon's range the vast expanse of sail and the web of rigging that supported it became a relatively small target against a background of endless sea and sky, and the inevitable error in elevation or angle caused by the motion of the firing ship would become greatly magnified by the time the shot actually reached the target. One contemporary went so far as to say that the difficulty involved in aiming an elevated gun meant that any gunnery at a greater distance than point blank was almost always aimed by chance, the gun being fired at the enemy simply with the intention of reaching the target, 'in the hope that they will strike it somewhere or other',[77] while another stated that elevated shot fired from one moving ship at another must be random.[78] Sir William Monson was a little more direct when he wrote: 'he that shooteth far off at sea had as good not shoot at all.'[79]

The problem of gunnery in chase was particularly acute if the two ships were in each other's wake. In this scenario a bow-chaser could be fired from the chasing ship, or a stern-chaser from the escaping ship, but chase guns were usually single guns, or possibly pairs, and it therefore required a large degree of luck for them to have a severe effect on the enemy. In one example, a bow-chaser of the frigate *Crescent* brought down the studding sail booms and mainsail of an escaping brig, but it took the gunner a total of seventy-two shots to do so.[80] It was also quite easy for a chasing ship to 'hide' on the quarter of his enemy in a position where neither the chase guns nor those of the broadside could do any execution. This protected the chasing ship, but did prolong the chase.[81]

Bow and stern chase guns were lighter but longer than the main guns, and generally of brass rather than iron construction, as this offered greater accuracy. They were usually situated on the poop deck and forecastle, although the largest ships had chase ports cut in the gun deck level of the bow or stern. It was not until the late eighteenth century that chase guns became a permanent and regular feature of warship armament, however. By 1799 frigates, being more likely to be involved in chases than ships of the line, were equipped with four chase guns, two in the bow and two in the stern.[82] Before that date the captain might rig any gun temporarily to be trained on the chasing or escaping ship. In this way the captain of HMS *Aimable,* in chase of a strange schooner off Antigua in September 1796, slung a gun between the fore rigging and foremast, a proceeding which so alarmed the captain of the escaping schooner that he bore up and surrendered.[83] If no such invention was possible, or the chasing ship determined to 'hide' on the quarter of the escaping ship, both ships would be forced to yaw one way or another to present their broadside and target the enemy.

A broadside gun could be angled towards the bow or stern, but it was restricted by the size of the port through which the gun was fired and by the system of tackles with which it was restrained. Some merchant ships were known to expand the size of their gun ports to increase the potential angle of fire,[84] but the equation between angle of fire and broadside protection was more sensitive on warships than on merchantmen, who were obliged to maximise the potential of a limited number of guns. The solution for the Navy, therefore, was not found through alteration to the size of the ports, but through design changes to the tackles. Sir Charles Douglas introduced a system in 1779 by which gun crews manœuvred guns with tackles secured to the hull between each gun, rather than by the traditional method of manhandling the guns with handspikes. He also had the timber beam knees known as 'standards' cut away if they interfered with the carriages at extreme angles. In combination, these amendments allowed the gunners to point the guns a 'full four points before or abaft the beam ... a degree of obliquity until now unknown in the Navy'.[85]

A warship directly in the wake of an escaping enemy therefore did not have to yaw a great deal to present her broadside; turning just a few degrees either side of her course would suffice. Nevertheless, any alteration in course, however minor, was highly significant in chase. Only a few degrees change of course would necessarily increase the distance between the two ships,[86] and would also bring with it an unknown and unpredictable alteration in the heel of the ship. For both these reasons a yaw, however minor and however brief, brought with it a requisite alteration in the elevation of the cannon which were to be fired. A cannon elevated to fire long distances was notoriously difficult to aim, as the muzzle of the gun itself, raised a full $7°$ to fire at maximum effective range, blocked the gunner's view of his target.[87] The gunner below decks was often unable to see either his target, or where his shot landed, and it was also notoriously difficult to judge distance from below decks.[88] In practice, therefore, although the gunner firing alone might hear his shot hit the hull of an enemy, there was a continual dialogue between the gunners below decks and those officers on the weather deck who could observe the effect of the shot. If the shot failed to make its mark it would make 'ducks and drakes' in the water, and the tell-tale splashes would be noted. Often the shot themselves could be seen.[89]

Elevated fire was therefore difficult enough, but alteration of the elevation made aim even more uncertain. Altering the elevation of cannon was not a scientific process. The guns were manhandled using iron spikes and then lowered onto a wedge-shaped piece of wood known as a quoin. The quoin would then be pushed in or out to adjust the angle of the gun. Any alteration in range was therefore difficult to adjust accurately in perfect conditions, and almost impossible in a rush; a random volley was usually the inevitable result. 'It is almost incredible', wrote Howard Douglas (son of the gunnery innovator Charles Douglas), '... how little effect is produced by this sort of raking fire,'[90] and he appears to have been right. In a chase between an unidentified French frigate and the *Melampus* in November 1796 Captain Graham Moore positioned himself carefully on the quarter so that the Frenchman was forced to yaw to present his broadside. Though the French frigate did indeed yaw a number of times to fire at the *Melampus*, she hit her target only once and caused no damage.[91]

With the likely extension in the distance of chase caused by gunnery, there was a greater emphasis on the success of that shot. If the aim of the ship seeking to escape was awry, the chasing ship would have closed a significant distance; if, on the other hand, it was the chasing ship that failed in her attempt, the escaping vessel could have crept once more out of range. Captain Lobb of the frigate *Crescent* tried this in the spring of 1800 in chase of a strange brig, and in doing so demonstrated the potential negative impact on a chase of such an attempt: in rounding to and firing at the escaping ship, all of the foremost main deck guns were fired without any of them hitting their target, which, by the time they had resumed their original course, had gained more than a mile.[92] The same applied to an escaping ship. 'An hundred times I was tempted to manœuvre in order to cripple her from fighting', wrote Captain Saunier of the French eighty-gun *Guillaume Tell* as he was hunted down by Henry Blackwood in the thirty-six-gun *Penelope* in March 1800, 'but as the wind blew fresh, and I observed, notwithstanding the darkness of the night, several ships at the extremity of the horizon in full sail to support her, I was sensible that by lying to, I should be giving them all time to come up, and that my escape would be impossible.'[93] The problems that yawing to fire caused a ship in chase, therefore, ensured that it remained in the interest of a captain in chase to fire only those guns that he could bring to bear without changing course.[94] On the other hand, it was in the interests of the escaping ship to force the chasing ship to yaw if they were going to open fire. This was simply achieved by keeping the chasing or pursuing vessel's masts 'in one'.[95]

Excessive speed was also highly disadvantageous to accurate gunnery. The frequent and significant 'jerks and lurches' in the motion of a ship, inseparable from the use of a heavy press of canvas, would necessarily render any attempted gunnery more hurried and inefficient.[96] Any attempt to engage under full sail would only 'give double celerity to his flight, absolute inefficiency to your practice, and shorten the duration of the cannonade'.[97] It was also believed by some that the gunfire itself was potentially detrimental to the progress of the firing ship. It was an established belief in the late eighteenth century, and there is evidence that this was believed as early as 1742, that the firing of the bow guns checked the speed of the vessel 'so much as may occasion the loss of your expected prize', and conversely that the firing of the stern-chasers increased the speed of a vessel.[98] No explanation is offered in the few instances where this appears, and it was a belief that appears to have fallen out of fashion by 1836.[99]

Not only was gunnery difficult in chase, but wayward gunnery was also considered encouraging to the enemy.[100] For both practical and psychological reasons, therefore, it was often in the interests of the captain of each ship to withhold fire completely until the enemy had come within pistol shot.[101] In turn this placed a greater emphasis in chase on the importance of maximising speed, on weather prediction, reaction to changing sea and weather conditions, the harnessing of tides and currents, and analysis of the enemy's course and destination.

These, therefore, are the tactics of chase that have survived, but other tactics and techniques were undoubtedly also used, and much would have been passed down by word of mouth. Incomplete as this record is, however, it is clear that a complex system of tactics existed in chase to aid escape or increase the likelihood of capture. These tactics and the unpredictability of performance under sail ensured that the crew of a chasing ship who had lost sight of their prey would not lose hope, and that the crew of an escaping ship could never relax. All of this, it must be emphasised, was peculiar to the age of sail: it is why chase is a distinguishing feature of sailing warfare; it is why contemporaries gave much thought to the tactics of chasing and forcing battle; and it is why sailing warfare is so suited to fiction: the cat and mouse games of hunting and hiding, of chasing and escaping, were real.

CHAPTER 4

Station Keeping

At ½ past eight this morning the Commodore made the signal for the line abreast. Such a confusion ensued as I never before saw.[1]

At this stage of the engagement, if two fleets had sighted each other, the maintenance of cohesion was critical. In cohesion lay security and power but its achievement was a multi-layered and permanent problem in the age of sail. Its foundations were the ability of a ship to maintain her station in a fleet, and then to continue do so when manœuvring in the face of the enemy, under fire, in unpredictable wind, weather and sea conditions, and with a damaged rig and a crew depleted in numbers and strength through injury and fatigue. The potential problems of such manœuvring when in contact with the enemy are obvious; less apparent are the inherent and formidable problems of station keeping under sail in a gentle breeze, with no swell, good visibility and no enemy in sight. When understood, they throw the challenge of station keeping in battle into a bewildering perspective and illuminate a hitherto ignored aspect of seamanship that must be appreciated in its own right.

It has already been explained that a fleet maintained cohesion by sailing at the speed of its slowest performer.[2] The need for cohesion dictated speed and had a considerable effect on the problems of fleet manœuvrability – particularly on those manœuvres which included a tack or a wear. To manœuvre efficiently, with a minimum of time and leeway lost in the process, a ship needed good speed to maximise the efficiency of the rudder.[3] However, sailing in a fleet was all about keeping station in relation to other ships; it did not necessarily follow that a ship carrying only enough canvas to maintain her position had sufficient speed to tack successfully or wear efficiently. A fleet would therefore have to open up to a sufficient distance to allow each ship enough sea room to gather speed and perform the evolution, and then close again as soon as the evolution had been executed.[4] The paradox is clear: to reduce the risk of collision, each ship needed space for manœuvre, but the effectiveness of fleet formation in battle relied upon cohesion and concentration of force. Tacking a single ship could take as much as fifteen minutes or as little as five.[5] Any type of evolution could therefore take some considerable time, even if the fleet was at the peak of its capability. Prior to the first Battle of Finisterre, Anson's well-trained fleet still took two hours to manœuvre from line abreast to line ahead.[6] Even without the pressure of battle, this was a considerable challenge. In May 1781 Pasley recalled that an untrained fleet laboured all day, and without success, to answer the signal for 'Line of Battle abreast at two cables distant' that was made in the morning.[7]

Performing the evolution was itself far from reliable, and the dangers associated with a failed tack, an inefficient wear, or even only a poorly timed manœuvre were particularly significant in a fleet, as other ships would be quickly thrown into disarray.[8] Collision was thus likely even in fine weather, and the biggest danger to a fleet at any time was the fleet itself, as Admiral Matthews found to his cost in 1744, when the *Warwick* fell on the *Nassau* as he beat thirty ships to windward in the confined waters of Hyères Bay.[9] In 1793 Lord Howe was unable to get his fleet down the Channel in fine weather in the middle of summer without two ships running foul of each other.[10] Light winds and a great swell were particularly difficult for station keeping. The large ships became almost completely unmanageable, and would roll deeply and heavily. The guns would have to be secured as if for a storm, while the sails flogged themselves to pieces against the rigging. In such conditions ships had to be at least three-quarters of a mile from each other to remain safe, and if they drifted too close to each other, boats would have to be used to tow them apart.[11]

The unwieldy nature of the line was further compounded by its sheer size. It needed to be compact to maximise its strength, but at the same time there had to be sufficient intervals between the ships to allow a damaged vessel to leave the line without falling aboard the next astern and throwing the whole line into confusion.[12] Ships would therefore take their position in the line at a distance of between one and two cables from each other, depending on the wind and sea conditions.[13] The most common distance was two cables (200 yards or 182 metres), and the greatest, for cruising formation, was 3 miles.[14] It did not, therefore, take many ships to be in the line for it to assume a significant length. At the Battle of Ushant in 1778, it is not surprising that the fleet of thirty-one ships of the line was estimated by Captain Robinson of the *Worcester* to be a full 3 leagues (9 nautical miles) in length and, in one instance, when the order to anchor was given, the entire rear third of the fleet was so far behind the van that they were unable to come to anchor in the desired place until the next day.[15]

The problem of size would be further compounded if the fleet was split into more than one line, as, for safety's sake, each line or squadron would be at least half a mile from its neighbour.[16] With the fleet scattered over such an expanse of ocean, weather conditions could easily differ from one part of the fleet to another. In the skirmishes prior to the Battle of the Saints in April 1782, the van of the British fleet stood on in a good breeze, while the centre and rear divisions were becalmed.[17]

Even without the added complications of local wind conditions when spread over such a distance, variations in the general direction and force of the wind would cause ships to fluctuate in both course and speed with little warning.[18] This was enough to ensure that entire sections of a fleet were often under different sail plans, backing to ease congestion or making sail to close a gap. Lord Mulgrave, captain of the *Courageux* at the Battle of Ushant (1778), claimed that this was always the case 'where fleets keep company together'.[19] Chaos ensued. At the Battle of the Saints the two fleets were completely deranged by a change in the wind alone, each being divided into three parts.[20] This was the nature of fleet performance and, as such, signals for making or reducing sail and closing of the line could be made to any division without the slightest censure intended for the admiral or captains in that squadron.[21]

In battle the problems of fleet cohesion were further compounded, as to cope with the unpredictability of the weather, sea and battle conditions, and the difficulties of fleet manœuvre, each ship had to be at the very peak of its powers of manœuvrability if it was to maintain its position in the line and not endanger the efficacy of the line as a tactical weapon. To ensure cohesion of the line a captain had to be able to keep the ship balanced, to fill, shiver or back sail, to enable the ship to yaw, shoot ahead or back astern as the occasion demanded.[22] Damage to the rig and injuries to the crew quickly threatened the ability of a ship to do this.

At the Battle of Ushant (1778) the heavily damaged *Formidable* was considered capable of getting into her station in line, could wear and steer, but was 'by no means in a manageable state and condition ... to preserve her distance between two ships of the line',[23] and the *Ramillies*, though leaking badly, continued to attack the enemy, but Captain Digby was specific that she could not be fought in line.[24] In the skirmishes before the First of June (1794) the *Invincible*, having suffered damage to her masts, signalled her readiness to engage the enemy, but her inability to keep the line of battle.[25] A ship that could not maintain her position, yet persevered in the line could endanger the defensive efficiency of the line and the survival of the fleet itself. Sir Richard Bickerton, captain of the disabled *Terrible*, was repeatedly shouted at to get out of the way of other ships in the line at the Battle of Ushant.[26]

Not only were the movements of ships in a line governed by those of their own fleet, however, but also by those of the enemy. Each ship, by constantly juggling sail plan, backing, shivering and filling, had to keep station in line and also stay abreast of her opponent.[27] This became even more taxing as a fight developed and the ships became disabled. A ship might have to leave the line altogether to repair her damage,[28] but a ship with only a slight reduction in her capability could still have an immediate and significant knock-on effect on those both ahead and astern, which would cause the whole structure of the fleet formation to evolve. Thus at the Battle of Ushant (1778) the *Ramillies* fell to leeward and obliged the *Ocean* to back her maintopsail to prevent the two ships falling aboard each other. This in turn forced the *Victory* to leave her position in the line, an opportunity of which she took advantage by coming alongside the French admiral, and forced the *Formidable* to back her topsail to prevent her from shooting ahead straight into the line of fire of the *Ocean*.[29]

Damage was not the only cause of a ship acting unpredictably and altering the characteristics of fleet formation. Fear, cowardice and confusion in the noise and smoke were all significant. Even the ability of a ship to react by backing or filling as necessary was often unreliable; with so many ships in such close proximity, it was common for ships to lie becalmed in each other's lee, as at the First of June, when the *Jacobin* lay in the lee of the huge 120-gun flagship *Montagne*.[30]

The problems of station keeping by day were so formidable that at night it was all but impossible, and fleets would simply close to prevent separation as much as possible.[31] Even Kempenfelt, a constant innovator and not one to shirk a challenge, resorted to issuing an instruction for ships to pay great attention to their positions at daybreak, rather than making further attempts to keep station at night.[32] He also claimed that a large fleet could never hope to tack or wear in a dark and stormy night without risking great damage, and he proposed using this truism to strategic advantage by keeping the English fleets in port in such conditions, leaving the enemy to the mercy of long nights and hard gales as, in his words: 'They'll do more in favour of you than your fleet can.'[33]

Unless the fleet was in chase and needed to remain 'invisible', ships in company would light their lanterns. From 1690 these were made from stone-ground glass, which replaced the earlier green plastic mica and allowed the lights to be seen at a far greater distance. The number of lights a ship carried altered a little throughout the century. Before 1722 ships of a third rate and above carried three lights, and after 1722 fourth rates also carried three lights, but after 1804 it was decided that only two lights were necessary for all ships other than flagships, who would retain the central light so that they might be identified at night. In any case, more than one light was always carried when in company because the lights could be used by other vessels as a transit. By viewing the two stern lights in relation to each other, the following ship gained some indication of how far away the leading ship was and her relative aspect. A lantern hung in the tops was also used by flagships or ships in charge of a convoy, the lantern being placed in the maintop for a full admiral, in the foretop for a vice-admiral, and in the mizzen top for a rear-admiral.[34] Even with these lights, fleet manœuvres remained particularly problematic at night, as it was hard to discern at what speed a vessel was manœuvring. To ease this problem Howe issued a signal in 1762 that, if tacking at night, each ship was to hoist a light to be kept visible until she had completed the manœuvre.[35] In a fog no such luxury was possible which necessarily led to considerable anxiety for those in command while the fog lasted. In this situation guns were fired every hour, with volleys of musketry at frequent intervals accompanied by the constant ringing of bells to reduce the likelihood of collision.[36]

TECHNIQUES FOR KEEPING STATION

The particular problem of station keeping lay in relative manœuvre. To maintain position, a ship had to manœuvre in relation to at least one other ship, and the position of those ships would in turn be dependent on the position and behaviour of more ships, and so on. The nearest any fleet could come to having a fixed point was the commander-in-chief, but he was as susceptible to the vagaries of wind, weather, tide and battle as anyone else. Position, therefore, was conditional on a complex equation of unpredictable variables, and maintaining it demanded immediate and subtle control of speed and direction. Contrary to popular belief, sailing warships were capable of such manœuvrability through subtle control of the sail plan and rudder,[37] but that capability was subject to certain conditioning factors, the most significant of which was point of sail and sail plan.

In practice the best way of achieving subtlety and immediate control of speed was to sail under reduced canvas. This was usually achieved by the entire fleet sailing semi-hove-to, usually with the mizzen topsail aback,[38] which allowed for mutual support even between ships of widely differing performance. Thus at the Battle of Toulon, Captain Williams of the *Royal Oak*, despite being a poorer sailer, was able to haul up to support the *Rupert*, a fine sailer.[39] In terms of point of sail, it was always sensible for a fleet to sail a few points off the wind. This allowed the fleet to change course to windward or to leeward without the time consuming and risky process of tacking or wearing. A fleet to leeward could haul their wind and close on a fleet to windward,[40] and any ship that might happen to fall to leeward could easily haul up to regain her station, which was almost impossible if the fleet were close-hauled.[41] Sailing close to the wind also had its advantages, however, not least that it was easier to control speed, as the yards only had to be braced a short distance to be shivered or backed. An effective compromise that was widely practised was to sail with the wind abeam.[42]

The difficulty of maintaining position posed a substantial problem to all captains in a fleet, but it was not the end of their troubles. Indeed, their ability to maintain position rested on one key assumption: that the prescribed position could be recognised once achieved, and the methods by which captains judged their position were often uncertain, and at best imprecise.

Judging position was a twofold problem, requiring a determination of bearing and distance. For ships in line ahead, there was a very simple practical solution to the problem of bearing. At the court martial of Captain Ambrose after the Battle of Toulon, the quarter-master of the *Rupert* was asked: 'What rule have you for a ship's being in a line?' He replied: 'When a ship is in the wake of another, and has her three masts in one.'[43] Earlier in the trial there is evidence of this being used in practice. Captain Ambrose, frustrated at not being in line, directly ordered the helmsman to keep up until the admiral's masts were in one.[44] If performed correctly by every ship in the fleet, one would only be able to see the ship directly ahead and that directly astern.[45] This method of rapidly judging a bearing was also used at night. To identify the course of an enemy at night, the headmost ship in chase would keep a light in the middle poop lanthorn and one at the topmast head.[46] By lining up the lights of the ship in chase, the rest of the fleet could ascertain the course of the enemy.

This technique only worked for line ahead, however, and no such quick method of judging bearing existed for ships in any other formation. Measurements had to be taken by instrument, always using the mainmast as the point from which bearings were taken.[47] The instruments available for measuring distance were the sextant and quadrant, which were to be used thus:

> The interval from ship to ship, at the distance directed by signal, is regulated by observing the angles subtended by the masthead above the water line, of each adjoining ship, which angles, being calculated for the various distances that may be signalled, are entered into a table, whence by setting the limb of a sextant or quadrant to the angle corresponding to the distance ordered, it may be ascertained in every ship whether she is drawing ahead, or dropping astern, or steady to distance.'[48]

Most commonly, however, position and speed were simply judged by eye; absolute mathematical accuracy with regards to bearing and distance was neither obtainable nor expected.[49] Each ship kept at the same distance as the immediate neighbours of the commander-in-chief, regulating her motions by those of the ship preceding her,[50] but this was not a straightforward process. In fact the difficulty of judging any distance at sea, particularly for those with little previous experience, was so notorious that it was used to explain away disparity between testimonies in courts martial, the most common illusion being that a fleet of ships at a great distance would appear further from each other than they actually were. It was also remarkably difficult to tell at a distance if a fleet of ships was in a regular line or not.[51] Ships in extended cruising formation would use the appearance of their immediate neighbour on the horizon as a rough guide, ensuring that they did not keep further than hull-down from each other,[52] but this was of no use in close formation. Line ahead seems to have been particularly problematic. Young, in a letter to Middleton, stated his preference for line abreast in which: 'the officers are better judges of their distance than in forming in a line ahead',[53] but offered no explanation as to why.

Added to these problems of measuring distance were further ambiguities in the description of distance that made the process even more unreliable. Seamen most often used cannon fire as a measure of distance, even for navigational directions or fleet orders, the most common terms being 'point blank' and 'random shot'.[54] There were, however, no fixed rules as to the exact distance each term represented, and there was frequent disagreement over the distances implied. Some stretched point blank to as much as three-quarters of a mile, whereas many saw it as no more than a quarter of a mile.[55] Others judged it purely on the effect of cannon, point blank being 'as far as a gun will carry without elevating the metal', and random shot being 'as far as a gun will carry when the metal is elevated'.[56] In a published collection of courts martial after the Battle of Toulon, eight separate people were asked for their definition of point blank, and each provided a different answer.[57] Sometimes no specific distance was even ordered, rather the ships were simply to keep 'nearer or farther off the leading ship according to the state of the weather'.[58]

The problems of maintaining distance were further compounded by changes of speed, as uniform change of speed throughout the fleet at exactly the same time was impossible. To reduce the likelihood of large gaps appearing in the line, the commander-in-chief or leading ship of each line or squadron was used as an official template from which to base all changes in speed. The proportion of sail he carried was the visible statement of his intent, to be observed by all so that they might better judge what sail to keep company with him.[59] Exactly the same technique was used to stay abreast of the enemy. Thus at the trial of Captain Molloy for his conduct in the First of June, 1794, the *Caesar*, van ship of the English fleet, reacted immediately to changes in sail plan in the enemy fleet: 'Mr Cleverley from the forecastle came aft and said the van ship had hoisted her jib, upon which Captain Molloy ordered him immediately to go forward and do the same.'[60]

The impression this gives is oversimplified, however. To sail at the same speed as another ship, even of similar size and construction, required far more than copying the sail plan. In Keppel's Channel squadron of 1779, for example, it was well known that the admiral's flagship *Victory* always outsailed his vice-admiral in the *Formidable* when under the same sail plan.[61] To allow for the inevitable disparity in performance, captains had to acquire a perfect knowledge of the comparative rate of sailing of their ship in relation to that of the commander-in-chief under all variations of sail plan and, in all weather, day and night,[62] a skill which could only be acquired through lengthy practice and experience, and only then by those with sufficient aptitude. To help them, certain rules, both written and unwritten, existed regarding station keeping. It was, for example, customary for the ship on the starboard tack to keep her wind, while that on the larboard passed to leeward,[63] and there were similar rules for ships being taken aback, or missing stays in a fog.[64] If changing course in line ahead, it was customary for the leading ship to be signalled the new course, and for all others to follow in her wake.[65] Furthermore, captains did not operate in total isolation and were not afraid to hail each other to clarify a situation.[66]

CHANGE OVER TIME

Many of these logistical problems of station keeping and fleet manœuvre were inherent in the very nature of sailing warfare, yet with time came experience and innovative tools and techniques that made fleet cohesion less problematic. The most significant of these improvements was a steady growth in the standardisation of performance. Uniformity of performance meant predictability of sailing capability, and any improvement in the predictability of sailing capability was of immediate practical assistance in station keeping.

The most significant change in this direction was the standardisation of ship type in the fleet. In 1719 and 1733 'Establishments' were created which laid down the dimensions and armament of each class of ship. The object of these establishments was to simplify the task of the administrators in supplying the necessary spares, and ease the problems of fleet control by standardising ship type.[67] In practice, however, it was not until the advent of the two-decked seventy-four-gun ship which first started to appear in the 1750s that standardisation in ship-type had a significant impact on fleet cohesion and control. Fast, highly manœuvrable, but also strong enough to provide the backbone of a battle fleet, these ships gave a much-needed homogeneity to the fleet, and soon replaced the motley collection of ship types that characterised the early years of the eighteenth century.[68] Thus there were seven different rates of ship of the line in the English fleet of thirty-nine at the Battle of Malaga in 1704, and five different rates in the British fleet of twenty-eight at Toulon in 1744, whereas at the First of June in 1794 sixteen of the twenty-five British and nineteen of the twenty-six French were 74s, and at the Nile in 1798 nine of the thirteen French and all bar one of the fourteen British ships were 74s.[69] Such homogeneity was of considerable advantage, since in practice it was impossible to get two-decked ships to sail on parity with those of one deck, or three-decked ships to sail on parity with those of two, particularly when by the wind.[70]

There were also other design improvements and innovations that helped standardise ship performance. The cumbersome lateen mizzen was gradually replaced by a gaffsail, which made the process of changing tack easier (Fig. 17).[71] The spritsail topsail, and eventually the spritsail itself, were found to be cumbersome by many and particularly frustrating when sailing in company with other ships, owing to the restriction in visibility they caused.[72] In practice, and particularly in battle, spritsails stopped being used long before the spritsail yard itself was removed as a basic design feature.[73]

Undoubtedly, the most noteworthy design improvement of the century was the advent of copper. By reducing the negative impact of worm in the tropics and marine growths in cooler climates, copper increased the standardisation of performance. Certainly there were teething problems, which in retrospect can be attributed to electrolytic corrosion,[74] and these ensured that the advent of

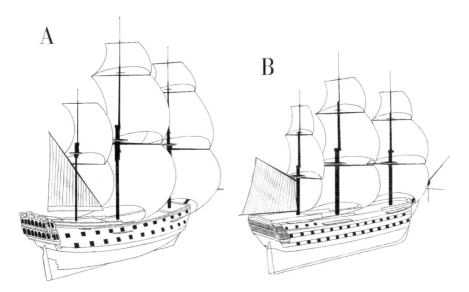

17 The lateen mizzen (A) was replaced by the more efficient gaffsail (B).

copper did not completely remove the symptoms of performance deterioration over time. Captain Sheen wrote to Captain Rotherham in the summer of 1801, complaining of the defects of his ship: 'She steers very ill, refuses stays very often, a thing she never used to do ... there is no material defect except that of her copper which is otherwise very bad.'[75] Overall, however, ships became faster, less leewardly, easier to manœuvre, and could be maintained in better condition for longer. One contemporary noted its particular advantages in station keeping: '... its greatest effect is in sailing large; we have frequently made the signal for a line of battle ahead ... when going with the wind near aft, our topsails on the caps, the yards braced contrary ways, and the uncoppered ships with every sail they could set, and have not been able to form, though six hours at it, but obliged to give it up.'[76]

In practice the standardisation of ship-type and the advent of copper could only go so far in securing uniformity of performance. Copper was introduced slowly, and it was common for fleets to consist of both coppered and uncoppered ships. This further diversified the performance of ships and increased the problems of station keeping. Hughes's fleet suffered particularly badly from this off the coast of India in the early 1780s,[77] as did the combined British and Swedish fleet that operated in the Baltic in the early years of the nineteenth century: all of the British ships but none of the Swedish ships were coppered.[78]

The design of a ship and the state of her bottom was only part of the equation, however. Ship performance in the age of sail was fundamentally dependent on human input and seamanship skill. One contemporary goes so far as to say that 'mechanical improvements' were entirely irrelevant if the officers and seamen were not united and acting together.[79] Any improvement in standardisation, therefore, had as much to do with improvements in training and ship seamanship as design innovation.[80] Seamanship skill in its purest form was simply not enough, however; to be a good fleet captain required much more.

The skills required for fleet seamanship needed structured nurturing to gain the best results. The captains needed to know their own ships, and be experienced at the skills of station keeping, but they also had to understand the art of fleet manœuvre, which was only possible by learning from long practice the results of certain angular bearings and relative rates of ships and columns: fleet captains needed to learn to think and act in squadrons.[81] This required the ability to judge instantly and accurately by eye the relative rates of ships and columns, their angles, bearings and distance. This could rapidly become complex. A fleet sailing in three columns could be formed in a line in six different ways on each column, thus comprising eighteen separate formations.[82] Each captain then had to react by eye with accuracy and subtlety, often under extreme pressure, to maintain cohesion and unity in the fleet.

Fleet seamanship not only required a different set of skills, but also a different mindset. To work in a fleet, despite the constant need for individual manœuvre, was to work as part of a team; any movement of any ship would have repercussions throughout the fleet for the cohesion, and thus tactical efficiency, of the chosen formation. It was not enough to get any group of captains together, however talented, and expect them to work efficiently as a fleet at short notice, as to be a good fleet captain was an art and a talent in itself. These requisite skills were particular and peculiar to sailing in fleets and contemporaries were only too aware that they could only be learnt by long practice.[83] It is not therefore sufficient to explain the solution to the logistical problems of sailing in a large fleet in general terms of a need for practical experience and seamanship skill. Rather, a distinction must be made between seamanship – the art of managing a ship at sea, and fleet seamanship – the art of managing a ship in a fleet. Fleet seamanship was one of the root causes of the rust that so badly affected fleet efficiency in battle after long periods of peace. There were, for example, twenty-six years of peace before the fiasco at the Battle of Toulon in 1744; there were nine years of peace before the failure at the Battle of Minorca in 1756, and again there were nineteen years of peace before the indecisive Battle of Ushant in 1778. In all these actions a complete lack of fleet cohesion or an incapacitating concern over the maintenance of it was largely to blame. Inaugural successes are as rare as disasters are common: only the battles of Lowestoft (1665) and the Glorious First of June (1794) stand out as examples.

An exchange at a court martial after the Battle of Ushant (1778) explains the type of teething problem experienced. Coming up fast astern of the

Cumberland, the master's mate of the *Weymouth* hailed her and demanded that the *Cumberland* made more sail. The *Cumberland* in reply hailed the *Weymouth*, and demanded that *they* 'throw all aback or else we should be on board them'.[84] Codrington further explains the problem: 'If I am instructed to keep between two ships, each of which acts differently, and neither correctly, what am I to do but give way to the general indifference?'[85] In such cases the fleets were too busy observing their own movements to worry the enemy.[86]

Little could take the place of actual hands-on experience, therefore, but it soon became clear that leaving the acquisition of experience to the rare and peculiar conditions of battle itself was not conducive to acceptable progress in fleet efficiency. Regular programmes of practice in fleet manœuvre were needed to teach officers to work their ships by eye in the presence of the enemy. This required two things: an officer corps that believed this was the key to success, and a regular system of evolutions which laid down an entrenched set of rules by which fleets could manœuvre in safety.

Vernon encouraged daily practice for the inexperienced,[87] and Anson's passion for fleet training and discipline is well documented[88] and was certainly shared by some of his contemporaries. His close friend Commodore Curtis Barnett condemned 'the old stupid tracts of our predecessors, [which] leave all to chance and blunder on ad infinitum, without any regular system of discipline'.[89] This enthusiasm was continued by Warren, Hawke and Boscawen,[90] and in the 1770s both Britain and France sent out training cruises to practise simple manœuvres.[91] By 1780, however, still no 'regular system' existed, although Howe was certainly keen on fleet training.[92] Rodney for one loathed such exercises, describing them as 'sham cruises, disgusting the officers and seamen, and obliging them to constant fatiguing evolutions'.[93] This attitude was compounded by an atmosphere among the officer corps that was far from conducive to the acceptance of such a system. Vernon noted in 1745 how 'our sea officers despise theory so much',[94] and as late as 1808 Hamstead notes with surprise how a subject of such importance should be 'so little attended to by the generality of officers in the British Navy'.[95]

Towards the end of the century, possibly after the Battle of Ushant in which the French fleet was handled with a far greater degree of competence than the British fleet,[96] methods of fleet manœuvre came to be studied in a much more systematic way. Principally under Howe and Kempenfelt, the art of manœuvring a great fleet was brought to 'a degree of perfection never known before'.[97] Jervis and Hood continued their work.[98] Sailing in columns according to Hoste's plan was soon adopted, which allowed the line to be formed much more quickly and easily.[99] The fleets were more frequently worked in divisions, were kept more compact, and thus more in hand. Upon sighting the French fleet prior to the Battle of the Saints in 1782, Rodney's fleet formed the line of battle in an 'incredibly short time', and by the Battle of Cape St Vincent in 1797 a proud, and no doubt a little biased, British naval officer declared that the British fleet manœuvred as if it was performing at a fleet review.[100]

Under this programme of innovations, tactical systems were studied according to mathematical and geometrical principles. These benefited the processes of fleet manipulation by providing formulae for station keeping. For example, a formula was introduced by which ships would know how to alter course to regain the line after a change of wind, the rule being that: 'From the eight points of the compass, take half the number of points the wind has changed, and that will regulate your course, for example, the wind has come forward four points, take two, the half of four, from eight points, there remains six, the number of points the ships must bear away to recover the line.'[101] Similarly it was discovered that when a fleet had split from one line into two, one being to leeward, 'The half of the number of points that the two lines differ added to eight points, is the number of points you are to bear up, and gives a course that cuts both the lines at equal angles.'[102]

Moreover, through practice and experience, seamanship methods evolved that allowed for greater accuracy in station keeping. It was found, for example, that heaving-to by backing the mizzen topsail caused a ship to fall gradually to leeward through a want of her after sail, whereas shivering or backing the maintopsail when hove-to would better maintain her station.[103] The Fighting Instructions were added to, amended and consolidated until a fixed system of rules for fleet manœuvre existed. One of the real problems of fleet manœuvre, that of timing, was greatly improved, with additional instructions that explicitly stated when ships should tack in a manœuvre,[104] while preparatory signals were introduced which allowed every ship to prepare to tack, and then do so all at the same time upon another signal.[105] The introduction of the bow and quarter line (otherwise known as the line of bearing), believed to have been first practised by Anson in 1747 and established by Hawke as a squadron order in the Mediterranean in 1756,[106] was another marked breakthrough. The main advantage of the line of bearing was that a fleet could process under easy sail, making the most of a fresh breeze with the wind on the beam or the quarter, but at the same time be in a position to form a close-hauled line of battle quickly at the first sign of danger. To form a line of bearing each ship formed up on a pre-arranged compass bearing from each other – as opposed to forming up abreast or ahead of each other (Fig. 18). From this position the close-hauled line of battle could be formed simply by each ship hauling her wind (Fig. 19).[107]

Vernon was another great pioneer and innovator, and his additional instructions of 1740 made great advances in the logistics of fleet manœuvre. Of particular value was that which allowed a designated captain to lead, regardless of which tack was on board. Previously a change of tack caused by a shift of wind would have necessitated an inversion of the line to allow the commander designated to lead on the opposite tack to get into position.[108]

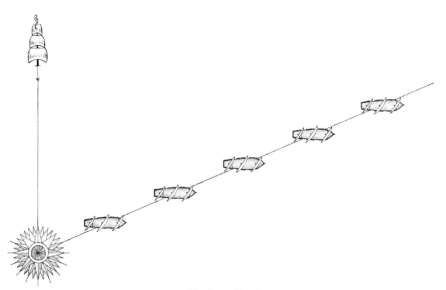

18 The line of bearing

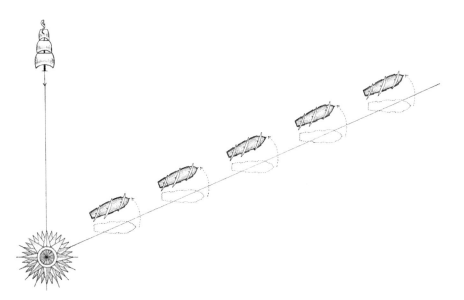

19 To form the close-hauled line ahead from the line of bearing, each ship must only haul her wind.

Yet all these changes took time to be accepted and consolidated. The continual changes that were made in the bow and quarter line instructions suggest that even during the American War of Independence they were imperfectly understood,[109] and Vernon's instruction for the rear to sail in the lead after tacking, introduced in the West Indies in 1740, had not filtered down to Matthews in the Mediterranean by 1744.[110] A system that relied so heavily on the accumulation of experience ensured that progress was not steady. Periods of peace time were particularly obstructive to progress in such skill-dependent activities that relied so much on first-hand experience. Often lessons and skills had to be learnt and relearnt many times. For some, no amount of training or experience would increase their skill at handling ships in company. In 1772 the French navy created an 'Evolutionary Squadron' under the command of the sieur d'Orvilliers, with specific orders to practice fleet manœuvres. D'Orvilliers cruised for a full seven months and reported on the ability of all of his captains. The report on the comte de Grasse, the future vice-admiral, read in part 'his collisions seem to show that there is something lacking in his judgement by eye'.[111]

These improvements must all be put into context, however. Taken either alone or together, they could not achieve pure uniformity in fleet performance, as the very nature of sailing ship performance was dictated by factors that were too fickle in nature to be controlled absolutely. As a consequence, the problems of station keeping were not restricted to certain periods in the history of the Navy, as has been asserted,[112] but were inherent to the very nature of any sailing fleet.

However highly trained a fleet was, it was never a homogenous and infrangible structure. The word 'fleet' is a collective noun for a group of ships; it is not itself a singular noun and it should not be treated as such. A fleet was not a single and solid physical entity, but a loose collection of ships which ebbed and flowed in shape, formation and structure, and required constant independent input of action and decision from all ships for it to retain any semblance of cohesion. This free-flowing and ever-changing formation demanded that each ship should be at the peak of her sailing capability and her captain and ship's company exercise considerable skill and initiative in her handling.[113] Fleet command was never a top-down power structure, with the fleet orchestrated with unerring control by the commander-in-chief. The practicalities of fleet command ensured that there was a lasting and potent bottom-up influence in fleet performance that took much of the control out of the commander's hands. This in itself may not come as a surprise to historians of warfare at sea across the ages, who understand that teamwork is the foundation of fleet efficiency, but what must be emphasised as peculiar to the age of sail is the exaggerated strength of this bottom-up influence. It was the nature of sailing warfare itself that made station keeping and fleet cohesion particularly difficult, and as such the reliance of a commander-in-chief on the relative skills, motivation and experience of his captains was of particular potency in, and peculiar to, the age of sail.

There is a tendency to view the last years of sail as the zenith of human potential in sailing warships, particularly with regard to the technology of their building and their handling,[114] but the inherent nature of the problems of sailing fleet cohesion and unity ensured that the problems of ship handling in a fleet were not solved by improvements over time, but merely eased. There was no glorious chapter of absolute control, because it was the very nature of sailing warfare that absolute control was unachievable. To attain unity and cohesion was the holy grail of fleet performance, not its defining characteristic. The best that could be expected in a sailing fleet was for '... vessels of nearly equal size, placed at nearly equal intervals from each other – sailing, at nearly equal angles from the wind, and going pretty nearly at the same rate',[115] and instructions issued 'in case of separation by bad weather or unavoidable accident'[116] do not represent over-cautious and pessimistic commanders covering all eventualities, but were a fundamental and principal requirement for any number of ships sailing in company. Fleet cohesion in sailing ships remained hard to maintain and impossible to guarantee. Vice-Admiral Moorsom, with the wisdom attained from a lifetime at sea, and able to enjoy the fruits of the innovations available in the final years of the age of sail, drives the point home by asserting in his study of naval tactics that the potential and frequency of variation in direction and strength of the wind was enough alone to baffle even the ablest of seamen.[117]

CHAPTER 5

Communication

I believe I cannot make any more signals. Every ship has had instructions what to do.[1]

The problems of fleet cohesion caused by the difficulty of station keeping were further compounded by the practical limitations of communication. The principal problem of signalling at sea was visibility. Fog, mist, rain, hail, sleet, snow, wind and even sunlight could be a nuisance, as it was difficult, if not impossible, to make out colours and patterns of flags if they were 'up sun'. A summer haze would have a similar effect, rendering colours very indistinct even at a short distance; as the sun went down, so colours became gradually more difficult to make out.[2] For a signal to be clearly visible there had to be sufficient wind for the flag to fly, which proved a considerable practical problem, as signal flags would not fly even at 3 knots if at all wet.[3] It is possible that in this situation a flag might be hung vertically,[4] but this raised problems of its own, not least the fact that a flag with horizontal stripes hung vertically changes into a flag with vertical stripes. A flag hung in a different orientation might also have a separate meaning. The national ensign hung upside down, for example, was a signal for distress.[5] To avoid such confusion, the greatest precautions were taken to keep the flags dry in flag lockers, and the signalman was personally charged with their upkeep, which included drying them if wet.[6]

Ideally the wind then had to blow at 90° to the viewing position, and that view had to be unobstructed by other ships. This was a particular problem for fleets in line ahead. At the Battle of Ushant (1778), with the signal for the line being on the mizzen peak of the *Victory*, Palliser in the *Formidable*, standing end-on towards the *Victory*, was unable to make out the signal until abreast of the flagship.[7] Moreover, when viewed directly from astern, it was virtually impossible to distinguish if a flag had been hoisted on the fore, main or mizzen masthead. For this reason, when two strange ships met and made the private signal it was always sensible for one ship to heave across the other's hawse to guarantee that their private signal was not obscured by the canvas. In battle the smoke of the guns that hung over the fleet made life particularly difficult for those ships to leeward. At the Battle of the Saints (1782) this was bad enough to render signals 'entirely useless'.[8]

The problems of visibility over distance were eased by a system of signal repetition through subordinate flagships and frigates stationed clear of the battle, though it was not set in stone that frigates alone could repeat signals. In the chaos of the Second Battle of Finisterre, Captain Hanway of the *Windsor*, suddenly finding himself astern of the flagship, repeated the signal flying for the

Kent.[9] The French fleet solved the problem in 1782 by enforcing every ship to repeat the signals of the admiral; this had a very fine effect, 'their fleet had the appearance of being dressed in colours'.[10] This method was suggested to the Admiralty in 1780 but never adopted by the Royal Navy.[11] A gradual reduction in squadron size throughout the century further improved matters by reducing the distances over which a signal would have to be seen. After 1777 the problems of visibility were further eased when the flag became the significant factor and not its position: it was now possible, therefore, to hoist the flag where it was most visible. The use of the rig as a complex signalling structure remained an advantage peculiar to the age of sail, however, and should not be routinely cast adrift by historians as a failed idea: the significance of position in the rig still continued to be used to great effect, particularly for night signals.[12]

During this innovative period in the 1770s, flags were also supplemented by pendants, which could be more easily fixed to any part of the rigging. An optimum size for flags was found, the standard approved by the majority of the officers being 9 yards by 5, anything larger being too hard to handle, particularly in strong winds.[13] Through repeat experiment it was also discovered that certain colours and patterns were more easily distinguished at a distance: they had rediscovered the heralds' 'Rule of Tincture'. Quartered, half, three-striped, striped corner-ways, half up and down, and pierced were the most favoured, chequered the poorest, and certain combinations of colours proved to be more effective in contrast to others, in particular white with red, and yellow with blue. Flags with white against the skyline were universally avoided.[14] It is instructive to remember that these flags were specifically designed for use at sea, and often worked to good effect. Captain Halkett recalled that at the Battle of Camperdown in 1797 the signals were still distinguishable despite its being very dark weather,[15] and a survey of the logs of those ships that fought in the infamous conditions of Quiberon Bay in 1759 records no difficulty with signalling on that most unpleasant of Atlantic winter evenings.[16] There was also a gradual, if uneven, service-wide progression towards two-way signalling throughout the century. By 1780 a captain in Rodney's fleet was able to signal to the flagship that he had not been able to make out or understand his signal, upon receipt of which Rodney promised to repeat the signal.[17]

The sailors themselves were not short of professional competence, and worked within the limitations of their system to make it work as effectively as possible. The use of lanterns may very well have been difficult, being blanketed by the canvas, but in practice it was not beyond the initiative of a captain to furl the mizzen topsail, topgallant or royal so that they would not obstruct the main-top light from the ships astern.[18] This practice was certainly customary in flag-ships, and in any case there were by 1778 instructions for lanterns to be placed 'where most easily seen'.[19] The problems of visibility of signals had not escaped Vernon in 1739, when he ordered that certain flag signals be fixed where they were most visible,[20] and at least two or three lookouts, usually on the poop, forecastle and occasionally aloft, were placed as a matter of course to observe the flagship and record any signals made.[21]

To have so many hands allotted to one task was a necessary precaution, as it was not unusual for a lookout to be injured in action.[22] These lookouts would have been trained to their task by the signalman, who remained the specialist.[23] The signal flags themselves were hoisted furled and then all loosed at once. William Dillon, signalman of the *Defence* in 1794 was even able to identify the signals of Lord Howe's flagship as they were run up the mast – before they were loosed; he was then able to tell the officer of the watch to prepare accordingly for the forthcoming manœuvre. The self-congratulatory air with which Dillon tells the story suggests that this may not have been a normal skill.[24] Long practice, anticipation of the signal that would next be made, and a good telescope were how this sleight of hand was achieved, but being long sighted like Lieutenant Codrington, signalman for Howe on the *Queen Charlotte* in 1794, certainly helped.[25]

The effect on signalling of battle damage to the rig is also cited as a problem peculiar to the era,[26] but in reality captains were well prepared for such eventualities. Numerous precautions were taken to reduce the potential damage to the rig,[27] but even when large sections of the rig had fallen, signalling capability did not have to go with it. After 1777 when the significance of a flag lay in its design, not its position, a flag could be secured to pretty much anything. At the First of June the *Marlborough*, under extreme pressure, hoisted the signal for assistance. It was immediately shot away, but hoisted again on a boat's mast.[28] Similarly, at the Battle of Copenhagen, Graves was required to repeat the signal to retire; all of the signal halliards were shot away except those at the cross jack yard, so he hoisted it there.[29] Fleet commanders were also sure to have spares to hand. Pocock recalled that, in action against the comte d'Aché off Negapatam in the summer of 1758, his flag for the line was shot away, but was replaced immediately by a spare, which in turn was shot away and yet again immediately replaced.[30] Such a luxury was only available to admirals, however, as captains would rarely have even one full set of flags. Admirals, moreover, enjoyed the perk of being able to move to another ship if the damage to their flagships were too bad to carry on fighting or make any signals.[31]

ORDERS AND INSTRUCTIONS

The signalling system cannot be considered in isolation from the body of ideas and instructions which it sought to convey, for it is by an appreciation of both that the characteristics of communication in the eighteenth century become clear. At the beginning of the century the system of instruction was very simple: a book of Fighting Instructions covered a large but by no means conclusive array of circumstances with corresponding instructions. Each instruction had its own signal, and the commander simply made his intention known by hoisting the corresponding signal.

This system posed three major problems. First, it was impossible to cover all eventualities. If no signal existed for the instruction that a commander wished to convey, he had no choice but to resort to the most similar, or least different instruction, often by combining signals.

The second problem was that no structure existed for *ad hoc* explanation of a signal. This proved a decisive weakness, for there was often disagreement between captains and commanders over the meaning of certain crucial terms. When confusion arose, there was little hope of dispelling it through signalling and hence of averting a loss of fleet cohesion or, at the very least, unity of purpose. In the General Fighting Instructions, for example, it was laid down that: 'when the Admiral would have the fleet draw into a line of battle one ship ahead of another' he would hoist a Union Flag at the mizzen peak. Rodney stipulated that this signal meant at two cables' length asunder, and when one cable's length was required, a blue flag with a red cross was hoisted under the Union. Arbuthnot, on the other hand, laid down that the Union at the mizzen peak was to be taken as a line ahead at half a cable's length asunder.[32] This lack of uniformity caused much confusion within the service, and was a significant barrier to smooth progress throughout the century.

The third problem was the piecemeal process of improvement through Additional Instruction. Any commander could augment the written Fighting Instructions by issuing his own Additional Instructions as he saw fit, but those additions were not applicable service-wide. So the Navy, which could be subdivided into seven separate commands with the potential for fleets in the Channel, North Sea, Baltic, North America, the Caribbean and East Indies, could not learn at the same speed.

Admiral Thomas Matthews, for example, when in command of the Mediterranean Fleet in the winter of 1744, found himself trapped in the dangerous confines of Hyères Bay, off Toulon. He attempted to beat to windward, but a shift of wind reversed the tacks, and in consequence the whole line had to be inverted in order that the commander ordered to lead with the starboard tack might get into position. He would have greatly benefited from the instruction which allowed a named captain to lead the fleet whichever tack was on board, which had been issued by Edward Vernon some five years previously when in command of the West Indies Fleet.[33] Similarly, the fiasco at the Battle of the Chesapeake in 1781 was caused to a great extent by Rear-Admiral Thomas Graves simultaneously hoisting the signals for the line ahead and close action. It was felt by Samuel Hood, who was leading the rear division, that the signal for the line negated the signal for close action, and he did not bear down and engage the enemy. Already aware of the potential for such confusion however, Admiral

Rodney had already issued an instruction to his West Indies fleet which allowed both signals to be flown without one rendering the other ineffectual.[34] Graves himself had to wait until he had experienced the potential for confusion at first hand before issuing a similar instruction in September 1781, after the Battle of the Chesapeake.[35]

CHANGE OVER TIME

Broadly speaking the signalling system experienced two major processes of reform and innovation, both at the very end of the century. The first was led by Howe, who introduced in 1790 a numerical system in which three-flag hoists made from any convenient position directly referred to the numbered paragraphs of the printed books. This allowed for greater versatility of command by expanding the potential to cope with situations unforeseen in the earlier system of prescriptive fighting instructions. The second major innovation was the introduction of the Popham Telegraph in the early years of the nineteenth century. This flag system contained letters, words and common phrases. It was an innovation that revolutionised command capability, allowing a freedom of expression between a commander and his subordinates never before experienced.

The years before these well-known innovations were introduced have become known by default as the Dark Ages of communication at sea, but in practice the relationship between the requirements of the instructions and the extent to which they fulfilled those requirements has been blurred. To understand that relationship, a distinction must first be drawn between the structure of the line as a tactical formation, which required rigidity, and the application of the line as a tactical weapon, which required flexibility.

To work within the unpredictable nature of sailing warfare, a commander needed to retain flexibility in his use of the line as a tactical weapon; he had to react to circumstance, to the manœuvres of the enemy, to shifts in wind and damage to his fleet or that of the enemy. The line itself, on the other hand, required rigidity to work as an effective tactical weapon. An effective line was tight and inflexible; it provided no opportunity for the enemy to break through, and the warships together presented a formidable and united broadside that would shatter any fleet that sought to approach it. The most effective line of battle was that in which the ships were not tied to each other in any metaphorical sense by restrictive instructions, but were literally tied to each other and the sea bed by warps and chains. Such a position, formed in a good defensive location, was formidable. The French fleet at Boulogne were formed up like this in 1801 to meet Nelson's attack, and he was easily driven off.[36] Moreover, because of the difficulty of achieving and retaining fleet cohesion, cohesion itself became a tactical goal. Disorder and irregularity in an enemy's line of battle was the one thing that commanders could depend on. To take advantage of such an opportunity the attacking fleet needed to be as compact as possible to make a powerful impression on the most vulnerable part of the enemy.[37]

There were also significant advantages to be had by certain ships taking up certain positions in the line, and the effectiveness of a line of battle could turn on the ships' being in their allocated station. Clean ships sailed faster, and were often put at either end of the battle line so they could lead in a chase.[38] Moreover, the role of the flagship as the platform of command and figurehead of the fleet meant that her protection was of the utmost importance. Regardless of where a flagship might be, in the middle of a fleet, as was Howe at The Glorious First of June in 1794, or at the head of a line, as Nelson was at Trafalgar, the need for reliable support remained the same. Reliable ships of similar size and firepower would consequently be placed nearby the flagship, a practice dating back well into the seventeenth century and undoubtedly beyond.[39]

Those supporting ships were also chosen for their sailing capabilities. As a general rule, flagships would be fine sailing ships, and it would not be sensible for a flag officer to appoint old, slow, leewardly ships near him in the line, as he might very soon find himself unsupported in the face of the enemy. Such was the fate of the Dutch commanders at the Battle of Lowestoft in 1665, when they engaged the enemy in their fine ships but left their squadrons without leadership and slowly drifting to leeward.[40] Certain positions within a line would also have 'specialist' roles. For example, a squadron in the van of a fleet would be aware of its duties as the van; of how to react upon sighting the enemy, or how to initiate a manœuvre starting with the van. If an inexperienced captain was thrown unexpectedly into a new role, chaos and collision were more likely to ensue. Prescribed position also allowed for easier identification of ships by the commander and provided a necessary level of continuity.

Undoubtedly, therefore, the preference would always be for joining battle with the ships in close formation and in the predetermined order in which they had trained, hence the strict wording of the instructions. Thus Anson took great care in ordering his fleet before the First Battle of Finisterre and Byng was explicit that he would only attack the French at the Battle of Minorca in close formation.[41] Such actions are not surprising or confusing, nor are they evidence of a dogmatic mindset as maintained by some,[42] but are clear, sensible and justified.

The inflexibility of the instructions, which has been criticised by generations of historians, has to some extent, therefore, been confused with a constant drive for cohesion. The line drew its strength from cohesion and unity of action, and those examples requiring strict station keeping were there to help provide that cohesion, not restrict mobility or aggression. The instructions were not dreamt up by bloody-minded and short-sighted administrators with little knowledge of the realities of sea warfare, but by battle-hardened veteran seafarers who knew their ships, knew the Navy, and knew war. Rigidity of tactical formation and a flexible command system are not necessarily a paradox, the characteristic of any tactical system being defined as much by the rules of which it consists as the way in which it is implemented. The mistake has been to assume that the instructions ensuring rigidity of tactical formation reflected or described a rigid and inflexible system of command; the two must be seen as existing interdependently.

It is also important to recognise the flexibility explicitly built in to the system of Instructions for its use as a tactical weapon. There was in practice nothing to prevent, and much to encourage, an admiral from issuing his own Additional Instructions, and the temporary nature of these Instructions allowed for the very real influences of geography, weather, strategy and personality of command, without impinging on the service as a whole.[43] Instructions with which a commander was not happy could easily and simply be changed. Thus Captain Webb of the *Surprize* in February 1748 turned his mind to the signal for discovering danger. The Fighting Instructions required that this signal was a weft of the jack or ensign.[44] A weft was defined as 'any flag or ensign stopped together at the head and middle portion, slightly rolled up lengthwise, and hoisted at different positions at the after-part of a ship'.[45] Webb realised that no sailor would have time to 'slightly roll up a flag lengthwise' when in immediate danger of sinking or capture, and issued an Additional Instruction that required the endangered ship to hoist the ensign half-mast and fire two guns.[46] On the other hand, advances in tactical thought beneficial to the service as a whole, but introduced as a temporary instruction, could and did remain to be entrenched in stone: Sir John Norris, when commander-in-chief of the Mediterranean, issued eight signals for chasing in 1710, the first four of which were added to the permanent instructions.[47]

Further allowance for flexibility can be seen in the wording of the instructions themselves, most clearly in an 'allowance for circumstance', and an acknowledgement of the impossibility of absolute control being written into them. This is most visible in the specific and detailed references to flexibility introduced during the American War. Most notably, Howe had a signal to 'form line as most convenient', a signal he used seven times in four days prior to the First of June,[48] and another to 'engage as circumstances required'.[49] His signal for cutting the enemy's line from the windward position included the additional clause: 'the different captains and commanders not being able to effect the specified intention in either case, are at liberty to act as circumstances require'.[50] Equally liberal were his Additional Instructions, which allowed ships to steer independently from the prescribed distance and course.[51]

There was also allowance for position in line to be manipulated according to circumstance to ensure, for example, that ships of a similar firepower would face each other in the line. In this way Howe allowed some ships to change places in the line before the action began on the First of June 1794. Captain Berkely recorded that the *Marlborough* (74) changed places with the *Royal Sovereign* (100) before battle, allowing the latter to engage the 110-gun *Terrible*,[52] and the *Royal George* exchanged places in the British line with a 74 whose position in line had fallen opposite a French three-decker.[53] In fact Howe emphasised the importance of such flexibility of fleet structure in writing as early as 1762, and included orders which allowed him to place himself opposite the commanding officer of the enemy, or to allow for more subtle tactical performance by which he might conceal from the enemy his principal tactical aim.[54]

Unquestionably the majority of the evidence from the written instructions that clearly demonstrates or even hints at a certain level of flexibility within the system of command comes from the years after 1760, specifically with the tactical tinkering of Howe. However, not all examples come from the end of the century, the period traditionally seen as the stronghold of evidence for a more flexible command system.

Hawke acknowledged in 1759 the 'great inconveniences [that] may arise from every particular ship in the squadron strictly preserving her situation in the line, either immediately at the beginning of, or during an action', and provided an instruction authorising independent action for that circumstance.[55] Boscawen in the same year issued similar instructions,[56] and Anson in 1758 had an instruction to engage 'without any regard to the situation which was prescribed to themselves by the line of battle'.[57] Preceding those instructions of Anson by almost another twenty years are those of Vernon from July 1739, in which he acknowledged in written orders that:

> As it is morally impossible to fix any general rules to occurrences that must be regulated from the weather and the enemy's disposition, this is left to the respective Captain's judgement that shall be ordered out of the line to govern himself by, as becomes an officer of prudence and resolution ...[58]

In written orders from February 1740 he continued this pattern of decentralisation, writing:

> ... as I am apprehensive that it can't be well expected, you should be able to discern such signals through the cloud of smoke we may then be in, I principally rely upon your prudence and resolution in observing where such service lie open for your execution, or require your relief, in all which cases you are hereby required and directed to govern yourself in the execution of them as becomes an officer of prudence and resolution, and as you expect to answer for your neglect therein at your peril.[59]

Although these instructions are directed in the first instance to his specially created *corps de reserve*, and in the second to captains of fireships, bomb tenders and bomb ketches, the acknowledgement of the impossibility of absolute control and the corresponding allowance for unpredictable circumstance is clearly visible here in the 1740s. There is indeed evidence from as early as 1688 of the need for an allowance of flexibility. Instruction 5 of Lord Dartmouth's instructions states:

> If the Admiral should have the wind of the enemy, when other ships of the fleet are in the wind of the Admiral. ... every such ship is to bear up into his wake. ... In this case, whether the line hath been broke or disordered by the shifting of the wind, or otherwise, each ship or division are not unreasonably to strive for their proper places in the first line of battle given, but they are to form a line, the best that may be with the Admiral, and with all the expedition that can be, not regarding what place or division they fall into or between.[60]

BEYOND THE SIGNAL BOOK:
ALTERNATIVE METHODS OF COMMUNICATION

Our understanding of the signalling system is also marred by a tendency to consider flag signalling in isolation from those methods of communication that existed alongside it. The traditional approach either does not deal with the question of alternative methods of communication at all, or does so only in passing.[61] Such brief discussion can only serve to give the impression of minor and auxiliary methods, used only to augment the system of flag signalling, existing by default of its weaknesses. Such a conclusion is certainly unfair.

After the Battle of Toulon Captain George Burrish of the *Dorsetshire* was acquitted of blame at his court martial for not supporting the fireship *Anne*, as 'he had no orders to cover the fire-ship, either by signal or otherwise',[62] and Captain Williams defended his actions in the same battle on account of only having joined the fleet an hour or two before the battle, and therefore had 'no other instructions from the Admiral, than the printed ones'.[63] Prior to the Second Battle of Finisterre, Hawke similarly prepared his captains by issuing specific instructions, but added as a postscript 'For all other signals, I refer you to the General Printed Sailing and Fighting Instructions, with the Additional Signals thereunto annexed, and to such other Signals and Instructions as you shall receive from me.'[64] These examples certainly suggest the existence of methods of issuing instructions alongside that of flag signalling. So what were these alternative methods of communication?

Meetings conducted prior to battle for a commander to inform his captains of his plans, if not openly discuss them, are an ancient practice. Some of the earliest evidence we have of signalling, the 'Black Book of the Admiralty' of 1338, includes only two real instructions; one to notify the presence of the enemy, the other to call the captains aboard the flagship.[65] In the early sixteenth century

Thomas Audley's orders from 1530 required that 'Whensoever, and at all tymes the Admyrall doth shote of a peace of Ordnance and set up his Banner of Council on Starborde bottocke of his Shippe, everie shipps capten shall with spede go aborde the Admyrall to know his will.'[66] Similarly Frobisher's fleet orders of 1578 declared that 'Upon sight of an Ensigne in the mast of the Admirall ... the whole fleet shall repaire to the Admirall, to understand such conference as the Generall is to have with them.'[67]

In the seventeenth century Wimbledon, Digby and Allin all spoke with their captains regularly, Wimbledon twice daily;[68] and Boteler is clear that such interaction was part and parcel of the instruction process.[69] Recent research has suggested that professional dialogue between eighteenth-century naval officers was more common than is traditionally held to be the case.[70] To the names of those commanders who are known to have regularly consulted their captains can be added Charles Knowles (the elder).[71] By the 1780s, and there is evidence from as early as 1761, it was established practice when sailing under Howe, Kempenfelt and Rodney for all officers to be provided with an orderly book into which they entered all verbal orders and instructions received, and signed their names in evidence of receipt of those orders.[72] Verbal instruction was thus in no way less significant or in any way less 'official' than any other type of order.

There are certainly examples of this not happening, however. Before the Battle of Cape Passaro in 1718 Byng failed to call a council of war, and believed that a commanding officer should only call a council of war 'to screen him from what he has no mind to undertake'.[73] Perhaps the most famous example of a commander not holding a council of war (with chaotic repercussions) is that of the Battle of Toulon in 1744, when Admiral Thomas Matthews refused to entertain his vice-admiral, Richard Lestock, with his tactical ideas and intentions.

There is, however, sufficient evidence to believe that both of these examples are aberrations from the expected norm. Most tellingly, one of the charges against Matthews at his court martial, and on which he was found guilty, was that he did not hold a council of war 'consistent to the constant practice of all Admirals and Commanders in Chief.'[74] It is no surprise that in September 1808, as the united English and Swedish fleet prepared to engage the Russians in the Gulf of Finland, the plan of attack was arranged beforehand and, to facilitate further the communication between the two fleets, two high-ranking officers were exchanged, the English lieutenant chosen to join the Swedish fleet, going equipped with the English signal books and flags.[75] Similar practical problems would have been experienced at the battles of Malaga (1704), Marbella (1705), Toulon (1744) and Trafalgar (1805), in each of which one of the two fleets was made up of ships of more than one nation. But the practical reality of warfare at sea ensured that, even among fleets of one nationality, without such regular contact before battle, in which plans might be presented, explained and discussed, and instructions or orders given, a captain could not hope to know the intentions of his commander, and a commander could not begin to rely on the actions of his captains. Captains and commanders were only too aware of the limitations of their system. Regular contact between a captain and his commanders did not begin in the late eighteenth century. Indeed, it seems most likely that regular contact between a captain and his commander was an acknowledged functional necessity of sailing warfare and a centuries-old practice.

If there was insufficient time to call a council of war, or if extra instructions needed to be passed, it could be done by voice from one ship to another. The admiral would summon a ship by hoisting its distinguishing pendant, and that ship would pass under the stern of the commanding officer to receive the instruction.[76] If a lengthier conversation was required, both ships would heave-to, but in slightly different ways: to reduce the possibility of a collision, the windward ship would heave-to with the maintopsail aback so that she might more easily fill and stand on without losing ground to leeward. The ship to leeward, on the other hand, would heave-to with the fore-topsail aback, so that she could quickly fill her foresail and turn sharply to leeward if in danger.[77] If the two ships were not near enough for the human voice to carry unaided, speaking trumpets were used to amplify the voice. These devices could reach a significant size, the largest being 6 feet long. Manufacturers of the earliest models, made in the 1670s, claimed that they could project a voice at sea well over a mile.[78] Some carried off an audience with their admiral with more dignity than others. After an impromptu discussion prior to the Battle of the Nile, Nelson took his hat off to wish Hood success on leading the fleet into battle. Hood, in an attempt to return the elegant and gentlemanly gesture, dropped his overboard.[79]

If it was impractical for the commander to communicate directly with his captains, he could pass on specific oral instructions by frigate or boat. The use of frigates for communication is usually passed over as a hopelessly impractical and unreliable method to which commanders were 'reduced' by the flaws in the signalling system.[80] Their role has been described only in terms of flag-repeating stations, but that was only one part of their official duty as command aids. Frigates were frequently sent throughout the fleet delivering specific and detailed instructions to one, some or all of the captains. At Trafalgar Nelson kept his frigate captains aboard the *Victory* right up until he went into battle for precisely that purpose.[81] One of the best-documented cases of the use of frigates for the relaying of specific instruction comes from the Battle of St Kitts in January 1782. The French, having drifted to leeward overnight, gave Hood the opportunity to seize their anchorage. He dispatched a frigate to explain to every ship in the van his exact intentions.[82] The plan was carried out so successfully that Robert Manners, commander of the *Resolution*, called it 'the most masterly manœuvre I ever saw'.[83]

In these examples frigates were used to relay and explain extraordinary or unexpected instructions, but they were also a regular feature of everyday fleet command, used to smooth the logistical problems of the daily functioning of the fleet. Howe and Duncan, for example, used frigates to keep the fleet informed in minute detail of intended sail plans during the night, the desired position of certain ships and changes in order or battle formation.[84] Frigates were most often dispatched on this duty, though in their absence a commander could make use of any ship for the purpose. Nelson, for example, used the *Swiftsure* (74) to relay specific instructions at the Nile.[85]

The number of frigates or other ships available was necessarily limited, but there was an abundance of boats and smaller craft that could be used for a similar purpose. It has been argued that the use of boats in this way was limited by the difficulty of launching them under gunfire or in any considerable sea.[86] Certainly, launching boats in the heat of battle would be far from ideal, but there is ample evidence to suggest that such an operation would rarely be necessary, as the boats would be launched before battle as a matter of course, both to make space and save them from damage.[87] In battle, smaller craft were also launched to carry out their function of protecting the fleet from, or escorting their own, fireships[88] and towing to safety damaged or becalmed warships.[89] The final, yet principal, reason for boats being launched prior to battle was their inevitable use as an aid to communication.

If, indeed, boats had to be launched quickly, the operation was not too problematic. Before the introduction of davits in the 1790s, boats were hoisted using tackles attached to the yards.[90] Certainly, they were heavy, but compared to the weight of the anchor or the topsail yard complete with wet canvas, it was relatively easy and could be done quickly. The boat itself was usually kept amidships on top of the spare masts and yards, so it was only necessary to hoist it *up* a few feet or just to take its weight to allow it to be swung over the side and launched. Once the boat had cleared the ship's rail, it could be swung over the side and lowered rapidly on the sheltered lee side of the ship.[91] If the sea was rough and the warship rolling, fenders, wooden skids and inhauls passed through the gun ports gave added control to the launch.[92] None of this had to be done stationary; a boat could be launched with headway, if care was taken to drop the stern first. The introduction of davits undoubtedly made this process faster, but their real value lay not so much in the ability to launch, as in recovering men overboard, where seconds represented the difference between life and death.

Once launched, there are examples of the weather being so bad that boats could not pass,[93] or of having a difficult time of it,[94] but these were rare, and fleet battles were in any case never fought in such conditions. Even at the Battle of Quiberon Bay, which was fought in appalling conditions, Keppel in the *Torbay* hoisted out his ship's boats to save twenty-two French sailors,[95] and Captain McBride, veteran of the Battle of Ushant, claimed at the court martial of Admiral Keppel that he had frequently passed between ships of a fleet in a cutter in conditions where it was not proper to open the lowest gun decks of the warships.[96] The biggest problem seems to have been coming alongside another large ship,[97] but in all but the most extreme conditions, boats could be launched and used as a method of communicating specific instruction and to reprimand, encourage, instruct or explain.[98] In the heat of battle this was certainly a terrifying prospect for the officer charged with this duty. 'In case of battle with the fleet', Howe said to Edward Codrington, 'when it may not be in my power to make signals, I may have occasion to send you with a message in a boat; and if you can carry that message between two ships in battle without making any mistakes, you will show more courage than if hand to hand with the enemy.'[99]

The use of sails as a means of conveying information is also much overlooked. Indeed, only a handful of modern historians have considered it at all, and then only too briefly.[100] Yet it is of the very first importance, for it was a tool that was part and parcel of the communication process, used in many different and valuable ways, and – most significantly – peculiar to the age of sail; its continued use until steamships no longer required their rigs must not be dismissed simply as a 'quaint survival'.[101]

The height of the masts and the size of the sails ensured that they remained visible at considerable distance. The ability to manipulate the sails, setting them in different shapes or at different heights made them valuable signalling tools in their own right. They were of particular use for signalling over large distances. Three-masted ships with their lofty sails set could be seen from each other's mast heads at 7 leagues (21 miles) distance,[102] though to make out detailed signalling, even with sails, they would have to be significantly closer. Scouts and lookout vessels, often stationed far from the main body of the fleet, used their topgallant sails to signal the presence of enemy vessels, the sail being hoisted and lowered repeatedly according to the number of vessels sighted.[103] If two scouts saw one another at the extremity of each other's vision, and they too were at the extremity of their own vision from the main body of the fleet, both fleets could be aware of each other's presence, though still 100 kilometres apart. In exactly this way Nelson used a chain of communication to keep him informed of Villeneuve's manœuvres on the night before Trafalgar through a system of signalling with coloured lights. It proved most effective. In the words of Lieutenant Browne of the *Victory*: 'As the enemy tacked or wore we had immediate intelligence of it, and regulated our conduct accordingly, tacking occasionally to preserve a relative situation with the enemy and ensure a meeting in the morning.'[104] Sails were also used for private signals, as a ship could establish if another was friend or foe without having to reveal her own colours, a practice dating back at least to the seventeenth century.[105] Howe's private signals of March 1762 provide a fine example from the mid-eighteenth century:

When any ship loses company, upon discovery of the squadron again, the ship to windward is to be made known by clewing the foretopsail sheets up, with the yard aloft; and the ship to leeward by clewing up the mizzen-topsail in the same manner.[106]

Sails could be used in place of signals in one very peculiar and particular way, as the very action of setting, furling or heaving-to was descriptive of intent. An instruction from 1778 illustrates the point:

> Instead of making the signals appointed by the second and third arti-cles of the general printed instructions for unmooring and weighing in the day-time: the commander in chief when he would have the squadron unmoor will loose the topsails and fire a gun; and when he would have them weigh he will fire a gun and haul home the topsail sheets.[107]

In this case, by loosing a sail a commander was stating his intent to make sail, and the setting of the sail was the completion of that intent, the instigation of action. Thus, through only a few minor alterations – in this case the addition of gunfire to draw attention to the flagship and the added specifics of instruc-tion – the action itself became a signal. In exactly the same way, the ship itself could be used as a means of communication. Arbuthnot's instructions of 1780 required a ship which had sighted the enemy to let the topgallant sheets fly, fire guns, and lay the ships head towards the enemy.[108]

These methods beyond the flag-signalling system did not exist because of a poor flag-signalling system alone, nor should they be seen as necessarily 'alter-native' to it. The system of flag-signalling, itself significantly less restrictive than is widely appreciated, was used to augment a much broader, simple, well-understood and well-entrenched structure for communication that was used on a day-to-day basis for the running of the fleet. It could even be argued that the flag signalling process was used to augment these processes and not vice versa. The most effective way of understanding the system of communication in the eighteenth-century Navy is not to consider each method of communication in isolation, for they were not used in isolation, but in conjunction with each other to provide a network for information exchange across the fleet.

The practical restrictions of any signalling system are central to our under-standing of its effectiveness, but it is not sufficient just to explore the practi-cal limitations of that signalling system without any explanation of how such an apparently flawed system worked in practice, yet this has been the accepted approach of generations of historians.[109] It is inevitable that our understand-ing of the system of communication has become unbalanced. By emphasising the difficulties, it has been both easy and convenient to find a culprit for fail-ure. We are left with an unrealistic picture of captains and commanders forever constrained in mute frustration by the limitations of the signalling system. In practice, the considerable problems of communication were often balanced by a practical problem-solving work ethic that eased many of the difficulties of communication and made fleet cohesion and unity of action less problematic than we might expect. To concentrate on exceptional innovators as agents of radical change in the signalling system is to fail to appreciate the daily input of those captains with less innovative minds who sought and achieved solutions to, or at least eased the negative impact of, the problems they were faced with on a daily basis. In the hands of those practical men these tools of command were not as restrictive as we have been led to believe, either for the commander or for his subordinate.

CHAPTER 6

Unwritten Rules

It wanted neither signal nor instruction to tell him what he should have done ...[1]

A large part of the challenge in trying to understand fleet battle lies in determining why captains acted as they did; it is the root cause of understanding success or failure in any battle. The signalling and communication system is, of course, a very important part of that, but it is only a part. The inherent problems of station keeping alone dictated that fleet captains were required to use their own initiative constantly when in company with other ships, and the flaws in the signalling system similarly required a degree of interpretation of signals that was permanent and significant: the limitations on what could be said by signal highlighted the importance of what was not said. But captains were not left in complete isolation, with no clue of what was expected of them. In practice, formal orders received by signal, written or verbal instruction formed only a part of the body of opinion and knowledge which underpinned the principles of action and determined the methods to be used. Known to more modern analysts of military efficiency as 'doctrine', this body of knowledge received no such formal recognition in the eighteenth century, although its influence was pervasive and permanent. Notions of duty in battle were determined by a composite amalgam of formal and informal doctrine. The formal doctrine consisted of Fighting Instructions, signals and written and verbal instruction: the body of informal doctrine consisted of uncodified law, custom and convention regarding collective identity and behaviour. It existed within the approved system of command hierarchy and worked in parallel with, and was frequently more influential than, official instruction. Together they formed that body of doctrine which defined subordinate duty.

The existence of that body of influence is easy to demonstrate, for it permeated all aspects of seafaring throughout the century. One of the most important was the expected behaviour of two strange ships when they met at sea. Nathaniel Boteler wrote in detail at the end of the seventeenth century of what he describes as the 'custom of the sea', which dictated that the inferior ship should pass under the lee of the superior.[2] Over a century later at the court martial investigating the behaviour of the *Leander* in 1807, it transpired that the *Leander* had opened fire on some vessels which were acting suspiciously, not bringing to in the 'customary manner' on the same tack and with the ship's head towards the challenging vessel.[3]

These unwritten rules were no less significant with regard to fleet command and control. The failure at the Battle of Toulon (1744) is a particularly valuable source for the detail of unwritten convention in fleet command and control, as the majority of contemporary commentators were concerned with what *should* have occurred. A young Hugh Palliser reminded the court at the trial of Vice-Admiral Richard Lestock that, in the case of two apparently conflicting signals, the last signal was always to be obeyed, 'according to the constant rule of the Navy',[4] and Rodney was explicitly critical of Lestock's action in the night preceding the action. Lestock hove-to for the night without closing the gap with his commander-in-chief. Rodney firmly believed he should have brought-to in the immediate wake of his commander-in-chief, which Rodney described as being 'agreeable to the known practice'.[5] The methodological point is clear: nowhere in the Instructions or the Signal Books are any of these examples stipulated, but here they are – rules governing behaviour throughout the century.

It is a much more difficult task to offer a detailed analysis of what principles such an unwritten doctrine actually embodied at any one time. Not only is it a methodological problem – by definition, this doctrine was never recorded in a written and isolated format – but also the principles of what determined 'duty' at any one time were open to change and circumstance. Nevertheless, contemporary discussions of the expectation of behaviour, most commonly found in the minutes of courts martial or in correspondence in the aftermath of controversial actions like the battles of Toulon (1744) or Ushant (1778), are particularly revealing, and they strongly suggest that, regardless of specific instruction, captains and commanders were expected to know how to behave regarding certain key issues: the distance of engagement, strength of firepower, tenacity, bravery, mutual support, how to keep station, and when to leave station.

FLEET COHESION AND ENGAGING THE ENEMY

The maintenance of fleet cohesion was the most basic priority of all fleet captains and a fundamental of fleet warfare. It maximised the defensive efficiency of any formation and was the starting point from which to launch any offensive tactic. The inherent difficulties of station keeping ensured that it remained of magnified significance throughout the century and was reflected in the expected duty of each captain. For example, the fleet captain who failed to close a gap in a line if the ship leading him had been damaged 'would deserve and justly incur the most severe punishment'.[6] It was an established maxim that a ship should not sacrifice line cohesion unless specifically signalled so to do,[7] and, in order to maintain cohesion, it was perfectly acceptable for a ship that wore very badly to tack if the signal for the whole fleet to wear was made.[8] Similarly, it was acceptable for a ship that took a long time in tacking to initiate the manoeuvre before she was explicitly ordered to do so.[9]

Another guiding principle which drove captains to act in lieu of, or even contrary to, specific instruction was a duty to engage the enemy. 'In my profession,' wrote Captain Graham Moore, 'whenever it is a disputed point whether to fight or not, it is best to fight.'[10] Some years earlier, Vernon had gone further in his description of this duty. Not only was a British ship expected to fight a single enemy, but she should not refuse a fight with two equal in force to her own. He magnanimously conceded, however, that a British ship might be allowed to run from three enemies.[11] This rule, Vernon argued, 'has no establishment in our laws, but is very well established in honour and reason'.[12]

The significance of this sense of duty in the structure of the command system is made clear in a series of exchanges at the trial of John Byng in 1757. Captain Durell of the *Trident* was quizzed over the potential confusion that might arise if the signals for engaging and that for the line of battle ahead were flown concurrently. He maintained that if the fleet was at too great a distance from the enemy and the signal for engaging was made, it was still his duty to bear down to an appropriate distance before hauling up and forming the line ahead, if still required by signal. He was quizzed further: 'But do not ships that put themselves in a line of battle abreast, when a signal is out on board the Admiral for a line of battle ahead; I say, do not they disobey the Admiral's orders?' He replied: 'I apprehend not, if the signal for engaging is made, and they are at too great a distance from the enemy.'[13]

For Durell, the duty of engaging outweighed any potential confusion caused by apparently conflicting signals. At the Battle of Ushant in 1778 the same sense of duty led Captain Bickerton of the *Terrible* to act contrary to his orders to chase a French ship. Having set off on his chase, the wind suddenly changed, which allowed the entire French fleet to be brought to action. Bickerton returned immediately to the fleet.[14] In similar fashion at Martinique in April 1780 Rowley, too far from Rodney to receive direct and specific instruction, followed the French in their unexpected wear. It was his duty to follow the enemy and renew the engagement that determined his action.[15]

Such a duty as engaging the enemy – however many of them there were – could not exist in a vacuum, however, and certain methodological doctrine existed to help captains do their duty.

MUTUAL SUPPORT

Officers knew that their best chances of success in a sea fight lay in unity of action. As a result, mutual support was expected by and of each and every captain during fleet engagement. For merchant ships in convoy, the masters of each ship had 'the strongest obligations incumbent upon them to stand by one another' if attacked.[16] In a description of how a good naval officer should behave, Lieutenant George Ryall was explicit that he should encourage the people, do his utmost to engage the enemy and 'make all haste that ever he could to the assistance [of whoever] he thought wanted it'.[17]

The example of Captain Fox at the Second Battle of Finisterre (1747) is itself particularly revealing of the high professional regard in which this duty was taken. Fox had clearly failed to support his fellow captains, and, in particular, had failed to relieve the *Eagle* when hard pressed and trapped between two fires. The other captains refused to sit with Fox during a council of war held immediately after the battle. He was later found guilty of misconduct at his court martial, and dismissed from his command of the *Kent*.[18] Cochrane was so confident of being able to rely on this sense of duty that he used it to advantage during the Battle of Basque Roads in 1809. He was astonished to find his frequent messages detailing the helplessness of the French fleet ignored, so he set to and embroiled himself in a battle against three French battle ships, knowing full well that his actions would, in his words, 'compel' ships to come to his assistance.[19]

Again, however, this responsibility did not exist in a total vacuum. Support was particularly expected by each ship's immediate neighbours in the line. When formed in line, a ship's responsibilities lay with her immediate neighbours as they ensured her security; thus the line maintained its strength, like a chain. It was acknowledged that, in time of action, the admiral was not always the best judge of the relative damage to his fleet and, correspondingly, of who to appoint to the relief of any ship in distress. That responsibility fell to the immediate neighbours of the damaged ships.[20] Thus Captain Ambrose recalled of the Battle of Toulon that, when the masts of the *Marlborough* fell, he did not expect support from the nearby *Rupert*, but from his two immediate neighbours, the *Dorsetshire* and *Essex*, although he did acknowledge that the *Rupert* could have helped.[21] In the same trial the captain of another ship was excused going to the help of the *Marlborough* as he was too far away, and was waiting to receive four upcoming Spanish warships.[22] When this system worked, it worked well. At Robert Calder's action in July 1805 the *Windsor Castle* (90) lay isolated in the face of a number of enemy ships. Her immediate neighbour, Calder's flagship the *Prince of Wales* (90), made sail to her support and engaged two of the enemy ships. This took the fire from the *Windsor Castle* and prevented her from being raked. Meanwhile, the captain of her other immediate neighbour, the large frigate *Egyptienne* (44), launched a boat, ready to tow the crippled *Windsor Castle* away from danger.[23]

The two immediate seconds to the commander-in-chief were specifically required to work as a unit with their flagship, together both attacking the enemy flagship and defending their own from any attack together; indeed, one contemporary believed that the seconds should be more focused on defence of the flagship than their own ship, 'as they must sacrifice every other consideration to the honour of their flag'.[24] Interestingly, this requirement for three ships to work together as a unit depended as much on the position of the enemy flagship as their own. If, for example, any other ship than the flagship was to engage the enemy flagship, then the two ships closest to her would act as seconds, thus trapping the enemy flagship between three fires so that she might strike sooner.[25] It was a convention based on a mixture of mutual support and considered aggression directed at the hierarchy and command structure of the enemy fleet.

One further and distinct aspect of mutual support was the responsibility of captains to support the commander of their division. Captain Barnet was explicit that he considered his duty 'never to leave the flag, or officer representing one, *in whose division I am,* without a particular order or signal'. [26] In another letter, he adds:

> I presume there are instances both of whole divisions going down to the enemy too soon, and of coming in so late as to have no part in the action; but I never heard that the private captains who kept their stations in those divisions fell under the least censure …[27]

The Battle of Ushant in 1778 illustrates how this worked in practice. The potential confusion arose when Sir Robert Harland, in charge of the van division, stood on towards the French after Admiral Keppel had made the signal to form the line of battle. This had a particular impact on Captain Brereton of the *Duke*, whose prescribed position in line depended on Sir Robert Harland assuming his. Brereton was thus in a quandary – to obey the fleet admiral's signal for the line as best he could or to go down in support of the leader of his division. In the end, it was his duty to support his divisional leader, which won through, and a collective decision was made by the officers aboard that, as their ship, the *Duke,* was not damaged, they were to follow the example of Sir Robert 'with all the sail they could bear'.[28] In turn, it was the sight of Admiral Keppel heavily embroiled and imminently outnumbered that had made Sir Robert Harland bear down to his assistance without orders.[29]

The most potent example, however, comes from the Battle of Copenhagen. Admiral Hyde Parker had given Nelson command of a division, and ordered him to attack one end of the Danish defences. After heavy fighting, Parker, in the belief that Nelson's division were failing to gain the upper hand, ordered a retreat. The signal was seen by Nelson but he chose to ignore it, realising that an attempted retreat in shoal water with damaged ships would be fatal. Some believe that he raised his telescope to his blind eye and said to his flag-captain 'I have a right to be blind sometimes. … I really do not see the signal.' Whether or not that is true, Parker's signal is well documented, along with the reaction of Nelson's division: every one followed Nelson's example, choosing to support the actions of their divisional commander over the explicit orders of the fleet admiral.[30]

THE ROLE OF EXAMPLE

The actions of the fleet commander were in fact used as a model for behaviour in a much broader, more subtle and sophisticated sense than simply for general support. The role of example as a means of conveying intention and methodology were of critical significance, due above all to the practical liabilities of the signalling system. Quite simply, to show what was required was often the easiest and best way of maintaining cohesion and unity of action.

In battle the commander-in-chief was always taken as the point of direction for the forming and preserving of formation, regardless of the position of any other ships.[31] His actions were 'of course' to be used as an example to be followed, engaging close or at a distance.[32] Indeed, if he was to tack, wear or heave-to without signal, it was required that he be copied.[33] At his trial in 1750 Rear-Admiral Knowles was explicit that *all* actions and motions were to be taken from the admiral or commander-in-chief, and subordinate ships were to keep a close and permanent eye on all his movements.[34] The admiral could not indicate in advance at what precise moment a manœuvre was to be expected, but the timing of that manœuvre was always regulated by his actions. If for any reason the admiral did not want his ship to be the model to be copied, he would designate another ship as the 'leading ship' on which all others should base their movements.[35] If a captain was unable to see the movements of the commander-in-chief or the leading ship, he could be guided in his own movements by the rest of the fleet. Thus at the Battle of Ushant (1778), Captain Brereton brought-to following the example of the rest of the fleet, despite the lack of a signal (or a visible one) explicitly detailing him or the fleet to do so.[36]

There is plenty of evidence of this working in practice. At the Battle of Ushant, those aboard the *Formidable* regulated all their actions in setting and taking in sails by what they saw in Keppel's flagship, the *Victory*,[37] and at the Trial of Captain Molloy in 1795 over his conduct at the First of June in 1794, Captain Seymour makes specific reference to tacking the *Leviathan* the moment he was informed that the flagship the *Queen Charlotte* was in stays, 'without attending to what the ship ahead of me did on that subject'.[38] This whole scenario was brought about by Howe repeatedly signalling for the leading ship, the *Caesar*, to tack and engage the French rear. With no response from the *Caeser*, Howe tacked in the *Queen Charlotte*, and those near him, including the *Leviathan*, followed his example.[39] In similar fashion, at the Battle of the Saints in 1782, in spite of the signal to engage to leeward flying clearly aboard Rodney's flagship, the *Formidable*, he was followed through the French line to windward by the five ships in his immediate wake. His manœuvre was also copied by the *Duke*, next ahead of Rodney, and by Hood's entire division.[40] With such an emphasis on the movements of the commanding officer, it was an established maxim of sea discipline that a commanding flagship would never get out of her way for any ship whatever, unless that ship was disabled or taken by a sudden shift of wind.[41] The commanding officer knew that all of his movements were carefully watched, so everyone had to be deliberate and well considered.

With his movements being followed so closely, bringing on a general fleet engagement required a good deal of decisiveness and bravery from the commander-in-chief. In 1702 Benbow, writing from sorry experience, lamented the poor state of professionalism in the service, and suggested leading by example, with the commander at the head of the line as a reliable but last-stop cure for those ills 'that our people for shame would not fail to follow a good example'.[42] Rodney's captain, Walter Young, was explicitly critical of his admiral's conduct at Martinique in April 1780 because 'for want of example in him other people erred'.[43] In direct contrast, St Vincent said of Duncan's victory over the Dutch at Camperdown in 1797: '[Lord Duncan] attacked, without attention to form or order, trusting that the brave example he set would achieve his object, which it did completely'.[44] From the subordinate's perspective, Captain Codrington of the *Orion* was explicit that his action at Trafalgar was 'in imitation of the noble example before us',[45] referring to Nelson and Collingwood leading the two divisions into battle.

In line ahead, the ship leading the fleet also had an important role to play in setting example, particularly regarding the timing of manœuvres or change of course. If the fleet were to change course without tacking or wearing, for example, the new course was to be taken from the leading ship, to which changes of course were signalled to sail a point to starboard or port as was required, the rest then following in her wake.[46]

The potency of the dual responsibilities for mutual support and for following the lead of a designated 'leading ship' is brought to light by the confusion at the Battle of Martinique in April 1780. Rodney's intention was to bring his entire force down on to the centre and rear of the enemy, thus overwhelming them with his numerical superiority. He had issued additional instructions regarding attacks to the van, centre or rear of the enemy accordingly. The wording of the permanent instructions, however, stated that upon the signal to engage, the van should bear down to the van of the enemy fleet – not to its centre as Rodney intended. Captain Carkett, leading the van of the fleet in the *Stirling Castle,* was unaware of or confused by Rodney's intentions, and bore down to the van of the enemy. Carkett, although mistaken in his admiral's intention, set a fine and brave example by slowly bearing down to the van of the enemy, thus exposing his ship to the fire of the entire enemy van. He was followed and supported by those in his squadron. Rodney was quite specific that Carkett's actions induced the entire van to follow him, in the face of his intended mode of attack.[47]

SUBORDINATE INITIATIVE AND THE BATTLE OF TOULON

The evidence presented so far also hints at one further unwritten rule and convention which was present in the operations of any fleet at any time: an allowance for subordinate initiative. Hierarchy, respect, obedience and discipline are essential to the efficient functioning of a military body, but victory itself remains the ultimate aim. It is in this rather murky area that insubordination becomes acceptable.

To help officers negotiate this dilemma in the eighteenth century, it was accepted that 'signals were sacred things, and should ever be attended to, and more particularly so in action'.[48] However, there was a parallel acknowledgement that station keeping required constant input of independent action from captains, and that specific instruction could be confusing or inaccurate because of rapidly changing circumstances and signalling inadequacy. Correspondingly, it was recognised and expected that captains and commanders had to think and act outside of their specific instruction as and when necessary.

The Battle of Toulon in 1744 and its aftermath highlight these questions of duty, signalling and initiative. Indeed, it has become known as 'the starting point, the zero of the scale from which the progress of the century is to be measured', as evidence of 'the greatest degradation in naval tactical thought'.[49] Having failed to follow his admiral into action, Lestock defended himself by taking a 'letter of the instructions' approach which confined itself purely to the wording of the Fighting Instructions, which he claimed prevented him from leaving his station. He was subsequently acquitted. The historian must, however, be cautious in taking the outcome of these trials as evidence of a particularly rigid system of command. There are certainly many more questions raised than answers provided by Toulon and its aftermath, but the answers we do have suggest that Lestock's acquittal must be treated with extreme care as evidence of the inherent inflexibility of the command system of the 1740s.

The simple fact that there are so few similar examples of captains or commanders being exonerated for similar behaviour should, in itself, have raised some eyebrows among naval historians, but for years it has not. Although it has been argued that the court was run fairly,[50] the evidence points to the unavoidable conclusion that the trial was conducted under heavy political pressure, the Navy itself being split, in the words of Sandwich, into 'private cabals ... parties and factions'.[51] There is general agreement that the trial was conducted with extraordinary partiality, and that the former opposition Whig government, in favouring the Whig Lestock, had conducted nothing short of a travesty of justice.[52]

There is also direct evidence that Lestock understood the significance of 'duty' as a motivational factor alongside that of the instructions. In 1742, two years before the Battle of Toulon, he wrote a letter to a subordinate, rebuking him for exactly the same crime as he was later to commit himself.

> ... is it your duty to see two-thirds of the squadron sacrificed to the enemy, when you could, but did not join in the battle? Such an account would tell but ill to our country after the loss of a battle ... the punishment inflicted on a breach of the 12th article of the Statute of Charles the Second upon those who withdraw, or keep aback, or do not come into the fight to engage would be what must follow in such a case. So I will say no more of trifling nor misunderstanding of a line of battle; as these are, and must be the consequences of a not trifling want of duty in the weighing of circumstance in regard to battle ... The 13th Article of the Fighting Instructions leans that way also.[53]

There is further evidence from the series of trials after Toulon that suggests Lestock's acquittal was extraordinary. The defence of Captain Burrish of the *Dorsetshire* included the following exchange:

> Q: Did you engage as an English Man of War ought to have done, to succour the *Marlborough* from the *Real* and the *Hercules*?
> A: I cannot say – We must be governed by lines; and we were in a line with the Admiral.
>
> Q: Did your Captain engage the enemy so close as he could have done, or as near as an English Man of War ought to have engaged?
> A: I think he must obey instructions.[54]

Although it might be tempting for historians, seeking to support an argument for the inherent inflexibility of the system, to take these examples out of context, the fact remains that Burrish's arguments were *not* accepted by the court; he was permanently cashiered, one of only four captains of a fleet of forty ships found to have exercised insufficient initiative.[55] The court believed that what he ought to have done was his duty, which was defined as 'to have done his utmost to take, fire, kill and endamage his Majesty's said enemies',[56] and, more specifically, to have gone to the support of the *Marlborough* and *Namur*. That, it argued, was more important than being governed by lines or instructions.

Another of those captains was Captain Ambrose of the *Rupert*. The mainstay of the argument was over his position in the line and whether he should have engaged the enemy closer, even if that meant leaving his position. In the evidence, Ambrose bemoaned his misfortune in being in a part of the line with no immediate opponent. He 'swore and stamped' on finding himself with no ship to engage, and 'he had a great mind to break the line to go down and engage those five ships'. At this stage the master, pointing to a book that lay on the arm-chest, said: 'Then you'll be hanged for breaking your Fighting

Instructions: consider you are in the line.'[57] After another extended episode of swearing and stamping, Ambrose declared forcefully that: 'It's better to be blamed for breaking the line than to lie thus and have no ship to engage.'[58] He was unable to make up his mind, however, and merely engaged at too long a distance.

In defence of his inactivity, he quoted the example of Rooke at Malaga, whose division was hard pressed and, though Shovell was in full view of what was happening, judged it inadvisable to leave his station without a signal or particular orders for that purpose. This, he said, proved that 'no ship can leave her station to go to the assistance of another without the proper signal or orders for that purpose; tho many ships may at that time lie in their stations inactive.'[59] At that battle, however, Shovell *did* receive specific orders by boat from Rooke to keep his station.[60] The court were unmoved by Ambrose's defence, and found him guilty of not doing his utmost to engage, take, fire and kill, and he was cashiered during the King's pleasure.[61]

There are more examples that tend towards the same conclusion of expected initiative. At the court martial of Richard Lestock, Captain Powlett of the *Oxford* described the instructions as 'discretional', did not think obedience to the instructions alone was sufficient authority to comply with a signal that was plainly wrong, and firmly believed there were certain instances in which a ship could leave her position in the line without fear of censure.[62] Captain Pett of the *Princessa* had charges brought against him by Lestock, who applied the technique of his own defence – a 'letter of the instructions' approach – to their prosecution. On that day the *Princessa*, an uneasy ship at the best of times but now heavily damaged, lay-to to repair her damaged rigging. In the light winds and big swell, the damaged rigging was likely to cause further damage if not secured and, with no immediate enemy to engage nor friend to support, it was decided that the best service Pett could render was to put his ship in a fighting condition in case the action was renewed as expected.[63] In the face of repeated and aggressive questioning in an attempt to ascertain if Captain Pett had received orders to go from his station and withdraw from battle, and was therefore justified in his action, the court upheld his defence and he was acquitted.[64] The pattern was repeated at the trail of Captain Sclater, who was acquitted of charges of misconduct for withdrawing from action with the *Poder*. It came to light in the trial that the *Somerset*'s braces were all broken, and as the *Poder* became disabled, she stopped dead in the water. The *Somerset*, unable to brace any of her yards, could not heave-to, tack, wear or make sternway, and shot past the crippled *Poder*.[65]

There is even evidence to suggest that too much initiative was taken at the Battle of Toulon. Captains Cooper, Lloyd and West of the van division were found to have exercised an excess of initiative by stretching ahead of Rowley's line to keep the French from doubling it, contrary to Matthews's additional instruction requiring each ship to keep station at the same distance from each other as those either side of the admiral. The van ships were faced with a clear dilemma: if they left the French van ships and bore down to the French line as the signal required, some seven or eight ships would remain unopposed and free to double the British line. Each captain, finding himself in a situation different from that which the instructions allowed for, firmly believed it was their duty to ignore them and do their duty as they understood it.[66] They believed the immediate requirement was to prevent the French from doubling. They therefore stretched along to the van of the French fleet to contain them. All three were cashiered, but all restored to their rank soon after. Captain Temple West in particular remained an officer of 'conspicuous merit' who fought with distinction at the Battle of Minorca in 1756 as a rear-admiral.[67]

SUBORDINATE INITIATIVE POST-TOULON

It is thus clear that the evidence from the Toulon trials does not overwhelmingly suggest that rigid interpretation of the instructions and lack of initiative were the expected norm in 1744. But what of the impact of the Toulon trials on the operational methodology of the Navy? Historians have long believed that Lestock's acquittal set an unhealthy precedent in the Navy for rigid interpretation of the instructions. This can be traced right back to Clerk, who believed 'that sentence of the court martial which broke Mr. Mathews ought virtually to be condemned as the source of all the many naval miscarriages since.'[68] There is not total agreement, however,[69] and it is certainly a complex problem. Did the service see the outcome of the trials as politically motivated and ignore it, or did it alter its professional practices to favour a rigid interpretation of the instructions? More work needs to be done before this question can be answered with any satisfaction, but some important points can be made nonetheless.

First, it is important that the trials are considered together as a body of evidence. As has been shown, the results were far from unanimous in their condemnation of initiative, and that of Lestock was extraordinary indeed. Furthermore, it was the minutes of those trials which favoured a liberal interpretation of 'duty' that were published, and were therefore most accessible to naval officers. The details of Lestock's own trial were kept secret by the Admiralty,[70] a fact significant in itself in terms of the impression the Admiralty wished to make on its officer corps. Although the result, if not the detail, of Lestock's trial was itself public knowledge, naval officers were well aware that results of courts martial might be unjust, and it is reasonable to assume that they were aware that something like this had happened after Toulon.[71]

The conduct of Admiral Byng at Minorca in 1756 is the most often used example of the negative impact of the Toulon trials.[72] With the fleet somewhat fragmented in its approach to the enemy, Byng's flag captain suggested he should set more sail to clear the confusion and get into action more quickly. Byng is reported to have replied: 'It was Mr. Matthews misfortune to be prejudiced by not carrying down his force together, which I shall endeavour to avoid.'[73] This quote must not, however, be taken out of context to argue for a particularly rigid system, for it was simply reflecting the long standing, respected and sensible convention of fleet tactics that stressed the importance of cohesion and unity of action. This was merely confirmed by the Toulon trials, which were certainly correct in this instance. Regardless of what happened at Toulon, Matthews *should* have brought his fleet down together, that being 'the usual practice of flag officers commanding in chief'.[74] In the same way, at Minorca, although it has been argued that Byng's complaint that his fleet was much weaker than the enemy is not justified,[75] it is more certain that the French fleet was faster, well formed and well conducted.[76] Byng realised quite sensibly that maintaining cohesion against such an enemy was of the highest priority.

In the years immediately after Toulon there is indeed little evidence to suggest a negative impact on the command structure. There are no further examples of commanders or captains being exonerated by court martial for failing to use initiative and adopting a 'letter of the instructions' defence. There is, on the other hand, continuing evidence for a liberal interpretation of duty, retaining its significance. Vernon's ideas about decentralisation, liberal interpretation and initiative, so clear in his command of the West Indies squadron,[77] were not affected by the outcome of Toulon. On the contrary, writing as an anonymous sea officer in the defence of Captain Mostyn in 1747, he launched a thinly veiled attack on the outcome of the Toulon trials:

> All formality ... only tends to keep the main point out of the question, and to give knaves and fools an opportunity to justify themselves on the credit of jargon and nonsense, whereby they think to perplex superiors and get acquitted with honour, for what they deserve to be hang'd.[78]

At Byng's trial, held in 1757, Lieutenant R. Boyle of the *Revenge* was quite sure that a ship was allowed to leave her station without a signal if certain circumstances arose, and offered the example of a ship in need of assistance.[79] Similarly Captain Durell of the *Trident* saw nothing wrong in disobeying specific orders if he considered them to conflict with his duty.[80] In general those in authority agreed, and a course of individual action that directly contradicted the signal book could always be overlooked. Although article xvii of the fighting instructions of 1782, for example, insisted that 'no ship or particular part of the fleet whatsoever, shall presume to tack, or wear, whilst in action unless by signals or order from the Admiral so to do',[81] at the trial of Admiral Keppel in 1778 Captain Robinson of the *Worcester* was explicit in his understanding of the command system that if he thought it proper he could tack his ship without the admiral making a signal specifically for him to tack. The court agreed.[82]

With regards to command method, in finding Matthews guilty, the Admiralty had merely reconfirmed the expectation that a commander clarify his views of tactical doctrine prior to an action. Rowley took over the Mediterranean command on Matthews's return to England, and immediately amended the Fighting Instructions to clarify certain points of doctrine with regard to station keeping and mutual support, drawing on Vernon's experience in the West Indies. Anson, Hawke and Knowles continued the process, concentrating particularly on the need for a clear and common doctrine.[83]

The weight of the evidence suggests, therefore, that Lestock's behaviour was not the norm at the time of Toulon, nor did his acquittal set an immediate precedent for a rigid interpretation of the instructions and a lack of initiative. Examples of captains taking the responsibility in battle to act contrary to specific signal, or in lieu of the necessary signal, are not examples of epoch-defining brilliance and inspiration, but of an everyday part of fleet warfare, born of necessity. A system with limited command flexibility needs subordinate initiative to work, but it does not in itself restrict or hinder the taking of that initiative. It is important to distinguish between a signalling and instructional system that did not provide flexibility of command expression, and a system which stifled subordinate initiative. The two are very much separate, but have traditionally been linked. In fact the primary flaws of the signalling system, allied to the practical difficulties of fleet capability, increased rather than reduced the scope for initiative. By definition, a system that does not provide flexibility of command provides too much potential for subordinate initiative as, unaware of or unclear about his commander's intentions at any particular time, the subordinate has no choice but to rely on his own initiative to fill in the gaps. Even Rodney, the finest example of an arch-authoritarian commander, acknowledged in a very matter of fact way that, at the Saints, his captains 'must have been guided entirely by their own judgement in the measures they were to pursue'.[84]

COMMAND INITIATIVE

This level of expected and approved flexibility was not restricted to subordinate behaviour, but also extended to command method. It was Anson's firm belief that 'a person trusted with command may and ought to exceed his orders and dispense with the common rules of proceeding when occasions require it',[85] a sentiment mirrored almost word for word by Captain Byam Martin some fifty years later.[86] It was this view which led Matthews to bear down on the Spanish fleet at Toulon, once he was aware that if he waited for the rear to join him as the Instructions prescribed, the opportunity for engagement would be lost.[87] At his court martial after Ushant, Keppel defended his action in not endeavouring to maintain the line of battle and assuming a more haphazard formation by invoking centuries of tradition of flexible command, in which 'strict orders give way to reasonable enterprise'.[88] In exonerating him, the court emphasised an admiral's responsibility to choose his own tactics and not blindly follow the Fighting Instructions. At Camperdown in 1797 Duncan had no qualms in admitting that he was obliged by his proximity to land to lay all regularity and tactics aside.[89]

The problems and solutions of fleet command mirrored the wider problems and solutions of communication in the eighteenth-century Navy. Commanders were given very broad objectives and an allowance for discretion because situations rapidly changed and communication was slow, and often impossible. It took, for example, an average of nine weeks for a military dispatch to get from London to New York;[90] securing a reply would take twice as long. Matthews's instructions upon his receiving the Mediterranean command in the spring of 1742 begin: 'It must in great measure be left to your discretion how and where to employ your squadron the most effectually for these purposes.'[91] The summing up of the trial of Captain Lumsdaine, court martialled in 1793 for disobeying direct orders to deliver a letter to Consul Magra in Tunis harbour illustrates perfectly the wider problem. Lord Hood was intent on provoking the French into attacking a British ship. In his own words, this would allow him to make a 'general sweep' of the French ships of war out of every neutral port. In full knowledge that there was a large squadron of French warships in Tunis harbour, he sent Lumsdaine, who was wholly ignorant of the trap he was sailing into, to deliver the letter. Upon discovering the French squadron, and with a valuable ship under his convoy, Lumsdaine determined to disobey his specific instructions concerning the letter. He argued:

> I had always conceived a certain degree of discretionary power was vested in a commander of a King's squadron, or any person holding a responsible situation. It must be very evident to every member of the court that orders delivered from a commander-in-chief do not provide against unforeseen events or accidents that may occur in the course of service.

And the court's verdict:

> And the court ... is of opinion that the said Captain George Lumsdaine did not comply with the orders of the commander-in-chief, in as much as he did not deliver to Mr. Consul Magra the letter in question; yet, from the testimony before the court, it clearly appears that his conduct upon that occasion did not proceed from any neglect, but, on the contrary, was owing to the information he had received of the superiority of the enemy's force in Tunis bay ... [it concludes] the court is of opinion that, however unjustifiable it is in an officer not strictly to comply with orders,

yet circumstances may sometimes arise in which his discretionary conduct may be found necessary ...[92]

Lumsdaine was subsequently acquitted of all blame. His understanding of
'duty', determined by custom, tradition and convention, and allowed for by a
flexible and tolerant system, was what counted at his trial.

The view that initiative was 'virtually forbidden',[93] must therefore be reconsidered, for it was clearly not the case. On the contrary, obeying orders and
doing one's duty were the two parallel fundamentals of naval discipline, but for
too long historians have overlooked the significance of the latter in favour of
the former. In practice, obeying direct orders was only one part of doing one's
duty, and as a general rule success pretty much justified any measure, a phrase
used by contemporaries as official, and acceptable, defence at trial.[94] Indeed,
of all of the unwritten rules, perhaps the most important was an acceptance
of the flaws in the signalling and instructional system. Once the complexities
and practical difficulties of fleet battle are fully appreciated, it is clear that
nothing could have been achieved without the body of unwritten knowledge
and influence which provided a sort of cartilage within which the bluntness
and inadequacy of specific instruction rested. The use of initiative to act above
and beyond specific instruction for the accomplishment of one's duty has been
viewed from the wrong end of the telescope: it should not have been the examples of initiative that became famous, but the cases where initiative was not
taken that should have become infamous.

CHAPTER 7

Command

I have acted by the spirit, not the dead letter, of [my orders] ... I have endeavoured to enthuse the like spirit into the breasts of people around me, but did not always succeed.[1]

The inherent problems of fleet cohesion and unity of action were formidable, and translated into a magnified significance in the 'upwards' power, influence and role of the subordinate in determining fleet efficiency. There was a constant need for initiative from each captain, both to keep station and to act in the absence of signals or to interpret those made. That is why one anonymous contemporary was careful to include subordinate initiative in his explanation of how to achieve success in a sea fight:

> The success of a sea-fight depends on the talent of the commander-in-chief for making arrangements, on that of the captains for executing orders, and supplying by their own intelligence what is wanting in them, and on that of the crew for managing and manœuvring the vessel and directing the artillery.[2]

To work efficiently, command style must always compliment command structure, and not define it. Successful command method in the eighteenth century was therefore determined by the ability of the commander to work within this enigmatic and unpredictable framework. To retain any semblance of control, the commander was required to adopt a flexible method of command which made allowance for unforeseen circumstance, acknowledged the impossibility of absolute control, and allowed for and encouraged a constant input of subordinate initiative. This required a detailed, easily understood and common doctrine, shared between a commander and his subordinates. The formal orders, signals and instructions, cushioned by a network of informal notions of duty, provided that common doctrine. The basis of the problem, therefore, was not the absence of doctrine, but its effectiveness.

It is only possible to understand efficiency in terms of requirement, and our understanding of what was required first needs a little attention. From the late nineteenth century to the present day, commentators have generally agreed that the problems of centralised control in eighteenth-century sea battles dictated a need for a flexible and decentralised command system.[3] In essence, this is correct, but very few have offered any detailed definition of that 'ideal' system. Yet a detailed definition of that 'flexibility' remains critical as confusion over the exact nature of that flexibility has led to many going astray. The adjective 'flexible' is particularly misleading, as it can be taken to imply much that it should not in the context of the tactics of command.

FLEXIBILITY AND CONTROL

The principal requirement for a flexible system was allowance for subordinate initiative, but we must be very careful in our definition of that initiative. The implication of personal choice that comes with it is particularly unhelpful. For the system of command to work effectively, to use initiative did not mean to do what a captain thought best, but to do what was expected of him by his commanding officer within a recognised and respected hierarchical structure and a framework of detailed doctrine. It was not enough for initiative to exist simply by default of a flawed system of signalling and instruction. Real efficiency and tactical capability were only born when a commander could use that initiative as part of a broader tactical plan, rather than accepting it as an inevitable frustration of sea warfare. To understand how it worked in practice, it is necessary to draw a distinction between a captain straining to grasp the gist of his commander's intentions and essentially improvising, and one using his initiative within the controlled confines of a detailed structure of specific and sophisticated tactical ideas elucidated by the commander-in-chief.

Under the first model, a breakdown of common methodology and shared purpose would be likely, leaving too much to chance, with chaos the most likely result. Indeed, Byam Martin laments the potential chaos of such a system, and ponders in his diary: 'What would become of all system and combination of action if every captain was to be at liberty to adopt his own opinion instead of that of the admiral?'[4] Such a system was also unsettling for the captains who were anxious not to bring blame on their heads, but did not know exactly what was expected of them.[5] If, on the other hand, the subordinate was armed with a detailed knowledge of his commander's intentions and tactical philosophy, the commander was able to make use of the initiative of his subordinates and cohesion could be maintained under an umbrella of common purpose and methodology.

For a commander to be able to use initiative in this way, he first had to know how his captains would react in any given situation. That level of effective reliability could only be achieved through exercising a considerable degree of control over the actions of his subordinates. If it could not be guaranteed that captain and commander were thinking alike, a commander could only hope that a captain would use his initiative to do what was expected of him, in the way that was expected. Hope, it must be remembered, is not a method.[6] A concentration on the need for flexibility can therefore easily act as a red herring, masking the real issue of a need for control. But how could this need for control co-exist with the need for a flexible command system?

The common perception is that it could not; that a flexible style of command would necessarily dilute the level of control in the system of command,[7] and it is on this basis that certain instructions delegating power to captains have been criticised.[8] The mêlée, it has been argued, was the very negative of tactical science.[9] In practice, however, flexibility and control were not mutually exclusive. Delegation and decentralisation do not necessarily have to imply a loss of control. Effective flexibility was controlled flexibility and, in practice, the decentralisers did not achieve this requisite controlled flexibility by diluting their command with the personal influence of other captains. Quite the opposite. They imposed their ideas of how to react in any situation on their subordinates. In the words of a twentieth-century admiral on the problems of command: '[it] resolved into teaching the subordinate how to react and act in situations similar to the [way] the task force commander would in the same situation.'[10] In June 1747 Warren described this process under Anson: 'Mr Anson having called them [his captains] all on board him the morning before the action, and given them directions what *he* believed would be right for them to do, supposing they should not be able to see, or he to change the signals.'[11]

Nelson's approach was identical. Sir Edward Berry famously wrote of Nelson's methods prior to the Battle of the Nile:

> It had been his practice during the whole of the cruise, whenever the weather and circumstances would permit, to have his captains on board the *Vanguard*, where he would fully develop to them his own ideas of the different and best modes of attack, and such plans as he proposed to execute upon falling in with the enemy ... With the masterly ideas of their Admiral, therefore, on the subject of Naval tactics, every one of the Captains of his squadron was most thoroughly acquainted.[12]

In a much less well-known, but highly significant aside, Codrington recalled how Nelson sent for Collingwood to consult with him about tactics, but joked to Hardy that he would not be guided by Collingwood's opinion unless it coincided with his own.[13]

Through his teaching and discussion, Nelson, like Anson before him, imposed on his captains his perceptions of how the battle might develop and his ideas of how to react accordingly. Both these commanders made sure that any initiative taken by a captain would be based on their own tactical ideas. Thus, by retaining subordinate initiative within a very precise and detailed framework, the tight personal control still remained but was transmitted via each fleet captain, according to circumstance. The successful commander exercised his control in a flexible manner; he did not dilute it with the ideas of his subordinates.

The principal requirement to achieve this level of control was a common doctrine which was explicit in its definition of duty and methodology in a variety of situations. Only once that detailed and dependable superstructure was in place could a flexible command system in the true sense of the word exist. But the existing system was inadequate in its provision of that reliable common doctrine. It was inadequate because it was unreliable, and it was unreliable because so much of it was unwritten.

THE WEAKNESS OF UNWRITTEN RULES

A system based on a combination of oral tradition and practical experience will always be fragile, because the knowledge being passed down can become obfuscated or even lost altogether through the passage of time. This was of particular significance in the eighteenth century, as there were long periods of peace between wars, and even longer gaps between full-scale fleet battles. Lestock claimed that no one could be expected to remember the manœuvres for forming lines of battle after a gap of two years.[14] But before assuming command in the Mediterranean and commanding the British fleet at the Battle of Toulon in 1744 Admiral Thomas Matthews had been ashore for some twenty years, twelve of them tending his estate in Wales.[15] Prior to the Battle of Ushant, Keppel had been ashore for fifteen years,[16] and James Gambier, who took command of the *Defence* in 1793, had been ashore for thirteen years. It is likely that this accounted to some extent for the marked absence of realism which distinguished him as captain of a line of battle ship.[17]

The fact that the Navy did not learn, remember or forget at the same speed encouraged the growth of individual pockets of doctrine. Kempenfelt's main criticism in his frequent and lengthy tirades about the state of tactics was not the absence of rules regarding behaviour, but the absence of a common rule.[18] Different fleets under different admirals had different methods of fighting. This frequently led to confusion, most famously at the Battle of the Chesapeake in 1781. Graves had recently taken command of the North American station, having come fresh from the Channel Fleet, where he had been well schooled in the tolerant command methods of Howe and Kempenfelt.[19] Before the battle he was joined by the West Indies squadron led by Samuel Hood, which had been schooled in unquestioning obedience to the exact wording of signals by the intolerant Rodney.[20]

There was, therefore, not just a clear contradiction in doctrinal understanding of command methodology between Graves and the West Indies squadron, but even the detail of that doctrine was different. The West Indies squadron worked with a signal book altered by Rodney, while the North American squadron used those altered and issued by Arbuthnot in 1779–80, to which Graves had supplemented a list of forty-nine signals in 1781.[21] With only five days elapsing between the fleets joining for the first time and the engagement, there was insufficient time to achieve a shared doctrine in either detail or application.

The result was that Hood felt unable to comply with Admiral Graves's signal to engage when it was hoisted simultaneously with that for the line. Hood argued that the line should be followed to the letter, not interpreted in the spirit of it, as Graves clearly intended. However, the signal that so confused Hood and his colleagues was obeyed exactly by those who knew Graves, his signals and his methods.[22]

The weaknesses of unwritten doctrine also placed an extraordinary emphasis on the personality of each commander, for if a commonality of doctrine was to exist at all it had to be created and nurtured by each and every commander. The success or failure of any naval battle throughout the century can be traced back to the ability of the commander to achieve this common understanding prior to battle.

A commander had to be sufficiently receptive to acknowledge the need to share his ideas. Although it is now likely that this was a more widespread practice than we have previously assumed,[23] a commander also had to be able to transmit those ideas and that facility could not be relied upon. The ability to do so required a commander to achieve a certain level of psychological contact with his captains, for which the principal requirement was an adequate command of his native language. It is significant that Nelson praised Hood as 'the best officer I ever saw', not principally for bravery or heroism, but for the clarity of his expression: 'Everything from him is so clear it is impossible to misunderstand him.'[24] In contrast, Rodney's manner of talking was, in the words of Hood, 'very extravagant and extraordinary, but without much meaning'.[25] Although Rodney seems to have presented his plan of action to his captains prior to the Battle of Martinique, for example, it is equally clear that no one to whom Rodney explained his intention had the faintest idea of what he wanted them to do or how he wanted it to be done.[26] Howe could and did invite his officers to state their opinions, but did not always share his own in return.[27] When he did, usually in written format, his riddling verbosity was infamous.[28]

This ability to command, however, turned on much more than a simple ability to convey ideas. The structure of command in the eighteenth century was significantly more complicated than our modern assumptions of hierarchy and discipline in the armed forces lead us to believe. Notably, it does not logically follow that someone who did not do his duty was, in spite of any spirited arguments to the contrary, necessarily ignorant of it. In the first half of the century, and in many instances for another generation, a fleet captain's primary allegiance was to his King and to his own personal honour; there was no impersonal concept of duty.[29] The problem of command efficiency was as much to do with subordinate professionalism and personal motive as it was with the understanding of that duty.

A large part of the problem lay in the system of promotion. The promotion of a senior lieutenant to command of a ship was always a very uncertain affair, dependent on excellent contacts and influence. As the century progressed, however, distinction in battle became an established way of grabbing a commanding officer's attention. After the Glorious First of June 1794, all senior lieutenants of ships that were engaged were promoted to the rank of commander, and this became an established rule in the Navy thereafter. In the same battle a midshipman from every ship engaged was also promoted to lieutenant.[30] Promotion to command therefore gradually shifted away from patronage and connections, and came to depend more fully on skill and bravery, known in the eighteenth century as 'zeal'. Although this was excellent for the service as a whole, one young lieutenant lamented its introduction, claiming that 'a fellow has now no chance of promotion unless he jumps into the muzzle of a gun and crawls out of the touch-hole.'[31]

Promotion beyond post-captain, on the other hand, was simply a matter of seniority; nothing a captain could do would advance his career any more quickly. Those captains that fought with bravery fought for their own pride and for that of the nation, for the men aboard and for the commanding officer. In return, they expected some form of recognition, usually a medal. To be overlooked for such a medal could cause irretrievable offence. Cuthbert Collingwood, for example, was furious to be overlooked for a medal after the First of June, 1794. He had fought with distinction and bravery, but only those captains who were actually within sight of the flagship received commendation from the fleet admiral, Howe. Collingwood and a number of others were simply not mentioned in his dispatches to the Admiralty, and did not receive the commemorative gold medal. When he was awarded a medal for his actions at the Battle of Cape St Vincent some three years later he refused to accept it while that for the First of June was withheld. Eventually he received both.[32] Otherwise exceptional bravery and success might be rewarded with a title: after the Battle of St Vincent, Nelson was rewarded with the Order of Bath, and Jervis with the Earldom of St Vincent.

Nevertheless, such a reward was exceptional, and the prospect of a medal uncertain and, for many, irrelevant. The prospect of prize money would galvanise most into action, but as a general rule the structure of ship discipline which was bound together more by links of patronage, service and mutual obligation rather than the structure of rank,[33] was mirrored in that of a fleet. Fleet cohesion and fighting efficiency was not achieved through order and hierarchy, but through the command of loyalty and trust, won through mutual ties of obligation, service and patronage.

One important way in which those ties were augmented and solidified was through psychological contact between a commander and his subordinates, which enabled doctrine to be taught and explained, and a sense of duty instilled.[34] The ability of a commander to achieve that psychological contact was threatened on many fronts, however. One significant problem was the lack of any formal training in command skills. The shore-based academy for officers opened at Portsmouth in 1729, and included a curriculum that covered arithmetic, writing, gunnery, fortifications, mathematics, drawing and dockyard repairs. Navigation and seamanship were learnt through a mixture of teaching and experience aboard ship. Command skills, either of men or of fleets of ships, on the other hand, were acquired solely through practical experience. A lack of published material to help or advise the aspiring officer exacerbated this want of formal training. Although O'Brien wrote his *Essay on the Duty of a Captain* in the 1740s,[35] there was nothing available pertaining to the duties of an admiral other than Falconer's entry under 'Admiral' in his *Universal Dictionary of the Marine* (London, 1771) until Grenfell published his *Art of the Admiral*, over a century and a half later, in 1937.

As a result, the only good commanders were those who had it in their nature to be good commanders, and those with that inherent skill were instantly recognisable. An insight to the effect this could have comes from the diary of Charles Darwin, writing of his first impressions of Robert Fitzroy, the young naval captain of the exploration ship *Beagle*.

> ... he is a very extraordinary person. I never came across a man whom I could fancy being a Napoleon or a Nelson. I should not call him clever, yet I feel convinced nothing is too great or too high for him. His ascendancy over everybody is quite curious; the extent to which every officer and man feels the slightest praise or rebuke would have been before seeing him incomprehensible ... his candour and sincerity are to me unparalleled; and using his own words, his 'vanity and petulance' are nearly so ... his many good qualities are numerous: altogether he is the strongest marked character I ever fell in with.[36]

This reads like the many and better-known eulogies of well-loved commanders like Nelson or Duncan, and could not contrast more with surgeon Peter Cullen's description of St Vincent, who was 'haughty and imperious, rigidly and unnecessarily strict, on many occasions, in carrying on duty, which made him very much disliked by his captains and officers'.[37] Another contemporary remembered that it was an invariable rule with St Vincent not to do what anybody asked, and it made no difference whether the sufferer was friend or foe.[38] Even more to the point, Pasley described Rodney as a 'madman' and a 'rough, rude blackguard'.[39]

Despite Fitzroy's clear ability to transmit his personality and sense of duty to those working with him, we will never know if he would have become a talented fleet commander. It certainly did not follow that a good captain made a good admiral, and those promoted over and above their abilities frequently ended up performing beneath them. Thomas Matthews, architect of the failure at

Toulon in 1744, had an exemplary record as a good aggressive fighting captain. His conduct at the Battle of Cape Passaro in 1718 under Byng was particularly noteworthy.[40] Rodney's command style was also a dead end, but when he fought as one of Hawke's captains at Finisterre in 1747 he showed bravery, initiative and enterprise.[41]

The ability to make psychological contact was also threatened by the peculiar behavioural traits of the era. Although major differences in culture make it difficult to evaluate the behavioural dilemmas of military leaders who learnt their trade 200 or 300 years ago, it is clear that many contemporaries found it both psychologically and practically difficult to confide in their captains.[42] This could be complicated by the mistrust that can so easily grow with a generation gap, a problem the Navy regularly encountered after long periods of peace. Then the choice for command was stark; between the inexperienced and the old. The old were most often chosen.

Of course, old age does not necessarily imply incompetence in fleet command – at the Battle of Toulon the French were handled quite competently by the seventy-eight-year-old Admiral Court de La Bruyère[43] – but youth remained the ideal, since a commander had to be both physically and mentally strong to withstand the rigours of battle. Illness and fatigue had a deeply corrupting influence in a ship or fleet. At the best of times the motion of a ship could be exhausting for the unfit; at the worst the atmosphere became airless and stuffy, or cold and damp and debilitating to the infirm. Howe was so exhausted after the First of June, following five days and four nights of fighting, that he had to be physically supported by his staff to prevent him falling on deck.[44] Many illnesses could be dealt with quickly. Pasley recorded how he was seized in the night by a violent flux, which, bizarrely, seems to have calmed down after a little rhubarb,[45] but some illnesses such as the continual pain of gout from which Lestock suffered, and the discomfort of a urinary infection which plagued Matthews, could confine a man to his bunk at short notice and for long periods of time. On the night before the Battle of Toulon, for example, Lestock went straight to bed on receiving Matthews's signal to heave-to, despite the large gap between his division and that of his admiral[46]. Similarly, Rodney, who was ill with gout and the gravel, was in his bunk throughout the action off Cape St Vincent in January 1779 that became known as the Moonlight Battle.[47] Most strikingly, the master of the *Marlborough* at the Battle of Toulon had become so short-sighted in his old age that in his own words, 'I could hardly see anything.'[48] Illness could also cause long-term bad temper, a wholly corruptive and malign influence in a ship. Bad temper could lead to irrational behaviour and unfairness, and – with the possible exception of a thief – unfairness, real or imagined, was loathed more than anything in a ship.

One way of achieving a good level of contact with one's subordinates was through one's actions, and this required a high degree of personal bravery.

Commanders commanded from the quarterdeck. They were dressed in their formal uniforms and were easily distinguishable and easily targeted. Not only were they vulnerable, but they had nothing essentially practical with which to occupy themselves. Men are more likely to be overcome by fear when they are fully conscious of the risks they are running. A gunner, for example, was in a very poor vantage point, and would be preoccupied with doing his job properly as part of a team. A commander had no other recourse than to turn his mind to the job in hand as a form of escapism. Some took to this well, but others did not. In 1702, after an hour's fighting, Benbow's right leg was shattered by chainshot, but he insisted on continuing to conduct the battle. Contrast that with the behaviour of Captain Kirkby of the *Defiance*, who, in the same action, hid behind the mizzenmast or lay prone on the deck when there was any firing.[49] Nelson's own personal bravery is well documented. He wore his scars as medals, and this was undoubtedly one of the reasons why he was so loved by his men.

The personality of the commander was thus a key factor in determining his ability to make psychological contact with his captains, and hence in determining the efficiency of the command system. Whereas an older generation of writers has believed that the rigid system of instruction caused an 'annihaltions de personalités',[50] not only was personality significant, but the loneliness and freedom of command magnified its importance. Moreover, the conditions of intense pressure and fear in battle did not build character, but revealed it. Explaining anything as complex as a military success or failure in terms of personality alone is a dated concept, but it should not be overlooked, for it was a peculiarity of the era that the very nature of the command system was itself shaped by the personality of each commander.

CHANGE OVER TIME

In a number of ways, therefore, the system of unwritten doctrine prevented the emergence of a comprehensive service-wide doctrine, and was an obstacle to improvement in command efficiency over time. To achieve a more detailed and reliable concept of duty, the main priority was the reduction of the significance of unwritten doctrine in the functioning of the Navy. This was realised in two ways: first by changes in the methods of signalling to allow for greater freedom of expression, and secondly by an increase in the detail of written doctrine. The first of these has been well documented, but the latter process has not, even though it is visible in the contents of the signal books. Indeed, current perception regarding the identity of the Signals and Instructions as an historical source is understandably confused, owing in particular to the unacknowledged existence of three different types of Instruction. They can now be set out as follows.

1. Instructions that introduce innovative ideas and define new doctrine.

2. Instructions that clarify existing written doctrine.

3. Instructions that preserve or clarify unwritten doctrine in written form.

The first two categories are self-evident; it is the unacknowledged existence of the third category that has so often misled. Many of the unwritten rules were only recognised when they were broken, and that provided the motivation to record them in written form to ensure compliance with them in the future. This type of instruction is most visible in the last quarter of the century, when Howe and Kempenfelt among others were anxious to record as much unwritten doctrine in written format as possible to help prevent honest confusion, or to remove the possibility of confusion as an excuse for those with questionable motive. Examples include Howe's instructions of 1781–2, which read in part,

> ... Captains should be guided by the motions of the leading ships, and their seconds-ahead in their respective columns for preserving the necessary regularity in the conduct of the fleet ... [51]

And those of 1793, which read,

> When the Admiral tacks, wears, lies-to, makes or shortens sail &c., whether in consequence of the signal put abroad for such purpose, or otherwise, the ships of the fleet are to be regulated in the timely conforming thereto, as may best correspond with the means to preserve, or regain their appointed stations, with suitable expedition. [52]

These merely reflected two principles of naval warfare which required fleet captains to use their admiral or leading ships as a guide for their own behaviour, a practice already centuries old by the eighteenth century. His instruction of 1790 emphasising the need to maintain cohesion alongside the acknowledgement that,

> a strict adherence thereto may sometimes be found prejudicial to the service, by restraining the captains from taking advantage of the favourable incidents which may occur in the progress of a general action. [53]

... was a rehash of a 1777 instruction. As such it was the written embodiment of the already well-known and widely practised unwritten convention which saw the signalling and instructional system as being flawed in certain circumstances. In the same way his instruction which read,

> If any of the ships in the fleet are in distress and make the signal, which is a weft with the jack or ensign, the next ship to them is strictly required to relieve them. [54]

... records in written format the convention and methodology of mutual support. Similarly that of 1782, which reads,

> No ship in the fleet shall leave his station upon any pretence whatsoever, till he has acquainted his flag, or the next flag officer to him, with the condition of his ship, and received his direction herein; but in case any ship shall so do, the next ships are to close up the line.[55]

... is the written embodiment of the long-standing convention which required the maintenance of fleet cohesion at all times.

Again, it is clear that prior to issuing his instruction which allowed captains to take their stations to windward or to leeward of the enemy as they saw fit,[56] no instruction existed that specifically prevented such action, nor are there any examples of captains or admirals being reprimanded for engaging the enemy in a certain way, unless it was at too great a distance. It would be misguided, therefore, to use this particular example to argue for Howe's 'liberating effect' on the system.[57] It is also wrong to consider all instructions as permissive; it did not necessarily follow that the action described therein was unlawful prior to the issuing of that instruction. No example illustrates this better than Howe's instruction of 1777 which 'authorised' captains to 'act as they see best' if the fleet had been directed to disperse.[58] Once dispersed, it is difficult to see how they could do otherwise even before this signal had been issued.

These instructions are testament to the development and establishment of a detailed common doctrine. This process of improvement must not be taken as evidence of unnecessary or ill-advised centralisation.[59] Flexibility was not affected by increased detail. In fact, controlled flexibility required detail, as detail was uniformity, and uniformity was reliability. As Kempenfelt wrote:

> All general movements, without they are made by established rules known to all, must be disorderly and confused, subject the ships run foul of each other, be tedious in the performance, and imperfect in the execution. The fleet therefore whose motions are regulated by fixed rules, must have greatly the advantage of one whose motions have no rule to regulate them.[60]

Increased detail was also necessary to reduce the possibility of subordinates with questionable motive abusing the grey areas in written instruction. In 1739 and 1740, for example, Vernon was painfully aware of the ease with which this loophole could be exploited, and was careful to add as much detail as possible to his instructions to prevent his captains pleading ignorance.[61]

This process of increasing the detail of written doctrine helped improve the foundations for a common and dependable doctrine from which truly flexible and efficient command could blossom. The detail of doctrine, however, was only half of the problem; the other was discipline. There were important changes in the structure of discipline during the century. Courts martial were given more power, most notably by the Navy Bill of 1749, which introduced changes to the wording of the sentences that could be passed. The traditional punishment for cowardice, negligence and disaffection carried the death penalty, but included the escape clause for the well connected of 'or such other penalty as the court may determine'. This was amended, and the offending clause removed.[62] Further reforms were continued by Sandwich, who concentrated particularly on the military 'character' of naval officers.[63]

Much, however, remains to be discovered about the nature and development of the relationship between a fleet commander and the captains of his ships. It is a highly complex and little-researched question, combining ideas and ideals of honour and duty with notions of class and professionalism.[64] Very broadly, however, it can be argued that a sense of professionalism grew over time, and, as a sense of collective purpose and pride in being a naval officer also grew, so the enactment of subordinate duty could be more easily relied upon by those in command. Selfish motive became selfless motive, survival instinct came second to duty, and, most importantly, it became honourable to do that duty. It is nevertheless clear that, even at the very end of the century, the Navy had still not reached a level of professionalism where each and every officer could be expected to carry out his duty. At the Battle of St Vincent (1797), normally renowned for its great success, a significant proportion of the British officer corps did not behave as well as their admiral expected, and the same can now be said of Trafalgar.[65] Throughout the century, therefore, effective command still turned on persuasion as much as rank, and too much still depended on the personal skill of the commander to engender a common sense of obligation. To achieve effective command, the need to command culture through loyalty persisted.

There is a tendency to identify a continual increase in the standard of naval leadership, particularly in the last quarter of the eighteenth century.[66] However, if the commander was, as was claimed of Sir Robert Calder, 'wrong-headed',[67] or if his ideas were, in the words of Hood of his commander, Lord Rodney, 'big with absurdity',[68] the system of command would necessarily be inefficient. This problem of command incompetence was far worse before 1747, when the creation of the new rank of 'Rear-Admiral without distinction of squadron' – more commonly known as 'yellow admirals' – allowed elderly or incompetent captains to be bypassed in search of talent and potential,[69] but the most significant part of a navy's fighting doctrine, the doctrine of *how* to command, remained untouched by regulations throughout the period.

The best rules are those that do not stand in the way of the competent but which limit the negative impact of the incompetent. The Navy had not yet reached a stage of professional development where such rules existed. Quite the contrary, the disproportionate emphasis on personality to achieve command efficiency magnified the potential impact of the incompetent commander. Thus in a system that so clearly needed an allowance for subordinate initiative to flourish alongside a liberal interpretation of the instructions, Rodney did not learn from the exemplary precedent set by Anson, under whom he served for some nine months in the Western Squadron. It is entirely characteristic of the period that he could invoke Anson's style of command as 'the good old discipline of the Western Squadron',[70] and yet adopt a command style that was its very antithesis. He thus admonished Rowley for acting with necessary and unavoidable independence, claiming that: 'The painful task of thinking belongs to me.'[71] Of Captain Young he similarly wrote: 'My captain has presumed to think for me instead of obeying ... I have desired him never to do so again.'[72] It is in the same way entirely characteristic of the century that Howe, being unable to communicate his high ideals to his subordinates, was so poorly served by them,[73] and that Collingwood and those who succeeded him failed to learn from the precedent set by Nelson.[74] Despite these improvements, therefore, so much still depended on the personality and personal ability of the commander to achieve command efficiency, that a good deal of uncertainty, unreliability and unpredictability remained in the system of command throughout the century, and that was its greatest weakness.

There were problems, therefore, both with the detail of fighting doctrine – how ships were expected to behave in fleet battle – and also in the command method – how a commander chose to implement that fighting doctrine. Combined, these two flaws presented a formidable obstacle to operational efficiency. The real problem was that these flaws were self-perpetuating. The greatest lesson to be learned from the British experience is how difficult it is to change doctrine.[75]

First, new ideas had to be successfully introduced, but this was not always easy. Young reported, in a letter to Middleton in September 1780, how, on arriving at the West India station, he had issued new signals for chasing on every point of the compass and night signals for the same purpose, both much-needed technical improvements. He soon found, however, that the captains 'were adverse to them, therefore gave them up, though with much reluctance.'[76]

Once new doctrine had been introduced, the next test was to retain a common and accurate understanding of fighting doctrine as a whole, allowing for those improvements. To do so was, again, remarkably difficult. Relative strength of the forces; relative experience and competence of the crews; relative capability and, in action, disability; sea, wind and weather conditions; style of command; communication technology and current tactical theory all played their own part in determining doctrinal application and understanding. New doctrine could not therefore be learnt without a considerable investment in time and practice to achieve a level of continuity. If that continuity existed, experience would then lead to deeper understanding of its myriad applications and potential decision-making dilemmas. Without such continuity, practice and experience, confusion was inevitable. The common pattern in the operational history of the Royal Navy is, however, of different commanders with contrasting command styles using varying signal books based on dissimilar doctrine, which was permanently being tinkered with through the issue of Additional Instructions. With such a major lack of continuity it is no surprise that operational efficiency was difficult to achieve, let alone improve.

For any armed force to learn from the past, the detail of fighting doctrine and the culture of interpretation that exists alongside it must remain clear and united, and their relationship unambiguous. Without such a secure foundation, reliable and permanent improvement is impossible. Time, however, threatens the security of those foundations. Without a conscious effort to retain previous doctrine – both the bare facts and the interpretation of those facts – they quickly become clouded by time and liable to misinterpretation by newer generations. For obvious reasons, unwritten doctrine is even more susceptible to this ageing process. Not only is the culture of interpretation continually under threat, but so is the detail of the doctrine itself.

In the eighteenth-century Navy, interest in education and improvement in operational efficiency did not stretch to the systematic study of previous doctrinal failures or successes. Tradition was undoubtedly important, but the accuracy of the knowledge of that tradition was at best uncertain. Fashions and trends in command method and operational doctrine came and went, and with them important lessons for operational efficiency were learnt, forgotten, and, if lucky, relearnt. Moreover, any improvement tended to address the symptoms and not the cause of the problem. At the Battle of Martinique, for example, the failure of Captain Carkett to divine Rodney's intention was a failure at command level: Carkett did not understand Rodney's intention because of Rodney's distant and hermetic method of command. Instead of the Admiralty acknowledging this, and issuing a service-wide proclamation that commanders were expected to discuss their understanding of fleet tactics in detail with their captains before action, Rodney issued an amendment to the Instructions, making more explicit his intentions in written format.[77] Nothing was changed to address the wider problems of command method.

The relationship between the Admiralty and the commanders-in-chief was highly decentralised; very little was imposed on admirals in terms of how they chose to command their fleets. This ensured that the essential problem of a lack of understanding between a commander and his subordinates remained to rear its head time and again throughout the eighteenth century. Between 1744 and 1782 alone, a lack of communication between a commander and his subordinates adversely affected five of thirteen inconclusive actions – Toulon (1744), Minorca (1756), Ushant (1778), Martinique (1780) and Chesapeake (1782) – and marred two chase victories – Havana (1748) and Lagos Bay (1759).[78] Technical improvements in signalling and ship design made fleet performance and control easier. However, with no help or advice from the Admiralty, it still required the rare genius, intuition and foresight of a Nelson to understand the basic problems and synthesise the components of existing capability, think beyond their limitations, and create and then use an effective doctrine to achieve operational efficiency.

Nelson did this by achieving a high level of psychological contact with his captains and by developing a highly detailed doctrine based on his ideas and his understanding of tactics. Nelson turned his captains into models of himself. It is telling that Villeneuve remarked of Nelson's fleet before the Battle of Trafalgar that 'every Captain was a Nelson'.[79] Indeed, it is more helpful to understand the mechanics of fleet control in this way; Nelson's captains were more a 'Band of Nelsons' than a 'Band of Brothers'. Knowing that his captains would react as he would react and, therefore, how they would react in any given situation, Nelson was able to use the inevitable initiative and independence of action of his subordinates as part of his broader tactical plan. He demonstrated that the weaknesses of the system did not necessarily prevent it from working, and turned weakness into strength. His tactics of command led to high levels of control exercised in a flexible format. This outstanding achievement bore astounding results, most notably at Trafalgar, where Nelson still managed to achieve a commonality of doctrine, despite working with a combined force of the Mediterranean and Channel fleets, each with its own separate tradition of fighting doctrine.[80]

Under Nelson, therefore, these components reached an equilibrium, but that equilibrium was much more easily upset than maintained. Sustaining this level of competence and efficiency remained very difficult indeed. The Navy reached an astonishing level of operational efficiency, culminating in the Battle of Trafalgar, but many of the inherent problems remained. Fighting doctrine was insufficiently detailed, and a centralised doctrine of command method non-existent. The key to success remained elusive, and required a rare degree of genius to achieve. Any system that relies on genius to function is hopelessly impractical and unrealistic. Indeed, the whole concept of a requirement to 'sustain' what was achieved at Trafalgar misses the point, and carries with it a dangerous implication of completion, finality, even perfection of the command system in the age of sail. The foundations of command were still unstable after Trafalgar. The Navy had much to learn. It had to defy the myth it had created, to progress, innovate and develop. To sustain what had been achieved at Trafalgar, the Navy needed to sustain a continuous process of evolution.

CHAPTER 8

The Weather Gage

Relative position, which it is so vastly important to consider in naval tactics, [is] so difficult to allow for, involving so many uncertain results, and so fluctuating in degree.[1]

How a commander actually chose to attack an enemy was another matter entirely, and remained very much open to debate. The means by which a victory could be achieved, or, more often, an explanation of why it was not achieved, were popular topics among both naval officers and civilians, particularly in the aftermath of indecisive actions such as the battles of Toulon (1744) and Ushant (1778). One such heated discussion ended up with carefully ballasted models being sailed up St James's Canal to demonstrate an argument.[2] Central to any such discussion was position in relation to the wind. In any action one ship or fleet would necessarily be 'to windward' of the other. A ship or fleet lying in the direction *from* which the wind was blowing was said to be to windward or to hold the weather gage, and the ship or fleet in the direction *to* which the wind was blowing was said to be to leeward (Fig. 20). Each position carried with it certain advantages and disadvantages that informed tactical decision making. With the possible exception of gunnery, more has been written about this aspect of sailing warfare than any other: it is peculiar to the age of sail, and, for many, is its defining characteristic. It is somewhat surprising, therefore, that almost everything we know about it is wrong.

A

B

20 The weather gage (A) and lee gage (B)

INITIATIVE

Any investigation into this subject must begin with the vexing question of 'initiative' that is so often described as an advantageous, if not the most advantageous, characteristic of the windward position. To hold the windward position, it is argued, was to hold the power to engage at will.[3] In reality, however, the ability to force an enemy to battle was neither so exclusive nor so formulaic. The one crucial weakness that both modern historians and contemporary authors share in their discussion of initiative is a total lack of any definition of the term. This vague understanding is itself symptomatic of our confusion. Our uncertainty lies as much in the lack of a definition of the term 'initiative' as it does in the blind acceptance of the rigid understanding of ship and fleet capability upon which it is based. What is actually meant by initiative? Was it simply the ability of one fleet to force action on another? Or was it the ability of one fleet to force action on another at any point, in any way, whenever or, indeed, wherever it chose?

In any discussion of military tactics 'initiative' implies the power either to limit the enemy's freedom of action or to start operations of such a character that the enemy is compelled to take them into account and to make the necessary counter manœuvres under penalty of severe disadvantage to himself.[4] With sailing warfare, this thinking is based on the inability of a square-rigged ship to sail any closer than six points to the wind. The fleet to leeward, it is reasoned, was restricted in its ability to make ground to windward and could not force an engagement on a fleet to windward. It was thus reduced to a passive role, unable to influence the timing and initiation of the engagement. The fleet to windward, on the other hand, had simply to bear down to attack the enemy where and when it chose. What has been overlooked, however, is that, within this boundary, the actual capabilities of ships or fleets were relative in terms of the design of the ships, the weather and sea conditions, the skills of the sailors and the skills of the officers in charge. Beyond the basic law that a ship could sail no closer than six points to the wind, no rule was indisputable, and no advantage absolute.

Thus windward performance of ships or fleets, although limited, was never standard. It depended too much on ship design and condition, personal skill and experience, and sea and weather conditions. Windward performance varied between ships of the same nation, as it did between ships of different nations, and between fleets of the same nation and of different nations.[5] Significantly, therefore, a ship or fleet to leeward, but with superior windward performance, could overhaul and force an attack on a fleet to windward. Certainly, conditions would have to be particularly favourable to one ship or fleet for this to happen, but such conditions were not rare. On the contrary, it was rare indeed for two ships to be perfectly matched in their performance capability, and the multifarious nature of fleets ensured significant diversity in fleet perform-ance. Even a fleet with a majority of clean, weatherly ships could well contain one or more ships of a relatively poor capability. Moreover, a ship might easily have been damaged through battle or collision, and it is clear that the ability to make ground to windward, which required such a high degree of performance, was the first thing to be affected by most rig damage.[6] In this situation, the lee-ward fleet could force action on that to windward simply by setting its fastest and most weatherly ships on the slowest and most leewardly of the enemy, thus forcing the rest of the fleet to bear down in defence of those being attacked.[7]

This is exactly what happened at the Battle of the Saints. On the night of 10 April 1782, off the coast of Martinique, the French *Zélé* (74) ran foul of the *Jason* (64), losing her topmast.[8] The next night, the *Zélé* continued her path of destruction and ploughed into de Grasse's flagship, the *Ville de Paris* (106), this time losing her foremast and bowsprit, and damaging the rigging, sails and rudder of the *Ville de Paris*. These two incidents prompted one contemporary to assert that 'It is impossible to behave worse than this vessel did from the 8th 'til the morning of the 12th.'[9] The disgraced and disabled *Zélé* was then towed by a frigate back towards Basse Terre. The British fleet, meanwhile, had worked doggedly to windward, and by morning had the hapless *Zélé* in sight. Hood immediately sent a squadron of four of his finest ships to intercept her, prompt-ing De Grasse to bear down with his entire force to her protection, and forcing him into the general action that became known as the Battle of the Saints.[10]

This whole scenario, of course, relies on the escaping fleet being prepared to enter into a general engagement for the sake of one or two ships, and not all captains were as well supported by their admirals as Captain Gras-Préville of the *Zélé*. In 1708 an attempt to land the Pretender in Scotland was discovered by George Byng's fleet. Vernon, in command of the *Jersey* at the time, recalled that the enemy ships, being clean, made good their escape to windward, but, in doing so, sacrificed their two slowest ships to the only pair of clean frigates in Byng's otherwise foul squadron.[11]

If, however, the rare occasion presented itself in which the worst perform-ers of the fleet to windward had a better windward performance than the best of those to leeward, no such action could be forced. At Malaga in August 1704 the comte de Toulouse's fleet was fresh out of port, and had no trouble in escaping to windward of Rooke, no doubt to the relief of Rooke, who was fast running out of ammunition.[12] Come the spring of 1780, the French fleet sailed so much better than the British that, in the words of a despondent Rodney, 'They with ease could get what distance they pleased to windward.'[13] In this situation, the best that could be hoped for was for the lee fleet to use a squadron of its fastest and most weatherly ships to act as lookouts, keeping in contact with the wind-ward fleet and relaying details of its position and course back to the main fleet. Similarly, a lee fleet with a superior or equal performance off the wind could avoid action simply by drifting out of range to leeward, or, indeed, escaping entirely. This was a tactic used by the French to excellent advantage on numerous occasions, of which the battles of Toulon (1744), Minorca (1756) and Grenada (1779) are three of the best documented examples.[14]

The importance of relative capability therefore suggests that to hold the weather gage was not necessarily to hold absolute control over the engagement. That rested as much on the relative sailing capabilities of the combatants as it did on position in relation to the wind. The ever practically minded Kempenfelt summed up these realities of advantage at sea:

> The comparative force of two fleets depends much upon their sailing. The fleet that sails fastest has much the advantage as they can engage or not as they please, and so have it always in their power to choose the favourable opportunity to attack.[15]

Rear-Admiral Charles Knowles used an old English proverb to compare the challenge of forcing an engagement between fleets of different capabilities to 'the mouse proposing to put a collar round the cat's neck with a bell suspended to it.'[16] Indeed, the only conditions under which battle could be forced, and was in any sense inevitable, was when the aggressor was positioned on the *opposite* side from that on which he had a clear superiority of performance over his enemy. If an aggressor with a superior windward performance were to assume a position to leeward, the enemy could not escape to windward because of his inferior sailing performance, and his escape route to leeward was physically blocked by the superior ship.[17]

GUNNERY AND THE WEATHER GAGE

The second aspect of position in relation to wind concerns gunnery. The heel of the ship, it is claimed, frequently dictated that the ship or fleet to windward was unable to use its lowest tier of guns.[18] Following the same logic, it has also been argued that the ship or fleet to leeward was obliged by the heel of the ship to aim its guns high, at the masts and rigging of the enemy.[19] It has been explained that this might only happen in heavy weather,[20] but otherwise no allowance is made for circumstance, the weather conditions, the sea conditions, the motion of the ships or, most importantly, the skill of those aboard.

Heel was a characteristic of sailing warship performance that was dependent on a number of factors over which captains could and did exercise a degree of control through artful and judicious handling of the sail plan. For most ships, most of the time, heel could be remedied quickly and effectively by reducing the quantity of sail set. Indeed, one contemporary claimed that '[an] officer makes a wretched defence, who has only to say that his ship heels more than the enemy.'[21] Thus at the Battle of Quiberon Bay in 1756 the *Torbay* (74) was struck by a severe squall. In danger of flooding the lower gun ports, the sheets were let fly, thus instantly taking all the pressure out of the sails and reducing the angle of heel. The captain of the French ship she was engaging, the *Thesée* (74), was not so quick to react; her lower decks filled with water and she sank with all but twenty-two of her 815 hands.[22] It was not, therefore, in any sense inevitable that a ship to windward would be unable to fire her lee guns, or that the ship to leeward would be forced to fire high: to argue that is to presume that the captain was prepared to engage under highly unfavourable, if not impossible, circumstances.

When it became clear that a fight was inevitable, a reduction of sail plan was advisable for a variety of reasons. Once engaged, it was in the interests of a ship to adopt the 'classic' fighting plan, working under topsails and foresail. This would both reduce the likelihood of sails catching fire from sparks and burning wads from the guns, and reduce the potential impact of damage aloft from enemy fire. With the majority of hands stationed at the guns, and a reduced crew working the ship itself, a reduction in speed and quantity of canvas would also make sail handling, and therefore manœuvre, easier in the heat of battle. Because of the link between angle of heel and quantity of canvas set, the only occasion when this might not have been the case was during a running chase. Sailing under a heavy press of canvas to escape or to catch an adversary, even a judicious reduction of sail plan would naturally be inadvisable because of the inevitable loss of speed. Thus Captain Young recorded how the French fleet to windward of Rodney in May 1780 got within engaging distance of the British van, but, upon the British making sail to leeward, the French were forced to chase under full sail in a good breeze, and for that limited time were unable to use their lowest tier of guns.[23]

Ships in 'formal' fleet battle would not face the same dilemma as those in a running chase. They would be under fighting sail plan, and their speed would be reduced even further to aid station keeping. Travelling at such a sedate pace and under such reduced sail, heel would rarely pose a problem. More importantly, and most obviously, a reduction in canvas would reduce heel and allow the ship unrestricted use of her full complement of guns. It would also allow those guns to be fired at a decent rate. Fighting the leeward guns on a ship to windward, and heeling badly, the cannon would often run back out of the ports under their own momentum after firing. Before they could be fired again they therefore had to be bowsed in every time for loading.[24] On a similar ship fighting to windward, the guns would effectively have to be run out uphill which would require extra blocks to make it easier and safe.[25] An apparatus invented in 1781 was designed to make this process easier through the use of a counterweight, but it is unclear if it was ever trialled.[26]

For all of these reasons, a captain would only engage under a full press of canvas *in extremis*. The majority of the time a warship would engage upright, with access to all of her guns. The only ships for which this was still not possible were particularly crank ships – ships that were so tender that no such measure could prevent the lowest tier of guns from being submerged – or ships whose lowest tier of guns was very close to the waterline. The British eighty- and ninety-gun three-deckers of the 1740s were particularly notorious for this but by the 1750s the dockyards were building bigger and stiffer warships and were learning the mathematics of raising the gun deck sufficiently free of the waterline without endangering the stability of the vessel.[27] By the Revolutionary War, examples of ships suffering in this way are hard to come by,[28] but the problem did not entirely disappear. All ships with gun ports were necessarily at risk from down-flooding, and as late as 1869 the *Plyades* was caught in a squall off Pampero, and heeled over so far that water poured into her lower gun deck.[29]

If a ship did suffer in this way, there is reason to doubt the contention that *all* of the ports of the lower deck were affected. At the Battle of Toulon, the eighty-gun *Dorsetshire* rolled heavily in the large swell and light winds, and shipped large quantities of water, but only through the foremost ports.[30] This is not a lone example, and in all of the reports that are specific about which ports were affected, only the forward ports, and sometimes those in the waist, suffer.[31] To be unable to fire any of the lowest tier was rare indeed, but if such a situation did present itself, even a frigate with only a single gun deck would still be able to use her quarterdeck and forecastle guns. It is also entirely characteristic of the resourcefulness of eighteenth-century seamanship that a tendency to flood through the lower gun ports could even be turned to advantage. In March 1758, for example, the *Prince George* (90) caught fire, and the severity of the flames caused the captain to help douse the flames by opening the lower-deck gun ports.[32]

The argument that the ship or fleet to leeward was obliged by heel to aim its guns high is particularly misconceived. Not only does it overlook the ability of a captain to ease the heel of his ship through judicious use of the sail plan, but it also fails to consider the art and materials of the gunner. Wedge-shaped pieces of wood known as 'quoins' were inserted or removed from underneath the cannon to adjust the angle at which it fired. By raising the back of the gun, the muzzle could be lowered and the heel of the gun deck compensated.[33] The third lieutenant of the *Dorsetshire* recalled how this was done in practice at the Battle of Toulon, which was fought in high seas and light winds with the ships rolling heavily:

Q: Was your metal lowered during the engagement?

A: Yes; sometimes more, sometimes less, according to the swell. The quoins were sometimes out, to bring the guns to bear, according to the motion of the ship.[34]

This ability was, however, restricted to a certain extent by the vertical dimensions of the gun ports, and in 1790 the degree to which the muzzle of the gun could be depressed was still considered insufficient.[35] Nevertheless, unless the ship was in a chase and heeling excessively with a large press of canvas, the motion of the ship would provide recurring opportunities in which it would be upright and the guns pointing horizontally. It was 'the rule generally laid down for observance in action' that this was the point at which guns should be fired.[36] This certainly seems to have been the case aboard the *Rupert* at the Battle of Toulon. Rolling heavily in high seas and light winds, Lieutenant William Williams took his opportunity to fire the gun 'when the ship was steady and still'.[37]

Firing when horizontal and still would both prevent the shot from going high and ease the recoil of the gun. A gun recoiling downhill put terrible strain on the breechings and ringbolts that secured it in place, and thus heightened the risk of its being dismounted. This was a particular problem if the gun was double-shotted.[38] Moreover, it was certainly not in the interests of the captain to fight his ship while it was heeling to the extent that adjusting the angle of the guns would not compensate for the angle of heel. Not only would gunnery be extremely difficult and restricted, but the vulnerable hull underneath the waterline would also be exposed to enemy gunfire. Only in certain very specific and very disadvantageous circumstances, therefore, would the lee position cause guns to fire high, and this was in no way inevitable.

This traditional focus on the relative advantages or disadvantages of the windward and leeward positions actually overlooks a more widespread problem, and one that affected both friend and foe equally, regardless of position in relation to the wind and that is roll.

The tendency of a ship to roll could be eased to a certain extent, but this involved the setting of steadying canvas and the positioning of the ship in relation to the swell. In a sea fight neither of these luxuries could be relied on. The position of the ship in relation to its enemy, not the swell, became the primary consideration. Thus at Trafalgar the French were obliged to receive the swell on the beam if they were to meet Nelson's attack broadside-to. In the light winds and under only minimal canvas, their ships rolled heavily, and, as a result, their gunnery suffered.[39] Furthermore, as it was in the interest of a ship to engage under reduced canvas and at a slow speed, a ship would become more susceptible to the motions of the sea as the swell passed under her than if she was clipping along at 5 knots with a cloud of steadying canvas.

Roll was also unpredictable. Although a well-ballasted ship in fine engaging weather and sea conditions would have an easy and slow motion, it was not always this simple. Roll was caused by a complex combination of factors: the position of the ship in relation to the swell, the amount of canvas set, the positioning of the ballast, the design of the hull, and, not least, the swell, which does not come at regular intervals and sizes. There also seems to have been a distinction between a 'lee lurch' and a 'weather roll'. The shape of the wave combined with the pressure of the wind caused the difference in motion, the lee slope of the wave being considerably steeper than the weather side. The 'lee lurch' was an abrupt and awkward motion to leeward, whereas the weather roll was a slower and more measured motion to windward.[40] Both could affect gunnery, but the roll to leeward was usually worse.[41]

One of the most famous examples of a ship being unable to fire her lowest tier in battle, which sheds light on the whole question of heel, roll and gunnery, was the case of Captain Savage Mostyn in 1745. He was unable to bring two French ships carrying valuable cargo from Martinique to action, as in his words: 'The middle of the lower deck ports was under water.'[42] This case aroused a good deal of professional interest, and Vernon was most vociferous in calling for Mostyn's scalp, arguing firmly that as heel could be controlled, it was no reason for a ship to be unable to attack an enemy.[43] Soon after the trial had ended, a most interesting pamphlet entitled *A Vindication of the Conduct of Captain M-N* (London, 1745) was anonymously published. In this, the author made the important distinction between heel and roll, and firmly blamed Mostyn's troubles on the latter.

> The swelling surges of a hollow grown sea entirely baffles all regular dispositions and contemns all plans of theory. It was not therefore the *Hampton Court*'s lying along [heel] altogether that was the cause she could not fight her lower deck guns, but her disordered motion occasioned by a swelling sea, which forced her lower deck ports at uncertain intervals much deeper into the water than happened merely by her pressure of sail ...[44]

Ships, therefore, did not roll as a pendulum swings; the motion was neither uniform nor predictable. This unpredictability ensured that roll had a far greater negative impact on fighting capability than did heel, which was easier to predict and overcome. It is important, therefore, to distinguish between the two, as roll, not heel, seems to have been the primary cause of ships being unable to fire the lowest tier of guns (Fig. 21 and 22).

OTHER CHARACTERISTICS OF THE WEATHER GAGE

There is evidence of ships to leeward experiencing trouble with burning wads, and sparks from the guns being blown back towards the sails and the ship.[45] Indeed, it was advised that, in a chase, the ship to leeward should haul up her courses, the lowest sails, to prevent them from catching fire when the guns were fired.[46] By the Battle of the Saints in 1782, however, the practice of using wetted wads to reduce this risk of fire was slowly being introduced, the *Duke* and *Formidable* finding them most effective on that day.[47]

21 The accepted understanding of the weather and lee gages is that the wind affected two ships like this, with each heeling at the same angle.

22 In practice, the unpredictable roll of ships in battle was the major factor in gunnery, and it had little to do with position in relation to the wind. This image of the *Brunswick* sandwiched between the French *Vengeur du Peuple* and the *Achille* in the midst of the Glorious First of June 1794 is one of the most realistic images of sailing warfare ever painted. The artist was both a professional artist and a professional seaman, and, moreover, he witnessed this battle at first hand. Note how the ships are both in mid-roll and are heeling towards each other, and compare with Fig. 21.

23 The *Defence* at the Battle of the First of June 1794, by Nicholas Pocock

Accumulation of smoke from the guns was also a very real problem. There was a traditional belief that smoke caused the sea and wind to fall calm in action,[48] a phenomenon that was also attributed to the concussion of the guns.[49] Restriction of visibility is, however, a more readily proven contention. Hawke complained after the Second Battle of Finisterre in 1747 that the smoke prevented him from seeing what happened on either side for some time,[50] and the sketches and paintings of Nicholas Pocock, artist and eyewitness of the battles of 29–31 May and 1 June 1794, show huge clouds of smoke enveloping the ships (Fig. 22 and 23). Indeed, the smoke was so thick during that battle that Lieutenant Bennet of the *Caesar* was directed in his fire by the flashing of the enemy guns, a technique also used by Admiral Villeneuve's gun crews at Trafalgar.[51] Inevitably, such restricted visibility led to instances of friendly fire. At the Battle of Ushant in 1778 the smoke caused the *Thunderer* to fire into the *Egmont*.[52] At the First of June 1794 a midshipman aboard the *Orion* reported that the smoke was so thick that they were unable to make out those ships engaging ahead or astern,[53] and a number of English ships targeted the *Caesar*, which was obscured by smoke.[54] In exactly the same way, in the action between Duckworth and Leissègues in January 1806 the *Spencer*, obscured by smoke, was targeted by the *Superb* and *Northumberland*.[55]

Measures were taken, however, to reduce the likelihood of this happening. Even if visibility was limited to the extent that the surface of the water could not be seen, the masts of the enemy were often visible above the smoke,[56] and it was customary to paint the 'hoops' of each mast so that the masts might still indicate friend or foe.[57] In addition, both divisions of Nelson's fleet at Trafalgar hoisted the white ensign to prevent any confusion from a variety of national flags. Furthermore, each British ship of the line carried a Union Jack at her maintopmast stay and another at her foretopgallant stay.[58] Nearly fifty years earlier, at the Battle of Quiberon Bay, Hawke ordered Francis Geary, Rear-Admiral of the White, to replace his traditional white ensign in the forthcoming battle with red ensigns. All the commanders of the ships in his division were to do likewise, thus ensuring no confusion with the French fleet, who were known to fly white flags.[59] It was claimed by one contemporary in 1787 that the accumulation of smoke in the gun decks was as easy to remedy as it was to foresee,[60] but he provides no explanation of how this might be done, and we know that, in the calm at Trafalgar in 1805, the accumulation of smoke on the gun decks was still a significant problem.[61]

To concentrate on the immediate effects on gunnery capability is, however, to overlook the deeper significance that reduced visibility had on tactical performance which transcended the ability to see a target. Central to this was the increased difficulty of station keeping, as the ability to judge distance, speed and bearing by eye was restricted for obvious reasons.[62] One further problem created by the smoke was the loss of the considerable advantages that could be gained from studying the appearance and manœuvre of the enemy to glean information about intent and capability.[63] In this new light, Hood's orders after his encounter with de Grasse off St Kitts can be better understood. He ordered that all damage sustained during the day should be repaired at night, with the specific intention that: 'Owing to this judicious arrangement the enemy knew not the extent of the injury inflicted by them',[64] the unspoken addendum being that the French would not therefore be able to take any advantage from such critical intelligence.

The problem of how the windward fleet was actually to engage without exposing itself to untold damage from the fleet to leeward remained a serious problem. The ultimate goal was to bring the entire fleet to action simultaneously. To do this, however, the fleet to windward had to draw parallel to that to leeward, and then bear down straight towards the enemy, each ship keeping her opposite number on the same point of the compass.[65] This exposed the vulnerable bows and rig of the attackers to a punishing raking fire that could not be returned until the attacking fleet had reached its required engaging distance and could haul up into line, present its broadsides and return fire (Fig. 24).

One method used to get round this problem was known as 'lasking'. Rather than bearing down when parallel to the enemy and thus approaching at 90°, the manœuvre involved sailing past the waiting enemy before tacking or wearing and then bearing down. This brought the windward

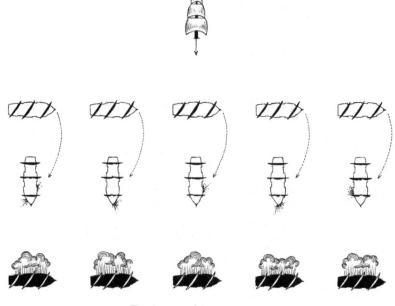

24 The dangers of the windward attack

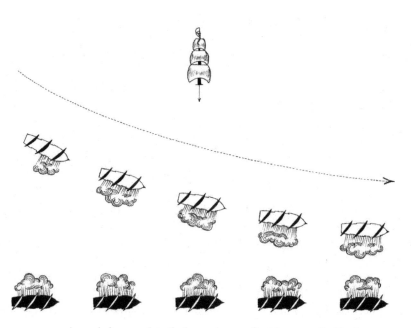

25 An angled approach to the leeward enemy fleet, known as 'lasking'

ships down on their enemy at a much shallower angle, helping to protect the bows and allowing a certain degree of gunfire from the ships to windward (Fig. 25).

No signal existed for this approach, so the success of any attempt rested on the pre-existence of unwritten doctrine, common to both the commander and his captains, which dealt with the lasking approach. At the Battle of Minorca in 1756 Byng suffered the inevitable consequences of an attempt at lasking without such a common doctrine. To windward of La Galissionière's fleet, he realised the danger of a perpendicular approach and determined to lask down. When the van of Byng's fleet passed the final ship of the French fleet, he signalled to tack, hoping that his captains would understand his intention and bear down on their opposite number at a shallow angle. Captain Andrews of the *Defiance*, leading the British line, failed to grasp Byng's intention and continued on a course parallel with, and at some distance from, the enemy. Understandably, the following ships of Rear-Admiral West's van squadron followed his misguided example.[66]

These disadvantages of the windward attack prompted John Clerk, the author on naval tactics, to describe it as 'a disadvantage almost beyond the power of calculation'.[67] He offered five examples of engagements in which the British fleet attempted the attack from to windward, but, after completing its approach, was so disabled as to be temporarily incapable of much further aggression. He cited the Battle of Minorca, 1756; Byron's engagement off Grenada, 6 July 1779; Rodney's action off Martinique, 17 April 1780; Arbuthnot off the Chesapeake, 16 March 1781; and the Battle of the Chesapeake on 5 September 1781.[68]

These obvious disadvantages of the weather gage so perplexed one contemporary that he sought to explain it as a hangover from an earlier age. The French commentator De Grenier argued that in the age of oared warships with rams secured to the prows, the windward position was a prerequisite for their tactics. The aim was to bear down with as much force as possible and ram the enemy before manœuvring alongside and boarding. The windward position facilitated this attack by adding speed to the ship. 'For want of reflection', he argued, the rule was passed down to the eighteenth century, whence it became entirely inappropriate for ships with their main armaments broadside-to.[69] His argument is certainly interesting, and, viewed alongside the practical difficulties of the windward attack and the significance of relative capability in fleet engagements, bears more than a little consideration. However, there remained some clear-cut advantages of the windward position and disadvantages of the leeward position that must also be understood to help us achieve a more balanced understanding of this complex subject.

A little-discussed advantage of the weather gage was that the fleet to windward would be able to make the dangerous approach to battle more quickly than having to force battle close-hauled, that being the slowest point of sailing for a square-rigged ship. This was an advantage because an increase in speed reduced the time in which the bows of the attacking fleet were vulnerable to the guns of the waiting enemy. A quick attack was also a valuable tactic, as it disrupted the aim of those being attacked. Captain Miller, writing to his wife of the Battle of the Nile, said that, running down the enemy's line in the wake of the *Zealous* and *Goliath*, he observed the shot of the enemy sailing clear overhead. He then deliberately closed with the Frenchmen as quickly as possible, 'knowing well that at such a moment Frenchmen would not have coolness enough to change their elevation'.[70] Such a rapid approach was clearly the intention of Nelson at Trafalgar; he wished to 'go at them at once',[71] and did so, contrary to tradition, under full sail.

There were, however, more significant advantages to the windward position than a marginal superiority in speed. To understand them, three fundamentals of fighting tactics in the age of sail must first be considered.

The first was the need to maintain cohesion when fighting in a fleet. A fleet divided or fragmented could offer little resistance to a well-organised and disciplined enemy. Although a long-established maxim of all forms of warfare, this was particularly significant in the age of sail because of the inevitability of the need for mutual support. In battle a warship could quickly turn from a bristling machine of war to a home of souls wholly concentrated on survival, at the mercy of the enemy and the elements. A disabled ship needed immediate support if it was not to be surrounded by the enemy, and a sinking ship needed to be towed to safety and given the necessary time, spares and extra labour to ensure her survival. It was also an accepted maxim that the more ships that were together, the less damage each would receive.[72] That requisite mutual support could only be achieved through the maintenance of cohesion. Modern navies are able to maximise the use of long-range guns and wide arcs of fire to effect the principle of concentration of numbers by the convergence of fire from widely dispersed positions. In the eighteenth century, however, the limitations in accuracy and range of gunnery meant that mutual support could only be achieved through physical proximity.

This need for mutual support was not a longed-for bonus, but a fundamental requirement of the highest priority for all entering into a sea fight. Nothing highlights this more clearly than Nelson's description of Hotham's action with a French fleet off the coast off Genoa in March 1795. On the morning of the 13th the *Ça Ira* (84) collided with the *Victoire* (80), carrying away her main and foretopmasts, and Nelson bore down to attack it in the *Agamemnon* (64). However, he uncharacteristically resolved to fire 'so soon as I thought we had a certainty of hitting', long before he had reached his preferred distance of point blank. In his report of the action, he explained that the decision was forced on him by the situation of the two fleets, citing in particular the certainty of his being severely cut up in the masts and the impossibility of receiving any support from the rest of the fleet.[73]

The second fundamental was to protect the vulnerable bows and stern of the ship, while at the same time trying to exploit that vulnerability in the enemy. The third was to avoid tacking under the guns of the enemy. It was a requirement born from a combination of the need to maintain cohesion and the vulnerability of the bows and stern. To tack in a fleet and retain cohesion was all but impossible.[74] Furthermore, in the process of tacking, the vulnerable bows and stern would be exposed to the enemy. To attempt to tack, and fail – to 'miss stays', an occurrence that became even more likely in the heat of battle with sail plan reduced and an inevitable degree of damage to the rig – was to leave the bows and stern at the mercy of the enemy's guns. In the summer of 1796 the French *Vengeance* suffered heavy losses in exactly this way when twice missing stays in a duel with the *Mermaid* (32).[75] At the Battle of Cape St Vincent the *Colossus* missed stays as Jervis ordered the fleet to tack in succession, and was badly mauled by the Spanish *Principe*.[76]

Herein lie the real practical advantages of the windward position. Regardless of relative ability to make ground to windward, it remained an indisputable fact that windward sailing took time and was difficult, particularly in a body. The principal problem was that a fleet trying to force action from to leeward would be sailing close hauled in order to gain as much ground towards the enemy as possible. If the enemy to windward were seeking to avoid action, it would no doubt also be close-hauled to keep its distance from the attacking fleet. The two fleets would therefore be very nearly parallel, and to force the enemy's hand, the fleet to leeward would have to tack and come at the windward fleet on the contrary tack in line ahead.[77] The leeward fleet would also need to have fore-reached, at least in part, on the enemy fleet before tacking since to tack earlier would have been to pass ineffectually to the rear of the windward fleet. A classic example of this is Howe's action on 29 May 1794; with the French fleet to windward, Howe tacked his fleet in succession and engaged the French rear.

Unless this manœuvre was performed at a considerable distance, the aggressive lee fleet therefore had to attempt the risky process of tacking directly under the guns of the windward fleet. For both ships and fleets to leeward, exposure of the vulnerable bows and sterns to the enemy was at some point inevitable in an aggressive attack, and, because of the need for manœuvre, the dislocation of fleet formation was a strong possibility, if not a certainty. To obtain the weather gage was, therefore, to facilitate forcing close action whilst retaining cohesion.

'Aggressive attack' and 'forcing action' are clearly key terms in understanding the value of the windward position for the Royal Navy. All the disadvantages of the leeward position depend on the fleet to leeward wishing to force close action. For a fleet prepared merely to withstand an attack, evade decisive encounters and preserve their ships, the disadvantages of the lee gage were of little consequence. Hence an author who served in De Grasse's fleet in the West Indies in 1781–2, which under no circumstances desired a decisive encounter with the Royal Navy, considered the windward position a 'very trifling advantage at sea'.[78] Reflecting an aggressive strategy, on the other hand, in 1704 the Englishman Robert Park thought it 'absurd' to think an enemy would chose to fight to leeward when he had the option of being to windward;[79] and almost exactly a century later, in 1803, Nelson brusquely wrote in a plan of attack that upon meeting the French 'of course I should weather them'.[80]

Once engaged, however, it was the leeward position that was particularly favourable for those wishing to force a decisive encounter, by, in effect, 'trapping' the enemy and preventing any escape. In his tactical memorandum of 1803 Nelson was specific that 'the great object is for us to support each other, and to keep close to the enemy and to leeward of him'.[81] The first characteristic of capability to be lost by any damage to the rig of any ship was windward performance, as the rig needed to be secure and fully functioning to withstand the rigours of sailing close hauled. The only possible escape of a damaged ship was, therefore, downwind. Not only would the lee fleet's damaged ships drift to safety behind their own line, threatening isolation to any enemy that dared to follow, but the damaged ships of the enemy to windward, unable to hold their wind, would drift down helplessly on to the guns of the waiting lee fleet. This would drastically affect their ability to repair damage. To be to leeward was thus to deny the enemy the time and opportunity to repair, a highly significant tactic. In consequence, it would be much easier for the leeward ship or fleet to press home any advantage once action had commenced.

It is clear that the advantages of position in relation to the wind cannot be divorced from issues of seamanship, gunnery and the relative performance capability of the ships or fleets in question. It is also intricately tied in to broader questions of strategy and, in particular, to the need to achieve or avoid a decisive encounter. Determined by so many variables, preference for one position or another could and did change according to circumstance as a sea fight evolved and a rigid explanation of the choice between the weather and lee gages should be avoided. The reality of the choice is neatly summed up by a contemporary American author on naval tactics: 'A general rule for the adoption of either the weather or lee gage cannot be laid down. Sometimes the one is preferable, and sometimes the other; and very often the commander-in-chief has it not in his power to make an option.'[82]

CHAPTER 9

Fleet Tactics

The most minute accident may turn the scales in favour of the party that humane reason was least inclined to.[1]

Position in relation to the wind was only one part of fleet tactics, and there was far more to occupy the mind of a fleet commander concerning the way he was going to use his fleet in battle. At their most basic, fleet tactics can be divided into two categories according to their intended offensive or defensive goal. The choice between the two was governed by strategic concerns such as the defence of a port, harbour or convoy, and also by circumstance. The relative size, design, performance and skill of the enemy; their numbers, geographical position, confidence and courage; their available resources of powder and shot, spare masts, yards and manpower: these were all influences on tactical choice. With such a large number of influential factors there was a corresponding variety of battles fought throughout the period. These included pitched fleet battles and chase actions; actions fought stationary with one or both fleets anchored; actions involving merchant ships and convoys; and actions between numerically equal or unequal fleets. In considering tactics it is therefore important to be aware of this variety of battle types, and not to compare battles of dissimilar kinds. To achieve a useful overview, tactics must be considered at the fundamental level of the ideas and principles upon which they were founded and the practical requirements upon which they rested.

For Lord Howe the object of all tactics was to develop the utmost power of his weapon against the enemy, while denying that same opportunity to his enemy.[2] At sea in the age of sail a principal requirement for achieving this objective was moderate sea and weather conditions. Although the Battle of Quiberon Bay, fought in mid-winter in a howling Atlantic gale and large swell, is recognised today as one of the greatest decisive fleet actions in the age of sail, such conditions were far from the norm, and were usually avoided at all costs. Nelson was explicit that fleet manœuvre in poor weather was almost impossible and would render any decisive action unlikely through a restriction of command capability.[3] It is also certain that very poor weather could preclude action of any sort: the battles of Ushant and the First of June were both delayed by poor weather and sea conditions.[4] Even when two fleets had successfully been brought to action, heavy, changeable and squally weather made it very hard for a captain to position his ship exactly as he would like, and gunnery was difficult and dangerous.[5]

Numerical superiority was also fundamental to decisive victory throughout the century. At its heart was the ability to engage a ship or a fleet on both sides.

To fire all of the guns on one side of a ship, tend the sails and repair damage was a challenge in itself, but to do so while exchanging fire on both sides put a significant strain on manpower as the gun crews simply divided in half.[6] Gunnery would be slower and harder work, and it could not be kept up for long at any significant rate of fire. With the wisdom of experience, Shovell wrote in 1702:

> 'tis without a miracle, number that gains the victory, for both in flesh, squadrons and single ships of near equal force, by the time one is beaten and ready to retreat the other is also beaten and glad the enemy has left him; To fight, beat and chase an enemy of the same strength I have sometime seen, but rarely have seen at sea any victory worth boasting where the strength has been near equal.[7]

He was right. All comprehensive victories in the age of sail were achieved through numerical superiority. It was either established from the moment that the two sides met, as at the two battles of Finisterre in 1747, in which Anson had fourteen sail to the enemy's five, and Hawke had fourteen to the enemy's eight, or one way or another numerical superiority was achieved through manœuvre. This required one fleet to bring a large force to bear on a smaller part of the enemy fleet. In those battles that were indecisive, numerical superiority could not be achieved or was not attempted. The question of decisive victory could therefore be reduced to the challenge of securing numerical superiority and overwhelming firepower over the enemy.

This principle was well known both among naval officers and civilian commentators on naval tactics. The idea of cutting off and separating a part of the enemy fleet to achieve numerical superiority was as alive in Holland in 1652 as it was at Trafalgar in 1805,[8] and in 1697 Hoste had detailed the methods by which this could be achieved in his *L'Art des armées navales.* Much of that work was repeated by Morogues in his 1763 *Tactique navale* and again by Clerk in his *Essay on Naval Tactics* (1797). What has continually perplexed historians, therefore, is Article xviii of the printed Fighting Instructions of 1691 issued by Admiral Edward Russell,[9] which required the commander of the attacking fleet to stretch his fleet the full length of the enemy and his van to attack the enemy van, thus removing the possibility of concentration of force. It was essentially a defensive tactic. The intention was to prevent the lead or rear ships of the enemy from doubling, and it persisted until tactical aggression and decisive action came to dominate the minds of naval officers in the late 1770s.

Howe and Kempenfelt issued orders to the Channel Fleet to attack certain parts of the enemy in 1777,[10] and in 1780 Rodney issued Additional Instructions to concentrate on the van, centre or rear of the enemy as directed. He argued that the traditional approach of engaging van to van and rear to rear was 'contrary to common sense' and 'absurd', and he made it a rule of his own to bring his whole force against a part of the enemy's.[11] His first opportunity to use these tactics came at the Battle of Martinique in April 1780, but his intention of massing his force on the enemy rear was misunderstood by his subordinates in his van division, who bore down to the enemy van according to the traditional method of engagement.[12]

Nevertheless, the shift towards aggressive tactics designed to create numerical superiority over the enemy had clearly been made, at least in the Channel and West Indies fleets. Just over a year later Rear-Admiral Thomas Graves tried to target the van of the French fleet with his entire force at the Battle of the Chesapeake in 1781.[13] Again, however, good aggressive tactics were undone by a failure of command method: the rear division led by Samuel Hood failed to understand Graves's intention, and did not engage until it was too late. The first successful application of this tactic in the eighteenth century came in the Battle of the Saints in 1782. Largely by accident and with the timely assistance of a wind shift, Rodney achieved numerical superiority on a part of the French fleet, and overwhelmed them. Five French ships, including the admiral and his flagship, were taken. With the success of this tactic so clearly proven, the British did not look back. Between the battles of Malaga (1704) and the Saints (1782) the Navy fought fourteen fleet engagements in which both sides were prepared to stand and fight (as distinct from chase actions), and all of them were indecisive.[14] In the years between the Battle of the Saints in 1782 and Trafalgar in 1805, every one of the five formal fleet actions was a victory for the British, and they were all achieved by the creation of numerical superiority.[15]

To understand this change some general points must be made to put it into context. The first is that the idea of achieving numerical superiority in naval warfare may have existed for some time, perhaps for centuries, but the practical problems of achieving it were severe, even prohibitive.

ATTACKING THE ENEMY FORMATION

One way of achieving numerical superiority was to actively disrupt the enemy formation. Once their cohesion had broken down, one part of their fleet could be isolated and overwhelmed. The most direct way of disrupting the enemy formation was to attack it. This, in turn, could be done in two ways. The first, and the basis of any attempt to disrupt the enemy formation, was gunnery.[16] It is too often overlooked that the aim of gunnery in the first few exchanges of fleet battle was not to target the men and the ships but their order and cohesion. A well-directed cannonade might disable a ship sufficiently to prevent her from maintaining position in line, or a ship might be driven from her position, her captain and crew being unequal to the task of a fierce gunnery duel. In either case, a break in just one link in the chain of the enemy line could cause significant problems for the cohesion and unity of their entire fleet. The loss of two or three from the line would create an opportunity for the attacking fleet to pass through the enemy line and trap it between two fires by engaging it on both sides.

The second method of attacking the enemy formation was through manœuvre, dislocating the enemy formation by breaking their line. To break the enemy's line carried with it considerable risks, however.[17] The line of battle itself, once formed and held, was a formation very strong in the defensive but very weak in the offensive. Modern fleets can achieve numerical superiority by the convergence of fire from widely dispersed positions. In the eighteenth century, however, limited accuracy, arcs of fire and range made achieving numerical superiority fundamentally a problem of ship or fleet movement. Therein lay the problem. The difficulties of station keeping and communication made cohesive manœuvre of any sort extremely difficult whilst maintaining a solid defensive formation. It was therefore far easier to turn the tables on oneself than it was for an enemy to do so, and the larger and more unwieldy one's fleet, the more likely it was to happen. 'It is a principle of warfare', wrote one French contemporary in 1781, 'that much is to be risked to defend one's own position, and little to attack the enemy's.'[18]

To break an enemy line would at some point also require the attacking ship to expose her vulnerable bows to the enemy, when they would be unable to return fire except perhaps with bow-chasers. At the Battle of the First of June (1794) the first ship to break through the French line, the *Defence*, received the fire of at least fifteen of the enemy's ships.[19] Once the two fleets had met, it was then likely, if not inevitable, that only some of the attacking fleet would make it through the enemy line. Now disrupted, the attackers themselves became vulnerable to defeat in detail. In similar fashion, moreover, if the attackers broke the enemy's line, thereby cutting off and isolating their rear (Fig. 26A), by the time the enemy's van had tacked to come and succour those hard pressed, the attacking fleet would have lost all tactical cohesion, and would not be able to present a united front to the counter attack (Fig. 26B). The attacker thus instantly became the defender, and was vulnerable to isolation and defeat in detail by a larger force. For all these reasons, breaking a compact enemy line was only advised in dire circumstance: for example, when the fleet was pressed against a lee shore by an enemy to windward.[20]

WAITING FOR OPPORTUNITY

Despite these problems associated with physically attacking the enemy formation, all was not lost for the commander intent on achieving decisive action by dividing the enemy fleet. To understand how and why that was so, it is first necessary to distinguish between actively dividing the enemy fleet by smashing through their defensive formation with an aggressive manœuvre, and taking advantage of a pre-existing gap to 'divide' their fleet simply by passing through

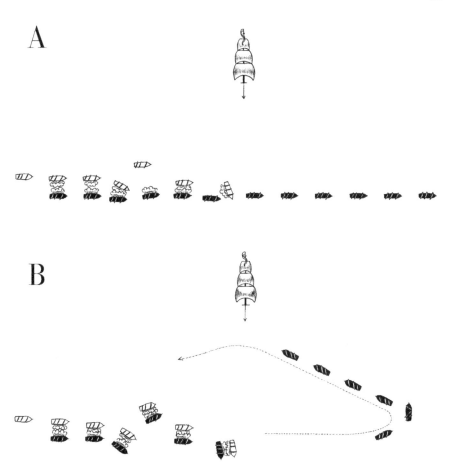

26 The dangers of breaking the enemy line. Once the attacking fleet has divided the centre and rear of the enemy from the van, in the process losing cohesion themselves (A), they are then vulnerable to counter-attack by the enemy van (B).

that gap. The latter was far more common and far less risky. For Admiral John Jervis it was the only way that a decisive result could be achieved. 'Two Fleets of equal Force', he wrote, 'never can produce decisive events unless they are equally determin'd to fight it out, or the Commander in Chief of one of them, bitches it, so as to misconduct his Line.' [21]

Fleet tactics in practice were characterised by the need for cohesion and the parallel difficulty of achieving it. The problems of station keeping, fleet man- œuvre and communication, the lack of teaching and training regarding the method of command, the unpredictability of wind and weather, and the varia- tion in performance capability of each ship, all ensured that a loss of cohesion of one or both fleets was highly probable at any time, and particularly so under the peculiar stresses of battle. Captains and commanders knew that nothing was certain other than uncertainty, nothing predictable other than unpredictability, and an alert commander could take advantage of the enemy's self-imposed or accidental dislocation of fleet formation to divide and impose overwhelming force on one part of the enemy's fleet. This was not tactical anarchy; on the contrary, it was a specific tactical idea elucidated by contemporaries. St Vincent put tactics down to '[taking] prompt advantage of disorder in the fleet of the enemy, by shifts of wind, accidents, and their deficiency in practical seamanship to the superior knowledge of which much of our success is to be attributed'.[22] That his contemporaries agreed is certain. In one of Kempenfelt's frequent tirades about tactics, he repeated St Vincent almost word for word,[23] and it is highly significant that Collingwood couched praise for Nelson's skill in exactly these terms:

> His success in most undertakings are the best proofs of his genius and his talents. Without much previous preparation or plan he has the faculty of discovering advantages as they arise, and the good judgement to turn them to his use. An enemy that commits a false step in his view is ruined, and it comes on him with an impetuosity that allows him no time to recover.[24]

The best examples of this working in practice come from the battles of the Saints (1782) and St Vincent (1797). Rodney divided the French fleet at the Battle of the Saints, but he did so by taking advantage of a shift of wind that caused great confusion in both fleets. Similarly, at the Battle of St Vincent, Admiral Jervis concentrated his force on one part of the Spanish fleet, but did not 'cut' through them; they were already divided, having been unable to maintain formation.

At their simplest and least risky, therefore, aggressive tactics were passive. They involved waiting for an opportunity to arise and then seizing it to create a position of numerical equality or superiority from which to attack. Thus a smaller but aggressive fleet could always retain a degree of optimism; they might easily find an opportunity to attack a larger fleet on their own terms. In a letter to Middleton in the summer of 1779, Kempenfelt thus describes an imaginary scenario:

> 'Tis an inferior against a superior fleet; therefore the greatest skill and address is requisite to counteract the designs of the enemy, to watch and seize the favourable opportunity for action, and to catch the advantage of making the effort at some or other feeble part of the enemy's line; or, if such opportunities don't offer, to hover near the enemy, keep him at bay, and prevent his attempting to execute anything but at risk and hazard; to command their attention, and oblige them to think of nothing but being on their guard against your attack.[25]

If such an opportunity for advantage did not present itself, or, as was more likely, if it did present itself but the fleet commander or his captains were unable to take advantage of it, then the battle would be likely to be indecisive, as happened at the Battle of the Chesapeake in September 1781. As the enemy van came out of Lynn Haven Bay on the morning of 5 September, the French were in no regular formation, their van greatly extended beyond the centre and the rear. Hood believed that a prompt attack would have allowed a full hour and a half to overwhelm the van before it could be succoured, but in the end nothing was done; the resulting battle was a confused and indecisive affair as both fleets had the time to get into a good line, and the opportunity for achieving numerical superiority was lost.[26] The mechanics of tactics in practice must therefore be understood in terms of working with the unpredictable nature of sailing warfare and command capability, and not in attempting to tame it. The unpredictability of sailing performance and weather was not just a source of frustration to commanders; it was also the key to success.

It is understandable, therefore, that the line of battle carried with it a naturally defensive and conservative mindset that was hard to shake off. Not to offer an opportunity to the enemy became the principal tactical goal, and was reflected in contemporary practice and beliefs; many naval officers were more concerned about the ability to enact a manœuvre than the tactical ingenuity of the manœuvre itself. Reducing evolutions in the face of the enemy and thereby minimising the likelihood of offering the enemy an opportunity to attack was an established tactical maxim in its own right.[27] In many respects fleet battle was primarily a contest of fleet seamanship: the admiral who could preserve his line the longest had the surest chance of finding an opportunity to create numerical superiority, and with it the hope of decisive victory.

DECEPTION AND THE CREATION OF UNCERTAINTY

If a commander was not prepared to wait for disruption to appear in the enemy line of its own volition, and did not wish to attack a compact enemy formation, he could still be pro-active in causing confusion in the enemy's line by deception.

The value of deception has already been discussed in terms of disguising performance and capability upon initial contact, but with fleet action it was deception regarding tactical intention that was particularly important. It was valuable because in the age of sail the ability to conceal a movement or method of approach was very difficult. Everything was visible; there were no woods, rivers, banks, hills or mountains to conceal one's movements, and, once in sight, every individual ship, and the line into which she belonged, was driven by the same weather pattern and confined to the same movements as her enemy. Moreover, in daylight the fleets were visible to each other over 10 miles away, and perhaps more in good weather. Their signals were visible and could be penetrated if one had a copy of their most recent signal book. If not, their movements involving changes of sail plan or course were clearly visible, and their sails signalled their intent.

After the Battle of Ushant, for example, Captain Peyton of the *Cumberland* explained at a court martial how the different manœuvres of the French gave away their intention:

> Q: Did you by the manœuvres they made in tacking and wearing, imagine it an indication to give us battle, or to avoid it?
>
> A: When they wore I had my eye on them, I then thought their intention was different to what they had shown the several days before, but when they tacked on the larboard tack, crowded sail and kept the wind close, I then thought they had an inclination to avoid it … it was a confirmation to me that they did not mean to come to battle, thinking they could get off when they thought proper.[28]

Of the same action, but of a different manœuvre, Captain Ross of the *Shrewsbury* believed that the French fleet, wearing twice when they might have tacked, indicated their intention of avoiding battle and pushing for Brest.[29]

Fleet movements themselves took a long time to perform, often requiring a number of hours even for a simple manœuvre, and that allowed a commander time to penetrate their intention and react accordingly. Based on clear geometrical principles, the effective parry was also obvious. It was an established tactical maxim, for example, that any positional advantage hoped to be gained by tacking could be nullified by the other fleet tacking in response. Similarly, a wear could be countered by a wear.[30] With so much always apparent to each side, the value of deception regarding tactical intention was magnified. Not only was it difficult to achieve, but because it was difficult to achieve, it was unexpected. 'Although the naval warrior cannot place his fleet in ambush, nor at all times press the foe in their weakest part', wrote one commentator on naval tactics, 'let it not be supposed that contrivance and surprise are excluded from this mode of battle.'[31]

Concealing intent was also valuable because it prevented the enemy from formulating a response until the very last moment. Owing to the inherent weaknesses of the command system, creating uncertainty by concealing the intended method of attack was particularly significant. To be able to react to any given situation at short notice required flexibility, and such flexibility required a command style based on a common doctrine that promoted initiative amongst the captains. To achieve this level of flexibility in command and still retain cohesion required years of training, the highest seamanship skill and exceptional leadership, and the successful combination of the three was rare indeed. To instil uncertainty, and hence prevent the enemy from preparing a response until the last possible moment, placed added stress on the pre-existing weaknesses of the command system, and was more likely to cause disruption in the enemy formation which could then be exploited. It is thus understandable that in 1665 the Dutch Admiral Johan de Witt became highly irritated by the fact that nothing that took place in The Hague was hidden, because at that time he was developing measures to bring the fleet to battle in a formation totally unexpected by the enemy.[32]

To conceal the chosen manner of attack for as long as possible was strongly advised by many contemporaries. Rodney believed that to force your enemy 'to depart from their original intention ... and attacking them in a different mode from that they offer you' would offer a manifest advantage[33] Hood was careful to deceive the enemy over his tactical intentions in the skirmishes off St Kitts in January 1782.[34] Nelson also based many of his ideas around deception. His tactical memorandum of 1803 included an order to head directly for the headmost ship of the enemy. He added as an explanation 'so as to prevent the enemy from knowing whether I should pass to windward or to leeward of him.'[35] He also acknowledged with an uncharacteristic lack of modesty that the real genius of his plan for attack at Trafalgar was that it would 'surprise and confound the enemy. They won't know what I am about.'[36] In that plan he intended to advance his van down towards the van of the enemy to deceive them into thinking that an attack there was his intention, while his real aim was to cut through their fleet in the middle and overwhelm their rear. In the attack itself, this is exactly what he did.[37]

These, therefore, were the methods by which a commander could overcome the practical problems of disrupting an enemy formation to create numerical superiority. They were all difficult and dangerous. Particularly significant in their capacity to achieve decisive victory, therefore, was the ability and the desire of the commander and his officers to take those risks which allowed one fleet to achieve numerical superiority over a section of the other. It is this ability and the desire for aggression that changed in the Royal Navy. The line of battle was far stronger in defence than attack, but that was only true in theory. For the line to be strong in defence still required considerable seamanship, courage and tenacity. As the century progressed, so a gap developed between British and French professionalism and seamanship skill, and the British demonstrated time and again their superiority. It was that difference in skill which enabled these aggressive tactics to be considered. British commanders realised that they could risk concentrating their force on one part of the enemy, thus exposing their own fleets to being doubled, confident that the enemy would not be able to make the necessary parry in time to support the part of the fleet that was being attacked. Even if they did, wrote Knowles, 'the battle will be reduced to a scramble, wherein British seamanship and courage will soon show their superiority.'[38]

This ability and the desire for aggression in formal fleet action did not come together until the Navy had repeatedly demonstrated in a number of chase actions its superiority in battle over its enemies. The astounding successes at the First and Second Battles of Finisterre (1747), Havana (1748), Lagos Bay (1759), Quiberon Bay (1759) and the Moonlight Battle (1779), all of which were chase actions, provided that foundation. In each case the enemy was overwhelmed by British numbers and skill. Kempenfelt acknowledged that superior skill might make up for a lack of numbers, 'But what', he ruefully asked, 'is to be expected when skill and address are wholly on the side of numbers?'[39] Well he knew the answer; it had been demonstrated time and again in these victorious chase actions. With the weight of history behind them, therefore, British fleet commanders came to realise what was possible, and to appreciate that the risk of aggressive action was worth taking in formal fleet battle. The confidence that grew below decks was mirrored in that of command. An anonymous Frenchman wrote of British sailors 'The habit of conquering ... makes them engage in battle with an enthusiasm and courage, which men accustomed to defeats and severe losses cannot have.'[40] Much the same can be said of those in command and the fleet tactics that they employed.

CHAPTER 10

Fighting Tactics

There is no strength and force without motion and direction.[1]

Once two fleets or ships became engaged, their behaviour was governed by an entirely separate type of tactic. The 'grand' tactics of fleet manœuvre and positioning made way for the tactics of fighting – the means by which two ships or fleets sought to inflict damage on each other.

GUNNERY TACTICS

It has long been accepted that British sailors preferred to target the hull of their enemy, and there is certainly a great deal of evidence for the British gunners targeting the hull alone. Captain Middleton's order book from August 1775 is specific that: 'In firing against an enemy, the guns are to be pointed on the hull, near the mainmast',[2] and Lieutenant Page of the *Dorsetshire* is equally explicit that he aimed solely at the hull during the Battle of Toulon.[3] There are numerous examples of sea fights throughout the century in which tallies of damage to French ships tell a similar story,[4] but in situations such as chase where targeting the rig was a sensible tactic, there are, unsurprisingly, numerous examples of British warships doing just that.[5]

That firing high was deliberate and actively encouraged by the British is certain. Knowles was explicit that the forecastle guns should be used specifically to disable masts or yards,[6] and at the Battle of Minorca Lieutenant Basset of the *Ramillies* deliberately aimed at the upper part of the hull so that any shot which missed was most likely to cause damage to the rigging.[7] By 1781 Arbuthnot issued detailed instructions for the gunners to reserve a portion of their fire for the enemy rig.[8] Carronades with grapeshot were favoured for use against the sails and rigging of an enemy, even if the majority of the main armament was aimed low.[9] Kempenfelt in particular was a vociferous supporter of firing high in the last quarter of the century,[10] and there is further evidence of this being a British practice dating right back to as early as 1702, gunners being instructed to fire 'alow and aloft'.[11] That the British frequently fired high itself questions the validity of the assertion that it was seen as dishonourable and an unfitting practice for an Englishman, as has been claimed,[12] but it can be disproved further still. Pasley promised a guinea to any man who might bring down the mast of an enemy in action, and Gunner Furlong was the happy recipient in May 1781 at the Battle of Porto Praya, claiming 'the honour' of carrying away the *Annibal*'s mizzenmast.[13] In the same vein, Lieutenant Buchanan of the *Sandwich* 'flattered himself' that he was the gunner who shot down the main yard of an unnamed enemy ship at the Battle of Ushant.[14]

French gunnery tactics have long been associated with targeting the rig of the enemy, and there is ample evidence of the French doing so,[15] but a close reading of contemporary accounts reveals that the French fired mostly, but not exclusively, at the rigging.[16] Nelson conceded, in a description of a skirmish with a French squadron off Fiorenzo in 1795, that although they 'only' fired high, his ship still received several shot underwater, enough to keep them at the pumps twenty-four hours after the engagement.[17] Damage reports from British ships are further persuasive of the French targeting the hulls of their opponents. In an engagement between Pocock and the comte d'Aché in September 1759, the *Elizabeth* received 119 shot in the hull, and the *Tyger*, 145.[18] Similar examples come from the battles of Ushant,[19] the First of June,[20] and the Nile.[21] Most interestingly, an anonymous letter published in the *Gentleman's Magazine* in February 1744 entitled 'the French way of Fighting at Sea' makes no reference at all to firing high, but suggests the real difference was that the priority of the French was to bear down and board as soon as possible.[22] A similar letter published in the 1801 edition of the *Naval Chronicle* argues that no order existed in the French navy for directing fire in one way more than another, but '... to fire ahead, in stern or in broadside, to dismast, at the hull or at the rigging, and to sink. In an engagement the guns are pointed in one or other of these manners, according to circumstances.'[23] Those 'circumstances' were largely dictated by strategic considerations, but of more immediate tactical significance was the construction of the enemy ship. Larger ships were always more strongly built than smaller ones. Thus in the summer of 1798 the much larger French 74, the *Généraux,* deliberately targeted the smaller and more weakly built British fifty-gun *Leander* in the hull.[24] Furthermore, as a general rule, British ships were more strongly constructed than their French counterparts, with larger and heavier scantlings, fastened more strongly. Their hulls offered good protection to the crews working the guns and to the ship itself. The gun decks of the French ships, on the other hand, were death traps.[25] Thus at the Battle of Quiberon Bay in 1759, one of the crew saved from the wreck of the French *Thésée* related that it was their captain's specific intention to target the British *Vengeance* in the hull, 'to have poured in a whole broadside, and to have sent her to the bottom at once; for he had perceived she was French built.'[26]

Another factor in choice of gunnery tactics was distance of engagement. To fire high was unwise, if not impossible, at very close range, and the apparent preference for the British targeting the hull of the enemy and the French for the rig was intricately linked with a British desire for close action and a French tendency to engage at distance. To withhold fire until point blank range had its drawbacks. To receive fire and not return it was psychologically hard on the men, and the lack of smoke from their own guns made their ships an easy target, but at the root of tactics was the practical problem of aim at distance.[27] One contemporary went so far as to say that 'If he did not bear down nearer the enemy he might as well throw the powder and shot out of one of the ports.'[28] Another was careful to distinguish between engaging at random distance, say half a mile, which he said was merely 'firing' at the enemy, and point blank – 200 to 300 yards – which was 'to engage'.[29] Nelson's intention was always to engage as soon as he was certain of hitting the enemy, which necessarily required him to be close to them.[30]

Reams of evidence support the desire of the British for close action,[31] but the most instructive in terms of how a sea officer believed that he should behave comes from a description of the Battle of Toulon in 1744. This action was the first taste of fleet battle for Edward Hawke, the future admiral and architect of the crushing victories at the Second Battle of Finisterre (1747) and Quiberon Bay (1759). At Toulon Hawke was the young and inexperienced captain of the *Berwick* (70). As the British fleet, still at some distance from their enemy, bore down on the combined French and Spanish fleet, some British ships began firing. It was suggested to Hawke by a number of his officers that this was too soon. 'Upon my word gentlemen I can not give an opinion', he replied. 'I dare not venture to do so, as I have never yet been in action. But when my turn comes I will try to prove to you how I think we ought to behave on these occasions.' Hawke withheld his fire, closed upon the *Poder*, his opponent in the enemy's line to within a few fathom's distance, and poured in such a well-directed fire that she struck her colours in a quarter of an hour. The *Poder* had 200 dead or wounded to the *Berwick*'s six. [32]

This method of gunnery, which required the men to withhold their fire until they could see the 'buckles on the men's shoes',[33] remained central to British fighting doctrine throughout the period. Although an engagement at pistol shot or 50 yards was considered close enough, some went even closer. An engagement between the *Magicienne* (36) and the French *Sibylle* (32) and *Railleur* (14) off San Domingo in January 1783 was fought so close that the men were 'making use of their half pikes and rammers to annoy the enemy from loading their guns during the engagement'.[34] More widely known is the description of the action between the *Brunswick* and the *Vengeur* at the First of June 1794, in which the *Brunswick* 'lay the *Vengeur*, an 84, alongside sometimes their guns running into our ports, at other times ours into theirs' (Fig. 22).[35]

To engage so close also had its drawbacks, however. At a short distance the velocity of cannon balls was so great that in penetrating a ship's side few or no splinters were torn off; they thus had less destructive effect than a ball reaching the enemy's hull at a slightly lower velocity.[36] To engage broadside to broadside was also to risk being boarded, and for that reason both Collingwood and Howe considered engaging so close always disadvantageous to the British.[37]

Moreover, the proximity of the cannons' muzzles so close to the enemy hull could start a fire which could then easily spread to both ships. The only way to prevent this was to station men either side of the gun to douse the enemy hull through the gun port after each broadside.[38] As a rule of thumb, it was said that ships should not be above two cables' length from the enemy, and a single ship ought to be nearer, preferably within half a cable's length.[39]

It is also important not to overlook the potential subtleties of gunnery tactics. There were, for instance, variations of targeting the hull. Gunners could concentrate on the hull at or below the waterline; on the gun ports or chainplates; or upperworks of the hull, a favoured target as it was the weakest part of the enemy ship and because shot that failed to strike the hull might still do damage in the rig.[40] The elevation of the guns could also be adjusted to provide different angles of fire within a single broadside. The lowest tier, for example, could fire with an upwards elevation into the hull, and the upper deck guns with a slight depression to catch the crews in the gun decks in a crossfire.[41] The guns might also be angled downwards to prevent shot going right through a ship engaged close, a tactic used by the *Victory* at Trafalgar when engaging the *Redoutable*, since another British ship, the *Téméraire*, was engaging the *Redoutable* on her other side.[42]

Not only could a captain select specific targets with his broadside, but he could split the aim of a broadside to concentrate on more than one target. The variety of a broadside can be seen in Admiral Parker's fleet orders of 1797, where he specifies how the guns are to be loaded and aimed in different ways.

> Quarterdeck and forecastle guns to have round and grape shot pointed at the gunwale of the enemy's ship. The first seven guns of the main and middle decks to have similar loads and targets. First and Second divisions of the lower deck to have round shot pointed at the bends of the enemy's ship. Third division to have round and double headed shot pointed at the gunwale.[43]

There was also a great deal of movement involved in effective gunnery tactics. Indeed, manœuvrability was nothing less than the key to tactical capability and advantage, as gunnery and manœuvre were intricately linked, principally due to the problems of oblique fire.

As a general rule oblique fire was far from ideal, being very uncertain and creating a huge strain on the ship's sides.[44] The actual process of shifting the gun with crowbars and handspikes was also cumbersome. Moreover, if the guns were canted round too far, their breechings would break, as Matthews found to his cost aboard the *Namur* at the Battle of Toulon, as did Hawke aboard the *Devonshire* at the Second Battle of Finisterre.[45] In 1779 this facility for oblique fire was improved by Sir Charles Douglas.[46] It proved of devastating effect at the Battle of the Saints in April 1782; the *Ville de Paris* believed herself safe from attack four points off the bow of the *Arrogant*, but 'to their infinite surprise' received a punishing broadside. Douglas, in extolling the virtues of his new system and his own self-professed genius in coming up with it, even claimed that few, if any of the enemy's masts would have been left standing if such oblique fire had been general.[47] These problems of oblique fire ensured that aim was most effectively controlled by manœuvring the ship itself: 'A principal thing in a gunner at sea', wrote William Monson, 'is to be a good helmsman ... and to call him to him at helm to loof, or bear up, to have his better level, and to observe the heaving and setting of the sea and take his aim at the enemy.'[48] The ideal position for one ship to attack another was not, therefore, 'to lie to like a log, and depend upon mere battering, with one side only',[49] but to use manœuvrability to advantage. There were a number of ways that this could be done.

The first and most basic method was to use manœuvrability to stay abreast of the opponent. However, to 'lie like a log' abreast of the enemy was far from straightforward, and required considerable seamanship skill and nous. Two ships of the same size under the same sail plan still would not travel at identical speeds, and, when engaging side by side, the relative effect of an inequality in speed was immediately and significantly felt, as the short length of each ship, only 200 feet or so for a First Rate, was the yardstick by which that difference in speed would be measured: a difference of only ¼ of a knot, for example, would mean that two ships 200 feet long would no longer be broadside to broadside in a little under 8 minutes. Such a short engagement was unlikely indeed to produce a decision. It was necessary, therefore, for sailors continually to juggle the sail plan, to back or fill, hoist and lower sails just to stay abreast of their enemy.[50] To stay alongside was, of course, particularly tricky if the ship being engaged was determined to avoid a prolonged fight. In March 1761 Captain Edward Jekyll of the *Ripon* (60) engaged the *Achille*, a French 64, but the frequently changing and squally weather made it hard to position his ship. The Frenchman, moreover, further sought to avoid battle by shooting ahead or dropping astern of the *Ripon* throughout the fight.[51]

Manœuvrability could also be used to create advantage through position. The best-known method of doing so was to position the attacking ship at right angles to the bow or stern of the enemy, a manœuvre known as 'raking'. The advantages of raking were twofold. On the one hand, the effect of raking fire was always disproportionate to its effect if broadside-to. The broadsides of line of battle ships were protected by oak walls 3 feet thick, and they were designed to receive fire. If a ship was raked at the stern, however, the raking fire would smash through the unprotected glazed stern, and, in the absence of transverse bulkheads, travel the length of the ship, killing and demolishing everything in its path. In such a situation, the crew of the ship being raked would all be ordered to protect themselves by lying down if they had advanced knowledge of such an attack from the weather deck.[52] The enemy crew were not the only intended target of raking fire, however. The enemy guns were also vulnerable as the carriages made an easy target and the guns could easily be dismounted by raking fire. The ship's pumps, which usually ran vertically either face of the mainmast (Fig. 27) and the ladders which ran between the decks were also vulnerable to raking fire. Damage to the ladders was particularly disruptive, as it made communication between the batteries and the upper decks extremely difficult.[53]

A ship could be raked effectively at either bow or stern, as both were poorly protected before the widespread introduction of the more heavily built 'round' bow and stern in 1817.[54] The stern, however, had the least protection, because of the elaborate windows which threw air and light into the officers' quarters. To rake the bow, on the other hand, had the advantage of damaging the bowsprit, upon which the security of the entire rig depended.[55] Nevertheless, raking the stern of the enemy seems to have been preferred, and it was a rule of Nelson's that, when breaking an enemy line, the cut should always be made under the stern of the ship to be engaged.[56]

The second principal advantage of raking was that the defending ship was unable to return fire other than from a handful of bow or stern chase guns, if she had any. To benefit from this advantage, the attacking ship did not necessarily need to be at exact right angles to the bow or stern of the enemy: in

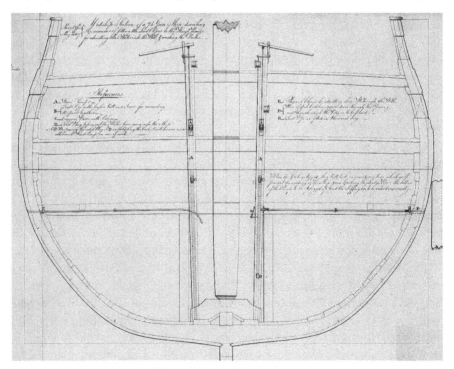

27 The positioning of the ship's pumps

practice it depended on what guns the ship being attacked mounted. French frigates, for example, rarely carried guns forward of the foremast.[57] Their arc of fire forward was therefore significantly limited, and an attacker might be safe from return fire if stationed slightly to port or starboard of her bow. In May 1777 the British *Fox* (28) was attacked by the American *Hancock* (32), lying on her port bow, and the *Boston* (30) on her starboard quarter and, being immobilised, was virtually unable to target either antagonist.[58]

The above example, however, hints at a significant difficulty with raking as a tactic. The ability of a ship to use her sails in combination with her rudder to make sharp and exaggerated movements allowed the main broadside armament to cover a large target area.[59] To assume such a position in which the enemy was unable to fire back, therefore, only seems to have been possible if the enemy was immobile. Thus Nelson claimed in his report of the engagement with the *Ça Ira* on 13 March 1795 that

> Within 10 yards of the *Ça Ira*'s stern I ordered the helm to be put a-starboard ... and the ship fell off, gave her our whole broadside ... the instant all were fired ... stood after her again. This manœuvre we practiced 'til 1 p.m., never allowing the *Ça Ira* to get a single gun to fire on us ...

... but his report of the damage received aboard his ship, the *Agamemnon*, betrays the reality of the situation: 'Our sails and rigging were very much cut and many shot in our hull and between wind and water.'[60]

To get into a position to rake an enemy required a high degree of manœuvrability from the aggressor, and, as has been made clear, the intention of a manœuvre was often 'visible' through alterations in sail plan and course, and the manœuvre itself was inevitably slow in the execution. It was, therefore, fairly easy to counteract any attempt to rake an enemy, usually by copying the manœuvre of the aggressive ship. If two ships started off sailing on the same course, and one intended to rake the other, a tack would be matched by a tack and a wear by a wear. Even a change of course of a few degrees would be matched.[61] One contemporary was quite specific regarding the ability to avoid being raked by an aggressive enemy. 'To me it seems impossible for a ship to lay his enemy thwart the hawse if there be a gale [a contemporary term of a good breeze], and the sails and rudder serviceable and the master a man of good conduct.'[62] The ease with which an aggressive raking manœuvre could be countered, combined with the inherent unpredictability of sailing warship manœuvre, particularly tacking, further ensured that any attempt to rake a mobile enemy could easily end up with him doing the raking.[63] Raking an enemy was therefore usually only achieved if the ship being attacked was in a line of battle and under strict orders not to manœuvre or break the line in the face of the oncoming attack, or if one of the ships was damaged in the course of an otherwise equal fight.

DAMAGE AND MANŒUVRABILITY

As a fight developed and the ships became damaged, they would necessarily become limited in very specific ways in their manœuvrability, course and speed. The sails of a square-rigged ship each exerted pressure on the hull at different points: the headsails a lateral and forward pressure on the hull at the bows; the mainmast, a lateral and forward pressure just aft of the centre of the ship; the mizzenmast and spanker, a lateral and forward pressure at the stern. For a ship to sail in a straight line it was important to balance these forces. A ship unable to do so would be perceptibly and significantly restricted in her capabilities. The captain of a ship with a damaged mainmast and mizzenmast, for example, would be unable to achieve such balance. With no sail aft to balance the effect of the headsails and those on the foremast, the ship would tend to point downwind. The captain would be unable to heave-to or tack, and would have great difficulty holding any course other than downwind.[64] Likewise, a ship with a damaged fore and mainmast would only be able to set the sails on the mizzenmast and the spanker, but canvas forward was essential to keeping a ship manageable, particularly when under reduced fighting canvas. The action of the wind on the sails at the stern of the ship would constantly drive the bows into the wind, and she would be unable to bear away, heave-to or wear.

Damage to the bowsprit was a particularly acute problem, as it would have serious repercussions for the structural integrity of the entire rig.[65] Damage to the hull was also significant, as it could restrict a ship to sailing on only one tack. The captain of a ship badly damaged at or below the waterline on one side would be obliged to keep that damaged side always to windward. If the damage was kept to leeward, the leak would be amplified by the heeling of the vessel and by leeway.[66]

The potential impact on a ship's manœuvrability therefore varied depending on what part of the rig was damaged and, crucially, much of this damage would be visible at the short distances over which these engagements took place. Damage to the enemy, therefore, was a valuable source of intelligence and an observant captain could, and was expected to, take immediate advantage of any significant incapacity in his enemy.[67] For exactly this reason one contemporary advised, after an initial attack, to: 'stand off on the other tack, ... keep clear of their lee broadside, and act according to their motions, and the experience of the effect your attack has had upon them'.[68]

In his report regarding the capture of the Indiaman *Warren Hastings* by the French frigate *Pie Montaise* in the summer of 1806, Captain Larkins described how this might have worked in practice. The two ships had clashed a number of times over a period of nearly 5 hours. Each time the French frigate bore down, engaged fiercely and then sheared off to consider the effects of her attack. After each onslaught, the *Warren Hastings* became more crippled in her rig. The turning point came when a shot from the *Pie Montaise* tore through the foremast of the *Warren Hastings* about a third of the way up, on the aft side of the mast. Larkins had no choice but to take in sail on the injured foremast for fear of losing it completely: a falling mast was likely kill many; the wreckage might obstruct and frustrate any further gunnery; and it was certain that the stability of the ship would be upset and endanger the lives of all aboard. The foremast, previously billowing with canvas, was quickly stripped of all sail; the fore-course hauled up; and the topsail lowered. To the French, the effect of their gunnery was clear: the *Warren Hastings* was unable to carry any canvas on her foremast, and her fate was sealed. Larkins wrote:

> Seeing, as I suppose they must have done, that I could do nothing but keep the wind with the sail I had set [only the maintopsail] they backed on my larboard quarter and kept there, without my being able to prevent her taking so advantageous a position.

The inability of the *Warren Hastings* to bear away led the French captain to stand and fight, to see the engagement through where his timidity had previously prevented him from laying her alongside. A passing scuffle thus became a decisive battle, and the *Warren Hastings* was taken.[69] In exactly the same way, Captain Colville Mayne reported that in a battle with a Spanish warship in April 1740 his position was governed by the loss of the Spaniard's foremast.[70] Any understanding of tactics must therefore allow for this type of situational empiricism, as in practice the recognition and exploitation of transient advantage defined a distinct aspect of seamanship that could alter the course of an engagement.

At this stage of the sea fight, therefore, relative manœuvre was not, as has been argued,[71] irrelevant but quite the opposite. Fighting tactics were more kinetic than we might suppose, and the skill of the crew in shiphandling had a great bearing on the outcome of any engagement. Advantage in sailing performance would give one party a greater element of control than the other. A greater element of control allowed for a greater freedom of choice, and a greater freedom of choice increased the tactical options and hence, given sufficient skill, of creating an advantage. Contemporaries granted the management of the sails equal status with the handling of the guns, and it was accepted that 'The difference in the management of such ships [ships of the line], to make them of the consequence they might really be, and others of lower and inferior rates, is much greater than generally is believed.'[72] It remains a pertinent point 260 years later.

BOARDING

Gunnery, of course, was not the only tactic used in a sea fight, and a duel was occasionally augmented or even decided by hand-to-hand combat. Much like raking, boarding one ship from another was difficult for a number of reasons. To evade a boarding attempt by manœuvre was relatively easy. It was in practice very difficult to get near enough to a ship to attempt to board her unless it was also her intention to settle the matter hand to hand.[73] A ship could be forced into a boarding action, but this usually required some measure of heroics. At the Battle of Trafalgar, the master's mate of the *Defiance* (74), upon finding the ship's boats shot through, leapt overboard and swam to the subdued *L'Aigle* (74). He climbed aboard with his boarding party and threw the *Defiance* some ropes. These were secured and the *Defiance* hauled herself alongside *L'Aigle*.[74]

Such extraordinary examples aside, the ship to be boarded was usually in some measure disabled or was prepared to settle the matter in this way.[75] The sailors nominated for the task would then be summoned by the ship's bell or, in the French navy, by a trumpet signal, and then armed with cutlasses, tomahawks and pistols like 'so many devils'.[76] In most contested instances of boarding, however, especially on small vessels, the initial onrush of people forcing themselves aboard would be met by a wall of armed defenders and would form a wedge so that, in the crush, there was little room for edged weapons to be swung.

The key problem, however, was to get across from one ship to the other. If the boarding party was not prepared to swim like that of the *Defiance* at Trafalgar, the basic requirement was for the two ships to be very close to each other, and this posed a number of challenges. Collision could cause severe damage to the rig or hull, injure crew and dismount guns. To be so close was also to risk the spread of fire. Indeed, one tactic used by a ship defending itself from being boarded was to raise as much smoke as possible to convince the enemy that she was on fire. It was then hoped that the attacking ship would haul off in self-preservation.[77]

There was in fact no way of boarding another ship safely. Damage was an accepted consequence of any attempt but some precautions could be taken to limit it. The lids of the gun ports, for example, could be hauled up, close against the side of the ship to prevent them from being ripped off as the two ships met.[78] A gun port without a lid was effectively a 2-foot square hole in the side of the ship, which could let in large quantities of water if the ship heeled or rolled suddenly. The lids were also important because they could be closed to prevent the enemy boarding through the gun ports.[79] To reduce potential damage a captain would normally attempt to board another ship only in calm sea conditions; in a heavy swell his ship would be harder to control, and the unpredictable roll more likely to damage his ship and endanger his men. A head sea was considered particularly dangerous for a boarding attempt.[80] The captain would also be careful to engage on the lee side of his enemy if at all possible, as the sea would be smoother where it was sheltered by the ship he was to board, and the lee position made it much more easy to haul off if the attempt failed.[81]

Once the two ships had been brought as close as possible, the challenge was to get a large enough body of men from one to the other. This is always difficult at sea, and, even without the peculiar pressures of battle, it could easily go wrong. In February 1796 the *Royal Sovereign* ran foul of the *Belisarius*, a transport ship full of troops. In an attempt to save themselves, 100 troops attempted to climb aboard the *Royal Sovereign*, but many fell to their deaths or were crushed in between the ships.[82] To make it harder for attackers, frigates and smaller craft carried boarding netting, but they do not appear to have been issued to line of battle ships.[83] Woven of tough line and sometimes reinforced with metal, this netting was secured at the bottom to the channels and then hoisted up.[84]

If, in the chaos of a fleet action, two ships had come stern to stern, then it was possible simply to step across from one to the other, using the gaff signal halliards as support.[85] If, however, as was much more likely, the ships were broadside to broadside, the problem was much greater. The tumblehome of both ships ensured that although they might be bilge to bilge with their gun ports more or less touching, at the level of the weather deck they would still be too

far apart to step across, or even jump (Fig. 28). This problem would have been far greater in the early years of the century, when tumblehome was much greater than at the end. By 1800 many ships were almost wall-sided.[86] To increase the difficulties of boarding broadside-to, a ship defending herself might run out spare yards horizontally from the gun ports on the endangered side.[87]

In every instance, to board a large ship from a small one was particularly difficult, as the levels of the decks would be

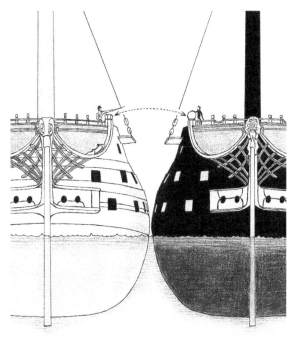

28 The difficulties of boarding

significantly different, and the crew of the smaller ship would at some point be forced to climb upwards to board their antagonist. The crew of the two-decked *Redoutable* particularly suffered in this way at the Battle of Trafalgar, as they struggled to board the three-decked *Victory*, which towered above them.[88] In such a situation, one solution was for the attacking ship to run in her guns, thus allowing the sailors free access to their gun ports, and then to board the enemy ship through their gun ports or climb the side of the ship.[89] Damaged and fallen rigging hanging over the ship's side might help a sailor to clamber up, and it was claimed in Falconer's *Marine Dictionary* (1780)[90] that the small axes issued to boarders could be used to sink into the ship's side to create a makeshift ladder. The practicality of this has recently been questioned, however, and it would appear that in this instance the civilian schoolmaster William Falconer is not to be trusted. It is far more likely that the axes were used to hook onto the shrouds or backstay chains, and on the way up they might be used to cut the lanyards of the enemy's gun port lids, so if the ships hauled off they would be unable to open the gun ports.[91] But however it was done, to climb up the outside of an enemy ship was extremely dangerous. Not only was the boarder at risk of death from enemy cannon and musketry fire from almost point blank range, but, with the ships so close, any sailor on the outside of the enemy hull could easily be crushed as the ships rolled into each other with the swell.

Most commonly, however, the bowsprit of the aggressive ship would be run on to the enemy. This had the distinct advantage that it could then be lashed in some way to the enemy ship to prevent the two from drifting apart. Ideally the bowsprit might deliberately be run into the enemy's main rigging in the hope that it would become tangled and hold fast without the inherent danger of having to lash it in place. Once the two ships were secured to each other, boarding became easier and safer. If they were secured by the bowsprit, it could itself be used as a makeshift bridge for men to cross from one ship to another.[92] Transferring a large number of men quickly over the narrow and circular bowsprit was still difficult, however, and one contemporary believed that a defensive force of ten stout men could repel a boarding party of 100 if the only means by which they could get on board was the bowsprit.[93] Usually large numbers of men would prepare to board in the waist or the shrouds and seize their opportunity as the ships came together.

Ideally one ship would board another from two directions, from the head and the waist for example, and thus force the enemy to fight on two fronts.[94] In any scenario, however, boarding was almost impossible in the face of a well prepared and steady enemy who could form defensive positions and sweep any boarding party with musketry and grape shot, and repel them with pikes.[95] Moreover, once a boarding party had made it on to an enemy ship, it was also very difficult for them to get back in retreat, help defend their own ship from boarding, or to receive reinforcements. Indeed, there appear to be as many examples of ships successfully defending themselves from being boarded as there are of being taken by boarding.[96]

The actual choice of boarding as a tactic is therefore an interesting one, and is certainly not clear cut. The party to be boarded would, more often than not, be disabled in some way. However, a disabled ship's only chance of victory lay in being boarded and winning the day through hand-to-hand combat. Otherwise she would lie adrift, and her enemy could take any position she chose and bombard her until she surrendered. To board a disabled enemy ship, therefore, was to give her crew a chance of victory that they would not otherwise have. As one contemporary wrote, 'the sole resource of the feeble is audacity'.[97] Another specifically recommended that, if the enemy was disabled, the attacker was not to risk getting too close in case the disabled ship attempted such a tactic.[98]

Boarding was therefore most likely to occur if the ships had inadvertently been driven together in the heat of battle and become entangled.[99] This was, of course, more likely if the ships were engaged closely, which goes some way towards explaining why so many captains were threatened by boarding at the Battle of Trafalgar, as, following Nelson and Collingwood's examples, the majority of British ships fought their enemies bilge to bilge.[100] Otherwise, boarding was the last option in a fight that could not be decided by gunfire alone, usually because a particularly obstinate enemy refused to strike her colours. On 19 January 1783 the *Leander* (50) attacked a hostile seventy-four-gunner, who promptly reduced her to a wreck, but the crew of the *Leander* repulsed all attempts to board and she was never taken.[101] In a similar example only four months earlier, Captain Latouche-Tréville from the *Aigle* (40) attempted to board the stricken British *Hector* (74), but was repulsed.[102]

In spite of the difficulties of successfully boarding an enemy, it remained a valid tactic for all navies, but was particularly favoured by ships that were well manned but poorly armed or poorly trained at gunnery. Privateers and the French fitted that description best. Privateers were particularly fond of boarding because they did not wish to damage their prizes, and the short-handed merchantmen they attacked posed little threat.[103] The French fleet commanders encouraged their captains to board the enemy throughout the century, 'this being the best method of reducing and of taking the enemy's ships'.[104] This was certainly true in many instances. The French generally carried larger crews, often took infantry to sea, and were encouraged to believe themselves superior at boarding. By the Battle of Trafalgar, an acknowledged inferiority in gunnery to the English further inclined them towards boarding as an effective tactic.[105]

CHAPTER 11

Damage

We know at sea men of resolution conquer at almost any odds.[1]

Essential to the debate over tactical choice is the question of damage. It was inevitable that performance capability fluctuated during battle, but the way in which it did so is largely unknown. If it is considered at all, then it is in the context of gunnery tactics. It is thus widely accepted that to fire high was to cause damage to the rig, disable and to target the manœuvrability of the enemy alone. It was the more defensive tactic,[2] and was even viewed by some as ineffective.[3] On the other hand, firing low was to cause damage to the hull and to target the manpower; as such, it was the more decisive tactic.[4] With such a polarised argument, the understanding of the effects of damage have been oversimplified and generalised to an unhelpful degree. There was, in practice, significantly more depth and subtlety to the effects of damage to the rig and the hull that in turn directly affected the choice and implementation of tactics.

The immediate and most obvious impact of damage to the rig was a reduction of manœuvrability, but, left to stand alone, this fact raises many more questions than it answers. To what extent, and exactly how, was manœuvrability affected? How quickly and effectively could repairs be made? How did this affect performance in battle? And how did this affect the tactics of engagement?

The ability to make ground to windward or at least to sail close-hauled, the ability to maintain station in a fleet and the ability to keep alongside an enemy were all crucial to the outcome of any battle, and all required a warship to be at the very peak of its manœuvrability. Damage to the rig therefore had significant implications for tactics.

An immediate loss of windward performance, for example, placed a ship at a serious disadvantage, as she would have to turn downwind, thus exposing her stern to raking fire.[5] A ship unable to sail close-hauled would also have to forgo any of the advantages that may have been inherent in the windward position, and would be forced to fight to leeward. An inability to maintain station in a line would leave the ships immediately ahead and astern outnumbered. Thus at the Battle of the Chesapeake in 1781, the *Shrewsbury,* having lost her fore and main topmasts, was unable to keep the line, leaving her neighbour, the hapless *Intrepid*, exposed to two ships of superior force.[6] A ship forced out of line would also endanger the cohesion, and with it the tactical efficiency, of the entire fleet. If the ships astern were unable to close the gap quickly enough, the enemy could break through the line and thus achieve the ultimate tactical goal of dividing the enemy fleet and trapping it between two fires.

A loss of manœuvrability did not, however, affect the ability to fire guns, as

Captain Digby astutely observed the day before the Battle of Ushant, claiming there was 'a great deal of difference between attacking and being attacked'.[7] Indeed, ships whose capability for manœuvre was damaged beyond hope could pay better attention to their guns, and it was not unusual for their gunnery to improve in such circumstances. Captain Wells of the *Lancaster* recalled how, at the Battle of Camperdown, one dismasted opponent resumed and kept up an astonishing rate of fire.[8] The significance of a loss of manœuvrability must, therefore, be considered in terms of the ability to carry out an aggressive strategy aimed at forcing an enemy to action and keeping them there until a decision had been reached.

To appreciate fully the impact of damage to the rig, one must also think beyond the obvious question of manœuvrability, and consider the broader question of performance. In practice, the rig provided speed and steering control but it was equally significant in determining the floating motions of the ship and, in particular, the tendency of a ship to heel, pitch and roll, all of which had a significant impact on sailing performance, gunnery and safety both on deck and aloft.[9] To target the rig, therefore, was directly to target this working efficiency, and hence the fighting capability, of an opponent. An imaginary scenario will best illustrate the point.

If a ship had lost a topmast, the steadying canvas would instantly be reduced by a third or even a half if the mizzen topsail was not set, and this reduction would cause the ship to roll heavily. At the Glorious First of June, for example, the dismasted *Marlborough* rolled so heavily that her lower deck ports could not be opened.[10] If the mast had not come clean away and was tangled in the rigging over one side of the ship, she would immediately start to heel towards the overhang. This could threaten the stability of the ship and cause it to heel over at a dangerous angle, further endangering flooding of the lower decks through the gun ports. A ship in this situation would almost certainly capsize if immediate action was not taken to cut away the fallen masts and man the pumps; this would draw men from the guns. The ship would also have been ballasted for the weight of three full sets of masts and all of the associated rigging, anything up to 120 tonnes for a seventy-four-gun ship. The immediate loss of even a fraction of this weight aloft would drastically alter the stability of the ship. Now with too much ballast for the corresponding weight aloft, the ship would begin to roll much more violently, tending to whip across rather than rolling steadily and smoothly, and further endangering the remaining masts. Gunnery would become more difficult, working conditions more hazardous for all, and the likelihood of downflooding through the lowest gun ports would further increase.

The knock-on effects of rig damage on sailing and gunnery performance were therefore considerable, but the direct effects on manpower of targeting the rig have also been overlooked. Falling masts were an effective way of killing people, of starting fires and of otherwise causing confusion aboard the enemy. When the British *Lion* fought the French *Elizabeth* in 1745, although the French fired mostly at the *Lion*'s spars, British losses were still heavy, with forty-five killed and 107 wounded, of which seven later died.[11] A fallen mast or spar with its associated rigging might also foul any guns on deck: at Trafalgar the collapse of the main and mizzen masts of the French 74 *Algésiras* prevented her from firing her entire starboard battery.[12]

HULL DAMAGE

The treasure ships and war junks of fifteenth-century China had compartmentalised hulls which could be partially flooded to transport trained sea otters for hunting fish. Northern European warships of the eighteenth century had neither trained otters nor compartmentalised hulls, and did not therefore enjoy the advantages of their Chinese predecessors, which were designed to stay afloat even if two large compartments were flooded. Nevertheless, it is widely accepted that to sink a warship through gunfire alone was very difficult, the sinking of the *Superbe* after only two broadsides from the *Royal George* at Quiberon Bay in 1759 being a notable and remarkable example.[13] Focus, therefore, has been placed on the psychological and physical impact on manpower of targeting the hull.[14]

It is certainly true that killing and wounding men was an express intention of those who fired at the hull,[15] but one aspect particularly notable in contemporary accounts is the resultant impact on morale of the fear of fire and flood. It was normal for any dangerous shot below the waterline to be reported in private to the captain, and it was recommended that, on pain of death, not a word was to be spoken of such damage unless it was to a superior officer. The same precaution was to be observed if any part of the ship had caught fire.[16] Although gagging a ship's company would have been all but impossible, this order reflects contemporary concern over the psychological impact of such damage. Not only was it an exhausting prospect – in one instance the crew was up all night pumping 2,400 strokes a watch[17] – but in the words of an anonymous contemporary, 'when a fear of sinking is induced, men are not much disposed to contend for victory'.[18] Indeed, there are numerous examples of officers keeping the true extent of a leaking ship from their men. Aboard the *Caesar* at the Glorious First of June, Captain Molloy severely admonished Bennett, the third lieutenant, for reporting in a loud voice that the ship was sinking. Bennett apologised sheepishly, and explained that he was unaware that he had spoken so loudly, having been deafened by the guns below.[19]

The effects of hull damage on performance capability must also be considered, but this requires some understanding of ship stability. In simple terms, anything afloat is in a state of stable equilibrium, the buoyancy of the hull being equal and opposite to the force of gravity.[20] To target the hull was to target this equilibrium – in particular the ability of a ship to recover from a roll – by moving the centre of gravity. One of the most dangerous phenomena was the ingress of water as it introduced a movable weight into the hull. As the ship rolled with the swell, so the water in the hull would move to the lowest point; this in turn would cause the centre of gravity of the ship to move, adversely affecting the effectiveness of the righting moment. Such a situation could rapidly spiral out of control. With each roll, more water would come in through the gun ports, and the ship would roll more deeply and become less and less able to right herself, so that she would eventually settle on her beam ends. The speed with which this could take hold was alarming, as was demonstrated in the sinking of the *Vengeur* at the First of June. Without masts to support canvas to steady her, she rolled heavily with her ports under water. She was taken possession of as a prize at 6.15 p.m., but sank soon after.[21] Even a mild ingress of water would cause a ship quickly to become unmanageable due to the added weight of water in the hull.[22]

To dismount guns was another specific intention of gunners aiming at the hull.[23] If a cannon had fallen off its trucks it could not be fired, and if it came entirely free from its carriage it could also roll around deck. The worst-case scenario was for the cannon to still be in its carriage with the wheels on, but the tackles broken. Loose cannon have traditionally implied confusion and immediate physical danger as the ordnance rampaged through an area of tightly packed humanity,[24] but this is to overlook the effect on the stability of the ship. Leaving aside the obvious potential danger of a loose gun breaching the hull,[25] dismounted guns could cause stability problems as severe as the ingress of water. Guns moving around on deck would cause the centre of gravity to shift significantly in the direction of a roll, affecting the ability of a ship to right itself in the same way as water within the hull. The effect might seem insignificant, given the size of the ships, but it must not be forgotten that a 32-pounder gun with its carriage and shot weighed over 3 tons, and French cannon even more.[26] A few dismounted guns would do more than just endanger those sailors in close proximity to them, but could endanger the ship itself by upsetting her stability or simply smashing through her side. One contemporary attributed the loss of the *Victory* in 1744 to this effect alone.[27]

To target the hull was also to target the masts. The strength and stability of the rig came only in small part from the wood of the masts and yards themselves; the majority derived from the complex rope superstructure that provided their support. The masts were given their stability by stays, secured sideways and aft by the backstays and shrouds, and forwards by the forestays (Fig. 29).[28] Quite simply, masts could not carry any sail without that support. There are examples of ships with perfectly healthy masts and spars being dismasted through poorly set-up rigging,[29] while conversely there are frequent

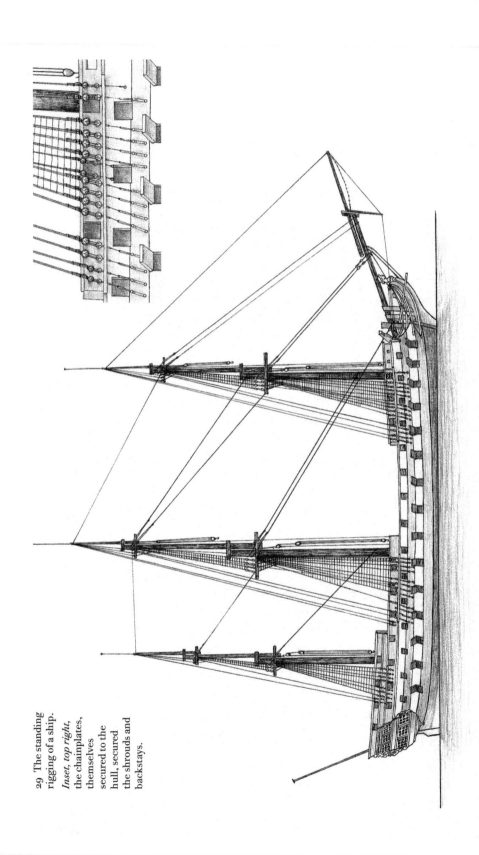

29 The standing rigging of a ship. *Inset, top right,* the chainplates, themselves secured to the hull, secured the shrouds and backstays.

mentions of masts remaining standing with shot clean through them, but their stays remaining undamaged.[30] At the court martial of Sir Hugh Palliser in 1779 Lieutenant Dickinson recalled how the foremast of the *Formidable* was secured with stays despite having a gunshot wound 6 feet above the forecastle deck, and being so rotten he could run his arm in 'near up to my elbow';[31] and after a warm action with the French frigate *Topaze* in the summer of 1805 Captain Zachary Mudge recalled how his foremast remained standing with ten shot in it.[32] Of those stays, the most important were the backstays, as they secured the mast aft, which provided the tension against which a sail would pull to drive the ship forward. The back stays were held taut by deadeyes and secured to the channels. These channels, therefore, were the critical point for rig tension, and to secure them was always the first step in securing a mast.[33] Most significantly, the channels were secured by chainplates which were bolted to the ship's hull, often below the guns of the upper deck and sometimes even lower down (Fig. 29). To target the masts in their support, therefore, an express intention of British gunners,[34] and a tactic described as the most efficient way of target-ing a mast,[35] was best achieved by targeting the *hull*. The masts could also be targeted directly by targeting the hull, as the masts were stepped at the keel and ran right through the decks (Fig. 30).

Targeting the hull also had the potential to disable a ship by damaging the steering, another specific intention of British gunners.[36] Without control from the wheel, not only would the ship be in a good part disabled, particularly in her ability to tack or wear, but it was rare for a ship to recover from such an acci-dent without causing further damage to herself and to those on board.[37] There are numerous examples of ships having their steering mechanisms destroyed in action,[38] and it was a common enough occurrence for a spare tiller to be kept in the wardroom during action, and for the relieving tackles which would replace the damaged tiller ropes to be 'stretched along' ready for use.[39] Reliev-ing tackles were, however, extremely inconvenient to operate,[40] and a number of ingenious solutions to the problem were proposed.[41] If no relieving tack-les were available, or if they had also been destroyed or lost, the only solution

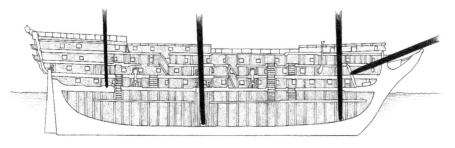

30 The masts of a sailing warship were stepped to the keel.

was to manhandle the tiller. A damaged rudder was even more problematic: even though a makeshift rudder could be fashioned out of spare timber, it would take at least a day, and usually several days, for it to be made and then hung.[42]

There was, therefore, significantly more depth and subtlety to the effects of damage to the rig and the hull than we have been led to believe by traditional studies of sailing warfare and tactics. However, the impact of those effects and their significance in determining tactics cannot be put into context without an understanding of how easy that damage was to cause and how easy it was to repair.

CAUSING DAMAGE

Sails could sustain a good deal of damage without losing all effectiveness. An anonymous writer commenting on tactics in the 1801 edition of the *Naval Chronicle* acknowledged that, 'notwithstanding the great number of balls which pass through the sails, they generally serve till the end of the engagement'.[43] Thus at the Battle of Toulon the *Rupert* suffered 'a great many' shot through the sails, but the Master, Frederick Breton, acknowledged that none were entirely disabled (Fig. 31). The sail-maker of the *Rupert* further explained how she even managed to wear with somewhere between forty and fifty shot holes in the fore and main courses and topsails.[44] Interestingly, this is just one of several instances in which heavily damaged ships were still able to wear. Most impressive of all is an example from a sea fight in June 1745. The *Jersey* listed her damage as:

> Two larboard main shrouds, four starboard and one larboard main top-mast shrouds, all the main topmast backstays, main and spring stays, main topmast and staysail stays, two of the starboard fore shrouds, one larboard foretopmast backstay, foretopmast and staysail stays. The braces, bowlines were shot away several times, also the staysail hall-yards, the running rigging in general very much shattered. The main topsail and flying jib and forestaysail shot all to pieces, and all the other sails very much shattered. The main topsail yard shot and [illegible] in the slings. The foremast shot through about the collar of the mainstay, and another wound in the after part of the mast in the head by a shot that passed through the foretop. The mainmast shot about two thirds up from the deck and divided the starboard cheek ... Ship making 11 inches of water an hour, occasioned by two shots in the counter, under the water line'

None of this, however, prevented her from wearing under the mizzen and fore-topsail, a little after 10 at night.[45] In fact, as long as a ship could point her bows

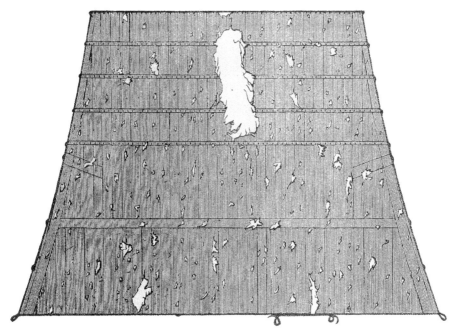

31 One of the most striking images of a damaged sail comes from this sketch of HMS *Victory*'s foretopsail, made shortly after the battle of Trafalgar when the topsail was returned into store at Chatham. The damage is surprisingly slight, with only one significant tear. The topsail itself can now be seen on display at the Royal Naval Museum in Portsmouth.

downwind, brace her masts, and had sufficient running rigging to reset the sails on a new tack, then she could be confidently wore.[46] One captain claimed that he could always retain at least a shadow of hope in battle with a much larger antagonist as long as at least one of his masts survived,[47] and another that he would not strike until his masts and rudder had been shot away.[48] The ability of a warship to absorb damage and retain manœuvrability suggests that there is more to these statements than bravado and heroic defiance alone, but to appreciate this properly it is first necessary to consider how a sailing warship could manœuvre without the use of her sails.

Captains could harness currents and tide to provide drive. Indeed, manœuvring a ship in a current and using the current itself to manipulate and manœuvre the ship were part and parcel of seafaring and sailing warfare. One of the most peculiar examples in practice can be found in Cochrane's *Autobiography of a Seaman* (1860), where he described how a large portion of the French fleet, panicked by an albeit clumsy attack of fireships the previous night, had run aground on the Île d'Oléron. Frustrated by the unwillingness of his commander, Lord Gambier, to bring the vulnerable French fleet to action, Cochrane deliberately drifted the *Impérieuse* toward the grounded enemy. He explains his movements thus:

I did not venture to make sail, lest the movement might be seen from the flagship [his own], and a signal of recall should defeat my purpose of making an attack; the object of this being to compel the commander-in-chief to send vessels to our assistance, in which case I knew their captains would at once attack the ships which had not been allowed to heave off and escape. [49]

If in sufficiently shallow water, a ship could further manœuvre without headway or wind by anchoring, running springs out to the anchor cable and using the anchor as a turning point. By hauling or slacking off the springs a ship was able to move towards or away from the anchor, and yaw sharply, entirely independent of the wind. This was particularly useful for freeing a ship that had run aground and for casting anchor in a fleet, when sharp turns independent from the wind were necessary to minimise the likelihood of collision.[50] It was also used in battle. In an engagement with a French frigate in the spring of 1746 Captain Noel anchored with a spring on his cable, his foretopsail tyes and most of his braces shot away. Although crippled in the rig, this allowed him to salvage a good degree of control and rake his antagonist every time he put about.[51] Samuel Hood's action at St Kitts in January 1782 is perhaps the most masterful example of the technique being used in a fleet action. Outnumbered and outgunned, Hood nevertheless resolved to occupy the anchorage recently deserted by de Grasse. Once anchored, and with springs run out to their anchor cables, Hood's fleet were able to yaw and present their broadsides at will, and with no hands needed for sail handling, more attention could be paid to the gunnery.[52]

Even without the help of currents and tides, canvas or anchors, a ship could still move. It was believed that the action of the swell and the shape of the hull caused a ship to forge ahead even in a flat calm. As a result, ships dismasted in action were advised to keep their heads towards each other to prevent separation.[53] In fact stopping a damaged ship was more of a problem. Ships actually stopped moving by heaving-to – backing the sails on the mainmast and leaving those on the foremast filled.[54] This required full control of the rig, and it is a peculiar idiosyncrasy of the sailing warship that one of the first aspects of its capability to be lost through damage to the rig was its ability to stop. It seems, therefore, to have been rare indeed for a ship to be motionless in a seaway, and, as it was generally accepted that warships had steerage way from as little as one knot,[55] there was almost always some degree of manœuvrability that could be harnessed, even by a heavily damaged ship.

Damage to the rig was peculiar, however, as there were a number of weak points which, if targeted, could drastically alter the working efficiency of the entire ship. The strength of the rig was determined more by its support than by the timber and ironwork, and so only a small degree of damage could have a disproportionate affect on sailing capability and performance. In turn, this would have much wider repercussions for fleet cohesion and the ability to create and take advantage of tactical opportunity as the battle evolved. If, for example, a ship under fighting canvas suffered the loss of only one topmast stay, the lack of support would increase the 'give' in the mast. If the ship then came to roll or pitch heavily, or there was a particularly strong gust of wind, the mast would not be adequately supported, and it would either be sprung or go by the board entirely, the victim of its own inertia. It was in exactly this way that so many ships came to lose masts and spars in the poor weather conditions in which the Glorious First of June was fought.[56] Similarly, if a ship lost the use of the topmast braces of only one mast, it would instantly lose a large degree of performance capability. Thus at the Battle of Toulon, the *Somerset* lost her braces and was instantly unable to heave-to or otherwise use her yards for subtle speed control. Nor could she tack or wear, and was only able to run downwind.[57] Weaponry was therefore designed to cause as much damage as possible in order to maximise the chances of a lucky shot. Of all the different types of shot, Kempenfelt believed langridge to be the most destructive, as it cut and tore the canvas, whereas grapeshot, he argued, left a smooth round hole.[58]

The strength and efficiency of the entire rig was particularly vulnerable in the bows, and could be compromised by the loss of only one rope – the bobstay. When rigging a ship the masts were held in place by securing them downwards and backwards by means of stays and shrouds. To do so the masts needed a secure point forward against which they could be tensioned, and that secure point was the bowsprit. Once the bowsprit was in place and firmly secured by the bobstay, which was in turn secured to the hull, the foremast could be secured by the forestays and then tensioned aft by the backstays. With the foremast secure, the mainmast could then be secured forward to it by the forestays and tensioned aft by its backstays, and the process repeated for the mizzenmast. The entire rig was thus like an inverted house of cards, with its tension, and thus its strength, dependent on the security of the bowsprit. If the bowsprit was endangered by damage to the bobstay, the structural integrity of the entire rig immediately suffered. For exactly this reason, in July 1740 the *Success* fireship with no other damage than to her bowsprit, was obliged to strike her foretopgallant mast, foretopmast and the fore course yard before being towed to safety.[59] Similarly when the *Russell* was caught in a storm in 1711, the bowsprit broke off, and the foremast and mainmast, lacking adequate tension in their support, fell soon after.[60]

The effects of damage to the hull depended on a number of variables, including range, hull construction, cannon and shot size, powder quality and angle of fire. It is, therefore, difficult to generalise about the effects of shot to the hull. Nevertheless, it *is* clear that the hull, like the rig, was characterised by an ability to absorb damage, combined with vulnerability in certain areas. Thus, while the hull itself might withstand a good deal of drubbing, a lucky shot might shoot off a channel or a chainplate, disabling the rig, or as with the *Vengeur* at the First of June, might catch the rudder at the exact angle so as to cause it to split.[61] There are also examples of ships forced to surrender because of relatively minor, but particularly inaccessible damage to the hull, which could neither be repaired nor the water pumped out with sufficient speed.[62]

With both the hull and the rig, therefore, chance played a major part in determining the effects of damage. On the one hand, the period was characterised by an ability to retain manœuvrability and a high quality of performance in the face of heavy damage. In this respect battle became attritional, and placed an increased emphasis on the value of high initial morale, staying power and tenacity of purpose.[63] It was a considerable advantage, therefore, that Nelson could say of his crew that they 'really mind shot no more than peas.'[64] On the other hand, it was perfectly possible for one lucky shot to alter the whole tactical nature of an engagement. Once in battle, sailing warship performance was in a constant state of fragile equilibrium. Any advantage that might be gained from superior sailing performance in terms of speed, windward performance or manœuvrability could be lost at a stroke by fortunate shooting. Knowledge of this certainly played a part in the tactical motivation of those who found themselves involved in mismatched engagements.[65]

REPAIRING DAMAGE

The inevitability of damage, and the impact which even minor damage could have on performance and capability, placed a considerable premium on the ability to ease or repair it. Frequently the outcome of an engagement was determined as much by the ability to absorb and repair damage as it was by the ability to cause it.

A significant factor in being able to repair damage was the rope construction of the running rigging, which moved the yards and sails, and the standing rigging, which provided the structural support. Rope could be easily mended, worked and adapted in use. A line cut by cannon fire or parted under excessive load could be mended in a matter of seconds by a knot or a splice or joined by a block and tackle. Splicing was essential for ropes that ran through blocks, as a splice – particularly a long splice – would not significantly change the diameter of the rope. However, knotting was faster, and in some situations more practical. Shrouds, stays and tackle pendants were often 'cable laid' – made up of nine-stranded rope consisting of three hawser-laid lines laid up together left handed, rather than the normal right handed,[66] and were in consequence much easier to knot than splice in a hurry.[67]

The key to understanding the significance of these repairs is strength. A cut line properly repaired with a knot or a splice would not lose a significant degree of its tensile strength, so repairs could be made rapidly and repeatedly without recourse to the spare parts required by more complex technology. In consequence, a large proportion of the damage to the rig was only temporary. At the trial of Captain Molloy, Mr. Lucky, Master of the *Caesar,* said it would take less than half an hour to resplice a mainsheet, and further added that it would only take ten minutes to reeve a new rope in its place.[68] At the Battle of Toulon Matthews rove new braces three times in the heat of the action,[69] and in 1745 the *London* repaired five main shrouds, the fore preventer stay, halliards and braces, the maintopmast and topgallant backstays, the main bowline, the mizzen staysail halliards, the starboard main brace and other miscellaneous rigging in only half an hour with as few as 'ten or twelve' men working in the rigging.[70]

If a line could not be immediately repaired or replaced, there was rarely a shortage of rope that could be temporarily sidelined to provide cover. Thus at the Battle of Ushant, Captain Bazeley was able to brace the yards of the *Formidable* using the yard tackle falls when the braces had been shot away.[71] In a similar situation at the First of June, Lieutenant Cleverly, fifth lieutenant of the *Caesar*, recalled how they managed to brace their yards with the preventer braces, though he acknowledged that using this method, the yards could not be braced as sharply.[72] A ship which lost a mainstay could secure the mast by hauling the main tack on board securing the main tackles to the bitheads and hauling the bowline taut. These ropes all led forward and secured the mast from leaning aft as the mainstay had done.[73] Similarly, a badly sprung mast could be given extra security by setting all of the lee backstays up to windward or even by attaching spare hawsers to the masthead and hauling them taut to provide further support.[74]

Considerable precautions were also taken before battle to prevent or at least reduce damage. Crucial parts of the rigging, such as the lifts that supported the yards and the braces that turned them in the horizontal plane, were doubled up to provide added security, and in some instances rope was replaced with chain. There are references to 'stirruping' the shrouds prior to action,[75] though it is unclear what this actually entailed. Puddings and dolphins – thick wreaths of wormed and parcelled rope – were secured around the masts to sustain the weight of the fore and main yards in case the lifts by which they were suspended were damaged.[76] Splinter netting was also fitted to protect the men from falling blocks, which were particularly dangerous because they were attached to ropes and could therefore 'swing' in a great arc and wreak havoc. A cask of water might also be hoisted aloft in case of fire.[77]

Only the minimum canvas was set for battle to reduce potential damage, but if the sails were split or were in danger of splitting, a number of options were available to limit the potential impact of the damage. This was crucial, since even a small cut in a sail could soon become a serious tear or even a complete split, particularly in high winds.[78] If the injury was near the head of the

sail, it could be reefed to protect the damaged area until such time as it could
be repaired, a technique used aboard the *Foudroyant* by Captain John Jervis
at the Battle of Ushant.[79] Although taking in the canvas hand over hand was a
tiresome process that required significant numbers of men aloft, it could still
be done despite damage to the running rigging.[80] A split sail could be sewn or
patched without unbending it but, if this proved impractical or the damage was
so bad that it needed replacing, it could still be unbent in relatively short order
by a well-trained crew. Mr John Lucky, master of the *Caesar* at the First of June,
recalled with nothing short of awe how she had a new topsail bent and two reefs
taken in so quickly that the *Caesar* was able to hold her place in the line.[81] This
is not an isolated example. At the Battle of the Saints in April 1782 the *Ville de
Paris,* flagship of the comte de Grasse, bent a new maintopsail after the original split in two, and then bore down to the aid of the *Glorieux*, which had lost
her main and mizzen masts.[82] Nothing is more indicative of this ability to repair
sails and rigging, however, than the statement of Captain Philip Durell of the
Trident, who, at the trial of John Byng, declared that damage to two of his main
shrouds, a fore stay cut, and some shot through the sails was 'trifling'.[83]

Undoubtedly some damage to the rig would be of more structural significance. There were, however, both temporary and permanent methods of cop-
ing with such structural damage. The first and most obvious was to acquire
replacements for the injured part of the rig, although this depended on the
resources being available. Specific wood – fir, pine and spruce – was needed
for masts and spars. Wood from the southern Baltic shore was preferred, and
that from Riga, around the banks of the River Dvina, was the best.[84] Without
the Baltic timber, the rigging would be of inferior quality, and a captain would
be forced to sail with greater prudence for fear of causing more damage. It was
customary to provide each ship with a spare set of topmasts and often topgallant masts, but these were usually kept under or on top of the boats and were
frequently damaged in action.[85] In 1777 Howe ordered spare spars to be lashed
alongside the hull, under the lower deck ports, or towed astern to protect them
from damage.[86] Damaged mainmasts and bowsprits were particularly problematic to replace because of their size, on average a yard in diameter.[87] The ships
themselves did not carry such sizeable spares.

These resources were far from inexhaustible and those which had to be
imported were often hard to come by.[88] Captured prizes were a prime source for
spares,[89] and captains would often lend their surplus to those in need. After the
Battle of the Nile, Captain Miller of the *Theseus* thus sent all of his unwounded
spars, a spare topsail and topgallant sails to the captured and badly damaged
Tonnant,[90] and the *Audacious* spared the *Bellerophon* her jib-boom, which
she used as a mizzenmast.[91] Once these resources had been exhausted, a crew
would have to make do with what they had on board, and masts and yards would
be taken from one part of the ship to be used in a more crucial role. Thus at

Trafalgar both the *Minotaur* and the *Revenge* used their spritsail yards as fore-topsail yards.[92] At the First of June, having lost everything above her mainmast, the *Orion* used a main topgallant mast for a jury maintopmast, a foretopgallant sail for a maintopsail, a foretopsail yard for a main yard and a foretopsail for a mainsail,[93] and at the Nile the *Culloden*, which so unfortunately ran aground before the action began, even made a new rudder out of a spare topmast.[94]

If the injuries to a mast or yard were not so severe as to need immediate replacement, the injured spar could be 'fished'. This involved using two pieces of timber, bound opposite each other, to splint the injured spar. Although seasoned Baltic timber was ideal, in an emergency any spare piece of sturdy timber would serve for a temporary repair. Captain Molloy recalled in his trial how they managed to secure the fore yard of the *Caesar* with capstan bars,[95] and after the Battle of Ushant the mizzenmast of the *Formidable* was fished with an anchor stock.[96] If there was no time for such carpentry, any piece of timber could be secured temporarily by tying a rope seizing known as a woolding around it. At Trafalgar the split and rotten neck of the rudder on board the *Defence* was secured in this way by a woolding of 3½-inch rope.[97] Such repairs were only temporary, however, and often inadequate. A fished mast might still remain weak, and a captain would often still be obliged to carry shortened sail if not to run before the wind.[98]

Damage below the waterline was particularly problematic because of the ingress of water. A leak at the bow was more dangerous than one at the stern. If the vessel had headway, a leak at the bow would be augmented in proportion to the headway, while one at the stern would be correspondingly diminished.[99] Damage below the waterline was paradoxically easy to identify but much harder to find and then access, particularly if it was by the keel, but precautions were taken to make this task as easy as possible. As early as the third quarter of the seventeenth century it was an established practice prior to battle to clear the holds along the ship's sides so that the carpenters could quickly and easily find the damaged area, which they would then plug and seal with wood and lead.[100] Special plugs for shot-holes seem to have been invented, although it is unclear how widespread they were or, indeed, whether they were used at all (Fig. 32).

If the damaged area was not too deep, it could be exposed by heeling the ship. In this way, the heavily damaged *Sandwich* was kept afloat at the Battle of Ushant in 1778,[101] as was the *Ville de Paris* after a skirmish with Hood in February 1782.[102] A stage could then be rigged over the side for carpenters to gain access to the damage, though this was not without its own dangers. In a letter to the Admiralty in the winter of 1805, Captain Morris recorded how the carpenter of the *Colossus* cut his legs badly on the ragged copper when over the side repairing the shot holes.[103] Nevertheless, it was possible. Indeed, it enabled Jervis's entire Mediterranean squadron to be caulked at sea during the

32 A specially designed plug for stopping shot holes

spring and summer of 1796, an astonishing feat of seamanship.[104] As an alter-native, a 'foddered' or 'fothered' sail, preferably number one canvas, tarred and with oakum stitched to it, could be sunk and held in place by the force of the water pressure trying to get into the hole in the hull. This was found to be a particularly useful method in ships short of carpenters or that, for one reason or another, worked a great deal and would repeatedly break open any attempted repair.[105]

Inevitably, much of this repair work was only temporary, and some damage needed the full facilities of a dockyard or a careening wharf. The replacement of lower masts was particularly problematic, since restepping such large masts usually required a mast-hulk.[106] Nevertheless, the ability to repair the great majority of damage at sea was a peculiar characteristic of sailing warfare, and the effects of damage were not, therefore, absolute once caused. Thus Nelson, having received considerable damage aboard the *Agamemnon* in a fierce skir-mish with a French squadron and with the maintopmast 'shot to pieces' and the mainmast, mizzenmast and foreyard badly wounded, was quite sure that 'a very few hours at anchor will repair all our damages, when the ship will in many respects be fitter for service than ever'.[107] Similarly, the damage and subsequent repair of the *Egmont,* as reported at the trial of Admiral Keppel after Ushant in 1778, deserves to be quoted in full, so impressive are the skills of the sailors and carpenters. Captain Allen lists the principal defects of the *Egmont*:

> We received six shot between the lower part of the whale on the starboard side, and five streaks below that; the head of the mainmast had two or three shot through it; the mizzen mast shot totally away; the head of the mizzenmast had two shot, the crotchet and mizzen topsail yard, the main yard, and the starboard yard arm shot through, one shot through the

slings of the main yard, one shot through the larboard, and most of the larboard yard-arm shattered. The head of the foretopsail shortened, the foreyard shot through in two places, the foremast and maintop sail yard shot through, one shot through the centre of the foremast and the head of the foremast much shattered, and the main stays.

The court accepted from this testimony that the ship was disabled, but Allen insisted that the ship was ready to renew the engagement in three and a half hours.[108]

It is important, however, not to consider repair in purely theoretical terms. Repair was made far easier – and was sometimes only possible – with calm sea and weather conditions and sufficient daylight,[109] but, above and beyond that, it was dependent on three vital elements.

The first of those was the requisite skill and experience of her crew. It required lengthy experience of seamanship to gain skill in repair and also experience of battle to understand the types of damage that could occur and the conditions of engagement under which it would have to be repaired.

A disabled ship also needed both time and distance to make repairs and would have little option but to stand clear of the action for some time. To carry out repairs under the guns of the enemy and in the sights of their sharpshooters was difficult, but not impossible; one contemporary noted in his diary how sailors were stationed aloft in battle for exactly that purpose.[110] The limited sail a fleet was under in action also allowed ships with minor damage to be repaired without causing too much disruption to the line.[111] Nevertheless, any serious damage took time to repair. The remarkable example of the repairs to the *Egmont* still took three and a half hours to carry out. Similarly, it took the carpenters of the *Formidable* all evening and night to fish the mizzenmast and mend three chainplates after Ushant,[112] and Captain Miller recalled how, after the Battle of St Vincent, labouring incessantly, it still took them until midnight to put the damaged and unsupported mainmast out of danger.[113]

With this sort of time and distance necessary for repairs, a ship could justifiably be out of action and at some distance from the enemy for a considerable length of time, and it was perfectly possible for it to miss the engagement altogether without a shadow falling on the aggressive reputation of her captain. At the Battle of St Vincent the *Colossus* lost her foreyard as the fleet tacked in succession to engage the Spanish fleet for the first time; forced out of the line, she was still struggling to repair her damage at the end of the battle.[114] Most famously, the heavy damage received by Palliser at Ushant in 1778 kept him out of the battle and unable to support his admiral.[115]

Time and distance were, therefore, crucial to the ability of a ship to repair its damage. Conversely, to *deny* an enemy the time and distance necessary for repair was a valuable tactic in its own right. Captains who 'stuck so close to their flying antagonists as to leave them no time to rally or repair any part of their damages'[116] were worthy of praise indeed.

The peculiar and symbiotic relationship between damage, capability and tactics in the eighteenth century was itself a defining characteristic of sailing warfare. The sailing warship was technologically complex, and the effects of damage on its performance necessarily mirrored that complexity. But the most striking characteristic of the impact of damage was the paradoxical conjunction of its ability to endure and absorb certain types of damage with an equal capacity to be hamstrung by other, relatively minor, injury. This undoubtedly influenced tactical choice, practice and the outcome of engagements. On one hand luck could play a significant part in the outcome of a gunnery duel, on the other, a gunnery duel could be purely attritional.

In practice, therefore, it is instructive to consider success in battle in terms of the ability of one ship to force the crew of another to change its priorities. A ship, it must never be forgotten, was not just an instrument of war; it was also a home, a shelter from the elements and the only thing that lay between a sailor and a salty grave. To fight a ship, therefore, was some way down a ladder of priorities for those aboard. The first priority was to float, the second to move, and only the third was to fight. With sufficient perseverance from an aggressive ship, these priorities could be shifted in the minds of the enemy crew, and in that shift lay the path to success. Thus, in Bridport's engagement with Villaret-Joyeuse on 23 June 1795, a ship at the rear of the French fleet was targeted in succession by a number of British ships as they came up with her. Her crew were not all killed, nor was the ship immobilised, but through some degree of fortune a fire started on the enemy poop. She immediately ceased firing, threw all her sails aback and the crew worked together to put out the fire. In the mean time she was surrounded by British ships and was forced to surrender.[117]

In this example the priority of the French crew changed completely and instantly from aggression to survival. In other examples where the impact was not so great, the effect of a change in priority of only a few men could still be felt like a ripple throughout the entire ship. If even a minor fire started, for example, men would immediately be taken from the guns both to fight the fire and to clear away any nearby rigging that might catch alight.[118] In exactly the same way, in a badly holed ship, men would be sent from the guns to the pumps. Then, if it became clear that the ship could not be saved without help, she would be struck. Thus when the French *Hector* finally surrendered at the Saints, all her pumps were constantly going, with nearly 4 feet of water in the hold.[119] This might have been seen as some kind of threshold beyond which a ship could not survive without significant help, as in April 1796 the *Virginie* also struck after a lengthy battle with three British frigates; she also had 4 feet of water in the hold.[120]

In these examples the manpower aboard the enemy ship was inadvertently targeted by forcing gunners and officers to shift their attention, but that pool of manpower itself was also targeted in battle. As men died or were injured, the gun crews had to work harder to cover for them. Gunnery slowed down, and the ship was manœuvred with less efficiency. The will to persevere was also threatened as men saw their shipmates die. It has been argued that the sapping of morale was more keenly felt on French ships, who did not heave their dead overboard as was customary on the English ships,[121] but in either case the value of high initial morale, staying-power and tenacity of purpose was crucial to helping crews get through and win a battle. In perseverance lay victory.

Conclusion

It is widely accepted that warfare at sea is very specific and exacting in its requirements, and warfare at sea under sail even more so, but our understanding of how and why that was the case is far from complete. The study of sailing warfare has existed for too long in a vacuum, divorced from the realities of practical capability; yet it is those realities which defined and described the nature of seafaring under sail, and which provide the key to understanding the nature and development of fighting tactics.

At the heart of these realities are the twin issues of seamanship and tactics. No one would deny their importance in the outcome of battles in the age of sail, or even in the outcome of wars and, in many instances, they are considered to be among the most important factors that determined victory or defeat. That prevalence, however, is matched by an equally conspicuous absence of any considered explanation of what they actually mean in context. 'Tactics', for example, is used rather carelessly as a single but amorphous subject to cover a whole range of subject matter associated with the methods of employing, or deploying, a ship or a fleet and its armament in battle, from signalling to gunnery. 'Seamanship' has been confused in a similar way. There are very few activities on board a ship – indeed, one could argue that there are none – that cannot be classed as 'seamanship' in their own right, or are not directly and significantly affected by seamanship skill. The seamanship skills of setting and furling sail and of rig and hull maintenance are obviously peculiar to shipboard life, but gunnery on board a ship is also different from gunnery on land, as is weather prediction at sea different from weather prediction on land. Furthermore anyone who has tried it will know that cooking at sea requires a very specific set of skills that does not come with cooking on land, not least the ability to carry a pot of boiling water in a rolling sea without scalding oneself. Even standing up at sea requires a different set of skills from standing up on land: one must learn to lower one's centre of gravity, bend at the knees and allow the legs to give with the motion of the ship. Seamanship has more to do with the environment – with *being* at sea – than any particular activity, and each activity, from station keeping to cooking and from gunnery to sleeping must be considered in that light.

If tactics and seamanship are indeed broken down into their separate components, some broader themes concerning fighting can then be identified. Particularly in need of emphasis is the mercurial nature of sailing warfare. Tactics were chosen to create and take advantage according to strategic priority, but this was a more subtle and fluid process than is usually allowed for. Much of the tactics of engagement were heavily dependent on circumstance. Tactical motivation and choice were dictated by relative capability, which was in turn determined by the variable factors of relative skill and ship design; of wind, weather and sea conditions; and of damage, morale and strategy. In practice tactics turned to a significant degree on the ability to judge those conditions and then react as circumstances changed to create and then to take advantage of transient opportunity. Excellent gunnery could, in some situations, be countered by speed and manœuvrability, yet speed and manœuvrability could in the right conditions be countered by excellent gunnery. At times, aggression could be rendered impotent by brilliant cautious and defensive tactics, while at others cautious and defensive tactics could be nullified by brilliant aggression. A continuous and relentless push to create and then make use of transient advantage was the nature of battle at sea in the age of sail.

Closely linked to this question of variety and unpredictability in capability, control and tactics was the marked preponderance of the human element over the material. The chaos of battle belied a system of subtlety and skill that directly affected the efficient and effective operation of ships and fleets that was of peculiar potency in the eighteenth century. To consider the ships without the sailors, the flags without the signalmen, and command without the commanders is only to get half the picture; one must be sure to splice together the dual strands of technology and its application. Tactics and behaviour in a sea fight were governed to a great extent by situational empiricism and intrinsically linked to 'seamanship skill' in all its definitions. In practice, sea fighting was as much an art as seafaring, for the two were inseparable.

Notes

Introduction

1 A. T. Mahan, *The Influence of Seapower on History, 1660–1783* (Boston, 1890), p. 2; J. Creswell, *British Admirals of the Eighteenth Century: Tactics in Battle* (London, 1972), pp. 21–2; M. A. J. Palmer, 'Lord Nelson, Master of Command', *Naval War College Review*, 41 (1988), pp. 105–16; W. C. B. Tunstall, *Naval Warfare in the Age of Sail*, ed. N. Tracy (London, 1990), pp. 1–10; M. A. J. Palmer, 'Sir John's Victory – The Battle of Cape St. Vincent Reconsidered', *MM*, 77 (1991), pp. 105–16; M. A. J. Palmer, 'Burke and Nelson: Decentralized Style of Command', *United States Naval Institute Proceedings*, 117/7 (1991), pp. 58–9; M. A. J. Palmer, 'The Soul's Right Hand: Command and Control in the Age of Fighting Sail, 1652–1827', *Journal of Military History*, 111 (1997), pp. 679–706; M. Depeyre, *Tactiques et stratégies navales de la France et du Royaume-Uni de 1690 à 1815* (Paris, 1998), pp. 57–74; N. A. M. Rodger, 'Weather, Geography and Naval Power in the Age of Sail', *Journal of Strategic Studies*, 22 (1999), pp. 178–80; N. A. M. Rodger, 'Image and Reality in Eighteenth Century Naval Tactics', *MM*, 89 (2003), pp. 283–4.

2 R. V. Hamilton and J. K. Laughton, eds., *The Recollections of Commander James Anthony Gardner, 1775–1814* (London, 1906), p. 105.

3 Tunstall, *Naval Warfare in the Age of Sail* relies almost entirely on a minute analysis of the Fighting Instructions and signal books, and Depeyre's *Tactiques et stratégies* analyses contemporary treatises on fighting tactics.

4 J. S. Corbett, *Fighting Instructions, 1530–1816* (London, 1905), p. 188.

5 See, for example, Mahan, *Influence of Seapower*; J. K. Laughton, 'The Scientific Study of Naval History', *Journal of the Royal United Services Institution*, 18 (1875), pp. 508–26; P. H. Colomb, *Naval Warfare: Its Ruling Principles and Practice Historically Treated* (London, 1895).

6 J. H. S. McAnally, 'The Purposes and Benefits of Doctrine: Why Go to All the Trouble of Having One?', in *Doctrine and Military Effectiveness*, ed. M. Duffy,

T. Farrell, and G. Sloan (Exeter, 1997), p. 7; R. Overy, 'Doctrine Not Dogma: Lessons from the Past', in *Doctrine and Military Effectiveness*, ed. M. Duffy, T. Farrell and G. Sloan (Exeter, 1997), p. 34.

7 See, for example, A. T. Mahan, *Types of Naval Officers* (London, 1902), p. 18; M. Lewis, *The Navy of Britain: An Historical Portrait* (London, 1948), pp. 481, 532–3. Also see R. Castex, *Les Idées militaires de la marine du XVIIIᵉ siècle, de Ruyter à Suffren* (Paris, 1911), p. 63.

8 Creswell, *British Admirals*, pp. 8–9, 27–30.

9 The minutes of any court martial enquiring into the behavior of a naval officer in action are testament to this. For a published example, see 'The Charges Against Admiral Matthews', in H. W. Richmond, *The Navy in the War of 1739–48*, 3 vols. (Aldershot, 1993), II, pp. 260–8.

10 A few copies were published privately in 1782.

11 Rodger, 'Image and Reality', pp. 280–96.

12 Depeyre, *Tactiques et stratégies*, p. 82; Tunstall, *Naval Warfare in the Age of Sail*, p. 59.

13 Rodger, 'Image and Reality', p. 281. Also see N. A. M. Rodger, 'Navies and the Enlightenment', in *Science and the French and British Navies, 1700–1850*, ed. P. van der Merwe (London, 2003), pp. 5–9.

14 P. Hoste, *L'Art des armées navales ou traité des évolutions navales* (Lyon, 1697), p. xv.

15 P. Hoste, *A Treatise on Naval Evolutions*, trans. J. D. Boswall (Edinburgh, 1834), p. xvi.

16 J. R. de Grenier, quoted in D. Steel, *The Elements and Practice of Rigging and Seamanship*, 2 vols. (London, 1794), II, p. 405.

17 Anon., *A Vindication of the Conduct of Capt. M-N by a Sea Officer* (London, 1745), p. 17.

18 J. Clerk, *An Essay on Naval Tactics* (London, 1790), p. 22.

19 T. Wareham, *Frigate Commander* (Barnsley, 2004), pp. 74–5.

20 S. Martin-Leake, *The Life of Admiral Sir John Leake*, 2 vols. (London, 1920), I, p. 179.

CHAPTER 1: Contact

1 F. Marryat, *Frank Mildmay or the Naval Officer* (London, c.1895), p. 61. Marryat's works are fictional, but he served in the Navy for twenty-four years between 1806 and 1830 and his books are scattered with detailed observations of fighting at sea such as this.

2 F. Marryat, *Mr. Midshipman Easy* (London, c.1850), pp. 258–9.

3 Journal of R. Wilson, H. G. Thursfield, ed., *Five Naval Journals, 1789–1817* (London, 1951), p. 130.

4 T. Pasley, *Private Sea Journals, 1778–1782* (London, 1931), p. 42. Also see R. C. Anderson, ed., *The Journals of Sir Thomas Allin*, 2 vols. (London, 1939), I, p. 160; G. Mason to W. Marsden 29 Sep 1805, TNA ADM 1/2149.

5 J. Harland, *Ships and Seamanship: The Maritime Prints of J. J. Baugean* (London, 2000), p. 31; N. A. M. Rodger, *The Command of the Ocean: A Naval History of Britain, 1649–1815*, II (London, 2004), p. 421.

6 Harland, *Ships and Seamanship*, pp. 14–31.

7 Harland, *Ships and Seamanship*, p. 36; T. Cochrane, *The Autobiography of a Seaman* (London, 1860), p. 176.

8 *Minutes of the Proceedings at a Court Martial Assembled to Enquire into the Loss of H.M.S. Ardent* (London, 1780), p. 18; Cochrane, *Autobiography of a Seaman*, p. 176; G. Mason to W. Marsden 29 Sep 1805, TNA ADM 1/2149; J. W. Maurice to W. Marsden 19 Jun 1805, TNA ADM 1/2150.

9 Chevalier de Goussencourt, 'A Journal of the Cruise of the Fleet of His Most Christian Majesty, under the Command of the Count De Grasse-Tilly in 1781 and 1782', in *The Operations of the French Fleet under the Comte De Grasse in 1781–2*, ed. J. G. O'Shea (New York, 1971), p. 103.

10 N. Boteler, *Sea Dialogues* (London, 1688), p. 345.

11 Spranger to Smyth 21 Nov 1805, TNA ADM 1/2513.

12 D. Bonner-Smith, ed., *The Barrington Papers, Selected from the Letters and Papers of Admiral the Hon. S. Barrington*, 2 vols. (London, 1937), I, p. 81.

13 J. Cornish to S. Barrington 18 Dec 1757, Bonner-Smith, *Barrington Papers*, I, p. 188.

14 See, for example, 'Signals and Instructions for Ships under Convoy', in W. Bunsford to Adm. Sec., TNA ADM 1/1525.

15 E. Vernon to Rentone Nov 1740, B. McRanft, ed., *The Vernon Papers* (London, 1958), p. 140.

16 J. K. Laughton, *Journal of Rear-Admiral Bartholomew James* (London, 1896), p. 328. For further examples, see Court Martial of Capt. Lumsdaine in R. V. Hamilton, ed., *Letters and Papers of Admiral of the Fleet Sir Thomas Byam Martin*, 3 vols. (London, 1898–1903), I, p. 351; Capt. Porter to Cleveland 26 Oct 1759, *The Annual Register* (1759), pp. 120–1.

17 J. Laforey to W. Marsden 23 May 1805, TNA ADM 1/2074.

18 T. Larkins to R. Patton 13 Sep 1806, *Naval Chronicle*, 16 (1806), pp. 479–80. Also see Palliser to Sandwich 29 Sep 1777, G. R. Barnes and J. H. Owen, eds., *The Private Papers of John, Earl of Sandwich, First Lord of the Admiralty, 1771–1782*, 4 vols. (London, 1932), I, p. 249; Journal of R. Wilson, Thursfield, *Five Naval Journals*, p. 207; M. A. Lewis, ed., *A Narrative of My Professional Adventures by Sir William Dillon*, 2 vols. (London, 1953), I, p. 90.

19 See, for example, Lewis, *Dillon Narrative*, I, pp. 277, 303.

20 Report of Latouche-Tréville 16 June 1804, R. Monaque, 'Latouche-Tréville: The Admiral Who Defied Nelson', *MM*, 86 (2000), p. 283.

21 Rodney's notes in his copy of Clerk's *Naval Tactics*, quoted in H. B. Douglas, *Naval Evolutions: A Memoir, Containing a Review and Refutation of the Principle Essays and Arguments Advocating Mr. Clerk's Claims in Relation to the Manœuvre of 12 April 1782* (London, 1832), appendix I, p. 2.

22 For examples of this being used in action, see *Minutes of the Proceedings at a Court Martial … For the Trial of Sir Robert Calder, Bart., Vice Admiral of the Blue* (London, 1806), p. 14; Anderson, *Allin Journals*, I, p. 242.

23 Russell's Instructions 1691, Corbett, *Fighting Instructions*, p. 191; J. S. Corbett, *Signals and Instructions, 1776–1794* (London,

1971), p. 222; J. H. Harland, *Seamanship in the Age of Sail* (London, 1985), p. 226.

24 W. Hutchinson, *A Treatise on Practical Seamanship*, 2nd edn (Liverpool, 1787), p. 225.

25 *The Trial of the Honourable John Byng at a Court Martial* (Dublin, 1757), pp. 84, 169, 249; W. Young to C. Middleton 24 June 1780, J. K. Laughton, ed., *The Letters and Papers of Charles, Lord Barham*, 3 vols. (London, 1907–11), I, p. 62; W. Falconer, ed., *Universal Dictionary of the Marine* (London, 1771), p. 138. For examples of this happening in practice, see Smyth to W. Marsden 26 Nov 1805, TNA ADM 1/2513; Pocock Journal Wed 2 Aug 1758, TNA ADM 50/21; Captured French report enc. in Byam Martin to Bridport 22 Oct 1798, Hamilton, *Byam Martin Papers*, I, p. 278; Falconer, *Universal Dictionary of the Marine*, p. 138.

26 K. Digby, *Journal of a Voyage into the Mediterranean, A.D. 1628* (London, 1868), p. 5.

27 Howe Add. Ins. 15 Apr 1762, Bonner-Smith, *Barrington Papers*, I, p. 368. Also see T. Graves, 'Minutes of an action of HM Ship *Magicienne*', 2 Jan 1783, TNA ADM 1/242.

28 F. Marryat, *The King's Own* (London, c.1896), p. 190. For a similar contemporary metaphor, see W. S. Lovell, *Personal Narrative of Events from 1799 to 1815 with Anecdotes*, 2nd edn (London, 1879), p. 44.

29 Digby, *Journal of a Voyage*, p. 5.

30 Douglas, *Naval Evolutions*, p. 69. See Chapter 4.

31 R. Lestock to T. Matthews 16 March 1743, TNA ADM 1/381; Sea-Officer, *An Enquiry into the Conduct of Capt. M-N (Mostyn)* (London, 1745), p. 15; *Minutes of the Proceedings of the Trial of Rear-Admiral Knowles* (London, 1750), p. 116.

32 T. Larkins to R. Patton 13 Sep 1806, *Naval Chronicle*, 16 (1806), pp. 479–80.

33 'The Tryal of George Burrish', in *Copies of All the Minutes and Proceedings Taken at and Upon the Several Trials of Capt. George Burrish, Capt. Edmund Williams, Capt. John Ambrose Etc. On Board H.M.S. London 23 Sept 1745* (London, 1746), p. 81; *The Case of William Brereton Esq.* (London, 1779), appendix D, pp. 78–9; A. Villiers, *Give Me a Ship to Sail* (London, 1958), p. 192.

34 Captain R. Miller's Account of the Battle of Cape St Vincent, C. White, *1797: Nelson's Year of Destiny* (Stroud, 1998), p. 154; J. Bourdé de Villehuet, *The Manœuverer, or Skilful Seaman* trans. J. N. J. de Sauseuil (London, 1788), p. 291.

35 J. Porter to Hawke (undated), R. F. Mackay, ed., *The Hawke Papers: A Selection, 1743–1771* (Aldershot, 1990), p. 328; *Minutes of the Proceedings at a Court Martial Assembled for the Trial of Vice-Admiral Sir Hugh Palliser* (London, 1779), p. 72; Hutchinson, *Treatise on Practical Seamanship*, p. 224; *Brereton Trial*, appendix D, pp. 57.

36 Pasley, *Private Sea Journals*, p. 13; Lewis, *Dillon Narrative*, I, pp. 68–9; *Knowles Trial*, p. 199; Report of 19 May 1760, TNA ADM 106/2508.

37 R. Adkins, *Trafalgar: The Biography of a Battle* (London, 2004), p. 75.

38 'Stratagems to be used at sea' from Sir W. Monson's Naval tracts in *Naval Chronicle*, 8 (1802), pp. 314–15.

39 The incident can be followed in letters between Spranger and Smyth, 21–6 Nov 1805, TNA ADM 1/2513, and in the Log of the *Amethyst* 22 Nov 1805, TNA ADM 51/1560.

40 Hutchinson, *Treatise on Practical Seamanship*, pp. 214–16.

41 Evidence of Rear-Admiral Knowles, *Knowles Trial*, p. 209.

42 R. Park, *Defensive War by Sea* (London, 1704), p. 147. For an earlier example still, see Boteler, *Dialogues*, p. 363.

43 Boteler, *Dialogues*, pp. 364–5. Also see *Minutes of the Proceedings of the Court Martial Assembled for the Trial of Captain John Moutray of H.M.S. Ramillies* (London, 1781), p. 14.

44 C. O'Bryen, *An Essay on Naval Military Discipline in General by a Late Experienced Sea Commander* (London, 1762), p. 81.

45 See, for example, Letter from 'A Seaman's Friend' undated, *Naval Chronicle*, 3 (1800), p. 42; Capt. Pierrepont to St Vincent 12 Jan 1798, TNA ADM 1/397; Capt. T. Rogers to St Vincent 15 Jan 1798, TNA ADM 1/397.

46 R. Gardiner, *The Line of Battle: The Sailing Warship, 1650–1840* (London, 1992), p. 118.

47 R. H. Gower, *A Treatise on the Theory and Practice of Seamanship* (London, 1808), p. 58. Douglas mourns the inefficiency in manœuvre of the ships of war in 1820 'being

48 Hutchinson, *Treatise on Practical Seamanship*, p. 220.

49 C. R. Moorsom, *On the Principles of Naval Tactics* (Birmingham, 1846), p. 1; Lewis, *Dillon Narrative*, I, pp. 303–4; Gower, *Treatise on Seamanship*, p. 75.

50 A. Hervey to Hawke 15 Jul 1759, Mackay, *Hawke Papers*, p. 245; R. F. Mackay, *Admiral Hawke* (Oxford, 1965), p. 233. Also see Lewis, *Dillon Narrative*, I, p. 277.

51 Quoted in M. Duffy, 'Jervis: St. Vincent', in *Great Battles of the Royal Navy as Commemorated in the Gun Room, Britannia Naval College, Dartmouth*, ed. E. Grove (London, 1998), p. 109.

52 P. K. Crimmin, 'John Jervis, Earl of St. Vincent, 1735–1823', in *Precursors of Nelson*, ed. P. Le Fevre and R. Harding (London, 2000), pp. 334–5. For another example, see R. Malcomson, *Warships of the Great Lakes* (London, 2001), p. 83.

53 Z. Mudge to W. Marsden 22 Jul 1805, TNA ADM 1/2149. For other examples of displaying false colours, see Laughton, *Journal of Rear-Admiral Bartholomew James*, p. 91; A. Wilkinson to T. Brodrick 17 May 1759, TNA ADM 1/384; M. Maxwell to W. Marsden 18 Nov 1805, TNA ADM 1/2149; Porter to J. Cleveland 26 Oct 1759, *The Annual Register* (1759), p. 120; M. Oppenheim, ed., *The Naval Tracts of Sir William Monson*, 5 vols. (London, 1914), V, p. 138.

54 Capt. K. Maxwell to W. Marsden 18 Nov 1805, TNA ADM 1/2149.

55 E. Boscawen to T. Corbett 25 Jul 1744, TNA ADM 1/1480; Digby, *Journal of a Voyage*, p. 76; C. Douglas to C. Middleton 28 Apr 1782, Laughton, *Barham Papers*, I, p. 275.

56 Digby, *Journal of a Voyage*, p. 82. Also see Anderson, *Allin Journals*, I, p. 46.

57 Lewis, *Dillon Narrative*, I, p. 167. Unfortunately Dillon offers no further

information regarding how a ship might be painted to make her appear smaller. Also see Hamilton, *Byam Martin Papers*, II, pp. 120–1, 125; Wareham, *Frigate Commander*, p. 142.

58 L. G. Carr Laughton, 'H.M.S. Victory: Report to the *Victory* Technical Committee of a Search among the Admiralty Records', *MM*, 10 (1924), p. 205.

59 See, for example, Lewis, *Dillon Narrative*, I, p. 73.

60 Lewis, *Dillon Narrative*, I, pp. 114, 167, 173–4.

61 Lewis, *Dillon Narrative*, I, p. 114; Lovell, *Personal Narrative*, p. 46.

62 J. Boudriot, *The Seventy-Four Gun Ship: A Practical Treatise on the Art of Naval Architecture*, 4 vols. (Paris, 1986–8), II, p. 89; Lovell, *Personal Narrative*, p. 46.

63 J. Allen, ed., *Memoir of the Life and Services of Admiral Sir William Hargood* (London, 1841), p. 138. Lovell claims they were painted white: Lovell, *Personal Narrative*, p. 46; W. P. Cumby, 'The Battle of Trafalgar (an Unpublished Narrative)', *Nineteenth Centur*, 96 (1899), p. 722.

64 Wareham, *Frigate Commander*, pp. 187, 198; J. B. Bourchier, ed., *Memoir of the Life of Admiral Sir Edward Codrington*, 2 vols. (London, 1873), I, p. 46; B. Lavery, *The Ship of the Line*, 2 vols. (London, 1983), II, p. 69.

65 Cochrane, *Autobiography of a Seaman*, p. 101.

66 Hamilton, *Byam Martin Papers*, II, pp. 120–1, 125.

67 Douglas to Middleton 5 Sep 1779, Laughton, *Barham Papers*, I, p. 269.

68 'Stratagems to be used at sea', extracts From Sir W. Monson's naval tracts, *Naval Chronicle*, 8 (1802), pp. 311–12.

69 Howe Add. Ins. 15 Apr 1762, Bonner-Smith, *Barrington Papers*, I, p. 369.

70 Cochrane, *Autobiography of a Seaman*, p. 189. Also see Oppenheim, *Naval Tracts of Sir William Monson*, V, p. 138.

71 Douglas, *Naval Gunnery*, p. 266.

so much slower in turning on account of their flat futtock and great length': H. B. Douglas, *A Treatise on Naval Gunnery* (London, 1820), p. 269.

CHAPTER 2: Chase and Escape I: Speed and Performance

1 Marryat, *Frank Mildmay*, p. 261.

2 Report of Latouche-Tréville 16 June 1804, Monaque, 'Latouche-Tréville', p. 283.

3 Hamilton and Laughton, *Recollections of James Anthony Gardner*, p. 186.

4 For examples of this in use, see Barrington to the Bosun of the *Romney* 3 June 1748, Bonner-Smith, *Barrington Papers*, 1, p. 39; Anderson, *Allin Journals*, 1, pp. 57–9.

5 See, for example, Cochrane, *Autobiography of a Seaman*, p. 177.

6 *The Minutes of a Court Martial Held on Board H.M.S. Lennox Enquiring into the Conduct of the Commanders of the Hampton Court and the Dreadnought* (London, 1745), p. 19; R. Lawrie to Adm. Sec. 25 Feb 1805, in *Bell's Weekly Messenger*, 28 Apr 1805, pp. 3–4; Lewis, *Dillon Narrative*, 1, p. 277; Wareham, *Frigate Commander*, p. 102.

7 Pasley, *Private Sea Journals*, p. 179. Also see Digby, *Journal of a Voyage*, pp. 2, 4, 46.

8 *Palliser Trial*, pp. 6–7. Unfortunately no detail is offered as to what these conditions might be.

9 D. K. Brown, 'The Speed of Sailing Warships, 1793–1840', in *Les Empires en guerre et paix, 1793–1860*, ed. E. Freeman (Vincennes, 1990), p. 162.

10 Gower, *Treatise on Seamanship*, p. 68; E. M. Blunt, *Theory and Practice of Seamanship; Together with a System of Naval Tactics*, 2nd edn (New York, 1824), p. 75; Bourdé de Villehuet, *The Manœuverer*, pp. 135, 154–5.

11 R. Gardiner, *The Heavy Frigate: Eighteen Pounder Frigates, 1778–1800*, 1 (London, 1994), p. 91.

12 Pasley, *Private Sea Journals*, p. 19.

13 E. Boscawen to T. Corbett 6 Jan 1744/5, TNA ADM 1/481.

14 A. Cochrane to E. Nepean 15 May 1799, TNA ADM 1/1627.

15 Hutchinson, *Treatise on Practical Seamanship*, p. 218.

16 *Brereton Trial*, appendix C, p. 22; F. L. Liardet, *Professional Recollections on Points of Seamanship* (London, 1849), p. 127; P. Brett to T. Corbett 18 Oct 1745, TNA ADM 1/481.

17 G. Collieron to E. Nepean 14 Dec 1799, TNA ADM 1/1627. Captain Walsh also re-stowed

his ship by the stern to counter a tendency to pitch heavily caused by the foremast being too far forward. P. Walsh to P. Stevens 19 Mar 1778, TNA ADM 1/2673.

18 Mostyn to T. Corbett 1 Feb 1745 and 14 May 1745, TNA ADM 1/2100. Also see Anderson, *Allin Journals*, 1, p. 92.

19 E. Boscawen to Adm. Sec. 25 Jul 1744, TNA ADM 1/1480; A. Lambert, 'Sir William Cornwallis, 1744–1815', in *Precursors of Nelson*, ed. P. Le Fevre and R. Harding (London, 2000), p. 360; F. Gardner to Adm. Sec. 13 Dec 1804, in *Bell's Weekly Messenger*, 17 Mar 1805, p. 3.

20 Laughton, *Journal of Rear-Admiral Bartholomew James*, p. 329. For other examples, see S. Hood to J. Nourse, in *Bell's Weekly Messenger*, 13 Jan 1805, p. 3; Commodore M. Michell to Adm. Sec. 26 Apr 1747, Bonner-Smith, *Barrington Papers*, 1, p. 10. For weight and size of guns, see Laughton, *Journal of Rear-Admiral Bartholomew James*, p. 329; P. Padfield, *Guns at Sea: A History of Naval Gunnery* (London, 1973), p. 69; A. B. Caruana, *The History of English Sea Ordnance, 1523–1875*, 2 vols. (Rotherfield, 1994–7), II, p. 261.

21 D. Lever, *The Young Sea Officer's Sheet Anchor*, 2nd edn (London, 1819), p. 74.

22 Lever, *The Young Sea Officer's Sheet Anchor*, p. 82. A ship said to be carrying helm must have her rudder kept at a certain angle for the ship to hold her course.

23 E. G. Martin, *Helmsmanship* (London, 1934), pp. 1–2.

24 Anon., *A Dialogue between Two Volunteers Belonging to a Ship Fitting to Sea from Chatham* (London, 1742).

25 'The Tryal of Captain John Ambrose', in *Copies of All the Minutes and Proceedings Taken at and Upon the Several Trials of Capt. George Burrish, Capt. Edmund Williams, Capt. John Ambrose, Etc. On Board H.M.S. London 23 Sept 1745* (London, 1746), p. 94. Also see S. B. A. Willis, 'The Capability of Sailing Warships, Part 1: Windward Performance', *The Northern Mariner*, 13/4 (2004), pp. 32–3.

26 Douglas, *Naval Evolutions*, p. 69.

27 Digby, *Journal of a Voyage*, p. 83.

28 *Knowles Trial*, p. 132. For an example of this in chase, see Hamilton and Laughton, *Recollections of James Anthony Gardner*, pp. 185–6.

29 Cochrane, *Autobiography of a Seaman*, p. 89.

30 R. Gardiner, ed., *Navies and the American Revolution, 1775–1783* (London, 1996), pp. 34–5; J. Glete, 'Sails and Oars: Warships and Navies in the Baltic During the Eighteenth Century, 1700–1815', in *Les Marine de guerre européennes XVIIᵉ–XVIIIᵉ siècles*, ed. M. Acerra *et al.* (Paris, 1985), pp. 381–405; R. C. Anderson, 'Mediterranean Galley Fleets in 1725', *MM*, 42 (1956), pp. 179–87; P. Bamford, *Fighting Ships and Prisons: The Mediterranean Galleys of France in the Age of Louis XIV* (Minneapolis, 1973), pp. 15, 36–7; J. Glete, *Navies and Nations: Warships, Navies and State Building in Europe and America, 1500–1860* (Stockholm, 1993), I, pp. 250, 304; II, pp. 416–17, 501, 706–12; J. Glete, 'The Oared Warship', in *The Line of Battle*, ed. R. Gardiner (London, 1992), pp. 98–105.

31 Wilkinson to Brodrick 17 May 1759, TNA ADM 1/384. See, for example, Hamilton, *Byam Martin Papers*, II, pp. 2, 45.

32 P. Durell 21 Aug 1761, TNA ADM 1/802, quoted in N. A. M. Rodger, *The Wooden World: An Anatomy of the Georgian Navy* (London, 1986), pp. 41–2.

33 Harland, *Seamanship in the Age of Sail*, p. 205; Hutchinson, *Treatise on Practical Seamanship*, p. 221; B. Lavery, *The Arming and Fitting of English Ships of War, 1600–1815* (London, 1987), pp. 207–11.

34 Journal of R. Wilson, Thursfield, *Five Naval Journals*, p. 154.

35 C. S. Forester, *The Naval War of 1812* (London, 1957), pp. 42–4; A. T. Mahan, *Sea Power in its Relations to the War of 1812*, 2 vols. (London, 1905), I, p. 328.

36 Digby, *Journal of a Voyage*, p. 2.

37 Douglas, *Naval Evolutions*, pp. 61–2.

38 Cochrane, *Autobiography of a Seaman*, p. 166.

39 Hamilton, *Byam Martin Papers*, I, p. 132.

40 *Knowles Trial*, p. 37.

41 Kempenfelt to Lord Colvill 23 Jul 1758, TNA ADM 1/2010.

42 Lewis, *Dillon Narrative*, I, p. 124.

43 Article xiv of the Additional Fighting Instructions of 1781–3 required that in chase each ship was to engage her opponent as they as they come up but 'on no pretence to quit them until they are so disabled that they cannot get away or submit'. Corbett, *Signals and Instructions*, p. 291, quoted in Richmond, *The Navy in the War of 1739–48*, III, p. 93 n. 2.

44 Richmond, *The Navy in the War of 1739–48*, III, pp. 91–3.

45 D. Syrett, *The Royal Navy in European Waters During the American Revolutionary War* (Columbia, SC, 1998), p. 87.

46 Wareham, *Frigate Commander*, p. 125.

47 For detail of the accident, see Log of the *Culloden* 12 Feb 1797, TNA ADM 51/1199.

48 Wareham, *Frigate Commander*, p. 125. Moore has the ships mixed up, claiming Troubridge commanded the *Colossus*; the *Colossus* was in fact commanded by Captain George Murray. T. S. Jackson, ed., *Logs of the Great Sea Fights, 1794–1805*, 2 vols. (London, 1981), I, pp. 199, 240–3.

49 G. Byng to J. Burchett 6 Aug 1718, Hattendorf *et al.*, eds., *British Naval Documents, 1204–1960* (Aldershot, 1993), pp. 360–2.

50 Richmond, *The Navy in the War of 1739–48*, III, pp. 91–3. For similar examples, see, the Second Battle of Finisterre, the Battle of Lagos Bay and the Battle of Quiberon Bay.

51 Syrett, *The Royal Navy in European Waters*, pp. 86–7; Rodger, *Command of the Ocean*, pp. 344–5.

52 J. R. Dull, *The French Navy and American Independence: A Study of Arms and Diplomacy, 1774–1787* (Princeton, 1975), p. 176 n. 15.

53 Sandwich to S. Hood 9 Nov 1781, Barnes and Owen, *Sandwich Papers*, IV, p. 201.

54 Lewis, *Dillon Narrative*, I, p. 155. A similar belief held by the English of their enemies during the Dutch Wars of the seventeenth century may account for the expression 'Dutch Courage'.

55 Kempenfelt to Middleton 18 Jan 1780, H. W. Hodges, ed., *Select Naval Documents* (Cambridge, 1922), p. 163.

56 Lewis, *Dillon Narrative*, I, p. 155.

CHAPTER 3: Chase and Escape II: The Tactics of Chasing

1 Hamilton, *Byam Martin Papers*, II, p. 3.

2 Moorsom, *Principles of Naval Tactics*, p. 1.

3 Martin-Leake, *Life of Admiral Leake*, I, p. 159.

4 R. J. B. Knight *The Pursuit of Victory: The Life and Achievement of Horatio Nelson* (London, 2005), pp. 483–92.

5 Nelson to Otway 10 Jul 1805, N. H. Nicholas, ed., *The Dispatches and Letters of Vice Admiral Lord Viscount Nelson*, 7 vols. (London, 1845–6), VI, p. 469, quoted in Knight, *Pursuit of Victory*, p. 493.

6 Rodger, 'Weather', pp. 189–90.

7 Hutchinson, *Treatise on Practical Seamanship*, p. 219. This seems a sensible estimate, if a little low. On a clear day France can be seen across the Channel at its narrowest point: 22 miles. It can also be estimated by the equation $D = 1.144 \times \sqrt{HE}$, where D = the distance to the horizon, and HE is the height of the eye above the waterline. Assuming a nominal HE of 100 feet, two lookouts could see each other on the horizon 11.44 miles away, when they would be 22.88 miles apart.

8 These figures have been chosen to illustrate two similar warships making their best way in a light breeze. The difference in speed of ½ a knot has been chosen as an example of a small difference in speed, perhaps down to better trim or sail balance.

9 See, for example, Journal of P. Cullen, Thursfield, *Five Naval Journals*, p. 100; Laughton, *Barham Papers*, I, p. 55.

10 W. Laird Clowes, *Royal Navy: A History from the Earliest Times to the Death of Queen Victoria*, 7 vols. (London, 1897–1903), III, p. 213.

11 Anon., 'Voyage d'un Suisse dans différentes colonies d'Amérique pendant la dernière guerre', in *The Operations of the French Fleet under the Count de Grasse in 1781–2*, ed. J. G. Shea (New York, 1971), p. 198.

12 See, for example, A. H. Alston, *Captain Alston's Seamanship* (London, 1871), p. 214. For a comparison with contemporary land-based weather-wisdom, in which shepherds excelled, see J. Claridge, *The Shepherd of Banbury's Rules to Judge of the Changes of the Weather* (London 1723).

13 A. D. Fordyce, *Outlines of Naval Routine* (London, 1837), p. 140.

14 Harland, *Seamanship in the Age of Sail*, p. 221.

15 J. Nisbet, *Half Hours at Sea: Stories of Voyage, Adventure and Wreck* (London, 1897), pp. 5, 75.

16 Laughton, *Journal of Rear-Admiral Bartholomew James*, pp. 329–30. Also see Hamilton and Laughton, *Recollections of James Anthony Gardner*, p. 186.

17 W. Mountaine, *The Seaman's Vade-Mecum and Defensive War by Sea* (London, 1744), p. 210.

18 Mountaine, *Seaman's Vade-Mecum*, pp. 209–10.

19 Hutchinson, *Treatise on Practical Seamanship*, p. 220.

20 D. J. Warner, 'Telescopes for Land and Sea', *Rittenhouse*, 12/2 (1998), pp. 45–6. For an example of a night telescope being used, see Journal of R. Wilson, Thursfield, *Five Naval Journals*, p. 143.

21 Lewis, *Dillon Narrative*, I, p. 313.

22 Lewis, *Dillon Narrative*, I, p. 412.

23 Lewis, *Dillon Narrative*, I, p. 314; Hamilton and Laughton, *Recollections of James Anthony Gardner*, p. 187.

24 See Chapter 5.

25 Lewis, *Dillon Narrative*, I, p. 122; Knight, *Pursuit of Victory*, p. 478.

26 'Lorsque le Général éteindra ses feux de poupe, on redoublera d'attention dans tous les vaisseaux pour ne laisser voir aucun feu', in Anon., *Signaux de nuit et de brume qui seront observés par l'escadre du roi commandée par M. de la Clue chef d'escadre des armées navales de Sa Majesté* (Toulon, 1757), p. 3.

27 J. S. Corbett, *England in the Seven Years War: A Study in Combined Strategy*, 2 vols. (London, 1918), II, pp. 35–6; Tunstall, *Naval Warfare in the Age of Sail*, p. 113; G. Lacour-Gayet, *La Marine militaire de la France sous le règne de Louis XV* (Paris, 1902), p. 285.

28 Cochrane, *Autobiography of a Seaman*, pp. 177–8.

29 Hamilton and Laughton, *Recollections of James Anthony Gardner*, p. 187.

30 Journal of R. Wilson, Thursfield, *Five Naval Journals*, p. 143.

31 Liardet, *Professional Recollections*, p. 84.

32 Captain's Orders, HMS *Amazon* 1799, B. Lavery, ed., *Shipboard Life and Organisation, 1731–1815* (Aldershot, 1998), p. 167; Journal of R. Wilson, Thursfield, *Five Naval Journals*, p. 244; Park, *Defensive War by Sea*, p. 158.

33 Hamilton and Laughton, *Recollections of James Anthony Gardner*, p. 73.

34 Journal of R. Wilson, Thursfield, *Five Naval Journals*, p. 130; Rodger, *Command of the Ocean*, pp. 503–4.

35 Hamilton and Laughton, *Recollections of James Anthony Gardner*, p. 108.

36 *Palliser Trial*, p. 85; *Brereton Trial*, appendix C, p. 24; Pasley, *Private Sea Journals*, p. 138.

37 Rodger, *Command of the Ocean*, p. 504.

38 J. K. Laughton, ed., *Memoirs Relating to the Lord Torrington* (London, 1889), p. 159.

39 D. Greenwood, 'James, Lord De Saumarez, 1757–1836', in *British Admirals of the Napoleonic Wars*, ed. P. Le Fevre and R. Harding (London, 2005), p. 259.

40 Mountaine, *Seaman's Vade-Mecum*, p. 203.

41 E. Hawke to Clevland 24 Nov 1759, Mackay, *Hawke Papers*, pp. 344–50.

42 Mackay, *Hawke Papers*, pp. 344–8; Mackay, *Admiral Hawke*, pp. 239–54; Creswell, *British Admirals*, pp. 109–19; Rodger, *Command of the Ocean*, pp. 282–3.

43 An anonymous writer from Rochefort 25 Nov 1759, Lacour-Gayet, *La Marine militaire*, p. 340, quoted in Rodger, *Command of the Ocean*, p. 283.

44 Blunt, *Theory and Practice of Seamanship*, p. 219.

45 G. Rickman, 'Mare Nostrum', in *The Sea and History*, ed. E. E. Rice (Stroud, 1996), pp. 5–6.

46 Goussencourt, 'Journal', p. 121; Laird Clowes, *Royal Navy*, III, p. 523.

47 *The Trial of Vice-Admiral Griffin* (London, 1751), p. 87.

48 Rev. J. Ramsey to C. Middleton 23 Apr 1779, Laughton, *Barham Papers*, I, p. 47; Anon., 'Journal of an Officer in the Naval Army in 1781 and 1782', in *The Operations of the French Fleet under the Comte De Grasse in 1781–2*, ed. J. G. Shea (New York, 1971),

p. 165; D. Spinney, *Rodney* (London, 1969), pp. 389–90.

49 *Griffin Trial*, pp. 31, 85.

50 Mountaine, *Seaman's Vade-Mecum*, p. 202.

51 S. B. A. Willis, 'The Capability of Sailing Warships, Part 2: Manœuvrability', *The Northern Mariner*, 14/3, pp. 66–7.

52 Gower, *Treatise on Seamanship*, p. 59.

53 Mountaine, *Seaman's Vade-Mecum*, p. 202.

54 *Minutes of a Court Martial Holden on Board H.M.S. Gladiator in Portsmouth Harbour, 20 June 1807, for the Trial of Captain Laroche* (London, 1807), p. 16.

55 Mountaine, *Seaman's Vade-Mecum*, p. 192.

56 Mountaine, *Seaman's Vade-Mecum*, pp. 192–202.

57 Mountaine, *Seaman's Vade-Mecum*, p. 209.

58 These issues are explored in greater depth in Willis, 'Windward Performance', pp. 29–39.

59 Kempenfelt Ins. 1781–2, Corbett, *Signals and Instructions*, p. 143.

60 Gower, *Treatise on Seamanship*, pp. 70–1.

61 Gower, *Treatise on Seamanship*, pp. 70–2; Kempenfelt Ins. 1781–2, Corbett, *Signals and Instructions*, p. 143.

62 Willis, 'Windward Performance', p. 39.

63 Hamilton, *Byam Martin Papers*, II, p. 34.

64 Digby, *Journal of a Voyage*, p. 83.

65 Moorsom, *Principles of Naval Tactics*, p. 3.

66 Moorsom, *Principles of Naval Tactics*, p. 4.

67 Alston, *Captain Alston's Seamanship*, p. 230; Douglas, *Naval Gunnery*, p. 274; Lewis, *Dillon Narrative*, I, p. 314; Moorsom, *Principles of Naval Tactics*, pp. 4–6; Gower, *Treatise on Seamanship*, p. 73. This is a technique that is still taught to mariners today: if the bearing of a nearby vessel does not change, you are heading for a collision.

68 Alston, *Captain Alston's Seamanship*, p. 230.

69 See, for example, Lewis, *Dillon Narrative*, I, pp. 303–4.

70 Douglas, *Naval Gunnery*, p. 274; Lewis, *Dillon Narrative*, I, p. 314; Moorsom, *Principles of Naval Tactics*, p. 6; Gower, *Treatise on Seamanship*, p. 73.

71 Moorsom, *Principles of Naval Tactics*, p. 4.

72 Gower, *Treatise on Seamanship*, p. 73.

73 Anon., *A Specimen of Naked Truth from a British Sailor*, p. 25.

74 Creswell, *British Admirals*, p. 93.

75 There are an enormous amount of references to this, but see for an example J. Brett to Adm. Sec. 8 Mar 1744, TNA ADM 1/1481.

76 Hutchinson, *Treatise on Practical Seamanship*, p. 224.

77 Anon. (French), 'French Naval Tactics', extracted from *Le Moniteur*, in *Naval Chronicle*, 4 (1801), pp. 223–4.

78 S. J. Pechell, *Observations upon the Defective Equipment of Ship Guns* (Corfu, 1825), p. 9.

79 Oppenheim, *Naval Tracts of Sir William Monson*, IV, p. 43.

80 Lewis, *Dillon Narrative*, I, p. 381.

81 R. Lawrie to Adm 25 Feb 1805, in *Bell's Weekly Messenger*, 28 Apr 1805, pp. 3–4; Wareham, *Frigate Commander*, p. 115.

82 Lavery, *The Arming and Fitting of English Ships of War*, p. 125.

83 Lewis, *Dillon Narrative*, I, p. 259.

84 Mountaine, *Seaman's Vade-Mecum*, p. 160.

85 C. Douglas to Middleton 12 Jul 1779, Laughton, *Barham Papers*, I, pp. 267–87; Padfield, *Guns at Sea*, p. 111. Douglas later claimed that this alteration to gunnery practice played a significant part in Rodney's victory at the Battle of the Saints in 1782. Laughton, *Barham Papers*, I, pp. 280–1.

86 Park, *Defensive War by Sea*, p. 162.

87 Anon., 'French Naval Tactics', p. 223.

88 *Byng Trial*, p. 209.

89 *Minutes of the Proceedings at a Court Martial, Assembled for the Trial of Anthony James Pye Molloy, Esq., Captain of His Majesty's Ship Caesar* (London, 1795),

pp. 112–13; E. Fraser, *The Enemy at Trafalgar: An Account of the Battle from Eye-Witnesses' Narratives and Letters and Dispatches from the French and Spanish Fleet* (London, 1906), pp. 271–2; 'Ambrose Trial', p. 52; Journal of R. Wilson, Thursfield, *Five Naval Journals*, p. 225; Lewis, *Dillon Narrative*, I, p. 129.

90 Douglas, *Naval Gunnery*, p. 254.

91 Wareham, *Frigate Commander*, p. 115.

92 Lewis, *Dillon Narrative*, I, p. 381. Also see Wareham, *Frigate Commander*, p. 115.

93 Vice-Admiral Decrès to the Minister of the Marine and the Colonies, 1st Floreal, 8th year (the engagement took place on the night of 29 March, 1800), *Naval Chronicle*, 4 (1801), pp. 233–6.

94 See, for example, H. Norris to Adm. Sec. 24 Jul 1744, TNA ADM 1/2217; Wareham, *Frigate Commander*, p. 115.

95 See Chapter 5.

96 Douglas, *Naval Evolutions*, p. 69.

97 Douglas, *Naval Evolutions*, p. 70.

98 Anon., *Dialogue between Two Volunteers*; Hutchinson, *Treatise on Practical Seamanship*, p. 223; Park, *Defensive War by Sea*, p. 162.

99 Liardet, *Professional Recollections*, p. 101; E. Howard, *Rattlin the Reefer*, ed. F. Marryat (London, 1836), vol. 2, p. 186.

100 Captain's Orders HMS *Amazon* 1799, Lavery, *Shipboard Life and Organisation*, p. 168.

101 J. Davie to K. Maxwell 27 Dec 1805, TNA ADM 1/2149.

CHAPTER 4: Station Keeping

1 Pasley, *Private Sea Journals*, pp. 123–4.

2 See Chapter 2.

3 Bourdé de Villehuet, *The Manœuverer*, p. 75.

4 Kempenfelt Ins. 1781, Corbett, *Signals and Instructions*, pp. 151, 165.

5 Lewis, *Dillon Narrative*, I, p. 121.

6 Tunstall, *Naval Warfare in the Age of Sail*, p. 93.

7 Pasley, *Private Sea Journals*, p. 146.

8 Arbuthnot Add. Ins. 1779, Corbett, *Signals and Instructions*, p. 237.

9 Richmond, *The Navy in the War of 1739–48*, II, p. 9.

10 Collingwood to E. Blackett 22 Jul 1793, E. A. Hughes, ed., *The Private Correspondence of Admiral Lord Collingwood* (London, 1957), p. 36.

11 Lestock Trial TNA ADM 1/5280.

12 Blunt, *Theory and Practice of Seamanship*, p. 207.

13 Howe Ins. 30 Jul 1778, Corbett, *Signals and Instructions*, p. 100; 'Ambrose Trial', pp. 10, 56; Blunt, *Theory and Practice of Seamanship*, pp. 206–7.

14 Rodney Add. Ins. 1780 and Howe Ins. 1781–2, Corbett, *Signals and Instructions*, pp. 148, 214; Byron Add. Ins. 11 Aug 1758, Bonner-Smith, *Barrington Papers*, I, p. 220.

15 *An Authentic and Impartial Copy of the Trial of the Hon. Augustus Keppel, Admiral of the Blue* (Portsmouth, 1779), p. 119; Goussencourt, 'Journal', p. 91.

16 Hardy Fleet Orders 16 Sep 1779, Corbett, *Signals and Instructions*, p. 127.

17 Allen, *Memoir of Admiral Sir William Hargood*, p. 33. For further examples, see Laird Clowes, *Royal Navy*, IV, pp. 514, 536.

18 Moorsom, *Principles of Naval Tactics*, p. 13.

19 *Keppel Trial*, p. 238.

20 T. White, *Naval Researches* (London, 1830), p. 107. For more detailed discussion of the influence of the weather on naval campaigns and encounters see D. A. Wheeler, 'The Influence of the Weather During the Camperdown Campaign of 1797', *MM*, 77 (1991), pp. 47–54; Rodger, 'Weather', pp. 179–200.

21 White, *Naval Researches*, p. 42.

22 For an example of what a ship might have to do to keep place in line, see Log of the *Culloden* 28 May – 2 Jun 1794, Jackson, *Logs*, I, p. 136.

23 *Palliser Trial*, pp. 50, 72.

24 *Keppel Trial*, p. 88.

25 Log of the *Invincible* 29 May 1794, Jackson, *Logs*, I, p. 118.

26 *Keppel Trial*, p. 182.

27 For examples of ships struggling to stay in position in battle, see *Molloy Trial*, p. 61; Log of the *Royal Sovereign* 1 Jun 1794, Jackson, *Logs*, I, p. 62; F. Maitland to Middleton 5 Jul 1780, Laughton, *Barham Papers*, I, p. 102.

28 One of the most notorious examples of this was the behaviour of Captain Molloy of the *Caesar* at the Glorious First of June 1794. See *Molloy Trial*; M. Duffy and R. Morriss, eds., *The Glorious First of June 1794: A Naval Battle and Its Aftermath* (Exeter, 2001), p. 60.

29 Anonymous account of the Battle of Ushant 1778, NMM HIS/33; *Keppel Trial*, p. 145.

30 R. Morriss, 'The Glorious First of June: The British View of the Actions of 28, 29 May and 1 June 1794', in *The Glorious First of June*

1794, ed. M. Duffy and R. Morriss (Exeter, 2001), p. 61.

31 Boscawen Add. Ins. 12 Aug 1755, Bonner-Smith, *Barrington Papers*, I, p. 128.

32 Kempenfelt Ins. 1781–2, Corbett, *Signals and Instructions*, p. 148.

33 Kempenfelt to C. Middleton 16 Nov 1779, Laughton, *Barham Papers*, I, p. 303.

34 Lavery, *The Arming and Fitting of English Ships of War*, p. 255; Lavery, *The Ship of the Line*, II, pp. 52, 62.

35 Howe Add. Ins. 8 Mar 1762, Bonner-Smith, *Barrington Papers*, I, p. 350.

36 Lewis, *Dillon Narrative*, I, pp. 23–4.

37 Willis, 'Manœuvrability', pp. 67–8.

38 For a detailed example of this in battle, see *Brereton Trial*, appendix D, pp. 44–6. There are other examples of the main topsail being used for this purpose: see Barrington Memo 19 May 1756, Bonner-Smith, *Barrington Papers*, I, p. 148.

39 'The Tryal of Captain Edmund Williams', in *Copies of All the Minutes and Proceedings Taken at and Upon the Several Trials of Capt. George Burrish, Capt. Edmund Williams, Capt. John Ambrose Etc. On Board H.M.S. London 23 Sept 1745* (London, 1746), p. 47.

40 C. H. Knowles, *Observations on Naval Tactics and on the Claims of Clerk of Eldin* (London, 1830), p. 10.

41 Blunt, *Theory and Practice of Seamanship*, p. 206 n. 1.

42 For an example of a fleet going into battle with the wind abeam, see *Knowles Trial*, p. 92.

43 'Ambrose Trial', p. 121. Also see Duke of Cumberland Add. Sig. 2 Aug 1769, Bonner-Smith, *Barrington Papers*, I, p. 400.

44 'Ambrose Trial', p. 109.

45 Hamilton and Laughton, *Recollections of James Anthony Gardner*, p. 60.

46 Rodney Add. Ins. 18 Dec 1779, Corbett, *Signals and Instructions*, p. 232.

47 Anon. Fighting Ins. 1781–3, Corbett, *Signals and Instructions*, p. 288; Duke of Cumberland Add. Sig. 2 Aug 1769, Bonner-Smith, *Barrington Papers*, I, pp. 399–400.

48 Douglas, *Naval Evolutions*, p. 62.

49 A. Schomberg, *A Sea Manual, Recommended to the Young Officers of the Royal Navy as a Companion to the Signal*

Book (London, 1789), p. ix; Pasley, *Private Sea Journals*, p. 45.

50 Regular Add. Ins. 1778, Corbett, *Signals and Instructions*, p. 220; Vernon Order to Captains 8 Aug 1739, McRanft, *Vernon Papers*, p. 291; O'Bryen, *Essay on Naval Military Discipline*, p. 73; Howe Add. Ins. 1781-2, Corbett, *Signals and Instructions*, p. 165.

51 *Molloy Trial*, p. 102; *Palliser Trial*, p. 14; 'Ambrose Trial', p. 48; *Keppel Trial*, p. 238.

52 Arbuthnot Add. Ins. 19 Aug 1780, Corbett, *Signals and Instructions*, p. 247; Rodney General Order 20 Mar 1782, Laughton, *Barham Papers*, I, p. 265. An earlier example can be found in Anderson, *Allin Journals*, I, p. 27.

53 Young to Middleton 24 Jul 1780, Laughton, *Barham Papers*, I, p. 66.

54 Hawke Add. Ins. 16 Jul 1759, Bonner-Smith, *Barrington Papers*, I, p. 260; T. Stanhope memo 31 Aug 1781, Bonner-Smith, *Barrington Papers*, I, p. 318.

55 'Burrish Trial', pp. 24, 53.

56 'Burrish Trial', p. 51.

57 'Burrish Trial', pp. 24, 51, 53, 84; 'Williams Trial', pp. 5, 15; 'Ambrose Trial', pp. 121, 155.

58 Trial of Lieut. P. Webber 1805, TNA ADM 1/5371, p. 5.

59 Vernon Order to Captains 8 and 9 Aug 1739, McRanft, *Vernon Papers*, pp. 291, 293; *Molloy Trial*, p. 38; Anon Add. Ins. 1778-81, Corbett, *Signals and Instructions*, p. 220; E. Pratten Add. Ins. 26 Apr 1758, Bonner-Smith, *Barrington Papers*, I, p. 199; *Palliser Trial*, p. 74.

60 *Molloy Trial*, p. 144.

61 *Palliser Trial*, p. 74. For an earlier example, see Anderson, *Allin Journals*, I, p. 143.

62 Howe Ins. 30 Jul 1778; Howe Exp. Ins. 1779, Corbett, *Fighting Instructions*, pp. 98, 271.

63 Howe Add. Ins. 1781-2, Corbett, *Signals and Instructions*, p. 141; E. Riou, Instructions and Standing Orders Oct 1799, Lavery, *Shipboard Life and Organisation*, p. 123.

64 Boscawen Add. Ins. 12 Aug 1755, Bonner-Smith, *Barrington Papers*, I, p. 131.

65 White, *Naval Researches*, p. 41.

66 Log of the *Spartiate* 21 Oct 1805, Jackson, *Logs*, II, p. 250; Kempenfelt to Lord Colvill 23 Jul 1758, TNA ADM 1/2010.

67 N. A. M. Rodger, *The Insatiable Earl: A Life of John Montagu, 4th Earl of Sandwich, 1718-92* (London, 1993), p. 25.

68 B. Lavery, *Building the Wooden Walls: The Design and Construction of the 74-Gun Ship Valiant* (London, 1991), p. 18; Lavery, *The Ship of the Line*, I, pp. 96-9; B. Lavery, 'The Origins of the 74 Gun Ship', *MM*, 63 (1977), pp. 346-7.

69 These figures come from the lists of ships present at battles printed in Laird Clowes, *Royal Navy*, v.

70 Patton to Middleton 29 Jun 1792, Laughton, *Barham Papers*, II, p. 388.

71 Harland, *Seamanship in the Age of Sail*, pp. 75-6; F. Howard, *Sailing Ships of War, 1400-1860* (Greenwich, 1979), pp. 204, 207.

72 'Burrish Trial', p. 81.

73 *Brereton Trial*, appendix D, p. 79.

74 B. Rosier, 'Fleet Repairs and Maintenance 1783-93 Reconsidered', *MM*, 84 (1998), p. 332; R. J. B. Knight, 'The Introduction of Copper Sheathing into the Royal Navy, 1779-86', *MM*, 59 (1973), pp. 300-4; R. Cock, 'The Finest Invention in the World: The Royal Navy's Early Trials of Copper Sheathing, 1708-1770', *MM*, 87 (2001), p. 454.

75 R. Sheen to Rotherham 6 Aug 1801, TNA ADM 1/1630. Also see Nelson to Rev. Nelson 24 Aug 1781, Nicholas, *Dispatches and Letters of Lord Nelson*, I, p. 43.

76 W. Young to C. Middleton 24 Jul 1780, Laughton, *Barham Papers*, I, p. 67.

77 Mahan, *Influence of Seapower*, p. 437.

78 Hamilton, *Byam Martin Papers*, II, p. 34.

79 Anon., *A Short Account of the Naval Actions of the Last War ... With Observations on the Discipline and Hints for the Improvement of the British Navy* (London, 1788), p. 123.

80 There is a series of letters from Kempenfelt to Middleton from 1779 that explain in detail changes in seamanship conditions and method necessary to achieve better fleet performance in Hodges, *Select Naval Documents*, pp. 162-5.

81 Moorsom, *Principles of Naval Tactics*, p. 14; Corbett, *Signals and Instructions*, p. 9.

82 Moorsom, *Principles of Naval Tactics*, p. 2.

83 E. Vernon to C. Ogle 16 Jan 1740/1, McRanft, *Vernon Papers*, pp. 164-5; Moorsom, *Principles of Naval Tactics*, p. 14.

84 *Brereton Trial*, appendix D, p. 55.

85 Bourchier, *Memoir of the Life of Admiral Sir Edward Codrington*, I, p. 38.

86 Oppenheim, *Naval Tracts of Sir William Monson*, I, p. 97.

87 Vernon to Ogle 16 Jan 1740/1, McRanft, *Vernon Papers*, pp. 164-5; Lewis, *The Navy of Britain*, p. 504.

88 Richmond, *The Navy in the War of 1739-48*, p. 90; N. A. M. Rodger, 'George, Lord Anson, 1697-1762', in *Precursors of Nelson*, ed. P. Le Fevre and R. Harding (London, 2000), p. 183; Rodger, 'Image and Reality', p. 293; Palmer, 'The Soul's Right Hand', p. 686; Spinney, *Rodney*, p. 72.

89 C. Barnett to G. Anson 16 Sep 1745, J. Barrow, *The Life of Lord Anson* (London, 1839), p. 405.

90 Rodger, 'Image and Reality', p. 293; Corbett, *Signals and Instructions*, p. 354; Mackay, *Admiral Hawke*, pp. 148, 211.

91 Castex, *Idées militaires de la marine*, pp. 121-34; Rodger, *Insatiable Earl*, p. 240; S. S. and M. L. Robison, *A History of Naval Tactics from 1530-1930: The Evolution of Tactical Maxims* (Annapolis, 1942), pp. 264-5.

92 'The Journals of Henry Duncan', in J. K. Laughton, ed., *The Naval Miscellany*, I (London, 1902), p. 215; Laughton, *Barham Papers*, I, pp. 292-327; Hodges, *Select Naval Documents*, pp. 162-7.

93 Rodger, 'Image and Reality', p. 292.

94 Sea-Officer, *Enquiry into the Conduct of Capt. M-N*, p. 20.

95 J. Hamstead, *A Treatise on Naval Tactics* (London, 1808), p. ix.

96 Kempenfelt to Middleton 18 Jan 1780, Hodges, *Select Naval Documents*, p. 163; Rodger, *Insatiable Earl*, p. 244.

97 Anon., *Short Account of the Naval Actions*, p. 133; Lewis, *Dillon Narrative*, I, pp. 22, 99, 119, 128; J. H. Broomfield, 'The Keppel-Palliser Affair, 1778-1779', *MM*, 47 (1961), p. 267.

98 Crimmin, 'John Jervis', pp. 332-3; Mackay, *Admiral Hawke*, p. 150; J. J. Tritten, 'Doctrine and Fleet Tactics in the Royal Navy', in *A Doctrine Reader*, ed. J. J. Tritten and L. Donolo (Newport, RI, 1995), p. 12.

99 Corbett, *Signals and Instructions*, pp. 117, 123, 150.

100 Spinney, *Rodney*, p. 395; White, *Nelson's Year of Destiny*, p. 49; R. Monaque, 'On Board H.M.S. Alexander (1796-9)', *MM*, 89 (2003), p. 210.

101 Schomberg, *Sea Manual*, pp. 63-4.

102 Kempenfelt to Middleton 6 Apr 1780, Laughton, *Barham Papers*, I, p. 323. For similar examples of methods to deal with shifts of wind, see Bourdé de Villehuet, *The Manœuverer*, pp. 253-4, 266.

103 Liardet, *Professional Recollections*, p. 48.

104 For details, see Vernon Ins. 8 Jun 1740, McRanft, *Vernon Papers*, p. 298; Hawke Add. Ins. 16 Jul 1759, Bonner-Smith, *Barrington Papers*, I, p. 259; J. M. Boyd, *Manual for Naval Cadets* (London, 1860), p. 426.

105 Kempenfelt first introduced a preparative flag in the channel fleet in 1779-80: Corbett, *Signals and Instructions*, p. 212 n. 2. Also see Arbuthnot's Add. Ins. 1779, Corbett, *Signals and Instructions*, p. 237.

106 Corbett, *Signals and Instructions*, p. 183.

107 Corbett, *Fighting Instructions*, p. 270; Tunstall, *Naval Warfare in the Age of Sail*, pp. 59-60, 99-101.

108 Richmond, *The Navy in the War of 1739-48*, I, p. 47.

109 Corbett, *Signals and Instructions*, p. 183.

110 Richmond, *The Navy in the War of 1739-48*, II, p. 10 n. 2; I, p. 47.

111 Robison, *History of Naval Tactics*, p. 265.

112 N. Tracy, *Nelson's Battles: The Art of Victory in the Age of Sail* (London, 1996), p. 50.

113 This constant need for individual input and initiative from the captains is reflected in the patterns of promotion through the requirement of first-hand experience of the use and advantages of highly manœuvrable ships. It has been shown that Frigate Command became the training ground for fleet seamanship, the finest frigate officers being 'creamed off' by the Admiralty to command ships of the line. T. Wareham, *The Star Captains* (London, 2001), p. 11.

114 J. Charnock, *An History of Marine Architecture*, 3 vols. (London, 1800-2), III, p. 234; Lavery, *The Ship of the Line*, I, pp. 132-3; Boudriot, *The Seventy-Four Gun Ship*, IV, p. 277.

115 Douglas, *Naval Evolutions*, p. 59.

116 Edgecumbe to Barrington 26 May 1748, Bonner-Smith, *Barrington Papers*, I, p. 37.

117 Moorsom, *Principles of Naval Tactics*, p. 15.

CHAPTER 5: Communication

1 Lewis, *Dillon Narrative*, I, p. 129.

2 Anon., 'Letter to the Editor', *Naval Chronicle*, 4 (1801), p. 133.

3 Liardet, *Professional Recollections*, p. 207.

4 Boudriot, *The Seventy-Four Gun Ship*, iv, p. 338.

5 Capt. M. Dixon? [illegible] to Adm. 16 Jul 1798, TNA ADM 1/398; Cochrane, *Autobiography of a Seaman*, p. 131.

6 Journal of R. Wilson, Thursfield, *Five Naval Journals*, p. 130.

7 *Palliser Trial*, p. 56.

8 For examples of this happening, see Hawke to Corbett 17 Oct 1747, Mackay, *Hawke Papers*, p. 51; 'Extract from the minutes of the Court Martial on Captain John Williamson ... of the *Agincourt*', in Jackson, *Logs*, I, p. 330; White, *Naval Researches*, p. 119.

9 'Fox Trial', in Mackay, *Hawke Papers*, p. 74.

10 Hamilton and Laughton, *Recollections of James Anthony Gardner*, p. 30.

11 Laughton, *Barham Papers*, I, p. 69.

12 For a good example see Corbett, *Signals and Instructions*, pp. 306–11.

13 Kempenfelt to Middleton (undated) Mar 1781, Hodges, *Select Naval Documents*, p. 183; Kempenfelt to P. Stevens 21 Mar 1780, TNA ADM 1/95.

14 Young to Middleton 24 Jul 1780, Laughton, *Barham Papers*, I, pp. 69, 72; Young to Middleton 20 Mar 1780, Laughton, *Barham Papers*, I, p. 314; L. E. Holland, 'The Development of Signalling in the Royal Navy', *MM*, 39 (1953), p. 20.

15 'Williamson Trial', in Jackson, *Logs*, I, p. 313.

16 *Torbay* TNA ADM 51/100; *Magnanime* TNA ADM 51/385; *Dorsetshire* TNA ADM 51/262.

17 Corbett, *Signals and Instructions*, p. 213. For earlier examples of two-way signalling, see Henry to Barrington 16 July 1769, Bonner-Smith, *Barrington Papers*, I, p. 399; Add. Signals by HRH The Duke of Cumberland 2 Aug 1769, Bonner-Smith, *Barrington Papers*, I, p. 401.

18 *Palliser Trial*, pp. 16, 17, 26; Hamilton, *Byam Martin Papers*, I, pp. 175–6.

19 *Palliser Trial*, p. 77; Corbett, *Signals and Instructions*, p. 233.

20 Vernon Add. Ins. 16 Jul 1739, McRanft, *Vernon Papers*, p. 291.

21 Vernon Add. Ins. 8 Aug 1739, McRanft, *Vernon Papers*, p. 291; *Byng Trial*, p. 31; Journal of R. Wilson, Thursfield, *Five Naval Journals*, p. 130; Journal of W. Cumby, Thursfield, *Five Naval Journals*, p. 332.

22 *Keppel Trial*, p. 136.

23 Bourchier, *Memoir of the Life of Admiral Sir Edward Codrington*, I, pp. 14–15.

24 Lewis, *Dillon Narrative*, I, p. 167.

25 Bourchier, *Memoir of the Life of Admiral Sir Edward Codrington*, I, p. 17.

26 Rodger, *Insatiable Earl*, p. 239.

27 See Chapter 12.

28 Master's Journal of the *Marlborough* 1 Jun 1794, Jackson, *Logs*, I, p. 130.

29 A. H. Taylor, 'Admiral the Honourable Sir George Elliot', *MM*, 35 (1949), p. 322.

30 Pocock Journal 4 Aug 1758, TNA ADM 50/21.

31 G. M. Bennett, 'The Fleet Flagship: A Problem of Naval Command', *Journal of the Royal United Services Institute*, 81 (1936), pp. 601–11.

32 J. A. Sulivan, 'Graves and Hood', *MM*, 69 (1983), p. 187.

33 Richmond, *The Navy in the War of 1739–48*, II, p. 10 n. 2; I, p. 47.

34 Sulivan, 'Graves and Hood', p. 189; Creswell, *British Admirals*, p. 160.

35 Graves Memorandum 6 Sep 1781, Corbett, *Signals and Instructions*, p. 260.

36 Monaque, 'Latouche-Tréville', p. 280.

37 S. Hood's comments on Graves memo 6 Nov 1781, Corbett, *Signals and Instructions*, p. 261.

38 At Toulon the three rearmost ships of Lestock's squadron were the cleanest. Mahan, *Types of Naval Officers*, p. 37.

39 Boteler, *Dialogues*, p. 384.

40 R. E. J. Weber, 'The Introduction of the Single Line Ahead as a Battle Formation by the Dutch, 1665–6', *MM*, 73 (1987), p. 9.

41 Tunstall, *Naval Warfare in the Age of Sail*, p. 110.

42 Creswell, *British Admirals*, pp. 89–91; Richmond, *The Navy in the War of 1739–48*, II, pp. 90–1. Also see Lewis, *The Navy of Britain*, p. 494; Corbett, *Signals and Instructions*, pp. 54–6; F. A. Chadwick, ed., *The Graves Papers* (New York, 1916), p. lxxiii; Tritten, 'Doctrine and Fleet Tactics', p. 11.

43 Creswell, *British Admirals*, pp. 8–9, 27–30.

44 Corbett, *Signals and Instructions*, p. 276.

45 W. H. Smyth, *The Sailor's Word-Book* (London, 1991), pp. 715, 726.

46 Bonner-Smith, *Barrington Papers*, I, p. 26.

47 Tunstall, *Naval Warfare in the Age of Sail*, p. 73.

48 Log of the *Queen Charlotte* 28 May–1 Jun 1794, Jackson, *Logs*, I, pp. 34–50. For earlier examples of similar instructions, see Howe Add. Ins. 8 Mar 1762, Henry Memo 12 Jul 1769, and Cumberland Add. Ins. 2 Aug 1769, Bonner-Smith, *Barrington Papers*, I, pp. 351, 398, 400.

49 For examples of this being used in action, see Log of the *Tremendous* 1 Jun 1794, Jackson, *Logs*, I, p. 87.

50 For examples of this being used in action, see *Molloy Trial*, p. 91; Nicholas Pocock's Notebook 1 Jun 1794 in Morriss, 'The Glorious First of June', p. 76.

51 Howe Add. Ins. 1777, Corbett, *Signals and Instructions*, pp. 113–14.

52 G. Berkely and J. Monkton to Howe 6 Jun 1794, Morriss, 'The Glorious First of June', pp. 97, 99 n. 3.

53 Lieut. J. Smith of the *Royal George* 3 Jun 1794, Jackson, *Logs*, I, p. 56. Unfortunately no detail is given as to the names of the British or the French ship. For similar examples of positional flexibility see Howe's Battle Order 11 Apr 1762, Bonner-Smith, *Barrington Papers*, I, p. 365, and Allen, *Memoir of Admiral Sir William Hargood*, p. 119.

54 Howe General Order of Battle 11 Apr 1762, Bonner-Smith, *Barrington Papers*, I, p. 365.

55 Hawke Add. Ins. 16 Jul 1759, Bonner-Smith, *Barrington Papers*, I, pp. 259–60.

56 Boscawen Add. Ins. 1759, Corbett, *Fighting Instructions*, p. 221.

57 Anson Add. Ins. 30 Aug 1758, Bonner-Smith, *Barrington Papers*, I, p. 232.

58 Vernon Order to Captains 16 Jul 1739, McRanft, *Vernon Papers*, pp. 290–1.

59 Vernon, Orders to Captains of Fireships 23 Feb 1740, and Orders to Captains of Bomb Ketches and Tenders 23 Feb 1740, McRanft, *Vernon Papers*, p. 295.

60 Dartmouth Ins. Oct 1688, Corbett, *Fighting Instructions*, p. 171.

61 See, for example, Holland, 'Development of Signalling', p. 23; Rodger, 'Image and Reality', pp. 288–90; Tunstall, *Naval Warfare in the Age of Sail*, pp. 8–9; Sulivan, 'Graves and Hood', p. 184.

62 Mahan, *Types of Naval Officers*, p. 35.

63 'Williams Trial', p. 69.

64 Hawke Ins. 27 Sep 1747, Mackay, *Hawke Papers*, pp. 40–2.

65 Holland, 'Development of Signalling', p. 5.

66 Quoted in W. G. Perrin, *British Flags* (Cambridge, 1922), p. 155.

67 Quoted in T. Wilson, *Flags at Sea* (London, 1986), p. 77.

68 Corbett, *Fighting Instructions*, p. 55; Anderson, *Allin Journals*, I, p. 244; Digby, *Journal of a Voyage*, pp. 5–6, 38.

69 Boteler, *Dialogues*, p. 344ff.

70 P. Le Fevre and R. Harding, eds., *Precursors of Nelson: British Admirals of the Eighteenth Century* (London, 2000), p. 15; Palmer, 'The Soul's Right Hand', pp. 684–90; Rodger, 'Image and Reality', p. 293.

71 *Knowles Trial*, pp. 80, 195.

72 Kempenfelt General Ins. 1781–2 and Rodney Landing Ins. 1761–2, Corbett, *Signals and Instructions*, pp. 140, 157.

73 J. L. Cranmer-Byng, ed., *Pattee Byng's Journal* (London, 1950), p. 23.

74 'The Charges Against Admiral Matthews', Richmond, *The Navy in the War of 1739–48*, II, p. 260.

75 Hamilton, *Byam Martin Papers*, II, p. 41.

76 Hamilton and Laughton, *Recollections of James Anthony Gardner*, p. 29.

77 Lever, *The Young Sea Officer's Sheet Anchor*, p. 94.

78 S. Morland, *Tuba Stentoro-Phonica: An Instrument of Excellent Use, as Well at Sea as at Land Etc. (a Short Discourse Touching*

the Nature of Sounds Etc.) (London, 1671); S. Morleand, 'An Account of the Speaking Trumpet as It Hath Been Contrived and Published by Sir Sam. Moreland Knight and Baronet; Together with Its Uses Both at Sea and Land', *Philosophical Transactions, 1665–1678*, 6 (1671), pp. 3056–8; P. M. Gouk, 'Acoustics in the Early Royal Society, 1660–1680', *Notes and Records of the Royal Society of London*, 36 (1982), pp. 155–75; Boudriot, *The Seventy-Four Gun Ship*, II, p. 124.

79 W. H. Webley Memo 21 May 1810, Jackson, *Logs*, II, p. 26.

80 Tunstall, *Naval Warfare in the Age of Sail*, p. 8; Rodger, 'Image and Reality', pp. 288–9; N. A. M. Rodger, 'The Exercise of Seapower and its Challenges in Maritime History', in *Maritime History*, II: *The Eighteenth Century and the Classic Age of Sail*, ed. J. B. Hattendorf (Malabar, FL, 1997), p. 180; A. Gordon, *The Rules of the Game: Jutland and British Naval Command* (London, 1996), p. 157.

81 A. T. Mahan, *The Life of Nelson: The Embodiment of the Sea Power of Great Britain*, 2 vols. (London, 1897), II, pp. 372–3; Logs of the *Euryalus, Phoebe* and *Sirius* 21 Oct 1805, Jackson, *Logs*, II, pp. 149, 307, 313.

82 Anon., *Short Account of the Naval Actions*, p. 51.

83 Quoted in M. Duffy, 'Samuel Hood, First Viscount Hood, 1724–1816', in *Precursors of Nelson*, ed. P. Le Fevre and R. Harding (London, 2000), p. 260.

84 Logs of *The Royal Sovereign, Culloden, Bellerophon, Valiant* and *Ramillies* 31 May 1794, and the *Russell* 11 Oct 1797, Jackson, *Logs*, I, pp. 61, 75, 92, 95, 140, 275.

85 Captain Miller to Mrs Miller (undated), Nicholas, *Dispatches and Letters of Lord Nelson*, VII, p. clvii.

86 Rodger, 'Image and Reality', p. 288.

87 For examples of warships launching their boats and towing them in battle, see Mitchell Trial 11 May 1748, TNA ADM 1/5290; Raleigh Ins. 1617, Corbett, *Fighting Instructions*, p. 43; *Brereton Trial*, appendix D, p. 61; *Knowles Trial*, p. 196; G. Williams, *The Prize of All the Oceans* (London, 1999), p. 35.

88 This role can be traced in the Instructions from the Commonwealth Orders of 1653 right up to Howe's Instructions of 1782. Corbett, *Fighting Instructions*, pp. 103, 248.

89 Blunt, *Theory and Practice of Seamanship*, p. 208; Steel, *Elements and Practice of Rigging*, II, p. 380.

90 W. E. May, *The Boats of Men of War* (London, 1974), pp. 10–11.

91 Anderson, *Allin Journals*, I, p. 188.

92 Harland, *Seamanship in the Age of Sail*, p. 283.

93 Hawke to Clevland 16 Nov & 18 Dec 1757, Mackay, *Hawke Papers*, pp. 187, 188; Mackay, *Admiral Hawke*, p. 141.

94 For a wonderful description of the difficulties of bringing a boat alongside a large warship in a rolling sea, see Hamilton, *Byam Martin Papers*, I, pp. 137–8. Also see Digby, *Journal of a Voyage*, p. 43.

95 Mackay, *Admiral Hawke*, p. 248. For another example of boats being launched in poor conditions, see A. Lindwall, 'The Encounter between Kempenfelt and De Guichen, December 1781', *MM*, 87 (2001), p. 167.

96 *Keppel Trial*, p. 378.

97 Anderson, *Allin Journals*, I, pp. 81, 279; Mitchell's Defence, p. 20, TNA ADM 1/5290; Hamilton and Laughton, *Recollections of James Anthony Gardner*, pp. 5, 159.

98 For examples of boats thus being used in action throughout the century, see Benbow's Deposition 8 Oct 1792, N. A. M. Rodger, ed., *The Naval Miscellany*, v (London, 1984), pp. 147–8; *Account of the Arraignments and Tryals of Col. R. Kirkby, Capt. J. Constable, Capt. Cooper Wade, Capt. S. Vincent, Capt. C. Fogg ... For Cowardice, Neglect of Duty ... Committed by Them in a Fight at Sea Commenced the 19th August, 1702* (London, 1757), p. 13; *Brereton Trial*, appendix D, p. 58; Log of the *Spartiate* 21 Oct 1805, Jackson, *Logs*, II, p. 250.

99 Bourchier, *Memoir of the Life of Admiral Sir Edward Codrington*, I, p. 14.

100 Tunstall, *Naval Warfare in the Age of Sail*, p. 8; Holland, 'Development of Signalling', pp. 20–1; Perrin, *British Flags*, p. 173.

101 Perrin, *British Flags*, p. 173.

102 See Chapter 3.

103 *Keppel Trial*, p. 231.

104 Jackson, *Logs*, II, p. 195; J. Brown to T. Windever 28 Dec 1805, Thursfield, *Five Naval Journals*, p. 364.

105 Digby, *Journal of a Voyage*, p. 5.

106 Howe Add. Ins. 8 Mar 1762, Bonner-Smith, *Barrington Papers*, I, pp. 326. Also see pp. 81, 125, 188, 221, 327.

107 Regular Add. Ins 1778, Corbett, *Signals and Instructions*, p. 191.

108 Arbuthnot Add. Ins. 19 Aug 1780, Corbett, *Signals and Instructions*, p. 147. For another

example of flags and sails used together, see Boscawen to Barrington 23 May 1755, Bonner-Smith, *Barrington Papers*, I, p. 125.

109 For examples of this approach, see Tunstall, *Naval Warfare in the Age of Sail*, pp. 8–9; Tracy, *Nelson's Battles*, pp. 49–51; Gordon, *Rules of the Game*, p. 188; Sulivan, 'Graves and Hood', p. 184; Spinney, *Rodney*, p. 321; Palmer, 'The Soul's Right Hand', pp. 681–2; Lewis, *The Navy of Britain*, pp. 480, 507.

CHAPTER 6: Unwritten Rules

1 Prince Rupert's 'A Brief relation of the Engagement of his Majesty's and the King of France's fleets under my command with the Dutch upon the 11th August 1673 near the Texel' (undated), Hattendorf *et al.*, *British Naval Documents*, p. 221.

2 Boteler, *Dialogues*, pp. 323, 335.

3 'Minutes Taken at a Court Martial Assembled on Board H.M.S. *Gladiator ... Regarding* H.M.S. *Leander*', *Naval Chronicle*, 18 (1807), pp. 170–1.

4 Deposition of Hugh Palliser, Lestock Trial, TNA ADM 1/5280.

5 Rodney's notes in his copy of Clerk's *Naval Tactics*, quoted in Douglas, *Naval Evolutions*, appendix 1, pp. ii–iii.

6 Douglas, *Naval Evolutions*, p. 62.

7 'Burrish Trial', p. 148. Also see Blunt, *Theory and Practice of Seamanship*, p. 211.

8 *Brereton Trial*, pp. 61, 67; *Keppel Trial*, p. 174.

9 *Brereton Trial*, pp. 61, 67.

10 Wareham, *Frigate Commander*, p. 94.

11 Anon., *Vindication of M-N*, p. 2.

12 Anon., *Vindication of M-N*, p. 2.

13 *Byng Trial*, pp. 171–2.

14 *Keppel Trial*, p. 180.

15 Rowley to Rodney 20 Apr 1780, TNA ADM1/311.

16 Mountaine, *Seaman's Vade-Mecum*, p. 232.

17 Fox Trial, Mackay, *Hawke Papers*, p. 79.

18 Fox Trial, TNA ADM1/5291.

19 Cochrane, *Autobiography of a Seaman*, p. 386.

20 *Byng Trial*, p. 178.

21 'Ambrose Trial', p. 11.

22 'Williams Trial', pp. 69–70.

23 'Lieutenant Nicholson's Relation of the Late Action' and 'Extract of a letter from an Officer on Board the *Windsor Castle*', in *Bell's Weekly Messenger*, 4 Aug 1805, pp. 3–4.

24 Blunt, *Theory and Practice of Seamanship*, p. 211.

25 Blunt, *Theory and Practice of Seamanship*, p. 211. For an example of this working in practice, see Journal of G. Pocock, entry for Sunday 30 Apr 1758, ADM 50/21.

26 My italics. C. Barnet to R. Lestock 15 Apr 1742, Laird Clowes, *Royal Navy*, III, p. 81. Also see Blunt, *Theory and Practice of Seamanship*, p. 211.

27 C. Barnet to R. Lestock 16 Apr 1742, Laird Clowes, *Royal Navy*, III, p. 81.

28 *Brereton Trial*, p. 25.

29 *Palliser Trial*, p. 57.

30 D. Pope, *The Great Gamble: Nelson at Copenhagen* (New York, 1972), pp. 370–417; Jackson, *Logs*, II, pp. 81–135; Nicholas, *Dispatches and Letters of Lord Nelson*, IV, pp. 299–309.

31 'Williams Trial', p. 68; Howe Add. Ins. 1782, Corbett, *Signals and Instructions*, p. 151; Lestock to J. Hodsell 14 Apr 1742, Laird Clowes, *Royal Navy*, III, p. 81.

32 Rodney to P. Stevens 26 Apr 1780, TNA ADM 1/311; Boscawen Add. Ins. 12 Aug 1755, Bonner-Smith, *Barrington Papers*, I, p. 132.

33 Howe Add. Ins. 1782, Corbett, *Signals and Instructions*, p. 177. Also see O'Bryen, *Essay on Naval Military Discipline*, p. 73; Pett Trial, TNA ADM 1/5282; *Keppel Trial*, p. 162.

34 *Knowles Trial*, p. 208.

35 Boteler, *Dialogues*, p. 382.

36 *Brereton Trial*, appendix D, p. 58.

37 *Palliser Trial*, p. 74.

38 *Molloy Trial*, p. 50.

39 Lewis, *Dillon Narrative*, i, p. 124.

40 D. A. Baugh, 'Sir Samuel Hood: Superior Subordinate', in *George Washington's Generals and Opponents*, ed. G. A. Billias (New York, 1994), p. 313; Spinney, *Rodney*, p. 399.

41 O'Bryen, *Essay on Naval Military Discipline*, p. 73.

42 Benbow to Nottingham 11 Sep 1702, Rodger, *Naval Miscellany*, v, p. 147.

43 Young to Middleton 31 Jul 1780, Laughton, *Barham Papers*, i, p. 71.

44 Creswell, *British Admirals*, p. 195.

45 Capt. Codrington to Lord Garlies 28 Oct 1805, Bourchier, *Memoir of the Life of Admiral Sir Edward Codrington*, i, p. 60.

46 Howe Add. Ins. 30 Jul 1778, Kempenfelt Add. Ins. 1781 and Rodney Add. Ins. 1781, Corbett, *Signals and Instructions*, pp. 95, 153, 284; White, *Naval Researches*, p. 42.

47 Rodney to Adm. Sec. 28 Apr 1780, TNA ADM 1/311.

48 *Molloy Trial*, p. 22.

49 Mahan, *Types of Naval Officers*, p. 18; Richmond, *The Navy in the War of 1739–48*, i, p. 253.

50 P. A. Luff, 'Matthews v Lestock: Parliament, Politics and the Navy in Mid-Eighteenth Century England', *Parliamentary History*, 10 (1991), pp. 51–4.

51 Sandwich speech in the House of Lords quoted in Rodger, *Insatiable Earl*, p. 246.

52 Richmond, *The Navy in the War of 1739–48*, ii, p. 271; D. A. Baugh, ' "Too Much Mixed in This Affair": The Impact of Ministerial Politics in the Eighteenth Century Royal Navy', in *New Interpretations in Naval History*, ed. R. C. Balano and C. L. Symonds (Annapolis, 1999), p. 23.

53 R. Lestock to C. Barnet 16 Apr 1742, quoted in Laird Clowes, *Royal Navy*, iii, pp. 81–2.

54 'Burrish Trial', pp. 95, 99, 144.

55 'Burrish Trial', p. 147.

56 'Burrish Trial', p. 14.

57 'Ambrose Trial', p. 91.

58 'Ambrose Trial', p. 109.

59 'Ambrose Trial', p. 187.

60 'Ambrose Trial', p. 187.

61 'Ambrose Trial', p. 195.

62 Testimony of Captain Powlett, Lestock Trial, TNA ADM 1/5280.

63 Deposition of Robert Harland, Pett Trial, TNA ADM 1/5282.

64 Pett Trial, TNA ADM 1/5282.

65 Testimony of Duncan Grant Master of the *Somerset*, Sclater Trial, TNA ADM 1/5282.

66 Richmond, *The Navy in the War of 1739–48*, ii, p. 35; i, p. 254.

67 Hamilton, *Byam Martin Papers*, i, p. 192.

68 J. Clerk, *An Essay on Naval Tactics, Systematical and Historical with Explanatory Plates in Four Parts*, 2nd edn (Edinburgh, 1804), p. 117. Also see Baugh, 'Too Much Mixed in This Affair', pp. 30–1; Rodger, *Insatiable Earl*, p. 30; J. Horsfield, *The Art of Leadership in War: The Royal Navy from the Age of Nelson to the End of World War II* (London, 1980), p. 30; Lewis, *The Navy of Britain*, pp. 500, 532; D. Hannay, *A Short History of the Royal Navy, 1217–1815*, 2 vols. (London, 1909), ii, p. 117; D. Hannay, ed., *Letters of Lord Hood, 1781–2* (London, 1895), p. xxxix.

69 Creswell, *British Admirals*, p. 79. Also see Tritten, 'Doctrine and Fleet Tactics', pp. 6–7; Tunstall, *Naval Warfare in the Age of Sail*, p. 91.

70 Baugh, 'Too Much Mixed in This Affair', p. 30.

71 Baugh, 'Too Much Mixed in This Affair', p. 31.

72 See, for example, Baugh, 'Too Much Mixed in This Affair', p. 30; Tunstall, *Naval Warfare in the Age of Sail*, p. 110; Laird Clowes, *Royal Navy*, iii, p. 160; Mahan, *Types of Naval Officers*, pp. 17–20.

73 Mahan, *Influence of Seapower*, pp. 286–7.

74 Matthews Trial, TNA ADM 1/5289.

75 H. W. Richmond, ed., *Papers Relating to the Loss of Minorca* (London, 1915), p. xx.

76 J. Byng to J. Clevland 25 May 1756, TNA ADM 1/383; *Byng Trial*, pp. 224, 280, 283.

77 McRanft, *Vernon Papers*, pp. 290–1, 295, 297.

78 Sea-Officer, *Enquiry into the Conduct of Capt. M-N*, p. 22.

79 *Byng Trial*, p. 178.

80 *Byng Trial*, pp. 171–2.

81 Corbett, *Signals and Instructions*, p. 274.

82 *Keppel Trial*, pp. 131–2.

83 Richmond, *The Navy in the War of 1739–48*, III, p. 261; *Knowles Trial*, p. 195.

84 Quoted in White, *Naval Researches*, p. 108.

85 Quoted in P. K. Crimmin, 'Anson: Cape Finisterre, 1747', in *Great Battles of the Royal Navy as Commemorated in the Gun Room, Britannia Naval College, Dartmouth*, ed. E. Grove (London, 1998), p. 77.

86 Hamilton, *Byam Martin Papers*, I, p. 189. Also see Wareham, *Frigate Commander*, p. 181.

87 Richmond, *The Navy in the War of 1739–48*, II, p. 23.

88 *Keppel Trial*, p. 281.

89 Duncan to Spencer 15 Oct 1797, J. S. Corbett, ed., *Private Papers of George, Second Earl Spencer, First Lord of the Admiralty, 1794–1801*, 4 vols. (London, 1913–24), II, p. 197.

90 D. Syrett, 'Count-Down to the Saints: A Strategy of Detachments and the Quest for Naval Supremacy in the West Indies, 1780–2', *MM*, 87 (2001), p. 152.

91 Richmond, *The Navy in the War of 1739–48*, I, p. 198.

92 Lumsdaine Trial, Hamilton, *Byam Martin Papers*, I, appendix B, pp. 179–90, 351–2.

93 W. Maltby, 'Politics, Professionalism and the Evolution of Sailing Ship Tactics, 1650–1714', in *Tools of War*, ed. J. A. Lynn (Urbana, Illinois, 1990), p. 62. Also see R. F. Weigley, *The Age of Battles: The Quest for Decisive Warfare from Breitenfeld to Waterloo* (Bloomington, 1991), pp. 126–7.

94 *Keppel Trial*, p. 341; Nelson to Lord Spencer 6 Nov 1799, Nicholas, *Dispatches and Letters of Lord Nelson*, IV, p. 90.

CHAPTER 7 : Command

1 S. Graves to Sandwich 2 Dec 1775, Barnes and Owen, *Sandwich Papers*, I, p. 80.

2 Anon., 'French Naval Tactics', p. 147.

3 Palmer, 'Lord Nelson, Master of Command', pp. 107–8; Palmer, 'Burke and Nelson', p. 59; Palmer, 'The Soul's Right Hand', pp. 680–1; Rodger, 'Image and Reality', pp. 292–4; Gordon, *Rules of the Game*, pp. 157–8; Richmond, *The Navy in the War of 1739–48*, III, pp. 252–3; Lewis, *The Navy of Britain*, p. 352; D. W. Knox, 'The Role of Doctrine in Naval Warfare', *United States Naval Institute Proceedings*, 41 (1915), pp. 328–9; Mahan, *Life of Nelson*, I, pp. 452–3.

4 Hamilton, *Byam Martin Papers*, I, p. 193.

5 See, for example, Bourchier, *Memoir of the Life of Admiral Sir Edward Codrington*, I, p. 38.

6 D. A. Jagoe, 'United States Military Doctrine and Professional Military Education', in *Doctrine and Military Effectiveness*, ed. M. Duffy, T. Farrell and G. Sloan (Exeter, 1997), p. 33.

7 Palmer, 'The Soul's Right Hand', p. 703; Tritten, 'Doctrine and Fleet Tactics', p. 17; Rodger, 'Image and Reality', p. 293.

8 Corbett, *Fighting Instructions*, p. 177.

9 Creswell, *British Admirals*, p. 243.

10 Narratives of Admiral Burke quoted in Palmer, 'Burke and Nelson', p. 59.

11 E. Yorke to J. Yorke 5 Jun 1747, quoted in Rodger, 'George, Lord Anson', p. 183.

12 E. Berry 'An Authentic Narrative' 1798, Nicholas, *Dispatches and Letters of Lord Nelson*, III, p. 49.

13 Bourchier, *Memoir of the Life of Admiral Sir Edward Codrington*, I, p. 59.

14 A Sea Officer, *A Narrative of the Proceedings of His Majesty's Fleet in the Mediterranean, and the Combined Fleets of France and Spain, from the Year 1741 to March 1744. Including an Accurate Account of the Late Fight near Toulon, and the Causes of Our Miscarriage* (London, 1744), pp. 83–4. Although anonymous, this pamphlet is generally accepted as being written or inspired by Richard Lestock. Hattendorf *et al.*, *British Naval Documents*, p. 370.

15 Richmond, *The Navy in the War of 1739–48*, I, p. 197.

16 Rodger, *Insatiable Earl*, p. 240.

17 Lewis, *Dillon Narrative*, I, p. 93 n. 3.

18 Kempenfelt to Middleton 6 Apr 1780, Laughton, *Barham Papers*, I, p. 322.

19 Corbett, *Signals and Instructions*, pp. 53–6.

20 Tritten, 'Doctrine and Fleet Tactics', p. 11.

21 Creswell, *British Admirals*, p. 154.

22 Breen, 'Graves and Hood at the
    Chesapeake', *MM*, 66 (1980),p. 63; Corbett,
    Signals and Instructions, p. 56.

23 See Chapter 6.

24 Nelson to W. Locker 1 Dec 1793, Nicholas,
    Dispatches and Letters of Lord Nelson, 1,
    p. 339.

25 Hood to Middleton 3 Apr 1782, Laughton,
    Barham Papers, 1, pp. 156–7.

26 Spinney, *Rodney*, p. 332; Laughton,*Barham
    Papers*, 1, p. 1.

27 Rodger, 'Image and Reality', p. 294.

28 Rodger, 'Image and Reality', p. 291.

29 Rodger, *Insatiable Earl*, pp. 31–3; N. A. M.
    Rodger, 'Honour and Duty at Sea', *Historical
    Research*, 75 (2002), pp. 430–1, 444–5.

30 Lewis, *Dillon Narrative*, 1, p. 150; Cochrane,
    Autobiography of a Seaman, p. 148.

31 Hamilton, *Byam Martin Papers*, 1, p. 66.

32 Lewis, *Dillon Narrative*, 1, pp. 150–2;
    H. Owen, 'Cuthbert, Lord Collingwood',
    in *British Admirals of the Napoleonic Wars*,
    ed. P. Le Fevre and R. Harding (London,
    2005), p. 147.

33 Rodger, *The Wooden World*, pp. 205–7;
    N. A. M. Rodger, 'The Inner Life of the
    Royal Navy, 1750–1800: Change or Decay?',
    in *Les Empires en guerre et paix, 1793–1860*,
    ed. E. Freeman (Vincennes, 1990), p. 171.

34 I am grateful to Professor Nicholas Rodger
    for bringing this idea to my attention.

35 O'Brien, 'Essay on the Duty of a Captain',
    The Naval Chronicle, 5 (1801), pp. 213–20.

36 P. Nichols, *Evolution's Captain* (London,
    2004), p. 145.

37 Journal of P. Cullen, Thursfield, *Five Naval
    Journals*, p. 105.

38 Taylor, 'Admiral the Honourable Sir George
    Elliot', p. 317.

39 Pasley, *Private Sea Journals*, p. 243. Also see
    Corbett, *Signals and Instructions*, p. 354.

40 Richmond, *The Navy in the War of 1739–48*,
    1, p. 197.

41 Creswell, *British Admirals*, p. 142.

42 Rodger, 'The Exercise of Seapower', p. 180.

43 Creswell, *British Admirals*, pp. 66–7.

44 Bourchier, *Memoir of the Life of Admiral
    Sir Edward Codrington*, 1, p. 27.

45 Pasley, *Private Sea Journals*, p. 62.

46 Creswell, *British Admirals*, p. 69.

47 Young to Middleton 24 Jul 1780, Laughton,
    Barham Papers, 1, pp. 65–6.

48 'Ambrose Trial', p. 34.

49 Deposition of T. Mollams, Boatswain of hms
    Defiance, 15 Sep 1702, TNA adm 1/5263,
    f. 66; *Kirkby (et al.) Trials*, pp. 9–15.

50 Castex, *Idées militaires de la marine*, p. 63.

51 *Molloy Trial*, pp. 115–16.

52 Howe Ins. 1793, Corbett, *Signals and
    Instructions*, p. 337.

53 Howe Add. Ins. 1790, Corbett, *Signals and
    Instructions*, p. 319.

54 Gen. Ins. 1781–3, Corbett, *Signals and
    Instructions*, p. 276.

55 Gen. Ins. 1781–3, Corbett, *Signals and
    Instructions*, p. 276.

56 Howe Add. Ins. 1777, Corbett, *Signals and
    Instructions*, p. 114.

57 See, for example, Robison, *History of Naval
    Tactics*, p. 274. The instructions Robison
    refers to are printed in full in Corbett,
    Signals and Instructions, p. 114.

58 Corbett, *Signals and Instructions*, p. 104.

59 See, for example, Palmer, 'The Soul's Right
    Hand', pp. 690, 695.

60 Kempenfelt to Middleton 18 Jan 1780,
    Hodges, *Select Naval Documents*, p. 162.
    For a similar view from Howe, see Corbett,
    Fighting Instructions, p. 240.

61 McRanft, *Vernon Papers*, pp. 301, 308, 413.

62 Rodger, 'George, Lord Anson', p. 186.

63 Rodger, *Insatiable Earl*, pp. 30–5, 60–2.

64 Rodger, 'Honour and Duty at Sea',
    pp. 441–76.

65 Duffy and Morriss, *The Glorious First of
    June*, pp. 68–9; M. Duffy, ' "… All Was
    Hushed up": The Hidden Trafalgar', *MM*, 91
    (2005), pp. 217, 236.

66 See, for example, Horsfield, *Art of
    Leadership in War*, p. 43.

67 Hamilton, *Byam Martin Papers*, 1, p. 74.

68 Hood to Middleton 16 Apr 1782, Laughton,
    Barham Papers, 1, p. 164.

69 Rodger, *The Wooden World*, p. 299; Rodger,
    Insatiable Earl, p. 33.

70 Rodney to Carkett 30 Jul 1780, G. B. Mundy,
    ed., *The Life and Correspondence of Lord
    Rodney* (London, 1830), p. 354.

71 Rodney to Sandwich 31 May 1780, Spinney,
    Rodney, p. 330.

72 Rodney to Hood 5 Feb 1781, Spinney, *Rodney*, p. 358.

73 Bourchier, *Memoir of the Life of Admiral Sir Edward Codrington*, I, p. 27; Horsfield, *Art of Leadership in War*, p. 40.

74 Corbett, *Fighting Instructions*, pp. 335–42; Palmer, 'The Soul's Right Hand', p. 703; D. W. Knox, 'The Great Lesson from Nelson for Today', *United States Naval Institute Proceedings*, 40 (1914), p. 317.

75 Tritten, 'Doctrine and Fleet Tactics', p. 32.

76 Young to Middleton 22 Sep 1780, Laughton, *Barham Papers*, I, p. 76.

77 K. Breen, 'George Bridges, Lord Rodney, 1718?–1792', in *Precursors of Nelson*, ed. P. Le Fevre and R. Harding (London, 2000), p. 236.

78 J. Sweetman, ed., *The Great Admirals: Command at Sea, 1587–1945* (Annapolis, 1997), p. 146.

79 Quoted in Gordon, *Rules of the Game*, p. 183.

80 The same can be said for the Battle of St Vincent, fought by the combined Channel and Mediterranean squadrons.

CHAPTER 8: The Weather Gage

1 Douglas, *Naval Evolutions*, p. 58.

2 Anon., *Vindication of M-N*, p. 12.

3 Mahan, *Types of Naval Officers*, p. 15; Mahan, *Influence of Seapower*, p. 6; Creswell, *British Admirals*, p. 45; B. Lavery, *Nelson's Navy: The Ships, Men and Organisation, 1793–1815* (Annapolis, 1989), p. 255; Gardiner, *Line of Battle*, p. 186; Tunstall, *Naval Warfare in the Age of Sail*, p. 61; Tracy, *Nelson's Battles*, p. 58; Maltby, 'Politics, Professionalism and the Evolution of Sailing Ship Tactics', p. 57; Schomberg, *Sea Manual*, pp. 109–10; S. F. Bigot de Morogues, *Tactique navale* (Paris, 1763), translated in Steel, *Elements and Practice of Rigging*, II, p. 386. Also see Blunt, *Theory and Practice of Seamanship*, p. 223.

4 Anon., 'Studies in the Theory of Naval Tactics I', *Naval Review*, I/1 (1913), p. 37.

5 Willis, 'Windward Performance', pp. 29–39.

6 Willis, 'Windward Performance', pp. 29–39.

7 Steel, *Elements and Practice of Rigging*, II, p. 383.

8 Laird Clowes, *Royal Navy*, III, p. 525.

9 Goussencourt, 'Journal', p. 119.

10 Hood to Middleton 13 Apr 1782, Laughton, *Barham Papers*, I, p. 160.

11 Vernon to the Duke of Bedford 28 Aug 1745, McRanft, *Vernon Papers*, p. 454.

12 Creswell, *British Admirals*, p. 54.

13 Rodney to P. Stephens 31 May 1780, TNA ADM 1/311.

14 Byng to J. Cleveland 25 May 1756, TNA ADM 1/383; Byron to Middleton 8 Jul 1779, D. Bonner-Smith, 'Byron in the Leeward Islands, 1779: Part II', *MM*, 30 (1944),

pp. 88–9; Tunstall, *Naval Warfare in the Age of Sail*, pp. 86, 109, 163.

15 Kempenfelt to Middleton 5 Sep 1779, Hodges, *Select Naval Documents*, p. 160; *Byng Trial*, p. 224; Kempenfelt to Middleton 5 Sep 1779, Laughton, *Barham Papers*, I, p. 296.

16 Knowles, *Observations on Naval Tactics*, p. 17.

17 Hutchinson, *Treatise on Practical Seamanship*, pp. 214, 220.

18 Hoste, *Treatise on Naval Evolutions*, p. 27; Tracy, *Nelson's Battles*, p. 58; Tunstall, *Naval Warfare in the Age of Sail*, p. 61; Depeyre, *Tactiques et stratégies*, p. 60; Maltby, 'Politics, Professionalism and the Evolution of Sailing Ship Tactics', p. 60.

19 J. Clerk, *An Essay on Naval Tactics, Systematical and Historical*, 3rd edn (Edinburgh, 1827), p. 39; Depeyre, *Tactiques et stratégies*, p. 90; A. D. Lambert, *War at Sea in the Age of Sail* (London, 2000), p. 41; Spinney, *Rodney*, p. 307.

20 Tunstall, *Naval Warfare in the Age of Sail*, p. 61; Tracy, *Nelson's Battles*, p. 58.

21 Sea-Officer, *Enquiry into the Conduct of Capt. M-N*, pp. 3–4. Despite Vernon's detailed attack, he fails to consider situations such as chase in which the reduction of canvas was not an option.

22 Creswell, *British Admirals*, p. 111; R. Mackay, 'Edward, Lord Hawke, 1705–1781', in *Precursors of Nelson*, ed. P. Le Fevre and R. Harding (London, 2000), p. 219. For other references to reducing heel in action,

see Boteler, *Dialogues*, pp. 360–1; Park, *Defensive War by Sea*, p. 165.

23 W. Young to Middleton 3 Jun 1780, Laughton, *Barham Papers*, I, p. 57.

24 Steel, *Elements and Practice of Rigging*, II, p. 380.

25 Mostyn to Adm. Sec. 28 Aug 1744 and 25 Jan 1745, TNA ADM I/2100.

26 Laughton, *Barham Papers*, I, p. 274.

27 W. Bertram, 'Investigating a Nineteenth Century Ship Design', paper presented at the New Researchers in Maritime History Conference, Royal Naval Museum, Portsmouth, 1995, pp. 6–8; Lavery, *The Ship of the Line*, I, p. 102.

28 Lavery, *The Ship of the Line*, i, p. 122.

29 Harland, *Seamanship in the Age of Sail*, p. 223.

30 'Burrish Trial', p. 125.

31 E. Jekyll to J. Cleveland 3 Apr 1761, TNA ADM I/1985; S. Colby to J. Cleveland 3 Apr 1759, TNA ADM I/1607; S. Mostyn to T. Corbett 23 Jan 1744, TNA ADM I/2100.

32 T. Brodrick to J. Clevland 22 Apr 1758, TNA ADM I/384.

33 For an example of this being done in practice, see 'Burrish Trial', p. 93.

34 'Burrish Trial', p. 103.

35 Douglas, *Naval Evolutions*, p. 72.

36 Douglas, *Naval Gunnery*, p. 236; Douglas, *Naval Evolutions*, p. 72.

37 'Ambrose Trial', p. 155.

38 Douglas, *Naval Gunnery*, p. 239.

39 Report [undated] of Captain Majendie, E. Desbrière, *The Naval Campaign of 1805: Trafalgar*, trans. C. Eastwick, 2 vols. (Oxford, 1933), II, p. 194; T. Contamine to Min. of Marine 20 Nov 1805, Desbrière, *Naval Campaign of 1805*, p. 145.

40 Douglas, *Naval Gunnery*, p. 245.

41 'Burrish Trial', p. 120; 'Ambrose Trial', p. 115; Deposition of Robert Harland, Pett Trial, TNA ADM I/5282.

42 Mostyn to T. Corbett 23 Jan 1745, TNA ADMI/2100.

43 Sea-Officer, *An Enquiry into the Conduct of Capt. M-N*, p. 17. Also see Douglas, *Naval Evolutions*, p. 72.

44 Anon., *Vindication of M-N*, p. 8.

45 'Ambrose Trial', p. 144.

46 Sea-Officer, *Enquiry into the Conduct of Capt. M-N*, p. 15. Also see Blunt, *Theory and Practice of Seamanship*, p. 209.

47 Douglas to Middleton 28 Apr 1782, Laughton, *Barham Papers*, I, p. 280.

48 Nelson to the Duke of Clarence 15 Jul 1795, Nicholas, *Dispatches and Letters of Lord Nelson*, II, p. 52.

49 Anon., *Short Account of the Naval Actions*, p. 63; Lewis, *Dillon Narrative*, I, p. 134.

50 For an example of this happening in practice, see Hawke to Corbett 17 Oct 1747, Mackay, *Hawke Papers*, p. 51.

51 *Molloy Trial*, p. 172; Villeneuve to Min. of Marine 27 Jul 1805, in *Bell's Weekly Messenger*, 25 Aug 1805.

52 *Keppel Trial*, p. 371.

53 W. Parker to his father 17 Jun 1794, Morriss, 'The Glorious First of June', p. 87.

54 *Molloy Trial*, p. 8.

55 Laird Clowes, *Royal Navy*, v, pp. 189–91. For other examples of friendly fire, see Jackson, *Logs*, I, pp. 73, 113, 130.

56 Douglas, *Naval Gunnery*, p. 219.

57 Allen, *Memoir of Admiral Sir William Hargood*, p. 139.

58 G. L. Craik, *The Pictorial History of England*, ed. C. Knight, VI (London, 1856), p. 291.

59 Mackay, *Admiral Hawke*, p. 214; Mackay, *Hawke Papers*, p. 242.

60 J. R. de Grenier, *L'Art de la guerre sur mer* (Paris, 1787), translated in Steel, *Elements and Practice of Rigging*, II, p. 410.

61 Fraser, *The Enemy at Trafalgar*, p. 270.

62 Douglas, *Naval Evolutions*, p. 64.

63 Boteler, *Dialogues*, pp. 360–1; S. Colby to J. Clevland 3 Apr 1759, TNA ADM I/1607, and see Chapter I.

64 Quoted in White, *Naval Researches*, p. 84.

65 Douglas, *Naval Evolutions*, p. 57.

66 D. Pope, *At 12 Mr Byng Was Shot* (London, 1962), pp. 120–1.

67 Clerk, *Naval Tactics*, p. 20.

68 Clerk, *Naval Tactics*, p. 43.

69 Grenier, *L'Art de la guerre sur mer*, translated in Steel, *Elements and Practice of Rigging*, II, p. 410.

70 Captain Miller to Mrs Miller (undated), Nicholas, *Dispatches and Letters of Lord Nelson*, VII, pp. cliv–clx.

71 Memo of a conversation between Nelson and Sir Richard Keats, Nicholas, *Dispatches and Letters of Lord Nelson*, VII, p. 241 n. 9.

72 *Keppel Trial*, p. 174.

73 'Transactions on board His Majesty's Ship *Agamemnon*, and of the fleet as seen and known by Captain Nelson 8–14 Mar 1795', Nicholas, *Dispatches and Letters of Lord Nelson*, II, p. 13.

74 See Chapter 5.

75 Log of the *Mermaid* 8 Aug 1796, TNA ADM 51/1169.

76 White, *Nelson's Year of Destiny*, pp. 49–50.

77 Douglas, *Naval Evolutions*, p. 58.

78 Goussencourt, 'Journal', pp. x, 119.

79 Park, *Defensive War by Sea*, p. 162.

80 Nelson plan of attack 1803, Corbett, *Fighting Instructions*, p. 314.

81 Corbett, *Fighting Instructions*, p. 314.

82 Blunt, *Theory and Practice of Seamanship*, p. 209.

CHAPTER 9: Fleet Tactics

1 Park, *Defensive War by Sea*, p. 73.

2 Corbett, *Signals and Instructions*, p. 85.

3 Corbett, *Fighting Instructions*, p. 314. Also see Villeneuve's Account of the Action with Sir Robert Calder, *Naval Chronicle*, 14 (1805), p. 170.

4 *Keppel Trial*, p. 233; W. Parker to his father 7 Jun 1794, NMM PAR/193, in Duffy and Morriss, *The Glorious First of June*, p. 85; The Journal of Henry Duncan, Laughton, *Naval Miscellany*, I, p. 162.

5 E. Jekyll to Adm. Sec. 3 Apr 1761, TNA ADM 1/1985; Anderson, *Allin Journals*, I, p. 193.

6 Journal of W. Cumby, Thursfield, *Five Naval Journals*, p. 348.

7 Shovell to Nottingham 18 Jul 1702, PRO SP 42/67, f. 28, quoted in J. B. Hattendorf, 'Sir George Rooke and Sir Cloudesley Shovell, c1650–1709 and 1650–1707', in *Precursors of Nelson*, ed. P. le Fevre and R. Harding (London, 2000), p. 64.

8 'Afsnijding en separatie van schepen', Weber, 'Introduction of the Single Line Ahead', p. 7. The principles can also be seen in the Duke of York's instructions of 1672, Corbett, *Fighting Instructions*, p. 149.

9 See Corbett, *Fighting Instructions*, p. 192; Sweetman, *Great Admirals*, pp. 138–41.

10 Corbett, *Signals and Instructions*, p. 122.

11 Corbett, *Signals and Instructions*, p. 14. For a similar contemporary view, see Wareham, *Frigate Commander*, pp. 74–5.

12 Barnes and Owen, *Sandwich Papers*, III, pp. 158–60; Tunstall, *Naval Warfare in the Age of Sail*, pp. 165–7; Creswell, *British Admirals*, pp. 143–51; Tracy, *Nelson's Battles*, p. 79.

13 Tunstall, *Naval Warfare in the Age of Sail*, p. 173.

14 These were Malaga (1704), Toulon (1744), Minorca (1756), Cuddalore (1758), Negapatam (1758), Pondicherry (1759), Ushant (1778), Grenada (1779), Martinique (1780), Cape Henry (1781), Martinique (1781), Chesapeake (1781), Sadras (1782).

15 The Glorious First of June (1794), Cape St Vincent (1797), Camperdown (1797), The Nile (1798), Trafalgar (1805).

16 Douglas, *Naval Evolutions*, p. 63.

17 J. S. Corbett, *England in the Mediterranean: A Study of the Rise and Influence of British Power within the Straits, 1603–1713*, 2 vols. (London, 1904), II, pp. 268–70; Corbett, *Fighting Instructions*, p. 153 n. 1; Corbett, *Signals and Instructions*, pp. 29–31, 373.

18 Castex, *Idées militaires de la marine*, p. 43.

19 Lewis, *Dillon Narrative*, I, p. 140; Cochrane, *Autobiography of a Seaman*, p. 89.

20 Corbett, *Fighting Instructions*, pp. 153, 175–87; Creswell, *British Admirals*, p. 42.

21 J. Jervis to G. Jackson 31 Jul 1778, BL Add. MS 9344, f. 36, quoted in Rodger, *Insatiable Earl*, p. 239.

22 Creswell, *British Admirals*, p. 195.

23 Kempenfelt to Middleton 18 Jan 1780, Hodges, *Select Naval Documents*, p. 162.

24 Hughes, *Collingwood Correspondence*, p. 130. For other contemporary views, see Douglas, *Naval Evolutions*, p. 68.n. 1.

25 Kempenfelt to Middleton 27 Jul 1779, Laughton, *Barham Papers*, I, p. 292. Also see Kempenfelt to Middleton 5 Sep 1779, Hodges, *Select Naval Documents*, p. 160, and Boteler, *Dialogues*, p. 308. These

arguments directly refute Boudriot's claim that 'Whatever talents of the commander, no squadron can attack another with any chance of success unless it is superior or equal in numbers': Boudriot, *The Seventy-Four Gun Ship*, IV, p. 277.

26 Hood to Jackson 16 Sep 1781, Hodges, *Select Naval Documents*, p. 175. For a similar example see *Griffin Trial*, p. 26. Debate over the reasons for failure can be followed in Breen, 'Graves and Hood at the Chesapeake', pp. 53–65; Sulivan, 'Graves and Hood', pp. 175–94.

27 Collingwood General Order 23 Mar 1808, quoted in Tunstall, *Naval Warfare in the Age of Sail*, p. 262; Cochrane, *Autobiography of a Seaman*, p. 88; Corbett, *Signals and Instructions*, p. 9; Robison, *History of Naval Tactics*, p. 259.

28 *Keppel Trial*, p. 227.

29 *Keppel Trial*, p. 217. For similar examples, see Testimony of Edward Jekyll, Lestock Trial, TNA ADM 1/5280; J. Byng to J. Clevland 25 May 1756, Laird Clowes, *Royal Navy*, III, p. 153.

30 Byng to Adm. Sec. 25 May 1756, TNA ADM 1/383.

31 Steel, *Elements and Practice of Rigging*, II, p. 347.

32 Weber, 'Introduction of the Single Line Ahead', p. 11.

33 Rodney's notes in his copy of Clerk's *Naval Tactics*, quoted in Douglas, *Naval Evolutions*, appendix 1, pp. ii–iii.

34 White, *Naval Researches*, p. 79.

35 Nelson, 'Plan of attack' 1803, Corbett, *Fighting Instructions*, p. 315.

36 Memo of a conversation between Nelson and Sir Richard Keats, Nicholas, *Dispatches and Letters of Lord Nelson*, VII, p. 241n. 9.

37 M. Czisnik, 'Admiral Nelson's Tactics at the Battle of Trafalgar', *Journal of the Historical Association*, 89 (2004), pp. 557–8. Also see Schomberg, *Sea Manual*, p. 109; Hutchinson, *Treatise on Practical Seamanship*, pp. 190, 214.

38 Knowles, *Observations on Naval Tactics*, p. 16.

39 Kempenfelt to Middleton 18 Jan 1780, Hodges, *Select Naval Documents*, p. 163.

40 Anon., 'French Naval Tactics', p. 146.

CHAPTER 10: Fighting Tactics

1 Kempenfelt to Middleton 28 Apr 1779, Hodges, *Select Naval Documents*, p. 159.

2 C. Middleton Order Book 1 Aug 1775, Laughton, *Barham Papers*, I, p. 44.

3 'Burrish Trial', p. 98.

4 For good examples, see Laird Clowes, *Royal Navy*, III, pp. 110–11; IV, p. 251; G. J. Marcus, *Quiberon Bay* (London, 1960), p. 152; Creswell, *British Admirals*, p. 151.

5 For a few choice examples, see Boteler, *Dialogues*, p. 357; Benbow to Nottingham 11 Sep 1702, Rodger, *Naval Miscellany*, V, p. 155; Vernon Orders to Captains of Bomb Ketches 23 Feb 1740, McRanft, *Vernon Papers*, p. 297; Frankland to T. Corbett 12 Aug 1742, TNA ADM 1/178; Capt. Hood to Viscount Hood 10 Aug 1798, Jackson, *Logs*, II, p. 24; Journal of Capt. F. Geary, in Admiral Medley's Correspondence No. 2, TNA ADM 1/382; O'Brien, 'Essay on the Duty of a Captain', p. 220; Laird Clowes, *Royal Navy*, IV, pp. 530–1.

6 Knowles to T. Corbett 6 Jan 1744, Hodges, *Select Naval Documents*, p. 122.

7 *Byng Trial*, p. 210.

8 Arbuthnot Add. Ins. 1781, Corbett, *Signals and Instructions*, p. 251.

9 J. MacBride to Navy Board 12 Jan 1781, Hattendorf *et al.*, *British Naval Documents*, p. 499. For more examples, see J. Newman to Kingsmill 19 Oct 1798, *Naval Chronicle*, 3 (1800), pp. 43–5; R. Bevan Narrative (undated), W. G. Perrin, ed., *The Naval Miscellany*, III (London, 1928), p. 163.

10 Kempenfelt to Middleton 28 Apr 1779, Hodges, *Select Naval Documents*, p. 159.

11 Benbow to Nottingham 24 Aug 1702, Rodger, *Naval Miscellany*, V, p. 165; Park, *Defensive War by Sea*, p. 151; Log of the *Kent* 8 Apr 1740, TNA ADM 51/4231.

12 Boudriot, *The Seventy-Four Gun Ship*, IV, p. 135.

13 Pasley, *Private Sea Journals*, p. 145.

14 *Keppel Trial*, p. 365.

15 A choice few are: Barrow, *Life of Lord Anson*, p. 252; Pocock to J. Clevland 22 Jul 1758, TNA ADM 1/161; S. Colby to J. Clevland 3 Apr 1759, TNA ADM 1/1607; A. Keppel to Sandwich 29 Jul 1778 in Rodger, *Insatiable Earl*, p. 245; Morriss, 'The Glorious First of June', p. 56 n. 12; Nelson to Locker 8 Jul 1795, Nicholas, *Dispatches and Letters of Lord Nelson*, II, p. 51.

16 Kempenfelt to Lord Colvill 23 Jul 1758, TNA ADM 1/2010; Pocock to J. Clevland 22 Aug 1758, TNA ADM 1/161.

17 Nelson to Locker 8 Jul 1795, Nicholas, *Dispatches and Letters of Lord Nelson*, II, p. 51.

18 'An Account of the Damages sustained … in an engagement with the French, off Tranquebar', 10 Sep 1759, TNA ADM 1/161.

19 *Keppel Trial*, p. 331; *Palliser Trial*, p. 69.

20 Log of the *Royal George* 29 May 1794, Jackson, *Logs*, I, p. 52.

21 Miller to Mrs Miller (undated), Nicholas, *Dispatches and Letters of Lord Nelson*, VII, p. clviii.

22 Anon., 'Letter to the Editor', *Gentleman's Magazine* (1744), p. 97.

23 Anon., 'French Naval Tactics', p. 147.

24 Laird Clowes, *Royal Navy*, IV, p. 514.

25 Rodger, *Command of the Ocean*, p. 414; N. A. M. Rodger, 'Form and Function in European Navies, 1660–1815', in *In het kielzog: Maritiem-historische studies aangeboden aan Jaap R. Bruijn bij zijn vertrek als hoogleraar zeergeschiedenis aan de Universiteit Leiden*, ed. L. Akveld *et al.* (Amsterdam, 2003), pp. 85–97; A. M. Gicquel des Touches, 'Souvenirs d'un marin de la République', *Revue des Deux Mondes*, 28 (1805), p. 424.

26 N. A. M. Rodger, ed., *Memoirs of a Seafaring Life: The Narrative of William Spavens* (London, 2000), p. 53. The *Vengeance* had been captured in 1758 and was a frigate of twenty-eight guns.

27 See Chapter 3.

28 'Ambrose Trial', p. 68.

29 'Ambrose Trial', p. 162.

30 Nelson narrative 8–14 Mar 1795, Nicholas, *Dispatches and Letters of Lord Nelson*, II, p. 13; M. Duffy, 'The Gunnery at Trafalgar: Training, Tactics or Temperament?' *Journal for Maritime Research* (2004), p. 7.

31 A choice few are: Byron letter (undated) quoted in Bonner-Smith, *Barrington Papers*, I, p. 89; Barrington to Adm. Sec. 24 Aug 1747, TNA ADM 1/1483; Hood to Middleton 13 Apr 1782, Laughton, *Barham Papers*, I, pp. 160–1; P. Warren to G. Anson 31 May 1747, quoted in Rodger, 'George, Lord Anson', p. 184; Fox Trial, Mackay, *Hawke Papers*, p. 76; Mackay, *Admiral Hawke*, p. 181.

32 Lewis, *Dillon Narrative*, I, p. 156.

33 Simpson narrative of the Battle of Martinique, NMM HSR/B/10.

34 T. Graves to Rowley 2 Jan 1783, TNA ADM 1/242.

35 R. Bevan to T. Morgan (undated), Morriss, 'The Glorious First of June', p. 94.

36 Douglas, *Naval Gunnery*, pp. 54–7; Anon., 'Advantages of Close Action', *Naval Chronicle*, 3 (1800), p. 363. This is also discussed in Duffy, 'Gunnery at Trafalgar', pp. 8–9.

37 Collingwood General Order 23 Mar 1808, quoted in Tunstall, *Naval Warfare in the Age of Sail*, p. 262; Bourchier, *Memoir of the Life of Admiral Sir Edward Codrington*, I, p. 31.

38 W. Beatty, *Authentic Narrative of the Death of Lord Nelson* (London, 1807), pp. 32–3.

39 'Ambrose Trial', pp. 10, 165.

40 Park, *Defensive War by Sea*, p. 156; Oppenheim, *Naval Tracts of Sir William Monson Tracts*, I, p. 94; J. Inman, *An Introduction to Naval Gunnery* (Portsea, 1828), p. 30; *Byng Trial*, p. 209; R. Gardiner, *The First Frigates, Nine and Twelve Pounder Frigates, 1748–1815* (London, 1992), p. 112.

41 Lewis, *Dillon Narrative*, I, p. 130.

42 Beatty, *Authentic Narrative of the Death of Lord Nelson*, pp. 32–3.

43 NMM RUSI/36. For other references to splitting broadside aim, see 'Burrish Trial', p. 93; Park, *Defensive War by Sea*, p. 156.

44 Douglas, *Naval Gunnery*, p. 174.

45 Creswell, *British Admirals*, p. 86.

46 Douglas to Middleton 12 Jul 1779, Laughton, *Barham Papers*, I, p. 268. Also see Chapter 3.

47 Douglas to Middleton 4 May 1782, Laughton, *Barham Papers*, I, p. 284.

48 Oppenheim, *Naval Tracts of Sir William Monson*, IV, p. 33.

49 Hutchinson, *Treatise on Practical Seamanship*, p. 214.

50 Hamilton, *Byam Martin Papers*, II, p. 35; Journal of G. Pocock 30 Apr 1758, TNA ADM 50/21.

51 E. Jekyll to Adm. Sec. 3 Apr 1761, TNA ADM 1/1985.

52 Lewis, *Dillon Narrative*, I, p. 132.

53 Desbrière, *Naval Campaign of 1805*, pp. 201–2.

54 A. Lambert, *The Last Sailing Battlefleet* (London, 1991), p. 64.

55 See Chapter 11.

56 Czisnik, 'Admiral Nelson's Tactics at the Battle of Trafalgar', p. 553.

57 Gardiner, *First Frigates*, p. 11.

58 Laird Clowes, *Royal Navy*, IV, p. 5.

59 Willis, 'Manœuvrability', pp. 62–3, 65, 68.

60 Transactions on Board HMS *Agamemnon* ... by Captain Nelson 8–14 Mar 1795, Nicholas, *Dispatches and Letters of Lord Nelson*, II, pp. 10–15.

61 See, for example, Hamilton, *Byam Martin Papers*, II, p. 35; Jackson, *Logs*, II, p. 265; Kempenfelt to Adm. 14 Dec 1781, TNA ADM 1/95; White, *Naval Researches*, p. 21.

62 Park, *Defensive War by Sea*, p. 154.

63 Park, *Defensive War by Sea*, p. 149.

64 For examples of this happening in practice, see Log of the *Queen* 1 Jun 1794, Jackson, *Logs*, I, p. 70; Digby, *Journal of a Voyage*, p. 79; Nelson to Linzee 24 Oct 1793, Nicholas, *Dispatches and Letters of Lord Nelson*, I, p. 336; W. Young to C. Middleton 24 Jul 1780, Laughton, *Barham Papers*, I, p. 67; *Molloy Trial*, pp. 26, 144.

65 See Chapter 11.

66 Gower, *Treatise on Seamanship*, p. 150.

67 Douglas, *Naval Evolutions*, p. 95.

68 Hutchinson, *Treatise on Practical Seamanship*, pp. 214–15.

69 'Capture of the Warren Hastings From the St. Helena Gazette Sep 18 1806', *Naval Chronicle*, 16 (1806), pp. 479–8

70 C. Mayne to J. Burchett 8 Apr 1740, TNA ADM 1/2098.

71 Anon., 'Studies in the Theory of Naval Tactics II', *Naval Review*, 1/2 (1913), pp. 163–4.

72 J. Steuart to Adm. Sec. 11 Jun 1746, D. A. Baugh, *Naval Administration, 1715–50*

(London, 1977), p. 76. Also see Anon., *Short Account of Naval Actions*, p. 37.

73 Anon., *Short Account of Naval Actions*, p. 91; J. N. Newman to V.-A. Kingsmill Oct 19 1798, *Naval Chronicle*, 3 (1800), pp. 43–5.

74 A. Murray, *Memoir of the Naval Life and Services of Admiral Sir Philip C. H. C. Durham, G.C.B.* (London, 1846), pp. 60–2.

75 See, for example, R. Lawrie to Adm. Sec. 25 Feb 1805, in *Bells Weekly Messenger*, 23 Apr 1805, p. 131; J. N. Newman to V-A Kingsmill, 19 Oct 1798, *Naval Chronicle*, 3 (1800), pp. 43–5.

76 Hamilton and Laughton, *Recollections of James Anthony Gardner*, p. 130; E. Desbrière, *La Campagne maritime de 1805: Trafalgar* (Paris, 1907), pp. 199–200; Park, *Defensive War by Sea*, p. 158.

77 Mountaine, *Seaman's Vade-Mecum*, p. 209.

78 Cumby, 'Battle of Trafalgar', pp. 723–4.

79 Desbrière, *La Campagne maritime de 1805*, pp. 200–1; Craik, *Pictorial History of England*, VI, p. 293.

80 Digby, *Journal of a Voyage*, p. 11.

81 O'Bryen, *Essay on Naval Military Discipline*, p. 81.

82 Lewis, *Dillon Narrative*, I, p. 218.

83 Carr Laughton, 'H.M.S. Victory: Report', p. 204.

84 W. Gilkerson, *Boarders Away: With Steel, the Edged Weapons and Polearms* (Providence, RI, 1991), p. 50.

85 Hamilton, *Byam Martin Papers*, II, p. 37.

86 Lavery, *The Ship of the Line*, I, pp. 25–7.

87 'Stratagems to be used at Sea' Extracts from Sir. W. Monson's Naval Tracts, *Naval Chronicle*, 8 (1802), p. 320.

88 Desbrière, *La Campagne maritime de 1805*, pp. 200–1, 215; O'Bryen, *Essay on Naval Military Discipline*, p. 81; Steel, *Elements and Practice of Rigging*, II, p. 379.

89 W. Hamilton to his father 12 Oct 1805, Thursfield, *Five Naval Journals*, p. 375; Desbrière, *La Campagne maritime de 1805*, pp. 200–1; R. Miller to his father 3 Mar 1797, White, *Nelson's Year of Destiny*, p. 154.

90 See entry under 'Pole-axe'.

91 Gilkerson, *Boarders Away*, pp. 28–9.

92 Hamilton, *Byam Martin Papers*, II, pp. 43, 47; W. Robinson, *Nautical Economy* (London, 1836), pp. 18–19; Laughton,

Journal of Rear-Admiral Bartholomew James, p. 351; R. Miller to his father 3 Mar 1797, White, *Nelson's Year of Destiny*, p. 154; Boteler, *Dialogues*, p. 368.

93 Boteler, *Dialogues*, p. 377.

94 See, for example, Cochrane, *Autobiography of a Seaman*, p. 113.

95 Wareham, *Frigate Commander*, p. 177; Cumby, 'Battle of Trafalgar', pp. 723–4.

96 See, for example, Laird Clowes, *Royal Navy*, II, p. 522; IV, pp. 480, 489, 492.

97 J. Bourdé de Villehuet, quoted in Robison, *History of Naval Tactics*, p. 264.

98 Mountaine, *Seaman's Vade-Mecum*, p. 230.

99 Desbrière, *La Campagne maritime de 1805*, p. 215; E. Pellew to Adm. Sec. 19 Jun 1793, TNA ADM 1/2310; W. P. Williams to Adm. Sec. 10 Aug 1780, TNA ADM 1/2675;

100 J. Drinkwater, *Narrative of Proceedings of the British Fleet Commanded by Admiral Sir J. Jervis 1797*, 2nd edn (London, 1840), pp. 42, 94.

100 'Interesting anecdotes relating to the Battle of Trafalgar', *Naval Chronicle*, 14 (1805), p. 457.

101 Laird Clowes, *Royal Navy*, IV, p. 92.

102 Laird Clowes, *Royal Navy*, IV, p. 87.

103 Rodger, *The Wooden World*, pp. 55–6.

104 Richmond, *The Navy in the War of 1739–48*, II, p. 258. Also see Anon., 'Letter to the Editor', *Naval Chronicle*, 4 (1801) p. 97; R. Gardiner, ed., *Fleet Battle and Blockade* (London, 1996), p. 35; Laird Clowes, *Royal Navy*, IV, p. 543n. 4.

105 Desbrière, *La Campagne maritime de 1805*, p. 199.

CHAPTER 11 : Damage

1 Sea-Officer, *Enquiry into the Conduct of Capt. M-N*, p. 23.

2 Lambert, *War at Sea in the Age of Sail*, p. 41; Boudriot, *The Seventy-Four Gun Ship*, IV, p. 135.

3 Anon., 'French Naval Tactics', pp. 142–8.

4 Anon., 'French Naval Tactics', p. 142; Depeyre, *Tactiques et stratégies*, p. 55; Tunstall, *Naval Warfare in the Age of Sail*, p. 3; Gardiner, *Fleet Battle and Blockade*, p. 35.

5 Liardet, *Professional Recollections*, pp. 143–4; Park, *Defensive War by Sea*, p. 27.

6 Hood to Jackson 16 Sep 1781, Hodges, *Select Naval Documents*, p. 175. Also see P. Le Fevre, 'Arthur Herbert, Earl of Torrington, 1648–1716', in *Precursors of Nelson*, ed. P. Le Fevre and R. Harding (London, 2000), p. 31.

7 Evidence of Captain Digby, *Keppel Trial*, p. 61. Also see *Keppel Trial*, p. 62; *Knowles Trial*, p. 90.

8 Log of the *Lancaster* 12 Oct 1797, TNA ADM 50/34. Also see C. R. Markham, ed., *The Life of Captain Stephen Martin, 1666–1740* (London, 1895), p. 129.

9 S. B. A. Willis, 'The High Life: Topmen in the Age of Sail', *MM*, 90 (2004), pp. 157–9.

10 G. Berkely and J. Monkton to Howe 6 Jun 1794, in Duffy and Morriss, *The Glorious First of June*, p. 98. For a similar example,

see Gardiner, *Fleet Battle and Blockade*, p. 138.

11 Richmond, *The Navy in the War of 1739–48*, II, p. 164.

12 Desbrière, *Naval Campaign of 1805*, appendix, p. 35.

13 Mackay, 'Edward, Lord Hawke', p. 219.

14 Laird Clowes, *Royal Navy*, IV, p. 543; Depeyre, *Tactiques et stratégies*, pp. 55–6; Tunstall, *Naval Warfare in the Age of Sail*, p. 3; Duffy, 'Gunnery at Trafalgar', pp. 6–9.

15 Anon., *Dialogue between Two Volunteers*; Douglas, *Naval Gunnery*, pp. 250, 255.

16 Cumby, 'Battle of Trafalgar', pp. 724–5; Bourdé de Villehuet, *The Manœuverer*, p. 192; Blunt, *Theory and Practice of Seamanship*, p. 209.

17 Digby, *Journal of a Voyage*, p. 5.

18 Anon., 'French Naval Tactics', p. 142. For an example in practice, see *Keppel Trial*, p. 87.

19 *Molloy Trial*, pp. 23, 111. Also see 'Burrish Trial', p. 103.

20 W. H. White, *A Manual of Naval Architecture* (London, 1900), pp. 80–5, 111–12, 186–92; K. C. Barnaby, *Basic Naval Architecture*, 2nd edn (London, 1954), pp. 65–8; F. Scott, *A Square Rig Handbook* (London, 1992), pp. 101–8.

21 Morriss, 'The Glorious First of June', p. 66.

22 An Officer of the *Experiment* 6 Oct 1805, *Naval Chronicle*, 14 (1805), p. 339; Lewis, *Dillon Narrative*, I, pp. 211–12.

23 Anon., *Dialogue between Two Volunteers*.

24 Lavery, *Nelson's Navy*, p. 297.

25 Oppenheim, *Naval Tracts of Sir William Monson*, V, p. 147.

26 Padfield, *Guns at Sea*, p. 69; Caruana, *English Sea Ordnance*, II, p. 261.

27 W. Hutchinson, *A Treatise on Practical Seamanship* (Liverpool, 1777), p. 161. Although entirely plausible, it remains unclear why the *Victory* sank: there were neither survivors nor witnesses. It is believed by some that she ran on the Casquets as her distress guns were heard on Alderney. The weather and faulty construction have also been blamed. Laird Clowes, *Royal Navy*, III, p. 108. Also see Journal of W. P. Cumby, Thursfield, *Five Naval Journals*, p. 374; Lewis, *Dillon Narrative*, I, p. 131; 'Stratagems to be used at Sea' Extracts from Sir W. Monson's Naval Tracts, *Naval Chronicle*, 8 (1802), p. 319.

28 R. C. Anderson, *The Rigging of Ships in the Days of the Spritsail Topmast, 1600–1720* (Salem, MA, 1927), p. 83; Harland, *Seamanship in the Age of Sail*, p. 22.

29 Nelson to W. Locker 17 Jan 1794, Nicholas, *Dispatches and Letters of Lord Nelson*, I, p. 348.

30 'Ambrose Trial', p. 184; 'Burrish Trial', p. 107.

31 *Palliser Trial*, p. 74.

32 Z. Mudge to W. Marsden 22 Jul 1805, TNA ADM 1/2149. Also see 'Ambrose Trial', p. 184; 'Burrish Trial', p. 107.

33 *Palliser Trial*, p. 71.

34 Inman, *Naval Gunnery*, p. 30.

35 Douglas, *Naval Gunnery*, p. 247.

36 Hutchinson, *Treatise on Practical Seamanship*, pp. 214–15; Laird Clowes, *Royal Navy*, IV, p. 543 n. 2.

37 Pasley, *Private Sea Journals*, p. 80.

38 For some select examples, see J. Kempthorne to J. Rowley 26 Oct 1782, TNA ADM 1/242; E. Hawke to J. Clevland 17 Oct 1747, TNA ADM 1/88; Log of the *Royal George* 2 Jun 1794, Jackson, *Logs*, I, p. 54; Journal of J. Jervis 15 Feb 1797, TNA ADM 50/79; W. P. Williams to P. Stevens 10 Aug

1780, TNA ADM 1/2675; A. Wilkinson to T. Brodrick 17 May 1759, TNA ADM 1/384.

39 *Molloy Trial*, p. 147; Journal of R. Wilson, Thursfield, *Five Naval Journals*, p. 253.

40 Anon., 'A Treatise on Practical Navigation and Seamanship', *The Naval Chronicle*, 5 (1801), pp. 421–4; Journal of P. Cullen, Thursfield, *Five Naval Journals*, p. 100.

41 C. Stirling to P. Stevens 10 Apr 1793, TNA ADM 1/2489; Lieut. E. Pakenham to P. Stevens 26 Jan 1793, TNA ADM1/2310.

42 Lewis, *Dillon Narrative*, I, p. 208; Anon., 'Engagement of the Nile Drawn up from the Minutes of an Officer of Rank in the Squadron', *Naval Chronicle*, 1 (1799), p. 58.

43 Anon., 'French Naval Tactics', p. 142.

44 'Ambrose Trial', pp. 87, 144. For a similar example, see White, *Nelson's Year of Destiny*, p. 63.

45 Log of the *Jersey* 19 Jun 1745, TNA ADM 1/382. Similar examples can be read in *Keppel Trial*, p. 154; Allen, *Memoir of Admiral Sir William Hargood*, p. 131.

46 *Keppel Trial*, p. 346.

47 Laughton, *Journal of Rear-Admiral Bartholomew James*, p. 328.

48 Bourchier, *Memoir of the Life of Admiral Sir Edward Codrington*, I, p. 66.

49 Cochrane, *Autobiography of a Seaman*, pp. 385–6.

50 Anderson, *Allin Journals*, I, pp. 71, 184–5; Howe to S. Barrington 15 Mar 1762, Bonner-Smith, *Barrington Papers*, I, p. 364.

51 T. Noel to T. Corbett 4 May 1746, TNA ADM 1/2217.

52 The action can be followed in detail in Mahan, *Influence of Seapower*, pp. 469–78; Laird Clowes, *Royal Navy*, III, pp. 510–19.

53 Liardet, *Professional Recollections*, p. 206; White, *Naval Researches*, p. 23.

54 See Chapter 1.

55 *Byng Trial*, p. 226.

56 Jackson, *Logs*, I, p. 6.

57 Testimony of Duncan Grant Master of the *Somerset*, Sclater Trial, TNA ADM 1/5282.

58 Kempenfelt to Middleton 28 Apr 1779, Hodges, *Select Naval Documents*, pp. 159–60.

59 E. Vernon to C. Wager 19 Jul 1740, McRanft, *Vernon Papers*, p. 112.

60 Markham, *Life of Captain Stephen Martin*, p. 126.

61 Duffy and Morriss, *The Glorious First of June*, p. 64.

62 Douglas, *Naval Gunnery*, p. 242.

63 Anon., 'Theory of Tactics II', p. 154.

64 Nelson to Lady Nelson 4 Mar 1794, Nicholas, *Dispatches and Letters of Lord Nelson*, I, p. 368.

65 Hutchinson, *Treatise on Practical Seamanship*, pp. 214–16; Boteler, *Dialogues*, p. 361; O'Brien, 'Essay on the Duty of a Captain', p. 220; Douglas, *Naval Gunnery*, p. 247.

66 Anderson, *Rigging of Ships*, p. 84.

67 *Palliser Trial*, p. 47.

68 *Molloy Trial*, p. 31.

69 Anon., *An Account of What Passed in the Engagement near Toulon between His Majesty's Squadron under the Command of Admiral Matthews and the Fleets of France and Spain* (London, 1744), p. 5. For a similar example, see *Loss of the Ardent Trial*, p. 20.

70 'Burrish Trial', pp. 94, 116–17, 120. For similar examples of speedy repair, see *Keppel Trial*, pp. 111, 221; Anderson, *Allin Journals*, I, pp. 103, 200.

71 *Keppel Trial*, p. 155.

72 *Molloy Trial*, p. 94.

73 *Molloy Trial*, pp. 98–9.

74 Bourchier, *Memoir of the Life of Admiral Sir Edward Codrington*, I, p. 24; *Calder Trial*, p. 26; Cochrane, *Autobiography of a Seaman*, pp. 177–8.

75 See, for example, Testimony of Duncan Grant, Master of the *Somerset*, Sclater Trial, TNA ADM 1/5282.

76 *The Minutes of a Court Martial Held on Board H.M.S. Lennox Enquiring into the Conduct of the Commanders of the Hampton Court and the Dreadnought* (London, 1745), p. 12; Falconer, *Universal Dictionary of the Marine*, pp. 126, 360.

77 Lewis, *Dillon Narrative*, I, p. 122.

78 Douglas, *Naval Gunnery*, p. 253.

79 *Palliser Trial*, p. 33; *Molloy Trial*, p. 7.

80 *Knowles Trial*, p. 84.

81 *Molloy Trial*, p. 22.

82 Captured Narrative of the action 9 and 12 the Apr 1782, Laughton, *Barham Papers*, I, p. 173. Also see Hamilton and Laughton, *Recollections of James Anthony Gardner*, p. 186.

83 *Byng Trial*, p. 175. For more nonchalant reaction to damage and repair, also see Markham, *Life of Captain Stephen Martin*, pp. 28, 61–2, 129.

84 R. G. Albion, *Forests and Seapower: The Timber Problem of the Royal Navy, 1652–1862* (Annapolis, 2000), pp. 29–34; Glete, *Navies and Nations*, I, p. 33.

85 T. Graves to P. Stevens 14 Sep 1781, TNA ADM 1/489; E. Hughes to P. Stevens 30 Sep 1782, TNA ADM 1/164; Log of the *Leander* 19 Jan 1783, TNA ADM 51/527; Log of the *Director* 12 Oct 1797, TNA ADM 50/34.

86 Corbett, *Signals and Instructions*, pp. 115, 326.

87 Albion, *Forests and Seapower*, pp. 304–5.

88 Albion, *Forests and Seapower*, p. 206; Mahan, *Influence of Seapower*, p. 443; E. Vernon to C. Ogle and R. Lestock, Jan 1741, McRanft, *Vernon Papers*, pp. 394–5.

89 Codrington to W. Bethell 15 Nov 1805, Bourchier, *Memoir of the Life of Admiral Sir Edward Codrington*, I, p. 71.

90 Miller to Mrs Miller (undated), Nicholas, *Dispatches and Letters of Lord Nelson*, VII, pp. cliv–clx.

91 Log of the *Bellerophon* 2 Aug 1798, Jackson, *Logs*, II, p. 63. Also see Journal of C. Collingwood 28 Oct 1805, Jackson, *Logs*, II, pp. 207–8. For more examples, see Arbuthnot to Sandwich 30 Mar 1781, Barnes and Owen, *Sandwich Papers*, IV, p. 167; Anderson, *Allin Journals*, I, p. 127.

92 Log of the *Revenge* 22 Oct 1805; Log of the *Minotaur* 21 Oct 1805, Jackson, *Logs*, II, pp. 241, 275.

93 Log of the *Orion* 1 Jun 1794, Jackson, *Logs*, I, p. 122.

94 Log of the *Culloden* 2 Aug 1798, Jackson, *Logs*, II, p. 74.

95 *Molloy Trial*, p. 27.

96 *Palliser Trial*, p. 71.

97 Log of the *Defence* 3 Oct 1805, Jackson, *Logs*, II, p. 264.

98 Albion, *Forests and Seapowe*, p. 297.

99 Gower, *Treatise on Seamanship*, p. 150.

100 Boteler, *Dialogues*, p. 359; Anderson, *Allin Journals*, I, p. 225; Journal of W. Cumby, Thursfield, *Five Naval Journals*, p. 346; W. Mountaine, *The Seaman's Vade Mecum* (London, 1757), p. 206.

101 *Keppel Trial*, p. 366.

102 S. Hood to P. Stephens 7 Feb 1782, Laughton, *Barham Papers*, I, p. 144.

103 J. Morris to W. Marsden 30 Nov 1805, TNA ADM 1/2149.

104 Crimmin, 'John Jervis', p. 332. Also see E. Boscawen to T. Corbett 25 Jul 1744, TNA ADM 1/1480; Journal of R. Wilson, Thursfield, *Five Naval Journals*, p. 156.

105 Liardet, *Professional Recollections*, p. 69; Gower, *Treatise on Seamanship*, p. 151. For an example of this being used in practice, see Hamilton, *Byam Martin Papers*, I, p. 108; Log of the *Culloden* 2 Aug 1798, Jackson, *Logs*, II.

106 Tracy, *Nelson's Battles*, p. 33.

107 Nelson to Lord Hood 22 Oct 1793, Nicholas, *Dispatches and Letters of Lord Nelson*, I, pp. 334–5.

108 *Keppel Trial*, p. 111. A similar example can be found in the same trial, p. 221. The *Shrewsbury*, recovering from substantial damage, is made fit for action in only half an hour.

109 E. Salter to Sandwich 20 Dec 1777, Barnes and Owen, *Sandwich Papers*, I, p. 256; Mitchell Trial, p. 76, TNA ADM 1/5290.

110 Journal of R. Wilson, Thursfield, *Five Naval Journals*, p. 253.

111 Blunt, *Theory and Practice of Seamanship*, p. 210.

112 *Palliser Trial*, p. 71.

113 Captain Miller to his father 3 Mar 1797, White, *Nelson's Year of Destiny*, p. 154. For similar examples, see Mitchell Trial, TNA ADM 1/5290, p. 22; Laughton, *Journal of Rear-Admiral Bartholomew James*, p. 92.

114 White, *Nelson's Year of Destiny*, pp. 50, 69.

115 For a good discussion, see Broomfield, 'The Keppel–Palliser Affair', pp. 195–209.

116 Douglas to Middleton 28 Apr 1782, Laughton, *Barham Papers*, I, p. 280.

117 Lewis, *Dillon Narrative*, I, p. 192.

118 Log of the *Goliath*, 2 Aug 1798, Jackson, *Logs*, II, p. 11; Log of the *Alexander*, 2 Aug 1798, Jackson, *Logs*, II, p. 67.

119 Account of the action of 12 Apr 1782, Laughton, *Naval Miscellany*, I, p. 232.

120 Laird Clowes, *Royal Navy*, IV, p. 497.

121 Robinson, *Nautical Economy*, p. 26; Duffy, 'Gunnery at Trafalgar', p. 6.

Appendix: Fleet Battles, 1688–1815

Of all the naval battles fought between fleets in this period, the Battle of Trafalgar is the best known, and there are perhaps ten in all that have regularly been reproduced and analysed in print or interpreted by artists since the day that they were fought. Those few battles have been plucked from historical obscurity for a number of reasons. All were crushing victories: indecisive skirmishes do not survive the test of time. All encapsulated astonishing bravery: cowardice is rarely remembered. All involved a high element of risk: decisive victories are rarely won through timidity. This is no formula for longevity, however; there are many battles that fulfil these criteria but which have not survived to be celebrated in the national consciousness as the bicentenary of Trafalgar in 2005. In more intimate circles the bicentenaries of the Glorious First of June (1794) and Cape St Vincent (1797) were also celebrated in modern times, but who remembered the ferocious battle fought between Vice-Admiral Hyde Parker and a highly skilled Dutch fleet under Rear-Admiral Zoutman off the Dogger Bank in the summer of 1781? For the historian of sailing warfare all actions are important in their own way. In some cases the sources are highly detailed, the commander eloquent, with a fair hand; in others all that remains is a terse paragraph in a ship's log. But to focus only on the better-known actions is to distort our understanding of the nature and development of sailing warfare. This appendix therefore covers all those significant actions fought between squadrons and fleets of four or more ships between 1688 and 1815.

THE NINE YEARS WAR, 1688–97

The Nine Years War was a wide-ranging conflict in Continental Europe, with important secondary theatres in Ireland and North America. Following the 'Glorious Revolution' of November 1688, William of Orange was not only Stadtholder of the Dutch Republic but king of England; England and the Dutch Republic joined the Holy Roman Empire, Spain, Sweden and Protestant German states in a coalition against France to counter the expansionist policies of Louis xiv. The English and Dutch navies combined to meet the threat of French control of the English Channel and Irish Sea. The naval conflicts were fleet actions on a large scale and were fought in English and Irish waters as Louis pursued his plans for invasion with the intention of reinstalling the Catholic James ii to the English throne. The war was brought to an end by the Treaty of Ryswick in September 1697.

1. The Battle of Bantry Bay, 1 May 1689

With the Glorious Revolution complete, and William and Mary safely on the throne, it was imperative that Louis xiv be prevented from sending troops or arms to either Ireland or Scotland, from where a campaign to reinstate James ii could be launched. A week before war was declared Admiral Arthur Herbert discovered the French fleet, commanded by Vice-Admiral the marquis de Château-Renault, landing troops in the south-west of Ireland. Herbert saw he was outnumbered and formed into line ahead to await the French attack from to windward. When it came, the fleets fought in parallel lines. Herbert's ships were badly damaged and were forced to retire.

3. The Battle of Beachy Head, 30 June 1690

French plans in 1690 did not centre on an invasion or control of the Irish Sea, as the English feared, but on a fleet victory and control of the Channel, and in May the combined Toulon and Brest squadrons were sited off Portland. Herbert, again, was badly outnumbered and engaged reluctantly. The Dutch formed the van of the allied fleet, and engaged the van of the French but were heavily beaten, the French doubling the Dutch line. The centre division commanded by Herbert remained at some distance from the enemy, while the rear division was closer, attacking the French rear. French numbers soon made the difference, and the heavily damaged English and Dutch ships anchored in the light winds, while the French drifted away with the ebb tide. It was a clear victory for the French; the Dutch lost thirteen of their twenty-two ships.

3. The Battle of Barfleur, 19–23 May 1692

James II and Louis XIV had developed a detailed invasion plan, the troops to be landed in Dorset under the cover of Admiral Tourville's fleet. As Tourville entered the Channel he unexpectedly met the allied English and Dutch fleet under the command of Edward Russell, but this time it was Tourville who was outnumbered. Nevertheless, and perhaps by mistake, Tourville bore down to the centre and rear of the allied fleet, and engaged close and fiercely. Soon, however, his ships were worn down, outnumbered and outgunned by the Allied centre and rear. Two allied divisions doubled the French in the centre and inflicted severe damage, which forced Tourville to retreat under tow in the light winds. Strong tides pulled the damaged fleets apart, and the battle ended in confusion. During the next three days some of the enemy's ships were driven ashore at Cherbourg, and twelve others into the bay of St Vaast-la-Hougue. They were all burned by an audacious boat and fireship attack by the Allies. Sixteen French men of war and a number of transports were destroyed, and with them the immediate plans to replace James II on the English throne.

4. The Smyrna Convoy, 17 June 1693

Rear-Admiral Sir George Rooke was under orders to escort an enormous and valuable fleet of English, Swedish, Dutch and Danish merchantmen into the Mediterranean, but the French knew of his plans. Admiral Tourville united the Brest and Toulon squadrons off Cadiz and launched a perfectly executed ambush as the convoy rounded Cape St Vincent. The Dutch squadron of Rooke's fleet of escorting warships met Tourville's attack and acted as a decoy as the main body of merchantmen fled. Three-quarters of the merchantman escaped, but ninety-two were sunk or captured, along with two Dutch warships, sacrificed by their captains as they held off the French fleet.

THE WAR OF THE SPANISH SUCCESSION, 1702–13

On the death of the Habsburg Charles II of Spain in 1700, all his possessions passed to the Bourbon grandson of Louis XIV of France, Phillip, duc d'Anjou, who thereby became Philip V of Spain. Leopold I, the Habsburg Holy Roman Emperor, took arms to protect his own claim to the Spanish throne. He was joined by England and the Dutch Republic, who feared Franco-Spanish expansion and unity. Naval conflicts in this war were markedly different from those of the Nine Years War: by 1692 the French navy had turned its focus away from major fleets to a privateering war on allied trade. There was thus only one major fleet action during this war: the Battle of Malaga (1704). The theatre of maritime conflict also changed. France and Spain were heavily dependent on the importation of Spanish silver from South America to finance their war. With no direct invasion threat, the allied fleets were able to focus their attention on the Caribbean and the Mediterranean to protect their trade, and target that of France and Spain. These years saw a dramatic increase of British power in the Mediterranean, with the capture of Gibraltar in 1704 and Minorca in 1708. The war was concluded by the treaties of Utrecht (1713) and Rastatt (1714). Philip v was recognised as King of Spain, but the union of the thrones of France and Spain was averted; Spain's European possessions were divided up, and Britain acquired various French North American territories.

1. Benbow's Last Fight, 19 August 1702

Powerful squadrons from France were sent to the Caribbean to escort Spanish silver back to Europe, the Spanish navy being too weak for such a task. Vice-Admiral John Benbow, with a squadron of seven ships, met one such French squadron off Santa Marta under the command of Vice-Admiral Jean-Baptiste du Casse. A running battle lasted for six full days, but Benbow was poorly supported by his captains, and no ships were captured. Captain Richard Kirby and Captain Copper Wade were later court martialled and sentenced to death.

2. The Battle of Malaga, 13 August 1704

Gibraltar had recently been captured by the English, and a large French fleet under the command of Admiral le comte de Toulouse was ordered to unite with the Spanish fleet to recapture it. The allied English and Dutch fleet, commanded by Admiral Sir George Rooke, was intent on stopping them, and after a long chase the French were brought to action off Malaga. The fleets were roughly equal, although the French had the added advantage of a galley squadron that helped them manœuvre in the light airs and calm sea conditions. The allies were badly short of ammunition and the battle was fought at some distance. No ships were lost on either side, and although the battle was a stalemate, Gibraltar remained in British hands.

3. The Battle of Marbella, 10 March 1705

Still intent on the recapture of Gibraltar, the territory was blockaded by a French squadron of five ships commanded by Rear-Admiral le baron de Pointis. They were intercepted by Admiral Sir John Leake in command of a powerful allied force of twenty-three English, Dutch and Portuguese ships. Leake gave chase and easily overhauled the enemy from the rear, capturing one ship. Two others were run ashore and destroyed.

4. Wager at Cartagena, 28 May 1708

Commodore Charles Wager in charge of the West India squadron received intelligence of a Spanish Squadron off Cartagena laden with South American silver shipped from Porto Bello. He gave chase, and the Spaniards were forced to come within his range to weather the island of Baru. Wager gave his captains orders to attack the flagships because he knew they carried the silver, but none of them obeyed. Wager engaged the Spanish Admiral alone and so fiercely that his flagship blew up, and then again another warship which struck. Wager ordered two captains to chase a group of ships as they sought to escape, but again his orders were not properly obeyed.

A DEFENSIVE ALLIANCE AGAINST SPAIN, 1716–18

Philip v of Spain was determined to regain his lands in Austria which had been lost at the end of the War of the Spanish Succession. The Spanish navy was expanded, and an invasion force landed in Sicily. France, Britain, Austria and Holland united to take action against Spain. France invaded Spain; the Austrians dealt with Spanish forces in Sicily; and the British attacked their fleet. Philip abandoned his plans.

1. The Battle of Cape Passaro, 31 July 1718

When Sir George Byng met the Spanish fleet commanded by Admiral Antonio de Gastañeta, his position was delicate. He was in the Mediterranean to force a Spanish retreat from Sicily, but war had not been officially declared and he was unclear if the Spanish fleet would be hostile. His mind was settled as the Spaniards opened fire first and then sought to escape. Castañeta's second-in-command, the Irish Jacobite Rear-Admiral George Camcock led some ships away, leaving the Spanish admiral with only nine ships against Byng's twenty-one. In the running chase that followed, seven Spanish ships, including three flagships, were captured.

THE WAR OF THE AUSTRIAN SUCCESSION, 1739–48

In 1739 Britain fell into armed conflict with Spain over merchants' access to South American markets. Meanwhile, the Holy Roman Emperor Charles VI died, and Britain and Spain were both drawn into the wider War of Austrian Succession. Britain, Hanover and the Dutch Republic supported the claim of his daughter, Maria Theresa, while France, Spain and Prussia supported that of Charles Albert, Wittelsbach Elector of Bavaria. Britain stationed a fleet in the Mediterranean to blockade the French and Spanish fleet in Toulon and to assist with the land campaigns in Sicily. Another force was kept in the Channel to counter an invasion threat from France in support the Jacobite uprising in Scotland. The war on trade also remained crucial, and the interception of French and Spanish convoys to and from the Americas remained a high priority along with the protection of British interests. The war concluded with the Treaty of Aix-la-Chapelle in 1748, in which Maria Theresa's claim was upheld.

1. The Battle of Toulon, 11 February 1744

The Mediterranean fleet under Admiral Thomas Matthews had been blockading both the French and Spanish fleets in Toulon. England had been at war with Spain since 1739 and French support for the Spanish was imminent. Both the French and the Spanish came out on the morning of 8 February and headed towards the British fleet. It was three days before the two fleets were close enough to engage. The French and Spanish struggled to maintain a strong line; the French led the fleet, but the Spanish Squadron were some way astern. The British fleet were also strung out, with Vice-Admiral Richard Lestock's division lagging some way behind Matthews in the van, who steadily closed with the allied fleet in the light airs. Despite frequent signalling to Lestock, he failed to close the gap, and Matthews's division led the attack alone. Matthews attacked the centre and van of the allied fleet, and there was some fierce fighting, notably by Edward Hawke in the *Berwick*. But without Lestock's support Matthews was forced to call off the engagement when the van of the allied fleet tacked: it was clear from such a manœuvre that he was in real danger of being isolated and defeated in detail. The only prize of the day, the *Poder*, was retaken by the French. Courts martial carried out under intense political pressure and with marked injustice followed.

2. The First Battle of Finisterre, 3 May 1747

The first action of the newly formed Western Squadron. Admiral George Anson intercepted a combined convoy bound for India and America under the protection of the marquis de La Jonquière. La Jonquière formed his force of six battle ships and three armed Indiamen into line ahead and prepared to hold off the British while the convoy escaped. Anson took the time to form his fourteen ships into line ahead before attacking, despite his second in command, Rear-Admiral Sir Peter Warren, urging an immediate pell-mell attack. As the British bore down on the French, La Jonquière broke up his line and retreated downwind. Anson chased and gradually overhauled the French from the rear. All the French ships were taken, and eighteen of the thirty-eight merchantmen.

3. The Second Battle of Finisterre, 14 October 1747

A similar battle in many ways to the First Battle of Finisterre. The western squadron of fourteen ships, now under the command of Edward Hawke, intercepted a large West-Indies-bound French convoy escorted by eight warships and an armed Indiaman under the command of the marquis de L'Etanduère. Unlike La Jonquière, L'Etanduère kept his line as the British bore down to attack. Hawke gradually overhauled the French line from the rear and engaged it on both sides. Six French ships were finally taken, and although the convoy escaped Hawke, he managed to warn the West Indies squadron of their arrival, and they were intercepted in the Caribbean.

4. Knowles and Reggio, 1 October 1748

Rear-Admiral Charles Knowles, stationed at Jamaica, intercepted a Spanish convoy bound for Havana from Vera Cruz. The fleets were evenly matched, and on first sight Admiral Don Andres Reggio mistook Knowles's squadron for merchantmen, and chased in disorder. When he realised his mistake he took time to form into line ahead and awaited Knowles's attack from to windward. Knowles determined to engage, but his signals were misunderstood by ships in the van and the rear of his fleet. After more confusion (it is unclear it if was real or feigned) some of the British finally engaged, and Knowles drove Reggio out of his line. The Spaniards followed their admiral, and they were chased long into the night as they fled for Havana. In the end one Spanish ship was captured, another sunk and Reggio's flagship was run ashore and burned by her crew. Much bitterness remained between Knowles and his captains.

THE SEVEN YEARS WAR, 1755–62

The first global conflict in history. Britain and France had failed to come to agreement over the extent and location of the boundaries between British and French possessions in North America, and along the Ohio River tension spilled over into armed conflict.

Prussia and Hanover allied with Great Britain; Austria, the Russian Empire, Saxony, Sweden, Spain and Portugal fought with France. War at sea, however, was carried out only between Britain and France. The French were anxious to curtail British power in the Mediterranean by capturing Minorca, the only British naval base there; the British responded by attacking French and Spanish interests in Canada, the Caribbean and the Philippines. The French, meanwhile, harboured invasion plans for England itself. The final theatre of maritime conflict was the Bay of Bengal, where France and Britain fought for control of the lucrative European trading colonies. The hostilities concluded with the Treaty of Paris of 1763, with important British gains of overseas territories.

1. The Battle of Minorca, 20 July 1756

Vice-Admiral John Byng (youngest son of Sir George Byng, hero of the Battle of Cape Passaro, 1718) was sent to the Mediterranean to reinforce Minorca against a possible French attack. The French landed 12,000 troops in mid-April, and began a lengthy siege, entirely dependent on sea-borne supply protected by the French fleet under Vice-Admiral the marquis de La Galissonière. Byng's thirteen ships of the line gave him a slight advantage over La Galissonière's twelve, but the French easily repulsed Byng's attack. Both fleets formed in line ahead, but there was confusion (again it is unclear if it was feigned or real) over Byng's signals. When they finally bore down to attack, the well-formed French simply drifted to leeward, targeting the masts of the British. Byng's fleet were soon crippled, simply unable to close the relatively undamaged and fast ships of the French. Byng made no further move to lift the siege of Minorca. He was relieved of his command, court martialled and shot.

2. The Battle of Cuddalore, 29 April 1758

The first of two battles at Cuddalore (the other was in 1783) and the first of three fought between Rear-Admiral George Pocock and Rear-Admiral comte d'Aché de Serquigny for control of the Coromandel coast of Southern India. The fleets were evenly matched and fought in parallel lines ahead. Neither admiral was well supported by his captains. D'Aché bore away after an explosion in his flagship, but the British were too disabled to chase. No ships were lost on either side.

3. The Battle of Negapatam, 3 August 1758

The second action fought between Pocock and d'Aché in India, again with evenly matched fleets. They fought again in parallel lines ahead, and after some hard fighting four French ships were forced out of the line, including d'Aché's flagship. They were chased into the night. No ships were taken on either side, but the French suffered 800 casualties to Pocock's 200.

4. Boscawen and La Clue-Sabran off Lagos, 18 August 1759

In May 1759 the British captured Guadeloupe from the French, who sent the Toulon squadron under Rear-Admiral La Clue-Sabran to retake it. Boscawen, refitting in Gibraltar, intercepted the French fleet as they left the Mediterranean. Boscawen had ten ships to La Clue's eleven larger vessels. To evade the pursuing British, La Clue extinguished all lights, but confusion over their destination then caused three of his ships to make for Cadiz. By morning Boscawen had numerical superiority and engaged the rear of the French fleet as they came up in chase. Confusion among Boscawen's captains over how to act in a lengthy running battle and La Clue's unwillingness to stand and fight ensured this was not the decisive affair that it could have been. Nevertheless, three French ships were taken, and two were driven ashore and burned.

5. The Battle of Pondicherry, 10 September 1759

The third action fought between Pocock and d'Aché in India, it shared a number of characteristics with the earlier battles of Cuddalore and Negapatam. The fleets were evenly matched, but Pocock's fleet was in general smaller and he was badly outgunned. They fought in parallel lines ahead, and once again a number of French ships were driven from the line by the fierceness of British gunnery. The French fleet retreated, but the British were badly crippled in the rig and were unable to follow. As at the Battle of Negapatam, French casualties (1,500) were far worse than British (570).

6. The Battle of Quiberon Bay, 20 November 1759

The French were determined on an invasion of Britain. To do so the Brest fleet had to be united with the invasion force in southern Brittany. The French under the comte de Conflans sailed in mid-November for the Morbihan to collect the transport vessels for the invasion. Hawke found out and chased. Conflans sought safety in the dangers of Quiberon Bay, relying on his local knowledge of the uncharted rocks and shoals. He did not believe Hawke would follow him, but he did. A fierce and chaotic battle was fought in heavy seas, and the British won a resounding victory. One French ship was taken and six were sunk or wrecked. Two British ships were wrecked and their crews saved.

THE WAR OF AMERICAN INDEPENDENCE, 1775–83

In 1775 the British colonies in North America rebelled against British rule, and proclaimed their independence as the United States of America. France, Spain and soon the Dutch joined the Americans, and contested British control of the sea. A British army was sent to quell the rebellion, and secured a number of coastal cities. Unable to control the countryside around these bases, they were forced to rely on supply from the sea. Protection of these supplies was crucial, as was preventing the Americans from benefiting from their trade and alliances with France, Spain and the Netherlands. The French and Spanish, meanwhile, attacked British interests in the Mediterranean, the Caribbean and India, and once again threatened the invasion of England itself. The Royal Navy had not been mobilised in time and was spread too thinly. The war ended with the Treaty of Paris of 1783, which recognised the independence of the United States, ceded Minorca and West Florida to Spain, and returned a number of Caribbean and African trading posts to France.

1. The Battle of Ushant, 27 July 1778

The comte d'Orvilliers was given orders to take the Brest squadron to sea for a month in the hope that he might damage British trade from the Caribbean. His orders implied that he should not seek direct conflict with the British fleet. Nevertheless, they met and fought. The British fleet under Augustus Keppel had more ships, but the French were well trained and managed their fleet well. After much manœuvring it was clear to Keppel that, unless he immediately attacked, the French would escape. They finally engaged on opposite courses, with the British fleet badly strung out and disjointed. The French then wore to follow the British rear, and the British van tacked to chase the French: in effect chasing each others' tails. The British centre did not follow, and all cohesion seems to have been lost. Keppel was anxious to regain some order, but his signals could not be seen by Sir Hugh Palliser, in command of the rear division; once he was notified of them, they could not be obeyed owing to the damage he had sustained. The French did not want to renew the engagement, and the British crippled by confusion, acrimony and damage could not. There was a heated fallout, with courts martial for both Keppel and Palliser.

2. The Battle of Grenada, 6 July 1779

Two days previously Admiral the comte d'Estaing had succeeded in capturing Grenada from the British, and he was expecting to be attacked by Vice-Admiral John Byron. Byron met the French as they were leaving Georgetown harbour, and endeavoured to get onto a parallel course with the enemy. In so doing the French rear was badly mauled, but British cohesion broke down. The French line was intact and their fleet was numerically superior, but d'Estaing did not take advantage of his situation. Concerned for the safety of the newly won Grenada, d'Estaing turned his fleet around and made for Georgetown harbour.

3. Parker and La Motte-Picquet off Fort Royal, Martinique, 18 December 1779

Rear-Admiral Hyde Parker, while refitting at St Lucia, received intelligence of a French convoy at Martinique. He set off in chase and soon sighted a convoy of supply ships in disarray. Rear-Admiral the comte de La Motte-Picquet came out of Fort Royal to their defence. There was nothing more than a skirmish between the battle ships, but nine merchantmen were captured and four forced ashore.

4. The Moonlight Battle, 16 January 1780

In December Admiral Sir George Rodney sailed for the West Indies via the besieged Gibraltar with a fleet of eighteen sail in protection of a merchant convoy. Off Cape St Vincent he sighted a smaller Spanish squadron under Don Juan de Lángara and chased him through the night. The Spanish were overhauled from the rear as Rodney's newly coppered ships were significantly faster than the sluggish Spaniards, and six of the eleven Spanish ships were taken. Rodney spent the entire action in his bunk, and much of the success must be attributed to his flag captain, Walter Young.

5. The Battle of Martinique, 17 April 1780

Vice-Admiral the comte de Guichen had been sent to Martinique to reinforce the French squadron. He set sail with the intention of attacking Barbados, but the winds were too light and Rodney intercepted him off Martinique. Rodney planned to create a numerical superiority by launching all of his force on to the rear of the enemy, defeating it in detail before the French van could tack and support its centre and rear. Rodney's plans were misunderstood, and his van stretched out to the enemy van. The action was fierce, particularly between Rodney and de Guichen's flagships, but also in the van and rear around the flagships of Vice-Admiral Hyde Parker and Rear-Admiral Joshua Rowley. Finally the French bore away, leaving Rodney fuming at everyone but himself.

6. Arbuthnot and Destouches off Cape Henry, 16 March 1781

The chevalier Destouches escaped from Rhode Island with seven ships, where he was blockaded by Vice-Admiral Marriot Arbuthnot, also with seven ships. Arbuthnot feared he would head to Portsmouth, a town in the Chesapeake Bay recently taken by Brigadier Benedict. The two fleets met off Cape Henry, and after some preliminary manœuvring the British fleet threatened to overwhelm the French rear. Destouches wore his fleet to avoid being outnumbered and Arbuthnot matched the manœuvre, but he did so under the guns of the enemy and five of his ships were badly damaged. He was unable to continue the action.

7. The Dogger Bank, 5 August 1781

Vice-Admiral Hyde Parker was returning to England with the Baltic convoy when he fell in with a Dutch squadron escorting their own convoy, commanded by Rear-Admiral Arnold Zoutman. With seven ships aside, the battle was evenly matched and the action fierce. Zoutman formed up in line ahead to protect his convoy, and Hyde-Parker chased until his force was parallel with Zoutman's, but still some way off. He then bore down in line abreast. Zoutman appears to have waited until the British had formed parallel with him at half-musket shot before opening fire. The action ended with both fleets severely damaged in the hull and unable to continue. One Dutch ship sank.

8. Hood and Grasse off Martinique, 29–30 April 1781

Rear-Admiral Samuel Hood was blockading four French ships of the line in Port Royal when he was surprised by a large and powerful French fleet under the command of Vice-Admiral the comte de Grasse, escorting a large convoy. Hood was badly outnumbered and outgunned, and to leeward of the French the whole time. A series of skirmishes was fought at long range over two days, with both sides claiming that the other avoided action. A number of Hood's ships were too damaged to keep their place in the line, and he retired to St Eustatius.

9. The Battle of the Chesapeake, 5 September 1781

General Charles Cornwallis was fortified in Yorktown in the Chesapeake Bay, and was in danger of being cut off by the French squadron under the comte de Grasse. Rear-Admiral Thomas Graves, temporarily in charge of the North American squadron, was sent to prevent it, but the French were anchored in the Chesapeake when Graves arrived. Grasse left the bay in poor order, the rear straggling far behind the van. Graves appears to have wanted to use this opportunity to overpower the French van. His fleet was still some miles away and not parallel, however, so to attack the French van required an angled approach. Graves signalled accordingly. Hood, commanding the rear division, failed to understand Graves's intention, and did not get into battle until it was too late. Only the van and some of the centre of each fleet was engaged. Debate, recrimination and bitterness followed.

10. Hood and Grasse at St Kitts, 25 January 1782

The French fleet, still under the comte de Grasse, were anchored at Basseterre, St Kitts (St Christopher), which was being besieged by French troops. Hood was determined to lift the siege. After an aborted surprise attack by Hood, Grasse left the anchorage to face him. Hood decided that the best way to save the island was to seize the anchorage. He feinted to seaward, and Grasse followed. Hood then darted inshore and anchored in a defensive line. Over the next few days Grasse's attempted attacks were repulsed.

11. The Battle of Sadras, 17 February 1782

The first of five actions fought between Rear-Admiral the bailli de Suffren and Vice-Admiral Sir Edward Hughes for control of the Coromandel Coast of Southern India, much as Pocock and d'Aché had in 1758–9. The two fleets met, and Hughes formed into an orthodox line ahead to await Suffren's attack. Suffren planned to overwhelm Hughes's centre and rear, but his instructions were misunderstood (or deliberately ignored). There was not enough wind for Hughes to take advantage of the French confusion. Battle ended when night fell.

12. The Battle of the Saints, 12 April 1782

The French aim was the conquest of Jamaica. Grasse set sail from Martinique to Cap François, where he was to rendezvous with his Spanish allies. They were seen by Rodney and followed. After some preliminary skirmishes, the French tried to escape to windward, but were forced to come to the aid of a damaged ship, the *Zélé*, which was being overhauled by the leading British ships. The fleets, both in line ahead, met on opposite tacks. A shift of wind then disrupted the formation of both fleets, and in the confusion and smoke Rodney broke through the French line by accident. He was followed by those nearest to him, and his manœuvre was copied by the rear division under Hood. Five French ships were captured, including Grasse's flagship the *Ville de Paris*.

13. The Battle of Provedien, 12 April 1782

On the same day, some 10,000 miles away, Hughes and Suffren fought their second battle in the Bay of Bengal. Again Suffren was the aggressor, but this time did not plan to concentrate his force, but to attack in orthodox fashion, ship for ship in line ahead. He was poorly supported by his captains, however. The French van and rear did not engage close, while the centre bore the brunt of the fight. Battle ended with the sunset, and once again no ships were taken on either side.

14. The Battle of Negapatam, 6 July 1782

The third action between Hughes and Suffren, but this time Hughes had the weather gage and bore down to attack Suffren. He planned a traditional ship-for-ship engagement in parallel line ahead. Cohesion was lost as the British manœuvred, and when battle was finally forced only the van and the centre engaged. A shift in wind disrupted the battle and the two fleets drifted apart. British casualties were twice those of the French.

15. The Battle of Trincomalee, 3 September 1782

The fourth action between Hughes and Suffren. Suffren had the weather gage once again, and bore down on the British fleet, with no special plan for concentrating his force on one part of the British line: the battle once more was in traditional parallel lines ahead. The French lost cohesion on their approach, as happened to the British at the previous battle, and once again the engagement was fiercest in the centre around the two flagships, while the centre and rear engaged at too great a distance, or not at all. Night fell, and the heavily damaged fleets separated. No ships were lost on either side.

16. The Battle of Cuddalore, 20 June 1783

The last of the series of battles between Hughes and Suffren. This time Hughes outnumbered Suffren eighteen to fifteen, but his crews were sickly and undermanned. Suffren's ships were also in a bad state of repair. Despite his original intention to revert to his tactical plan of their first encounter, a concentration on the rear of the British fleet, Suffren backed down and ordered a traditional attack, ship for ship in parallel lines ahead. Again, little ground was given on either side, and the weak and damaged fleets retreated to lick their wounds.

THE FRENCH REVOLUTIONARY WARS, 1792–1802

After the execution of Louis XVI on 21 January 1793, Britain, Spain, Naples, Austria, Prussia and Sardinia declared war against the French Republic. British maritime concerns in these wars were to defend the British Isles and her colonies against invasion, protecting her trading interests, and attacking those of France and her allies. The Brest and Toulon squadrons were blockaded, but French fleet activity could not be stopped absolutely, and a number of actions were fought in the Western Approaches. The Batavian Republic, declared in the Netherlands in 1795, became an ally of France; its navy posed another threat to British interests, and was blockaded in Den Helder and the Texel. The Mediterranean theatre gained extra significance after 1796, when Spain joined France and their navies united. Napoleon needed control of the Mediterranean for his planned invasion of Egypt. In 1801 British control of the sea was further challenged by a pro-French alliance of Baltic powers known as the 'Armed Neutrality', designed to challenge British access to naval stores. Despite such varied interests in different parts of the globe, control of the Atlantic and the Mediterranean came into British hands, with the Danes and the Dutch pacified. Peace was declared at the Treaty of Amiens in May 1802.

1. The capture of the *Babet*, *Pomone* and *Engageante*, 23 April 1794

Commodore Sir John Warren was placed in command of a squadron of five frigates based at Falmouth with orders to terrorise French trade in the Western Approaches. Cruising off Guernsey he fell in with a squadron of four French frigates in line ahead. Warren chased in line ahead, and a fierce running action ensued as the British frigates slowly overhauled the French. The *Babet* (20), *Pomone* (44) and *Engageante* (36) surrendered, severely damaged. At the time the *Pomone* was considered the finest frigate afloat.

2. The Glorious First of June, 1 June 1794

The Channel Fleet, under Admiral Lord Howe, was searching in vain for a large grain convoy destined from the United States to France. The convoy was never located, but Howe came into contact with the main French fleet, which had been sent out to ensure the convoy's safe arrival. After two days of manœuvring and skirmishes in foggy weather, the fleets met with Howe to windward. Each captain was ordered to cut through the French line under the stern of his opposite number. Only seven of Howe's fleet of twenty-five obeyed (or understood) their instructions. Nevertheless the fight became general, and after a relatively brief but fierce engagement the French commander, Rear-Admiral Villaret-Joyeuse, retreated and was followed by those French ships that were not too damaged. Twelve crippled ships were left, of which five later limped back to their fleet. The remaining seven were taken by the British. The French suffered their heaviest losses in one day since the Battle of Barfleur in 1692.

3. Hotham's action, 14 March 1795

Vice-Admiral William Hotham, in temporary command of the Mediterranean squadron pursued the Toulon squadron, believed to be heading for Corsica, recently captured by Samuel Hood. During the chase a large French eighty-gunner, the *Ça Ira*, was disabled, and Hotham's two leading ships pounced. The French fleet under Admiral Martin bore down to fight off the British ships, who were recalled to the main fleet. The next day the *Ça Ira* was being towed by a French 74 when the British attacked again, and once more Martin bore down to their defence. This time the two fleets passed on opposite courses and exchanged fire. Martin chose not to prolong the engagement and fled, abandoning the two ships he had set out to defend. Many of Hotham's ships were badly damaged, and he chose not to pursue.

4. Cornwallis and Villaret-Joyeuse, 17 June 1795

Vice-Admiral Sir William Cornwallis was blockading Brest when he came into contact with a French convoy. Cornwallis attacked and Villaret-Joyeuse was sent out with the Brest fleet to defend it. Cornwallis's fleet was markedly inferior, and when he realised the overwhelming strength of the French he formed into a wedge formation with his flag-ship at the point. The French chased and gradually overhauled the British, targeting the rearmost ships. The slowest ship (the *Mars*) started to lag behind, but Cornwallis wore round in his huge flagship to her support. This bold move surprised the French. The *Mars* regained the line and firing gradually ceased. Earlier in the day Cornwallis had dis-patched the frigate *Phaeton* to scout ahead of the squadron. On her return, seeing Corn-wallis harried by the French, Captain Stopford pretended to signal to the main Channel Fleet over the horizon, taking care to use signals known to the French. The ruse worked and the French retreated.

5. Bridport's victory off L'Orient, 23 June 1795

The Channel Fleet had been sent out under Admiral Lord Bridport to protect an expedi-tion bound for Quiberon Bay. The French fleet under Villaret-Joyeuse, meanwhile, had left Brest, been scattered by a gale, and was heading back to port. Villaret-Joyeuse had no desire for battle and Bridport chased. The British closed with the French rear, but both fleets, already strung out, were further disrupted by a calm. Nevertheless, there was a prolonged skirmish between the French rear and the British van. Three French prizes were taken before the British retreated, Bridport being unwilling to chase the French inshore.

6. The Battle of Cape St Vincent, 14 February 1797

The Spanish fleet sailed from Cartagena to Cadiz in escort of a merchant convoy. The British under Admiral Sir John Jervis, cruising off Cape St Vincent, heard news of the Spanish fleet's position and readied for battle. Jervis was outnumbered, with fifteen war-ships to Vice-Admiral José de Córdoba's twenty-three, but the Spanish fleet was divided. Jervis quickly formed a line and cut through the gap to attack the main body of the enemy from the rear. Córdoba in turn tacked his van squadron to attack the British rear; the fleets in effect now chasing each other's tails. Jervis determined to block this move by ordering his rear squadron to turn and attack the van of the enemy as they approached. Jervis's signal was seen by Nelson, but not by his divisional commander, Vice-Admiral Sir Charles Thompson. Nevertheless, Nelson immediately turned and was followed by Collingwood. A close mêlée action ensued and the Spanish were heavily beaten, with Jervis taking four prizes, two of which were personally boarded by Nelson.

7. The Battle of Camperdown, 11 October 1797

The Dutch fleet under Vice-Admiral Jan Willem de Winter was reluctantly sent to sea to face the British, principally to distract public opinion from a series of disasters in the Dutch colonies. He was intercepted off the Texel on his way back to port by Admiral Adam Duncan. Duncan tried to form a line ahead but it took far too long, and the Dutch were nearing the safety of port all the time. He therefore attacked in his cruising formation; in two divisions, roughly at 90° to the enemy. Duncan then signalled for each ship to break through the enemy line and engage from to leeward – as Howe had attempted at the First of June. But yet again, as Howe experienced, only a handful of his captains understood or were able to perform the manœuvre. Duncan's two divisions bore down and overwhelmed the van and the rear of the enemy; their centre was not engaged. The Dutch were heavily defeated. Three Dutch admirals were captured, with nine ships of the line and two frigates.

8. The Battle of the Nile, 1 August 1798

Napoleon had set his heart on a conquest of Egypt, and the British were determined to frustrate his plans. Nelson was sent in pursuit of the French fleet. He eventually found them at anchor in Aboukir Bay, near the Rosetta entrance to the Nile. The French Vice-Admiral de Brueys had neglected to take the necessary precautions for defending a fleet at anchor. They were at a single anchor and would therefore swing with the wind or tide. Moreover, most had not run out springs to their anchor by which their position could be controlled. On their approach, the captain of the leading British ship realised that the French line could be doubled – as they were only at single anchor, there had to be sufficient room for them to swing round. Captain Foley of the *Goliath* consequently ran down the inshore side of the French fleet, which had not even been cleared for battle. Some followed him while others took the seaward side, trapping the French between two fires. The van and centre of the French were overwhelmed, while their rear, under Admiral Villeneuve, offered no assistance and escaped at daylight. Eleven French ships of the line and two frigates were taken or sunk.

9. Warren and Bompart, 12 October 1798

In 1798 there broke out a large scale rebellion of the United Irishmen, an aggressively Catholic movement to whom the French offered assistance. A French squadron under Commodore Jean Bompart sailed for Ireland with troops to reinforce the French General Humbert, who had landed in August. Captain Sir John Warren intercepted them with a squadron of eight ships, and the two fleets engaged in a chase action over three days interrupted by appalling weather. The British fleet gradually overhauled and overwhelmed the centre and rear of the French. Seven of the ten French ships were taken, and with them a great deal of intelligence regarding French designs in Ireland.

10. The Battle of Copenhagen, 2 April 1801

Admiral Sir Hyde Parker was sent to the Baltic to strike against the neutral Danes, who were increasingly being drawn towards an alliance with France along with Sweden and Russia. The Danish fleet, boosted with floating batteries, was anchored at Copenhagen, reinforced from the rear by powerful shore batteries. Much like the French at the Nile, though, the Danish fleet had no springs run to their anchors, and could not therefore manœuvre. A British squadron under Nelson was dispatched to attack the weaker southern end of the Danish fleet, to clear a way for gunboats to bombard the city. A lack of navigational intelligence caused three ships to ground and the rest to engage further away than they would wish, but the Danes were gradually worn down in a brutal action. Before they struck, however, in the belief from his position some distance away that the British were being worsted, Parker ordered a retreat. Nelson realised that to retreat was to manœuvre disabled ships in shoal water under the guns of the enemy – a highly dangerous proposal. He ignored Parker's signal and continued the action. All the captains in Nelson's division followed his example, and the Danes struck.

11. Saumarez off Algeciras, 6 and 12 July 1801

A French squadron of three ships under Rear-Admiral C. A. Durand de Linois was bound for Cadiz, but when he found it blockaded he took shelter at Algeciras and anchored in line under the shore batteries. Rear-Admiral Sir James Saumarez attacked with five ships, but the attack failed in light and baffling winds and the British were forced to retreat to Gibraltar. Vice-Admiral Juan Moreno then arrived with five Spanish ships to escort Linois to Cadiz. Despite being outnumbered, Saumarez, whose pride was bruised from his earlier failed attack, gave chase. It was night before the leading British ship made it up to the allied fleet and opened fire on a Spanish three-decker. She responded by firing into another Spanish three-decker, mistaking her for an enemy. Both Spanish ships continued to fight each other until they collided and blew up together, losing all hands. One French 74 was taken, and the rest limped into Cadiz.

THE NAPOLEONIC WARS, 1803–15

The Treaty of Amiens satisfied neither side for long, and Britain and France were soon at war again. Napoleon, who had become First Consul of France after his coup in 1799, proclaimed himself emperor in 1804. His plans for territorial expansion included an invasion of England, for which he needed control of the Channel. The Royal Navy blockaded the French fleets with the aim of attacking them if they put to sea. This was done with devastating success at the Battle of Trafalgar. Napoleon's plans for an invasion having been thwarted, his naval policy shifted to one of commerce raiding while he rebuilt his fleet. The Royal Navy responded to the threat with powerful frigate squadrons of its own. The threat of invasion never completely receded, however, and as Napoleon's empire expanded he could either influence or directly control the navies of Spain, Holland and Denmark, which all became targets of British naval aggression. Finally the combined power of Prussia, Russia and Austria broke the back of Napoleon's empire on the battlefields of Russia and Germany. His final defeat came at Waterloo in 1815.

1. Moore and the Spanish treasure ships, 5 October 1804

It was believed in London that Spain's declaration of war against England was only waiting for the arrival of a treasure convoy from South America, so before war was declared with Spain, four British frigates under Captain Graham Moore were despatched to intercept the convoy. Four large frigates were sited off Cape Santa Maria (near Cadiz) and chased. The Spanish formed a line ahead and the British drew up parallel. Questions were exchanged and a lieutenant even sent aboard the Spanish flagship to explain that they were there to detain the squadron. The Spanish opened fire, and action became general. After a very short engagement one of the Spaniards blew up, and the remaining three surrendered soon after. The Spanish were quick to join Napoleon in his war with Britain.

2. Calder's action, 22 July 1805

Rear-Admiral Villeneuve, attempting to follow Napoleon's orders to prepare for the invasion of England, arrived off Ferrol from the West Indies, where he had failed to meet up with the Brest and Rochefort squadrons as intended. On his return he fell in with Admiral Sir Robert Calder. Calder was outnumbered, but still attacked, intending to overwhelm the centre and rear of the enemy. Villeneuve countered the manœuvre by tacking, which was again matched by Calder. Finally the fleets met in dense fog. Both fleets were heavily damaged and lost cohesion, but the British secured two Spanish prizes. With dusk the battle ended. The fleets remained in close proximity for two days, but Calder did not renew the action when he could, preferring to protect his crippled ships. He was strongly reprimanded.

3. The Battle of Trafalgar, 21 October 1805

In August Napoleon had abandoned his plans for an invasion of England, and the combined fleet under Villeneuve was ordered into the Mediterranean to assist with his campaign against Austria. Nelson learned of their movements and closed in off Gibraltar. The allied fleet formed a conventional line ahead to meet Nelson's unconventional attack. He attacked in two divisions, at right angles to the enemy line, the lines being led by Nelson and Collingwood in their flagships. No admiral had ever led his fleet (or division) into battle in this way. Nelson cut through the middle of the allied fleet and Collingwood through the rear. The van of the allied fleet under Rear-Admiral P. E. Dumanoir Le Pelley made no move to support the centre and the rear until too late. The British took seventeen prizes, and another was sunk; nine of those prizes were lost in the storm that followed the battle.

4. Strachan's action off Ferrol, 4 November 1805

After Trafalgar four ships of the allied van under Dumanoir escaped into the Atlantic. They were finally caught by Rear-Admiral Sir Richard Strachan off Cape Finisterre with a much stronger force. Strachan attacked the rear three French ships, but they tacked to counter this concentration. Strachan responded with less success, but soon gained the upper hand as the French were caught between two fires. All four French ships surrendered.

5. Duckworth at San Domingo, 6 February 1806

Napoleon's naval strategy after Trafalgar was to create powerful commerce-raiding squadrons. One of these, a squadron of five ships of the line and three frigates under

Rear-Admiral Corentin de Leissègues, had headed for the French West Indies with supplies. Admiral Sir John Duckworth followed, and discovered them in Santo Domingo Bay. Leissègues divided his fleet, the frigates forming a separate division while the ships of the line formed a defensive line ahead. Duckworth ignored the frigates, divided his force into two squadrons, and attacked the French ships of the line at van and rear. They were all taken or sunk, but the frigates escaped.

6. Hoste's action off Lissa, 13 March 1811

Rear-Admiral Edouard Dubordieu attempted to capture the island of Lissa in the Adriatic to secure local trade from the threat of British cruisers. Lissa was defended by a small squadron of British ships under the command of Captain William Hoste. Dubordieu divided his force of ten vessels, including six powerful frigates, into two divisions and bore down on the British line, but the closeness of the British formation and the ferocity of their gunnery drove him off. Being close inshore, Hoste then wore his fleet, and the battle continued in some confusion until the allied fleet retreated, with Dubordieu dead and half his ships wrecked or captured.

THE WAR OF 1812

While Britain was pursuing its war with Napoleon, American merchants saw potential profit in trading with the blockaded French ports. The British reacted by banning American ships from the lucrative West Indian trade. Moreover, the British need for seamen was as high as it ever had been; to meet the demand they exploited their right to impress British citizens from neutral ships. Thousands of Americans were pressed into the Royal Navy. Relations worsened, and with President Madison's Republican Party in crisis in 1812, the President saw war as an opportunity to unite his party and secure another term in office. By attacking the remaining British colonies in North America, the United States could also achieve full independence. Britain blockaded the eastern seaboard, and there were a number of single-ship engagements. Meanwhile, as the land war developed, control of the Great Lakes became a crucial strategic goal, and Britain and America became locked in a remarkable land-locked arms race to build navies to control the lakes.

1. The Battle of Lake Erie, 10 September 1813

The British squadron on Lake Erie comprised two ships, two brigs, a schooner and a sloop, and was commanded by Commander Robert Barclay. He was defending the harbour of Presque Isle, the source of supply for the British army and their Indian allies inland. Driven offshore by poor weather, he returned to find the American squadron under Master Commandant Oliver Perry in control of the harbour. Perry attacked the well-formed British fleet, but his squadron struggled to come into action together, and he was badly outnumbered. Although Perry's flagship surrendered, he escaped and transferred his flag. The remainder of Perry's squadron, meanwhile, had joined the battle. The British ships were badly damaged, lost all defensive cohesion and the senior officers aboard every British vessel bar one were killed. The entire British squadron surrendered.

Glossary of Nautical Terms

This glossary covers words and phrases in the nautical or historical senses which occur in this volume. Many of them bear or have borne other meanings.

abaft. *See* AFT.

abeam, *adj.* In the direction at right angles to the ship's centreline.

aboard, *adj.* 1. On board a ship. 2. Alongside, touching another ship.

admiral, *sb.* 1. The senior officer commanding a fleet of ships. — **of the Blue, Red, White**, an admiral of the Blue, Red or White squadron (ranking in seniority Red, White, Blue).

Admiralty, *sb.* 1. The administration directed by the Lord Admiral or Board of Admiralty. 2. The building occupied by the Admiralty. 3. — **Board**, the Commissioners for executing the office of Lord High Admiral.

aft, abaft, *adj.* Towards the stern or after part of the ship.

aloft, *adj.* 1. Relating to the masts and rigging, upwards. 2. On deck.

alongside, *adj.* Beside or against the ship's side or the quayside.

alow, *adj.* Below.

amidship(s), *adj.* Relating to the middle or centreline of the ship.

ashore, *adj.*, *adv.* Towards or on the shore.

astern, *adj.* Behind a ship, in the direction from which she is moving.

athwart, *adj.* Across.

athwartships, *adj.* Across, at right angles to the ship's centreline.

awash, *adj.* Level with the surface of the sea, with waves washing over it.

back, *vb.* 1. To trim the sails so that they catch the wind on the wrong side and check the ship's way. 2. (Of the wind) to change in an anti-clockwise direction.

ballast, *sb.* Stones, gravel or other weight stowed low in a ship to improve her stability.

barge, *sb.* 1. A small coastal or riverine cargo vessel. 2. A type of ship's boat.

battery, *sb.* 1. The broadside guns mounted on one deck, or one side, of the ship. 2. A group of guns mounted ashore. 3. **floating** —, a stationary raft or hulk mounting heavy guns.

beam, *sb.* 1. The width of the ship. 2. The direction at right angles to the centreline. 3. A timber running from side to side of a ship to support a deck.

bear, *vb.* 1. To lie or point in a particular direction. 2. — **away**, to bear up, to turn downwind. 3. — **down**, to bear up. 4. — **up**, to turn downwind.

bearing, *sb.* A direction.

beat, beat up, *vb.* (Of a ship) to work to windward by successive tacks, to proceed obliquely to windward with the wind first on one side and then the other.

before, *adj.* In front of, ahead of.

below, *adj.* Within the body of a ship.

bend, *vb.* To make a sail fast to its yard, mast or stay.

bilge, *sb.* 1. The angle of the ship's hull between side and bottom. 2. — **and bilge**, *adj.* close alongside, touching.

binnacle, *sb.* A locker containing the steering compasses, standing immediately before the wheel.

block, *sb.* 1. A pulley. 2. **double** —, a pulley with two sheaves. 3. **Single** —, a pulley with one sheave.

board, *vb.* To go aboard a ship.

boarder, *sb.* A member of the ship's company ordered to attack the enemy by boarding.

boatswain, *sb.* A ship's officer responsible for sails, rigging and ground tackle. 2. —'**s call**, a whistle used to convey orders.

bomb, bomb vessel, *sb.* A warship designed to carry one or two heavy mortars for shore bombardment.

bonnet, *sb.* A strip of canvas laced to the foot of a sail to increase its area.

boom, *sb.* 1. A light running spar, particularly one extending the foot of a sail. 2. A floating barrier protecting a harbour.

bow, *sb.* Either side of the foremost part of the ship's hull, as it widens from the stem. **on the —,** *adj.* said of a ship or object on a bearing somewhere between right ahead and abeam.

bowsprit, *sb.* A spar projecting over the bows, spreading various items of rigging and one or more sails.

brail, *sb.* A line or tackle which hauls a sail against its yard or spar to allow it to be secured.

brig, *sb.* A vessel square-rigged on two masts.

bring to, *vb.* (Of a ship) to heave to or stop, usually by backing one or more sails.

broadside, *sb.* 1. The side of the ship. 2. The number of guns mounted or bearing on one side. 3. the simultaneous fire of those guns. 4. The total weight of shot fired by all the guns of the ship. 5. **— on,** *adj.* of a ship showing her broadside at right angles to the observers line of sight, or to a named point of reference.

bulkhead, *sb.* A vertical partition within the ship.

bulwark, *sb.* A barrier around the side of a deck.

cable, *sb.* 1. A large rope or hawser, particularly the anchor cable. 2. The standard length of an anchor cable, 120 fathoms.

canister, canister shot, *sb.* Anti-personnel shot made up of musket balls enclosed in a tin canister.

capstan, *sb.* A mechanical device for hauling in cables, consisting of a vertical revolving drum turned by bars inserted in its rim.

captain, *sb.* 1. A post-captain. 2. A master and commander, later commander. 3. The form of address of the commanding officer of any armed ship or vessel. 4. **— of the fleet,** a captain or rear-admiral assisting the commander-in-chief.

careen, *vb.* To heel a ship over to expose one side of her underwater hull for cleaning or repairs.

carronade, *sb.* A type of short gun, of heavy calibre but small charge and short range.

cartridge, *sb.* A cloth or paper bag containing the propellant charge of a gun.

caulk, *vb.* To make seams watertight.

caulking, *sb.* Material for caulking, usually oakum and pitch.

chase, *sb.* 1. The pursuit of one ship or squadron by another. 2. The ship pursued. 3. **— gun,** a gun mounted to fire ahead or astern. 5. **general —,** order to a squadron to pursue a beaten enemy without regard to order. 6. **stern —,** pursuit in which the pursued lies dead ahead of the pursuer.

chaser. *See* CHASE GUN.

clew, *sb.* One of the lower corners of a sail.

close-hauled, *adj., adv.* Steering as nearly towards the wind as possible.

colours, *sb.* Flags, especially the national ensign.

commission, *vb.* To establish a warship as an active unit for command, administrative and financial purposes.

complement, *sb.* The total ship's company authorised for her size or rate.

con, *vb.* To steer or pilot a ship in confined waters.

corvette, *sb.* French term for a brig-sloop.

course, *sb.* 1. The direction of ship's movement. 2. The foresail or mainsail, the lowest square sails.

court martial, *sb.* A court held under naval or military law.

crank, *adj.* Unstable, excessively tender.

cringle, *sb.* An eye sewn into a sail.

cruiser, *sb.* A warship, of any size or type, sent on detached operations, especially against enemy merchantmen.

cutter, *sb.* A small vessel fore and aft rigged on a single mast.

dead, *adj.* Directly, straight.

deck, *sb.* A floor or platform within a ship. 2. **— head,** the underside of the deck overhead. 3. **gun —,** the deck carrying the main battery (17th-19th century). 4. **half —,** the after end of the main deck, below the quarterdeck.   5. **lower** —. (a) the gun deck or (in a two- or three-decker) lowest gun deck; (b) the ratings of the ship's company as a whole, those who berth on the lower deck.   6. **main** —, the highest deck running the whole length of the ship.   7. **quarter** —, a deck above the main deck over the after part of the ship.   8. **spar** —, a light deck connecting quarter deck to forecastle.   9. **upper** —, a continuous weather deck incorporating quarterdeck and forecastle.   10. **weather** —, a deck exposed to the sky.

double, double on, *vb.* To attack a ship or squadron from both sides.

draught, *sb.* The depth of water required to float a ship.

draw, *vb.* 1. To haul.   2. (Of a sail) to be filled with wind, to pull.   3. (Of a ship) to require a specified depth of water to float her.

driver, *sb.* A gaff sail set on the mizzenmast of a ship, or the mainmast of a brig.

easting, *sb.* Distance run or made good to the eastward.

ebb, *sb.* The falling tide.

embark, *vb.* To board or be loaded on board a ship.

ensign, *sb.*   A flag flown aft by warships and merchantmen to indicate nationality.

establishment, *sb.* A scheme fixing the number of guns, dimensions etc. of the ships of a Navy.

eye, *sb.* A circular or tear-shaped metal fitting let into a sail or splice.

falls, *sb.* The hauling part of a purchase, part of the running rigging led down to the deck.

fireship, *sb.* A small warship fitted with combustibles in order to destroy enemy ships by setting herself on fire and running alongside them.

fireshot. *See* SHOT.

flag, *sb.* 1. An admiral's distinguishing flag.   2. — **captain**, the captain of a flagship.   3. — **rank**, admiral's rank.   4. — **ship**, the admiral's ship.

flood, *sb.* The rising tide.

flotilla, *sb.* 1. A group of small warships.   2. Coastal warships considered as a whole.

foot, *sb.* The lower edge of a sail.

fore, afore, *adj.* Towards the bow of the ship.

fore-and-aft, *adj.* Of a type of rig in which sails of various shapes are bent to masts or stays and move about positions parallel to the ship's centreline.

forecastle, *sb.* A deck built over the forward end of the main deck.

foremast. *See* BEFORE *and* MAST.

foresail. *See* SAIL.

forward, *adj., adv.* Relating to the fore part of ship, or motion towards the bow.

foul, *adj.* 1. (Of rope etc.) obstructed, tangled.   2. (Of the weather) stormy.   3. (Of a ship's hull) weed-grown, in need of cleaning.

foul, *vb.* To obstruct, tangle or dirty.

fouling, *sb.* 1. The process whereby a ship's underwater hull becomes foul.   2. The weed, barnacles etc. responsible.

founder, *vb.* To sink.

freeboard, *sb.* The minimum height of the ship's side above the waterline.

frigate, *sb.* A cruising warship with an unarmed lower deck, mounting her battery on the main deck.

full, *adj.* (Of a ship's hull form) voluminous or capacious in proportion to length and beam.

furl, *vb.* To bundle up a sail to its yard, mast or stay.

gaff, *sb.* 1. A short spar hinged at the masthead, supporting the peak of a fore-and-aft foresail, mainsail or driver.   2. — **rig**, a form of fore-and-aft rig in which the principal sails are quadrangular, their peaks supported by gaffs.   3. — **sail**, one whose peak is supported by a gaff.

gage. *See* WEATHER GAGE.

galley, *sb.* 1. A type of small boat.   2. A small sailing warship or merchantman fitted to row with sweeps.   3. A type of inshore warship propelled primarily by oars.   4. The kitchen or cook-room of a ship.

gangway, *sb.* 1. A light bridge connecting forecastle and quarterdeck.

gear, *sb.* Rigging or equipment.

general, *sb.* A commander-in-chief (17th century).

get the wind, *vb.* To gain the weather gage.

gibe, *vb.* To shift a fore and aft sail to the other tack, as in wearing ship, hence to wear or turn abruptly.

glass, *sb.* 1. A half-hour glass, used to tell time aboard ship. 2. A measure of time, half an hour.

grape, grapeshot, *sb.* Anti-personnel shot made up of small shot secured together in such a way as to fly apart on firing.

ground, *vb.* 1. To run aground. 2. To beach a ship in order to work on her underwater hull at low tide.

gun, *sb.* 1. A piece of artillery. 2. — **deck**. *See* DECK. 3. — **lock**, a flintlock firing mechanism for a great gun. 4. — **port**, a port cut to allow guns mounted below decks to fire out. 5. — **shot**, the range of a gun. 6. — **tackle**, tackle rigged to run out the gun after firing. 7. **chase** —. *See* CHASE.

gunboat, *sb.* A small armed vessel mounting one or two carriage guns.

halyard, *sb.* A rope or tackle used to hoist a yard or sail.

hand, *sb.* A member of a ship's company, a sailor.

hand, *vb.* To reef or furl a sail.

handspike, *sb.* A wooden bar or lever.

handy, *adj.* Handling easily, manoeuvrable.

haul, *vb.* 1. To pull on a rope. 2. — **up**, to alter course into the wind, to be close-hauled.

head, *sb.* 1. The foremost part of the ship's hull, projecting outwards and forward of the stem and partly supporting the bowsprit. 2. The ship's heading, the direction in which she points. 3. — **sail**. *See* SAIL. 4. — **sea**. *See* SEA. 5. — **wind**. *See* WIND.

head, *vb.* (Of the wind) to blow from ahead, to stop the progress of a ship.

heave, *vb.* 1. To haul a rope. 2. (Of a ship) to rise and fall in a swell. 3. — **down**, to careen. 4. — **to**, (of a ship) to stop or lie to by backing some of the sails.

heavy, *adj.* (Of the weather) stormy.

heel, *vb.* (Of the ship) to incline or be inclined to one side or the other.

helm, *sb.* 1. The tiller. 2. The means of steering a ship.

hog, *vb.* (Of a ship's hull) to lose structural rigidity, to deform, so that bow and stern drop relative the middle of the hull.

hold, *sb.* The lowest internal space of a ship, below all the decks.

hull, *sb.* The body or main structure of a ship or vessel.

inboard, *adj., adv.* In, into the ship.

inshore, *adj., adv.* Near, towards the shore.

jack, *sb.* A type of national flag flown forward, particularly by warships.

jib, *sb.* A triangular headsail hoisted on a stay set between the foretopmast and the bowsprit.

jibboom, *sb.* An extension to the bowsprit.

keel, *sb.* The timber lying centrally along the length of the bottom of the ship, forming a spine upon which other parts of her frame are erected.

knee, *sb.* A timber angle-bracket connecting two or more ship's timbers.

landfall, *sb.* The point at which the navigator meets or intends to meet the coast.

landward, *adj., adv.* Towards the land.

langridge, *sb.* Anti-personnel and dismasting shot made up of irregular pieces of iron, nails etc.

larboard, *adj.* Relating to the port or left-hand side of the ship.

large, *adj.* Relating to a course with the wind abaft the beam.

lask, lask away, *vb.* To sail large, but not right before the wind (17th century).

lateen, *adj.* Of a type of fore-and-aft rig in which large triangular sails are bent to yards which are set so that the foot is made fast on deck and the middle hoisted to the masthead.

latitude, *sb*. A position lying on a line around the earth parallel to the Equator, hence fixed in a north–south direction.

lay, *vb*. 1. (Of a gun) to aim or point. 2. — **up** (of a ship) to place out of service, in reserve.

lead, *sb*. A weight on a marked line, used for sounding.

leads, *sb*. Inshore channels amongst the coastal islands of Norway, Sweden etc.

league, *sb*. A measure of distance, 3 miles.

lee, *sb*. 1. The direction towards which the wind is blowing. 2. The water sheltered from the wind by the land or by a ship. 3. — **shore**, a coastline towards which the wind is blowing.

leeward, *adj*. Relating to the direction towards which the wind is blowing.

leewardly, *adj*. (Of a ship) tending to drift rapidly to leeward when trying to sail close-hauled.

leeway, *sb*. The extent to which the wind blows a ship to leeward.

lieutenant, *sb*. 1. A commissioned sea officer immediately junior to the captain. 2. — **commander**, — **in command**, a lieutenant commanding a small warship. 3. **first** (**second, third** etc.) —, lieutenant ranking first (second, third etc.) in seniority after the captain.

line, *sb*. 1. — **abreast**, A formation in which the ships of a squadron sail on the same course abeam of one another. 2. — **ahead**, a formation in which one or more ships follow a leader, imitating his movements. 3. — **of battle**, a fighting formation in which the ships of a fleet form a straight line in a predetermined order. 4. — **of bearing**, a formation in which a squadron of ships lie in a straight line diagonal to their course. 5. **centre** —, a line down the middle of the ship from bow to stern. 6. **water** —. *See* WATERLINE.

longboat, *sb*. The largest of the ship's boats.

longitude, *sb*. A position lying on a straight line drawn around the earth's surface from one pole to the other, hence fixed in an east–west direction.

loose, *vb*. To hoist or let drop sails, to make sail.

luff, luff up, *vb*. To turn into the wind.

magazine, *sb* 1. A storehouse. 2. A storehouse for explosives. 3. A compartment in the ship for storing powder.

mainmast. *See* MAST.

mainsail. *See* SAIL.

maintop. *See* TOP.

mainyard. *See* YARD.

make sail, *vb*. To set sail.

mast, *sb*. 1. A vertical spar or spars supporting sails, rigging and other spars. 2. **fore** —, the foremost mast. 3. **lower** —, the lowest and principal element of fore, main or mizzen mast, on which the topmast is stepped. 4. **made** —, a mast made up of more than one tree assembled together. 5. **main** —, the tallest (usually second) mast. 6. **mizzen** —. *See* MIZZEN. 7. **topgallant** —, **top** —. *See* TOPGALLANTMAST, TOPMAST. 8. — **dock**. *See* DOCK. 9. — **head**, the top of a lower, top or topgallantmast.

master, *sb*. 1. The commanding officer of a merchant ship. 2. A warrant sea officer responsible for the navigation and pilotage of a warship. 3. — **and commander**, a quasi-rank intermediate between lieutenant and post-captain (1674-1794).

midshipman, *sb*. 1. An inferior or petty officer. 2. A boy or young man hoping to become a commissioned officer.

mizzen, *sb*. 1. The aftermost mast of a ship or ketch. 2. — **peak**, the upper end of the mizzen yard or gaff. 3. **mizzentop**. *See* TOP. 4. — **yard**, the yard of the lateen mizzen sail (17th – mid-18th century).

moor, *vb*. To secure a ship by two anchors, or by making fast to a buoy.

offing, *sb*. The open sea, as viewed from on shore or inshore.

onshore, *adj., adv*. Towards or on the shore.

ordinance, *sb*. 1. Heavy guns. 2. *adj*. Relating to the Ordinance Board.

outboard, *adj., adv.* Relating to, towards, the outside of the ship.

parallel, *sb.* A meridian of latitude or longitude.

pay, *vb.* (of a ship in stays) to fall off on to one or other tack.

peak, *sb.* 1. The after topmost corner of a gaff or sprit-rigged sail. 2. **mizzen —**. *See* MIZZEN.

pipe, *sb.* An order conveyed by the boatswain's call.

pipe, *vb.* To give an order by the boatswain's call.

pitch, *vb.* To dip head and stern alternately into the waves.

point, *sb.* 1. A point of the compass, one of the thirty-two divisions of the compass card. 2. The interval between two points, an arc of $11\frac{1}{4}°$. 3. A point of sailing, one of the directions relative to the wind in which a vessel may sail.

point, *vb.* 1. (Of a ship) to head in a particular direction relative to the wind. 2. To lay a gun on some particular target. 3. **— high** (of a ship) to lie particularly close to the wind when close-hauled.

poop, *sb.* A short deck built over the after end of the quarterdeck.

port, *sb.* 1. An opening cut in a ship's side. 2. **gun —**, a port out of which a gun is fired.

privateer, *sb.* A privately owned warship licensed by letter of marque to capture enemy shipping for profit.

pull, *vb.* To row.

purchase, *sb.* An arrangement of rope led through pulleys in order to haul at a mechanical advantage.

quadrant, *sb.* A navigational instrument capable of taking sights or angles up to $90°$.

quarter, *sb.* 1. The sides of the ship's stern. 2. (*pl.*) Each man's post or station in action. 3. Mercy, safety on surrender. 4. **— deck.** *See* DECK. 5. **on the —**, in a direction between abeam and right aft, diagonal to the ship's course.

quoin, *sb.* A wedge inserted between the breech of the gun and the bed of the gun carriage, to adjust the elevation of the gun.

rack, *vb.* (Of a ship's hull) to distort by twisting.

rake, *sb.* An angle from the vertical.

rake, *vb.* To fire down the length of an enemy ship from ahead or astern.

rate, *sb.* 1. One of the six classes into which the larger warships were divided.

razee, *sb.* A ship modified by being 'cut down' by one deck.

reach, *vb.* To sail with the wind abeam.

rear-admiral, *sb.* 1. An admiral third in command of a fleet (17th century). 2. The flag-officer commanding the rear division of a fleet (17th century). 3. A rear-admiral's flagship (17th century). 4. A flag-officer of the rank of Rear-Admiral of the Red, White or Blue (18th century).

reckoning, *sb.* 1. A calculation of the ship's position. 2. **dead —**, an estimate of the ship's position without the benefit of observations, by calculating course, speed and drift from a known point of departure.

reef, *sb.* 1. A tuck taken in a sail to reduce its area. 2. A line of submerged rocks. 3. **— point**, a short length of line secured through a sail in order to be made fast around the yard or boom to take in a reef.

reef, *vb.* To shorten sail by bundling part of the sail against yard or boom.

reeve, *vb.* To run or lead a piece of running rigging through a block, eye etc.

refit, *sb.* The process of repairing a ship and putting her in good condition for service.

ride, *vb.* To lie at anchor.

rig, *sb.* 1. The style or arrangement of a ship's masts and sails. 2. **ship —**. *See* SHIP.

rig, *vb.* To prepare or set up something, particularly a ship's masts and rigging.

rigger, *sb.* One who rigs ships, a seaman employed in a dockyard.

rigging, *sb.* 1. The ropes supporting and controlling the masts and spars. 2. **running —**, rigging controlling the movement of sails and movable spars.

3. **standing** —, rigging supporting the masts.

road, roadstead, *sb.* An open anchorage.

roll, *vb.* (Of a ship) to heel from one side to the other under the pressure of the waves.

ropeyard, *sb.* A naval rope factory.

rudder, ruther, *sb.* 1. A paddle or blade turned to steer the ship.   2. — **irons**. *See* IRONS.

run, *vb.* 1. To sail downwind, in the direction towards which the wind is blowing. 2. — **out**, to haul out a gun to its firing position.

running, *adj.* Hoisting, moving.

ruther. *See* RUDDER.

sag, *vb.* (Of a ship's hull) to lose structural rigidity, to deform, so that the middle of the hull drops relative to bow and stern.

sail, *sb.* 1. A piece of cloth spread aloft by masts and rigging to catch the wind and propel a ship.   2. Some number of ships. 3. — **cloths**, heavy canvas for sails. 4. — **plan**, an arrangement of sails. 5. **easy** —, a reduced sail plan, for slow speed.   6. **fore** —, the fore course, the lowest square sail set on the foremast. 7. **head** —, a sail set forward of the foremast.   8. **main** —, the main course, the lowest square sail set on the mainmast. 9. **stay** —, a triangular sail set on one of the stays supporting a mast from ahead. 10. **studding** —, a light sail temporarily spread outboard of a square sail in light airs.   11. **top** —, a square sail hoisted on the topmast, above the course.

sail, *vb.* 1. (Of any sort of ship) to move, to proceed.   2. **make** —, to hoist, spread sail.   3. **shorten** —, to reduce, take in sail.

scantlings, *sb.* The structure of the ship's hull.

schooner, *sb.* A small sailing vessel fore-and aft rigged on two masts.

scupper, *sb.* A port or channel to carry water off a deck and over the ship's side.

scuttle, *vb.* 1. To cut a hole in the ship's deck or side.   2. To sink a ship deliberately.

sea, *sb.* 1. A wave or waves.   2. — **board**, the coast.   3. — **boat**. (a) a ship considered as behaving well or badly in heavy seas; (b) a ship's boat kept prepared for immediate lowering at sea.   4. — **keeping**, the ability of a ship to remain at sea in all weathers.   5. — **legs**. The ability to stand or walk steadily on a moving deck. 6. — **mark**, a beacon, tower or other prominent object serving to assist the navigator to fix his position in relation to the coast.   7. — **officer**. *See* OFFICER. 8. — **way**, the open sea with a swell running.   9. **head** —, a wave or waves coming at the ship from ahead.

seaward, to seaward, *adj., adv.* In the direction of the open sea.

set, *sb.* The direction of flow of a current.

sextant, *sb.* A navigational instrument capable of taking sights or angles up to 120°.

sheer, *sb.* 1. The curve of the ship's hull along her length, as bow and stern rise from the horizontal.   2. The longitudinal rigidity of the ship's hull.   3. — **plan**, a draught of the ship seen from the side.

sheer, sheer up, *vb.* 1. To alter course sharply.   2. — **off**, to alter course away from something.

sheet, *sb.* A rope or tackle controlling the clew of a sail.

shift, *vb.* 1. To exchange, replace or move. 2. — **flag**, (of an admiral) to change flagship.

ship, *sb.* 1. A seagoing vessel.   2. A vessel square-rigged on three masts (17th-19th century).   3. — **handling**, the skill of manœuvring a vessel.   4. — **master**, the master of a merchant ship.   5. — **of the line**, a warship large enough to form part of the line of battle.   6. — **sloop**, a ship-rigged sloop.   7. **armed** —, an armed merchant ship on charter to the Navy, usually as a convoy escort.   8. **battle** —, a ship of the line.   9. **flag** —, an admiral's ship.   10. **guard** —, a warship kept in commission in port in peacetime. 11. **private** —, a warship not carrying an admiral.

ship, *vb.* 1. To bring inboard, to stow. 2. — **water**, to take in water through stress of weather.

shipworm, *sb.* The *teredo navalis*, a marine borer native to the Caribbean which infests timber.

shipwright, *sb.* 1. The carpenter skilled in shipbuilding. 2. **master —**, the yard officer responsible for all building and repairs.

shoal, *adj.* Shallow.

shoal, *sb.* A sandbank, reef or area of shallow water.

shorten sail, *vb.* To reduce the number or area of sails set.

shot, *sb.* 1. A bullet or (non-explosive) projectile fired from a great gun. 2. **canister —**. *See* CANISTER. 3. **chain —**, hollow shot formed in two halves containing and linked by a length of chain, designed to damage rigging. 4. **dismantling —**, one of a number of types of shot designed to damage masts and spars. 5. **grape —**. *See* GRAPE. 6. **fire —**, hollow shot filled with an incendiary compound.

shroud, *sb.* A stay supporting a mast from the side.

sling, *vb.* 1. To lift or hoist something. 2. To secure a yard with slings.

slip, *sb.* An inclined plane running into the water, on which a ship is built, or one up which vessels may be hauled for repairs.

slip, *vb.* 1. To haul a small vessel up a slip for repairs. 2. To cast off a rope, especially to cast off (and buoy) the cable, in order to sail without waiting to weigh anchor.

sloop, *sb.* 1. A small cruising warship, having only one internal deck, and mounting her main battery on the upper deck.

sound, *vb.* To take a sounding, to measure the depth of water beneath a ship.

sounding, *sb.* 1. A measurement of the depth of water. 2. **soundings**, the sea area within the 100-fathom line, capable of being sounded; the Western Approaches to the British Isles.

spar, *sb.* 1. A mast, pole or boom. 2. **— deck**. *See* DECK.

splice, *sb.* The union of two or more ropes or parts of ropes spliced together.

splice, *vb.* To marry two rope's ends, or two parts of the same rope, by parting the strands and weaving them into one another.

spring, *sb.* A hawser led from the capstan, out of the ship aft and made fast some way along the anchor cable, hauling on which will cant an anchored ship to bring her broadside to bear as desired.

spring, *vb.* (Of a mast or spar) to split along the grain.

spring tide. *See* TIDE.

spritsail, *sb.* 1. A sail set on a yard below the bowsprit. 2. **— topsail**, a sail set on a small mast stepped on the end of the bowsprit.

stand off, *vb.* To sail away from, to keep a distance from.

standing, *adj.* Fixed.

starboard, *adj.* Relating to the right-hand side of the ship.

stay, *vb.* 1. To tack. 2. **in stays**, *adj.* of a ship pointing into the wind while in the process of going about. 3. **miss stays**, *vb.* in tacking, to fail to turn into the wind and to fall back on to the original tack.

staysail. *See* SAIL.

stem, stempost, *sb.* 1. A timber rising in a curve from the keel and forming the centrepiece of the bows. 2. **stem for stem**, *adv.* head on.

stern, *sb.* 1. The after end of the ship. 2. **— post**, a straight timber erected on the after end of the keel, supporting both the rudder and the structure of the stern. 3. **— chaser**, a chase gun pointing aft.

stick, *sb.* A spar.

stiff, *adj.* Having large reserves of stability, heeling little to the pressure of the wind.

stow, *vb.* To put away.

strike, *vb.* 1. To lower a mast, spar, sail etc. 2. To strike colours, to surrender. 3. To run aground.

studding-sail. *See* SAIL.

surge, *sb.* Bodily movement of the ship ahead or astern.

sway, *sb.* Bodily movement of a ship from side to side.

sweep, *sb.* 1. A large oar. 2. The movement of something (e.g. the tiller) revolving about a fixed point.

tack, *sb.* 1. A rope or tackle serving to haul down the clew of a square sail. 2. The course held by a ship beating to windward. 3. **larboard —, port —**, the tack on which the wind blows from the left-hand side of the ship. 4. **starboard —**, the tack on which the wind blows from the right-hand side of the ship.

tack, *vb.* 1. To shift tacks, to go about, to turn into the wind and so onto the opposite tack. 2. To beat to windward by successive tacks.

tackle, *sb.* 1. A purchase formed of cordage rove through two or more blocks. 2. Rigging or gear in general. 3. **gun —**, a purchase used to handle a carriage gun.

take aback. *See* ABACK.

tender, tender-sided, *adj.* Having low reserves of stability, yielding easily to the pressure of the wind.

tiller, *sb.* A bar inserted in the head of the rudder by which the ship is steered.

top, *sb.* 1. A platform built at the head of the lower masts, serving to spread the shrouds of the topmast and provide a space for men working aloft. 2. **— gallant**. *See* TOPGALLANT. 3. **— hamper**, ship's structure or equipment carried high up, tending to increase windage or reduce stability. 4. **— man** (likewise **foretopman** etc.), a seaman skilled in working aloft. 5. **— mast**, a mast fitted to the top of the lower mast and extending it. 6. **— sail**, *See* SAIL. 7. **— sides**, the upper part of the ship's structure, clear of the water-line. 8. **— timber**, a structural timber forming the uppermost section of a frame on each side. 9. **— weight**, the weight of ship's structure or equipment carried high, hence tending to reduce stability. 10. **fore —, main —, mizzen —**. (a) the platform built at the head of the foremast, mainmast, mizzenmast; (b) the fore, main or mizzen topmast head, the head of the topmast or topgallantmast.

topgallant, topgallantsail, *sb.* 1. A square sail set on the topgallantmast, above the topsail. 2. **— mast**, a mast fitted to the top of the topmast and extending it.

3. **— yard**, the yard set on the topgallantmast, spreading the topgallant.

touch-hole, *sb.* A hole board into the bore of the gun at its inner end for the insertion of priming to fire the gun.

treenail, trenail, *sb.* A wooden peg or pin used to fasten together the parts of the hull of a wooden ship.

trim, *vb.* To adjust the set of the sails, or the angle at which the ship floats.

truck, *sb.* 1. The solid wheel of a naval gun carriage. 2. A disc of wood protecting the top of a mast.

truss, *sb.* A diagonal bracing timber.

tumblehome, *sb.* The inward slope of the ship's side above the waterline.

tye, *sb.* The pendant of the topsail halyard purchase, rove through a block or blocks at the masthead and so to the yard.

unhandy, *adj.* Unmanœuvrable, clumsy.

unmoor, *vb.* To weigh anchor, to cast off a mooring.

upperworks, *sb.* The upper portion of the ship's structure.

van, *sb.* The leading one of three divisions of a fleet.

veer, *vb.* 1. To pay out a cable. 2. To alter course sharply. 3. To wear. 4. (Of wind) to change in a clockwise direction.

vice-admiral, *sb.* 1. An officer second in command of a squadron (17th century). 2. The flag-officer commanding the van division of a fleet. 3. The deputy of the Lord Admiral in one of the maritime counties or colonies. 4. A vice-admiral's flagship (17th century). 5. A flag-officer of the rank of Vice-Admiral of the Red, White or Blue (18th century).

wake, *sb.* The track of the ship's passage through the water astern.

wall-sided, *adj.* Of a ship having no tumblehome, with vertical topsides.

watch, *sb.* 1. One of the seven divisions of the nautical day. 2. One of the two or three divisions of the ship's company, taking turns to be on duty. 3. The length of one watch, a spell of duty on deck. 4. **— bill**, a list of the ship's company divided into watches.

water, *sb.* 1. **high** —, **low** —, the tide standing at either end of its range.   2. **— line**, *sb.* The line of the water surface against the ship's hull.

way, *sb.* 1. The movement of a ship through the water.   2. **steerage** —, *sb.*, movement at a speed sufficient to allow the ship to be controlled by the helm.   3. **under** —, *adj.* moving through the water.

wear, *vb.* To alter course from one tack to the other by turning before the wind.

weather, *adj.* 1. Relating to the direction from which the wind is blowing.   2. **— gage**, *sb.* the windward position in relation to another ship or fleet.

weather, *vb.* To get to windward of something.

weatherly, *adv.* (Of a ship) tending to ship seas easily.

weigh, *vb.* To raise something (most often an anchor) from the seabed.

westing. *sb.* Distance run or made good to the westward.

whipstaff, *sb.* A vertical lever fixed to the inboard end of the tiller by which to steer the ship (17th century).

wind, *sb.* 1. The direction from which the wind blows.   2. The windward position, the weather gage.   3. **head** —, a wind coming from ahead, one making progress on that course impossible.   4. **off the** —, *adv.* sailing with the wind abaft the beam.   5. **on the** —, *adv.* sailing close-hauled.

wind and water, between, *adj.* on the waterline.

windage, *sb.* The ship's susceptibility to the lateral pressure of the wind, hence the extent to which she makes leeway.

windward, *adj.* Relating to the direction from which the wind is blowing.

work, *vb.* 1. To beat to windward.   2. (Of a ship's hull) to flex or move under the strain of the waves.

works, *sb.* 1. Parts of the ship's structure.   2. **upper** —, parts of the ship's structure above the main deck, not part of the hull structure.

yard, *sb.* 1. A spar hung horizontally from a mast to spread the head or foot of a square sail.   2. An establishment to build, repair and supply warships.   3. **— arm**, the extreme ends of a yard.   4. **main** —, the yard spreading the mainsail.

yaw, *sb.* Deviations from side to side of the ship's course under pressure of wind and sea.

Bibliography and Sources

MANUSCRIPT SOURCES

There are a great many references to battle in private letters and private journals, but finding them is a rather hit-and-miss process, and it is often sensible to go to the official Admiralty records first. They are held at The National Archives.

ADM 1 contains a great deal of information concerning sea fights. Captains' letters to the Admiralty contain accounts of single ship actions, while letters from commanders-in-chief to the Admiralty contain the accounts of fleet action. These usually include detailed reports from each ship involved, often with damage reports enclosed. Other miscellaneous interesting information is often included with these reports.

ADM 1 also contains the minutes of every court martial, which are a goldmine, offering detail on how ships and fleets worked, on how battles evolved, on thought process and practical problems, agenda and priority. Not only is action and behaviour described, but also it is explained at length, and often from a variety of standpoints. It is not unusual for the captain, the master and each lieutenant to be asked identical or similar questions. The evidence of these trails must be handled with care, however. A major problem was the time-gap between an action and the corresponding trial. Vice-Admiral Griffin's trial for misconduct in 1748 was held in 1751, two and half years after the event, a delay which was far from uncommon. Witnesses understandably had a good deal of trouble remembering specific details, such as the timing of certain signals or wind direction and strength. Inevitably, these trials were also the stage of passionate and complex disputes that reflected both political and personal bias, most notably in the aftermaths of the battles of Toulon in 1744 and Ushant in 1778. While minor detail regarding ship and fleet capability from these trials can be used with a certain degree of freedom, therefore, evidence with wider implications for the outcome of the trial, usually regarding questions of competence and expectations of behaviour, must be used with more care, and the evidence balanced as much as possible.

ADM 50 contains the Admirals' Journals. Every Admiral kept his own journal, which was like a log but with more detailed narrative. These often include information that is not mentioned in the official reports to the Admiralty.

ADM 51 and ADM 52 contain the Captains' and Masters' Logs. These include much of the day-to-day information of running a ship, and all fights are mentioned, although there is little room for lengthy narrative, and most entries are brief. Log books are remarkably dry sources, but provide some useful detail on signals, wind and weather conditions, damage and repair. At Keppel's trial in 1779, however, Captain Hood remarked, 'I do not think that log-books, which are kept in the manner in which ship's logbooks are, ought to be implicitly taken as evidence.'* The incautious historian is duly warned.

---

* W. Laird Clowes, *The Royal Navy: A History from the Earliest Times to 1900*, IV (London, Chatham Publishing, 1997), p. 95 n. 4.

PUBLISHED COURTS MARTIAL RECORDS

The Minutes of a Court Martial Held on Board H.M.S. *Lennox Enquiring into the Conduct of the Commanders of the Hampton Court and the Dreadnought* (London, 1745)

Minutes Taken at a Court Martial Assembled on H.M.S. *Torbay ... Being an Enquiry into the Conduct of Captain R. Norris* (London, 1745)

Copies of All the Minutes and Proceedings Taken at and Upon the Several Trials of Capt. George Burrish, Capt. Edmund Williams, Capt. John Ambrose Etc. On Board H.M.S. *London 23 Sept 1745* (London, 1746) [includes 'The Tryal of Captain John Ambrose', 'The Tryal of George Burrish', 'The Tryal of Captain Edmund Williams']

Minutes of the Proceedings of the Trial of Rear-Admiral Knowles (London, 1750)

The Trial of Vice-Admiral Griffin (London, 1751)

The Trial of the Honourable John Byng at a Court Martial (Dublin, 1757)

Account of the Arraignments and Tryals of Col. R. Kirkby, Capt. J. Constable, Capt. Cooper Wade, Capt. S. Vincent, Capt. C. Fogg ... For Cowardice, Neglect of Duty ... Committed by Them in a Fight at Sea Commenced the 19th August, 1702 (London, 1757)

An Authentic and Impartial Copy of the Trial of the Hon. Augustus Keppel, Admiral of the Blue (Portsmouth, 1779)

The Case of William Brereton Esq (London, 1779)

Minutes of the Proceedings at a Court Martial Assembled for the Trial of Vice-Admiral Sir Hugh Palliser (London, 1779)

Minutes of the Proceedings at a Court Martial Assembled to Enquire into the Loss of H.M.S. *Ardent* (London, 1780)

Minutes of the Proceedings of the Court Martial Assembled for the Trial of Captain John Moutray of H.M.S. *Ramillies* (London, 1781)

Minutes of the Proceedings at a Court Martial, Assembled for the Trial of Anthony James Pye Molloy, Esq., Captain of His Majesty's Ship Caesar (London, 1795)

Minutes of the Proceedings at a Court Martial ... For the Trial of Sir Robert Calder, Bart., Vice Admiral of the Blue (London, 1806)

Minutes of a Court Martial Holden on Board H.M.S. *Gladiator in Portsmouth Harbour, 20 June1807, for the Trial of Captain Laroche* (London, 1807)

'Minutes Taken at a Court Martial Assembled on Board H.M.S. *Gladiator* ... Regarding H.M.S. *Leander*', *The Naval Chronicle*, 18 (1807), pp. 160–73

OTHER PUBLISHED SOURCES

Adkins, R. *Trafalgar: The Biography of a Battle* (London, 2004)

Albion, R. G. *Forests and Seapower: The Timber Problem of the Royal Navy, 1652–1862* (Annapolis, 2000)

Allen, J., ed. *Memoir of the Life and Services of Admiral Sir William Hargood* (London, 1841)

Alston, A. H. *Captain Alston's Seamanship* (London, 1871)

Anderson, M. S. 'Russia in the Med, 1788–91: A Little-Known Chapter in the History of Naval Warfare and Privateering', *MM*, 45 (1959), pp. 25–35

—— *The War of the Austrian Succession* (London, 1995)

Anderson, R. C. *The Rigging of Ships in the Days of the Spritsail Topmast, 1600–1720* (Salem, MA, 1927)

——, ed. *The Journals of Sir Thomas Allin*, 2 vols., NRS, 79–80 (London, 1939)

——, ed. *Journals and Narratives of the Third Dutch War*, NRS, 86 (London, 1946)

—— 'Mediterranean Galley Fleets in 1725', *MM*, 42 (1956), pp. 179–87

The Annual Register (London, 1759)

Anon. *A Dialogue between Two Volunteers Belonging to a Ship Fitting to Sea from Chatham* (London, 1742)

—— *An Account of What Passed in the Engagement near Toulon between His Majesty's Squadron under the Command of Admiral Matthews and the Fleets of France and Spain* (London, 1744)

—— *A Vindication of the Conduct of Capt. M-N by a Sea Officer* (London, 1745)

—— *A Specimen of Naked Truth from a British Sailor* (London, 1746)

—— *Signaux de nuit et de brume qui seront observés par l'escadre du roi commandée par M. de la Clue chef d'escadre des armées navales de Sa Majesté* (Toulon, 1757)

—— *The Conduct of Admiral Knowles on the Late Expedition Set in a True Light* (London, 1758)

—— *A Short Account of the Naval Actions of the Last War … With Observations on the Discipline and Hints for the Improvement of the British Navy* (London, 1788)

—— 'A Treatise on Practical Navigation and Seamanship', *The Naval Chronicle*, 5 (1801), pp. 421–4

——(French) 'French Naval Tactics', *Naval Chronicle*, 4 (1801), pp. 142–8

—— 'Studies in the Theory of Naval Tactics I', *The Naval Review*, 1/1 (1913), pp. 26–47

—— 'Studies in the Theory of Naval Tactics II', *The Naval Review*, 1/2 (1913), pp. 146–67

—— 'Studies in the Theory of Naval Tactics III', *The Naval Review*, 1/4 (1913), pp. 351–75

—— 'The Place of Doctrine in War', *Naval Review*, 7 (1914), pp. 542–65

—— 'Journal of an Officer in the Naval Army in 1781 and 1782', in *The Operations of the French Fleet under the Count de Grasse in 1781–2: As Described in Two Contemporary Journals*, ed. J. G. Shea (New York, 1971), pp. 136–85

—— 'Voyage d'un Suisse dans différentes colonies d'Amérique pendant la dernière guerre', in *The Operations of the French Fleet under the Count de Grasse in 1781–2: As Described in Two Contemporary Journals*, ed. J. G. Shea (New York, 1971), pp. 196–202

Arnold-Forster, D. *The Ways of the Navy* (London, 1931)

Azar, G. *The Origins of Military Thought, from the Enlightenment to Clausewitz* (Oxford, 1989)

Bamford, P. *Fighting Ships and Prisons: The Mediterranean Galleys of France in the Age of Louis XIV* (Minneapolis, 1973)

Banbury, P. *Shipbuilders of the Thames and Medway* (Newton Abbot, 1971)

Barnaby, K. C. *Basic Naval Architecture*, 2nd edn (London, 1954)

Barnes, G. R., and J. H. Owen, eds. *The Private Papers of John, Earl of Sandwich, First Lord of the Admiralty, 1771–1782*, 4 vols., NRS, 69, 71, 75, 78 (London, 1932–8)

Barrow, J. *Navigatio Britannica: Or a Complete System of Navigation* (London, 1750)

Barrow, J. *The Life of Richard, Earl Howe* (London, 1838)

—— *The Life of Lord Anson* (London, 1839)

Baugh, D. A. *British Naval Administration in the Age of Walpole* (Princeton, 1965)

—— *Naval Administration, 1715–50*, NRS, 120 (London, 1977)

—— 'Sir Samuel Hood: Superior Subordinate', in *George Washington's Generals and Opponents: Their Exploits and Leadership*, ed. G. A. Billias (New York, 1994), pp. 291–326

—— ' "Too Much Mixed in This Affair": The Impact of Ministerial Politics in the Eighteenth Century Royal Navy', in *New Interpretations in Naval History*, ed. R. C. Balano and C. L. Symonds (Annapolis, 1999), pp. 21–43

Baumber, M. *General at Sea: Robert Blake and the Seventeenth Century Revolution in Naval Warfare* (London, 1989)

Beatson, R., ed. *Naval and Military Memoirs of Great Britain from 1727 to 1783* (London, 1804)

Beatty, W. *Authentic Narrative of the Death of Lord Nelson: With the Circumstances Preceding, Attending, and Subsequent to, That Event; The Professional Report on His Lordship's Wound; and Several Interesting Anecdotes* (London, 1807)

Bell's Weekly Messenger (1805)

Bellamy, R. R., ed. *Ramblin' Jack: The Journal of Captain John Cremer* (London, 1936)

Bennett, G. M. 'The Fleet Flagship: A Problem of Naval Command', *Journal of the Royal United Services Institute*, 81 (1936), pp. 601–11

—— *Nelson the Commander* (London, 1972)

Bertram, W. 'Investigating a Nineteenth Century Ship Design', paper presented at the New Researchers in Maritime History Conference, Royal Naval Museum, Portsmouth, 1995

Bigot de Morogues, S. F., *Tactique navale* (Paris, 1763)

Black, J. 'The Execution of Admiral Byng', *Quarterly Journal of Military History*, 11 (1999), pp. 98–103

—— and P. Woodfine, eds. *The British Navy and the Use of Naval Power in the Eighteenth Century* (Leicester, 1988)

Blunt, E. M. *Theory and Practice of Seamanship; Together with a System of Naval Tactics*, 2nd edn (New York, 1824)

Bonnefoux, P. M. J. de *Manœuvrier complet* (Paris, 1848)

Bonner-Smith, D., ed. *The Barrington Papers, Selected from the Letters and Papers of Admiral the Hon. S. Barrington*, 2 vols., NRS, 77, 81 (London, 1937–41)

—— 'Byron in the Leeward Islands, 1779: Part I', *MM*, 30 (1944), pp. 38–48

—— 'Byron in the Leeward Islands, 1779: Part II', *MM*, 30 (1944), pp. 81–91

Boteler, N. *Sea Dialogues* (London, 1688)

Boudriot, J. *The Seventy-Four Gun Ship: A Practical Treatise on the Art of Naval Architecture*, 4 vols. (Paris, 1986–8)

Bourchier, J. B., ed. *Memoir of the Life of Admiral Sir Edward Codrington*, 2 vols. (London, 1873)

Bourdé de Villehuet, J. *The Manœuverer, or Skilful Seaman: Being an Essay on the Theory and Practice of the Various Movements of a Ship at Sea as Well as of Naval Evolutions in General*, trans. J. N. J. de Sauseuil (London, 1788)

Boyd, J. M. *Manual for Naval Cadets* (London, 1860)

Breen, K. 'Graves and Hood at the Chesapeake', *MM*, 66 (1980), pp. 53–65

—— 'George Bridges, Lord Rodney, 1718?-1792', in *Precursors of Nelson: British Admirals of the Eighteenth Century*, ed. P. Le Fevre and R. Harding (London, 2000), pp. 225–48

Brenton, E. P. *Life and Correspondence of John, Earl St. Vincent*, 2 vols. (London, 1838)

Broomfield, J. H. 'The Keppel–Palliser Affair, 1778–1779', *MM*, 47 (1961), pp. 195–209

Brown, D. K. 'The Speed of Sailing Warships, 1793–1840', in *Les Empires en guerre et paix, 1793–1860*, ed. E. Freeman (Vincennes, 1990), pp. 155–94

Brown, R. H. *American Polearms, 1526–1865: The Lance, Halberd, Spontoon, Pike and Naval Boarding Weapons* (New Milford, CT, 1967)

Browning, O., ed. *The Journal of Sir George Rooke, Admiral of the Fleet, 1700–1702*, NRS, 9 (London, 1897)

Callender, G. A. R. 'With the Grand Fleet in 1780', *MM*, 9 (1923), pp. 258–70, 290–34

Callo, J. F. 'Nelson at Santa Cruz: A Minor Battle of Major Importance', *Sea History*, 79 (1996), pp. 19–21

Carr Laughton, L. G. 'H.M.S. Victory: Report to the *Victory* Technical Committee of a Search among the Admiralty Records', *MM*, 10 (1924), pp. 173–211

—— 'The Way of a Ship', *MM*, 14 (1928), pp. 132–48

—— 'Gunnery, Frigates and the Line of Battle', *MM*, 14 (1928), pp. 339–63

Caruana, A. B. *The History of English Sea Ordnance, 1523–1875*, 2 vols. (Rotherfield, 1994–7)

Castex, R. *Les Idées militaires de la marine du XVIIIᵉ siècle, de Ruyter à Suffren* (Paris, 1911)

Chadwick, F. A., ed. *The Graves Papers*, Naval History Society USA, 8 (New York, 1916)

Charnock, J. *An History of Marine Architecture*, 3 vols. (London, 1800–2)

Claridge, J. *The Shepherd of Banbury's Rules to Judge of the Changes of the Weather* (London, 1723)

Clerk, J. *An Essay on Naval Tactics* (London, 1790)

—— *An Essay on Naval Tactics, Systematical and Historical with Explanatory Plates in Four Parts*, 2nd edn (Edinburgh, 1804)

—— *An Essay on Naval Tactics, Systematical and Historical*, 3rd edn (Edinburgh, 1827)

Cochrane, M. 'Cochrane: Basque Roads, 1809', in *Great Battles of the Royal Navy as Commemorated in the Gun Room, Britannia Naval College, Dartmouth*, ed. E. Grove (1998), pp. 145–52

Cochrane, T. *The Autobiography of a Seaman* (London, 1860)

Cock, R. 'The Finest Invention in the World: The Royal Navy's Early Trials of Copper Sheathing, 1708–1770', *MM*, 87 (2001), pp. 446–59

Cogar, W. B., ed. *New Interpretations in Naval History* (Annapolis, 1997)

Colledge, J. J. *Ships of the Royal Navy: An Historical Index*, 2 vols. (Newton Abbot, 1969)

Colomb, P. H. *Naval Warfare: Its Ruling Principles and Practice Historically Treated* (London, 1895)

Corbett, J. S. *England in the Mediterranean: A Study of the Rise and Influence of British Power within the Straits, 1602–1713*, 2 vols. (London, 1904)

—— *Fighting Instructions, 1530–1816*, NRS, 29 (London, 1905)

—— *England in the Seven Years War: A Study in Combined Strategy*, 2 vols. (London, 1918)

—— *Some Principles of Maritime Strategy* (London, 1911)

——, ed. *Private Papers of George, Second Earl Spencer, First Lord of the Admiralty, 1794–1801*, 4 vols., NRS, 46, 48, 58, 59 (London, 1913–24)

—— *Signals and Instructions, 1776–1794* (London, 1971)

Cornwallis-West, G., ed. *The Life and Letters of Admiral Cornwallis* (London, 1927)

Coutau-Bégarie, H. *L'Évolution de la pensée navale*, 7 vols. (Paris, 1990–9)

Cowley, J. *The Sailors Companion* (London, 1740)

Craik, G. L. *The Pictorial History of England*, ed. C. Knight, VI (London, 1856)

Cranmer-Byng, J. L., ed. *Pattee Byng's Journal* (London, 1950)

Creswell, J. *British Admirals of the Eighteenth Century: Tactics in Battle* (London, 1972)

Crewe, D. G. *Yellow Jack and the Worm: British Naval Administration in the West Indies, 1739–48* (Liverpool, 1993)

Crimmin, P. K. 'Anson: Cape Finisterre, 1747', in *Great Battles of the Royal Navy as Commemorated in the Gun Room, Britannia Naval College, Dartmouth*, ed. E. Grove (London, 1998), pp. 71–8

—— 'John Jervis, Earl of St. Vincent, 1735–1823', In *Precursors of Nelson: British Admirals of the Eighteenth Century*, ed. P. Le Fevre and R. Harding (London, 2000), pp. 325–52

Cumby, W. P. 'The Battle of Trafalgar (an Unpublished Narrative)', *Nineteenth Century*, 96 (1899), pp. 717–28

Czisnik, M. 'Admiral Nelson's Tactics at the Battle of Trafalgar', *Journal of the Historical Association*, 89 (2004), pp. 549–59

Depeyre, M. 'Le Père Paul Hoste – fondateur de la pensée navale moderne', in *L'Évolution de la pensée navale*, 1, ed. H. Coutau-Begarie (Paris, 1993), pp. 57–78

—— *Tactiques et stratégies navales de la France et du Royaume-Uni de 1690 à 1815* (Paris, 1998)

Desbrière, E. *La Campagne maritime de 1805: Trafalgar* (Paris, 1907)

—— *The Naval Campaign of 1805: Trafalgar*, trans. C. Eastwick, 2 vols. (Oxford, 1933)

Dick, C., and O. Kretchmer *Handbuch der Seemannschaft* (Berlin, 1902)

Dickens, B. 'Merchantmen of War in Nelsons Day', *MM*, 53 (1967), pp. 35–38

Digby, K. *Journal of a Voyage into the Mediterranean, A.D. 1628*, Camden Society, o.s. 96 (London, 1868)

Douglas, H. B. *Naval Evolutions: A Memoir, Containing a Review and Refutation of the Principle Essays and Arguments Advocating Mr. Clerk's Claims in Relation to the Manœuvre of 12 April 1782* (London, 1832)

—— *A Treatise on Naval Gunnery* (London, 1820)

Drinkwater, J. *Narrative of Proceedings of the British Fleet Commanded by Admiral Sir J. Jervis 1797*, 2nd edn (London, 1840)

Duffy, M., ed. *The Parameters of British Naval Power* (Exeter, 1992)

'The Gunnery at Trafalgar: Training, Tactics or Temperament?', *Journal for Maritime Research* (2004)

—— 'Jervis: St. Vincent', in *Great Battles of the Royal Navy as Commemorated in the Gun Room, Britannia Naval College, Dartmouth*, ed. E. Grove (London, 1998), pp. 105–12

—— 'Samuel Hood, First Viscount Hood, 1724–1816', in *Precursors of Nelson: British Admirals of the Eighteenth Century*, ed. P. Le Fevre and R. Harding (London, 2000), pp. 249–78

' "... All Was Hushed up": The Hidden Trafalgar', *MM*, 91 (2005), pp. 216–40

—— and R. Morriss, eds. *The Glorious First of June 1794: A Naval Battle and Its Aftermath* (Exeter, 2001)

——, T. Farrell, and G. Sloan, eds. *Culture and Command*, Strategic Policy Studies, 3 (Exeter, 2000)

Dull, J. R. *The French Navy and American Independence: A Study of Arms and Diplomacy, 1774–1787* (Princeton, 1975)

Ekins, C. *Naval Battles from 1744 to the Peace in 1814, Critically Reviewed and Illustrated* (London, 1824)

Falconer, W., ed. *Universal Dictionary of the Marine* (London, 1771)

Fanning, A. E. *Steady as She Goes: A History of the Compass Department of the Admiralty* (London, 1986)

Farrell, T. 'Figuring out Fighting Organisation: The New Organisational Analysis in Strategic Studies', *Journal of Strategic Studies*, 19 (1996), pp. 122–35

—— 'Making Sense of Doctrine', in *Doctrine and Military Effectiveness*, ed. M. Duffy, T. Farrell and G. Sloan (Exeter, 1997), pp. 1–5

Fordyce, A. D. *Outlines of Naval Routine* (London, 1837)

Forester, C. S. *The Naval War of 1812* (London, 1957)

Fraser, E. *The Enemy at Trafalgar: An Account of the Battle from Eye-Witnesses' Narratives and Letters and Dispatches from the French and Spanish Fleet* (London, 1906)

Gardiner, R. 'The First English Frigates', *MM*, 61 (1975), pp. 163–72

—— 'The Frigate Designs of 1755', *MM*, 63 (1977), pp. 51–69

—— *The Line of Battle: The Sailing Warship, 1650–1840* (London, 1992)

—— *The First Frigates, Nine and Twelve Pounder Frigates, 1748–1815* (London, 1992)

—— *The Heavy Frigate: Eighteen Pounder Frigates, 1778–1800*, 1 (London, 1994)

——, ed. *Fleet Battle and Blockade: The French Revolutionary War, 1793–1797* (London, 1996)

——, ed. *Navies and the American Revolution, 1775–1783* (London, 1996)

Gat, A. *The Origins of Military Thought, from the Enlightenment to Clauswitz* (Oxford, 1989)

The Gentleman's Magazine, 103 vols. (London, 1731–1833)

Gicquel des Touches, A. M. 'Souvenirs d'un marin de la République', *Revue des Deux Mondes*, 28 (1805), pp. 177–201, 407–36

Gilkerson, W. *Boarders Away: With Steel, the Edged Weapons and Polearms* (Providence, RI, 1991)

Glass, R. E. 'Naval Courts Martial in Seventeenth Century England', in *New Interpretations in Naval History: Selected Papers from the Twelfth Naval History Symposium*, ed. W. B. Cogar (Annapolis, 1997), pp. 53–65

Glete, J. 'Sails and Oars: Warships and Navies in the Baltic during the Eighteenth Century, 1700–1815', in *Les Marines de guerre européennes XVIIe–XVIIIe siècles*, ed. M. Acerra, J. Merino and J. Meyer (Paris, 1985), pp. 381–415

—— 'The Oared Warship', in *The Line of Battle: The Sailing Warship, 1650–1840*, ed. R. Gardiner (London, 1992), pp. 98–105

—— *Navies and Nations: Warships, Navies and State Building in Europe and America, 1500–1860*, 2 vols. (Stockholm, 1993)

—— *Warfare at Sea, 1500–1650: Maritime Conflicts and the Transformation of Europe* (London, 2000)

Gordon, A. *The Rules of the Game: Jutland and British Naval Command* (London, 1996)

—— 'The Doctrine Debate: Having the Last Word', in *Doctrine and Military Effectiveness*, ed. M. Duffy, T. Farrell and G. Sloan (Exeter, 1997), pp. 46–50

Gouk, P. M. 'Acoustics in the Early Royal Society 1660–1680', *Notes and Records of the Royal Society of London*, 36 (1982), pp. 155–75

Goussencourt, Chevalier de 'A Journal of the Cruise of the Fleet of His Most Christian Majesty, under the Command of the Count De Grasse-Tilly in 1781 and 1782', in *The Operations of the French Fleet under the Count de Grasse in 1781–2: As Described in Two Contemporary Journals*, ed. J. G. Shea (New York, 1971), pp. 26–134

Gower, R. H. *A Treatise on the Theory and Practice of Seamanship* (London, 1808)

Greenwood, D. 'James, Lord De Saumarez, 1757–1836', in *British Admirals of the Napoleonic Wars: The Contemporaries of Nelson*, ed. P. Le Fevre and R. Harding (London, 2005), pp. 245–70

Grenfell, R. *The Art of the Admiral* (London, 1937)

Grimble, I. *Seawolf: The Life of Admiral Cochrane* (London, 1978)

Hamilton, R. V., ed. *Letters and Papers of Admiral of the Fleet Sir Thomas Byam Martin*, 3 vols., NRS, 12, 19, 24 (London, 1898–1903)

—— and J. K. Laughton, eds. *The Recollections of James Anthony Gardner, 1755–1814*, NRS, 31 (London, 1906)

Hamstead, J. *A Treatise on Naval Tactics* (London, 1808)

Hannay, D., ed. *Letters of Lord Hood, 1781–2*, NRS, 3 (London, 1895)

—— *A Short History of the Royal Navy, 1217–1815*, 2 vols. (London, 1898)

Harland, J. H. *Seamanship in the Age of Sail* (London, 1985)

—— *Ships and Seamanship: The Maritime Prints of J. J. Baugean* (London, 2000)

—— 'Darcy Lever as Inspiration for Jane Austen's "Mr Darcy" ', *MM*, 87 (2001), p. 76

Hattendorf, J. B. 'Benbow's Last Fight', in *The Naval Miscellany*, v, ed. N. A. M. Rodger (London, 1984), pp. 143–206

—— *England in the War of the Spanish Succession: A Study of the English View and Conduct of Grand Strategy, 1702–12* (New York, 1987)

—— 'Byng: Passaro, 1718', in *Great Battles of the Royal Navy as Commemorated in the Gun Room, Britannia Naval College, Dartmouth*, ed. E. Grove (Annapolis, 1994), pp. 63–71

——, ed. *Maritime History II: The Eighteenth Century* (Melbourne, 1997)

—— 'The Anglo-French Naval Wars (1689–1815) in Twentieth Century Naval Thought', *Journal for Maritime Research* (June 2001)

—— 'Sir George Rooke and Sir Cloudesley Shovell, c1650–1709 and 1650–1707', in *Precursors of Nelson: British Admirals of the Eighteenth Century*, ed. P. Le Fevre and R. Harding (London, 2000), pp. 43–78

—— and R. W. Unger, eds. *War at Sea in the Middle Ages and Renaissance* (Woodbridge, 2003)

——, R. J. B. Knight, A. W. H. Perasall, N. A. M. Rodger, and G. Till, eds. *British Naval Documents, 1204–1960*, NRS, 131 (Aldershot, 1993)

Hodges, H. W., ed. *Select Naval Documents* (Cambridge, 1922)

Holland, L. E. 'The Development of Signalling in the Royal Navy', *MM*, 39 (1953), pp. 5–26

Horsfield, J. *The Art of Leadership in War: The Royal Navy from the Age of Nelson to the End of World War II* (London, 1980)

Hoste, P. *L'Art des armées navales ou traité des évolutions navales* (Lyon, 1697)

—— *A Treatise on Naval Evolutions*, trans. J. D. Boswall (Edinburgh, 1834)

Hough, R. *Captain Bligh and Mr. Christian: The Men and the Mutiny* (London, 2000)

Howard, E. *Rattlin the Reefer*, ed. F. Marryat (London, 1836)

Howard, F. *Sailing Ships of War, 1400–1860* (Greenwich, 1979)

—— 'Early Ship Guns I: Built-up Breech Loaders', *MM*, 72 (1986), pp. 439–55

—— 'Early Ship Guns II: Swivels', *MM*, 73 (1987), pp. 49–61

Howard, G. F. 'The Early Steering Wheel', *MM*, 64 (1978), pp. 188–9

Hughes, E. A., ed. *The Private Correspondence of Admiral Lord Collingwood*, NRS, 98 (London, 1957)

Hughes, W. P. *Fleet Tactics, Theory and Practice* (Annapolis, 1986)

Hurst, A. A. 'Modern Square-Riggers: Fact and Fallacy', *Maritime South West*, 6 (1993), pp. 125–53

Hutchinson, W. *A Treatise on Practical Seamanship* (Liverpool, 1777)

—— *A Treatise on Practical Seamanship*, 2nd edn (Liverpool, 1787)

Inman, J. *An Introduction to Naval Gunnery* (Portsea, 1828)

Jackson, F. B. 'Clerk of Eldin and the British Navy', *Historian*, 23 (1961), pp. 303–15

Jackson, T. S., ed. *Logs of the Great Sea Fights*, 2 vols., NRS, 16, 18 (London, 1981)

Jagoe, D. A. 'United States Military Doctrine and Professional Military Education', in *Doctrine and Military Effectiveness*, ed. M. Duffy, T. Farrell and G. Sloan (Exeter, 1997), pp. 26–33

James, W. *Old Oak: The Life of John Jervis, Earl of St. Vincent* (London, 1930)

Kennedy, L. *Nelson and His Captains* (London, 1951)

Knight, R. J. B. 'The Introduction of Copper Sheathing into the Royal Navy, 1779–86', *MM*, 59 (1973), pp. 299–309

—— 'Early Attempts at Lead and Copper Sheathing', *MM*, 42 (1976), pp. 292–4

—— 'The Building and Maintenance of the British Fleet During the Anglo-French Wars, 1688–1815', in *Les Marines de guerre européennes, XVII*^{e}*–XVIII*^{e} *siècles*, ed. M. Acerra, J. Merino and J. Meyer (Paris, 1985), pp. 47–63

—— 'New England Forests and British Seapower: Albion Revised', *American Neptune*, 46 (1986), pp. 221–9

—— *Portsmouth Dockyard Papers, 1774–1783: The American War* (Portsmouth, 1987)

—— *The Pursuit of Victory: The Life and Achievement of Horatio Nelson* (London, 2005)

Knowles, C. H. *Observations on Naval Tactics and on the Claims of Clerk of Eldin* (London, 1830)

Knox, D. W. 'The Great Lesson from Nelson for Today', *United States Naval Institute Proceedings*, 40 (1914), pp. 295–318

—— 'The Role of Doctrine in Naval Warfare', *United States Naval Institute Proceedings*, 41 (1915), pp. 325–65

Lacour-Gayet, G. *La Marine militaire de la France sous le règne de Louis XV* (Paris, 1902)

Laird Clowes, W. *The Royal Navy: A History from the Earliest Times to the Death of Queen Victoria*, 7 vols. (London, 1897–1903)

Lambert, A. *The Last Sailing Battlefleet* (London, 1991)

—— *The Foundations of Naval History: John Knox Laughton, the Royal Navy and the Historical Profession* (London, 1998)

—— *War at Sea in the Age of Sail* (London, 2000)

—— 'Sir William Cornwallis, 1744–1815', in *Precursors of Nelson: British Admirals of the Eighteenth Century*, ed. P. Le Fevre and R. Harding (London, 2000), pp. 355–75

Laughton, J. K. 'The Scientific Study of Naval History', *Journal of the Royal United Services Institution*, 18 (1875), pp. 508–26

——, ed. *Memoirs Relating to the Lord Torrington*, Camden Society, n.s. 46 (London, 1889)

——, ed. *Journal of Rear-Admiral Bartholomew James*, NRS, 6 (London, 1896)

——, ed. *The Naval Miscellany*, 1, NRS, 20 (London, 1902)

—— 'The Journals of Henry Duncan', in *The Naval Miscellany*, ed. J. K. Laughton (London, 1902), pp. 105–211

——, ed. *Letters and Papers of Charles, Lord Barham, Admiral of the Red Squadron, 1758–1813*, 3 vols., NRS, 32, 38, 39 (London, 1907–11)

Lavery, B. 'The Origins of the 74 Gun Ship', *MM*, 63 (1977), pp. 335–50

—— *The Ship of the Line*, 2 vols. (London, 1983)

—— 'The Revolution in Naval Tactics', in *Les Marines de guerre européennes XVIIe–XVIIIe siècles*, ed. M. Acerra, J. Merino and J. Meyer (Paris, 1985), pp. 185–93

—— *The Arming and Fitting of English Ships of War, 1600–1815* (London, 1987)

—— *Nelson's Navy: The Ships, Men and Organisation, 1793–1815* (Annapolis, 1989)

—— *Building the Wooden Walls: The Design and Construction of the 74-Gun Ship Valiant* (London, 1991)

—— 'Nelson: Aboukir, 1798', in *Great Battles of the Royal Navy as Commemorated in the Gun Room, Britannia Naval College, Dartmouth*, ed. E. Grove (London, 1998), pp. 113–20

——, ed. *Shipboard Life and Organisation, 1731–1815*, NRS, 138 (Aldershot, 1998)

Le Fevre, P. 'Arthur Herbert, Earl of Torrington, 1648–1716', in *Precursors of Nelson: British Admirals of the Eighteenth Century*, ed. P. Le Fevre and R. Harding (London, 2000), pp. 19–42

—— and R. Harding, eds. *Precursors of Nelson: British Admirals of the Eighteenth Century* (London, 2000)

Lees, J. *Masting and Rigging of the English Ship of War, 1625–1860*, 2nd edn (London, 1984)

Legro, J. W. 'The Culture and Command Conundrum', in *Culture and Command*, ed. M. Duffy, T. Farrell and G. Sloan (Exeter, 2000), pp. 1–10

Lever, D. *The Young Sea Officer's Sheet Anchor*, 2nd edn (London, 1819)

Lewis, M. *The Navy of Britain: An Historical Portrait* (London, 1948)

——, ed. *A Narrative of My Professional Adventures by Sir William Dillon*, 2 vols., NRS, 93, 97 (London, 1953)

Liardet, F. L. *Professional Recollections on Points of Seamanship* (London, 1849)

Lindwall, A. 'The Encounter between Kempenfelt and De Guichen, December 1781', *MM*, 87 (2001), pp. 163–79

Llinares, S. *Marine, propulsion et technique: l'évolution du système technologique du navire de guerre français au XVIIIe siècle*, 2 vols. (Paris, 1994)

Lloyd, C., ed. *The Keith Papers: Selected from the Letters and Papers of Admiral Viscount Keith*, 3 vols., NRS, 62, 90, 96 (London, 1927–55)

Lovell, W. S. *Personal Narrative of Events from 1799 to 1815 with Anecdotes*, 2nd edn (London, 1879)

Luff, P. A. 'Matthews v Lestock: Parliament, Politics and the Navy in Mid-Eighteenth Century England', *Parliamentary History*, 10 (1991), pp. 45–62

Mackay, R. F. *Admiral Hawke* (Oxford, 1965)

——, ed. *The Hawke Papers: A Selection, 1743–1771*, NRS, 129 (Aldershot, 1990)

—— 'Edward, Lord Hawke, 1705–1781', in *Precursors of Nelson: British Admirals of the Eighteenth Century*, ed. P. Le Fevre and R. Harding (London, 2000), pp. 201–23

Mahan, A. T. *The Influence of Seapower on History, 1660–1783* (Boston, 1890)

—— *The Life of Nelson: The Embodiment of the Sea Power of Great Britain*, 2 vols. (London, 1897)

—— *Types of Naval Officers* (London, 1902)

—— *Sea Power in its Relations to the War of 1812*, 2 vols. (London, 1905)

Malcomson, R. *Warships of the Great Lakes* (London, 2001)

Maltby, W. 'Politics, Professionalism and the Evolution of Sailing Ship Tactics, 1650–1714', in *Tools of War: Instruments, Ideas and Institutions of Warfare, 1445–1871*, ed. J. A. Lynn (Illinois, 1990), pp. 53–73

Marcus, G. J. *Quiberon Bay* (London, 1960)

Markham, C. R., ed. *The Life of Captain Stephen Martin, 1666–1740*, NRS, 5 (London, 1895)

Marquardt, K. H. *Eighteenth Century Rigs and Rigging* (London, 1992)

Marryat, F. *Mr. Midshipman Easy* (London, c.1850)

—— *Frank Mildmay or the Naval Officer* (London, c.1895)

—— *The King's Own* (London, c.1896)

Marshall, J., ed. *Royal Naval Biography*, 12 vols. (London, 1828)

Martelli, A. *Seaman's Guide for Preparing Ships for Sea* (London, 1848)

Martin, E. G. *Helmsmanship* (London, 1934)

Martin-Leake, S. *The Life of Admiral Sir John Leake*, 2 vols., NRS, 52–3 (London, 1920)

May, W. E. *The Boats of Men of War* (London, 1974)

McAnally, J. H. S. 'The Purposes and Benefits of Doctrine: Why Go to All the Trouble of Having One?', in *Doctrine and Military Effectiveness*, ed. M. Duffy, T. Farrell and G. Sloan (Exeter, 1997), pp. 6–13

McRanft, B., ed. *The Vernon Papers*, NRS, 99 (London, 1958)

Monaque, R. 'Latouche-Tréville: The Admiral Who Defied Nelson', *MM*, 86 (2000), pp. 272–84

—— 'On Board H.M.S. Alexander (1796–9)', *MM*, 89 (2003), pp. 207–12

Moorsom, C. R. *On the Principles of Naval Tactics* (Birmingham, 1846)

Morland, S. *Tuba Stentoro-Phonica: An Instrument of Excellent Use, as Well at Sea as at Land Etc (A Short Discourse Touching the Nature of Sounds Etc.)* (London, 1671)

—— 'An Account of the Speaking Trumpet as It Hath Been Contrived and Published by Sir Sam. Moreland Knight and Baronet; Together with Its Uses Both at Sea and Land', *Philosophical Transactions, 1665–1678*, 6 (1671), pp. 3056–8

Morriss, R. 'The Glorious First of June: The British View of the Actions of 28, 29 May and 1 June 1794', in *The Glorious First of June 1794: A Naval Battle and Its Aftermath*, ed. M. Duffy and R. Morriss (Exeter, 2001), pp. 46–100

—— *The Royal Dockyards During the Revolutionary and Napoleonic Wars* (Leicester, 1983)

Mossel, G. P. J. *Manoeuvres met zeil-, en stoomschepen* (Amsterdam, 1865)

Mountaine, W. *The Seaman's Vade-Mecum and Defensive War by Sea* (London, 1744)

—— *The Seaman's Vade Mecum* (London, 1757)

Mundy, G. B., ed. *The Life and Correspondence of Lord Rodney* (London, 1830)

Murray, A. *Memoir of the Naval Life and Services of Admiral Sir Philip C. H. C. Durham, G.C.B.* (London, 1846)

Nares, G. S. *Seamanship*, 2nd edn (London, 1862)

The Naval Chronicle, 40 vols. (London, 1799–1818)

Newnham, G. L. *A Selection from the Public and Private Correspondence of Vice-Admiral Lord Collingwood* (London, 1828)

Nichelson, W. *A Treatise on Practical Navigation and Seamanship* (London, 1792)

Nicholas, N. H., ed. *The Dispatches and Letters of Vice Admiral Lord Viscount Nelson*, 7 vols. (London, 1845–6)

Nichols, P. *Evolution's Captain* (London, 2004)

Nisbet, J. *Half Hours at Sea: Stories of Voyage, Adventure and Wreck* (London, 1897)

Nosworthy, B. *The Anatomy of Victory: Battle Tactics, 1689–1763* (New York, 1992)

O'Brien 'Essay on the Duty of a Captain', *Naval Chronicle*, 5 (1801), pp. 213–20

O'Bryen, C. *An Essay on Naval Military Discipline in General by a Late Experienced Sea Commander* (London, 1762)

—— *Naval Evolutions* (London, 1762)

Officer, An. *A Treatise in the Theory and Practice of Seamanship, by an Officer* (London, 1793)

Oman, C. *Nelson* (London, 1947)

Oppenheim, M., ed. *The Naval Tracts of Sir William Monson*, 5 vols., NRS, 22, 23, 43, 45, 47 (London, 1902–14)

Overy, R. 'Doctrine Not Dogma: Lessons from the Past', in *Doctrine and Military Effectiveness*, ed. M. Duffy, T. Farrell and G. Sloan (Exeter, 1997), pp. 34–45

Owen, H. 'Cuthbert, Lord Collingwood', in *British Admirals of the Napoleonic Wars: The Contemporaries of Nelson*, ed. P. Le Fevre and R. Harding (London, 2005), pp. 139–64

Padfield, P. *Guns at Sea: A History of Naval Gunnery* (London, 1973)

Palmer, M. A. J. 'Lord Nelson, Master of Command', *Naval War College Review*, 41 (1988), pp. 105–16

—— 'Burke and Nelson: Decentralized Style of Command', *United States Naval Institute Proceedings*, 117/7 (1991), pp. 58–9

—— 'Sir John's Victory – The Battle of Cape St. Vincent Reconsidered', *MM*, 77 (1991), pp. 105–16

—— 'The Soul's Right Hand: Command and Control in the Age of Fighting Sail, 1652–1827', *Journal of Military History*, 111 (1997), pp. 679–706

Park, R. *Defensive War by Sea* (London, 1704)

Pasley, T. *Private Sea Journals, 1778–1782* (London, 1931)

Patoun, A. *A Complete Treatise of Practical Navigation* (London, 1762)

Pechell, S. J. *Observations upon the Defective Equipment of Ship Guns* (Corfu, 1825)

Perlmutter, A. 'Military Incompetence and Failure: A Historical, Comparative and Analytical Evaluation', *Journal of Strategic Studies*, 1 (1978), pp. 121–38

Perrin, W. G. *British Flags* (Cambridge, 1922)

——, ed. *The Naval Miscellany*, III, NRS, 63 (London, 1928)

——, ed. *Boteler's Dialogues*, NRS, 65 (London, 1929)

Pitot, H. *Theory of the Working of Ships*, trans. E. Stone (London, 1743)

Pope, D. *At 12 Mr Byng Was Shot* (London, 1962)

—— *The Great Gamble: Nelson at Copenhagen* (New York, 1972)

Rees, A. *Naval Architecture* (Newton Abbot, 1970)

Richmond, H. W., ed. *Papers Relating to the Loss of Minorca*, NRS, 42 (London, 1915)

—— *The Navy in the War of 1739–48*, 3 vols. (Cambridge, 1920)

Rickman, G. 'Mare Nostrum', in *The Sea and History*, ed. E. E. Rice (Stroud, 1996), pp. 1–14

Robinson, W. *Nautical Economy or Recollections of Events During the Last War Dedicated to the Brave Tars of Old England by a Sailor Politely Called by the Officers of the Navy Jack Nasty-Face* (London, 1836)

Robison, S. S., and M. L. *A History of Naval Tactics from 1530–1930: The Evolution of Tactical Maxims* (Annapolis, 1942)

Rodger, N. A. M., ed. *The Naval Miscellany*, v, NRS, 125 (London, 1984)

—— *The Wooden World: An Anatomy of the Georgian Navy* (London, 1986)

—— 'The Inner Life of the Royal Navy, 1750–1800: Change or Decay?', in *Les Empires en guerre et paix, 1793–1860*, ed. E. Freeman (Vincennes, 1990)

—— *The Insatiable Earl: A Life of John Montagu, 4th Earl of Sandwich, 1718–92* (London, 1993)

—— 'The State of Naval and Maritime History in Britain', in *Ubi Sumus? The State of Naval and Maritime History*, ed. J. B. Hattendorf (Newport, RI, 1994), pp. 41–57

—— 'The Exercise of Seapower and its Challenges in Maritime History', in *Maritime History*, II: *The Eighteenth Century and the Classic Age of Sail*, ed. J. B. Hattendorf (Malabar, FL, 1997), pp. 175–84

—— 'Patronage et compétences', in *Les Marines de guerre européennes, XVIIᵉ–XVIIIᵉ siècles*, ed. M. Acerra, J. Merino and J. Meyer (Paris, 1998), pp. 255–66

—— 'Weather, Geography and Naval Power in the Age of Sail', *Journal of Strategic Studies*, 22 (1999), pp. 179–200

—— 'George, Lord Anson, 1697–1762', in *Precursors of Nelson: British Admirals of the Eighteenth Century*, ed. P. Le Fevre and R. Harding (London, 2000), pp. 177–200

——, ed. *Memoirs of a Seafaring Life: The Narrative of William Spavens* (London, 2000)

—— 'Honour and Duty at Sea', *Historical Research*, 75 (2002), pp. 425–47

—— 'Form and Function in European Navies, 1660–1815', in *In het kielzog: Maritiem-historiche studies aangeboden aan Jaap R. Bruijn bij zijn vertrek als hoogleraar zeergeschiedenis aan de Universiteit Leiden*, ed. L. Akveld *et al.* (Amsterdam, 2003), pp. 85–97

—— 'Navies and the Enlightenment', in *Science and the French and British Navies, 1700–1850*, ed. P. van der Merwe (London, 2003), pp. 5–23

—— 'Image and Reality in Eighteenth Century Naval Tactics', *MM*, 89 (2003), pp. 280–96

—— *The Command of the Ocean: A Naval History of Britain, 1649–1815*, II (London, 2004)

Rosier, B. 'Fleet Repairs and Maintenance 1783–93 Reconsidered', *MM*, 84 (1998), pp. 328–33

Ryan, N. A. 'The Royal Navy and the Blockade of Brest, 1689–1805: Theory and Practice', in *Les Marines de guerre européennes, XVIIe–XVIIIe siècles*, ed. M. Acerra, J. Merino and J. Meyer (Paris, 1985)

Schomberg, A. *A Sea Manual, Recommended to the Young Officers of the Royal Navy as a Companion to the Signal Book* (London, 1789)

Scott, F. *A Square Rig Handbook* (London, 1992)

Sea Officer, A *A Narrative of the Proceedings of His Majesty's Fleet in the Mediterranean, and the Combined Fleets of France and Spain, from the Year 1741 to March 1744. Including an Accurate Account of the Late Fight near Toulon, and the Causes of Our Miscarriage* (London, 1744)

Sea-Officer *An Enquiry into the Conduct of Capt. M-N (Mostyn)* (London, 1745)

Sedgwick, J. *Golden Hints for Young Mariners* (London, 1855)

Simmons, R. *Sea-Gunner's Vade Mecum* (London, 1812)

Smyth, W. H. *The Sailor's Word-Book* (London, 1991)

Southey, R. *The Life of Nelson* (London, 1813)

Spinney, D. *Rodney* (London, 1969)

—— 'Rodney and the Saintes: A Reassessment', *MM*, 68 (1982), pp. 377–89

Steel, D. *The Elements and Practice of Rigging and Seamanship*, 2 vols. (London, 1794)

Stephens, T. J. *Memoirs of Admiral the Right Honourable the Earl of St. Vincent*, 2 vols. (London, 1844)

Sulivan, J. A. 'Graves and Hood', *MM*, 69 (1983), pp. 175–94

Sweetman, J., ed. *The Great Admirals: Command at Sea, 1587–1945* (Annapolis, 1997)

Syrett, D. *Shipping and the American War, 1775–1783: A Study of British Transport Organisation* (London, 1970)

—— *The Royal Navy in European Waters During the American Revolutionary War* (Columbia, SC, 1998)

—— 'Count-Down to the Saints: A Strategy of Detachments and the Quest for Naval Supremacy in the West Indies 1780–2', *MM*, 87 (2001), pp. 150–62

Taylor, A. H. 'Admiral the Honourable Sir George Elliot', *MM*, 35 (1949), pp. 316–32

Thursfield, H. G., ed. *Five Naval Journals, 1789–1817* (London, 1951)

Todd, J., and W. B. Whall *Practical Seamanship*, 5th edn (London, 1903)

Totten, B. J. *Naval Text-Book* (New York, 1864)

Tracy, N. *Nelson's Battles: The Art of Victory in the Age of Sail* (London, 1996)

Tritten, J. J. 'Doctrine and Fleet Tactics in the Royal Navy', in *A Doctrine Reader: The Navies of United States, Great Britain, France, Italy, and Spain*, ed. J. J. Tritten and L. Donolo (Newport, RI, 1995), pp. 1–36

—— and L. Donolo, eds. *A Doctrine Reader: The Navies of the United States, Great Britain, France, Italy and Spain* (Newport, RI, 1995)

Tunstall, W. C. B., ed. *The Byng Papers*, 3 vols., NRS, 67, 68, 70 (London, 1930–2)

—— *Naval Warfare in the Age of Sail*, ed. N. Tracy (London, 1990)

Van Creveld, M. *Command in War* (Cambridge, MA, 1985)

Villiers, A. *Give Me a Ship to Sail* (London, 1958)

Wareham, T. *The Star Captains* (London, 2001)

—— *Frigate Commander* (Barnsley, 2004)

Warner, D. J. 'Telescopes for Land and Sea', *Rittenhouse*, 12/2 (1998), pp. 33–54

Warner, O. *The Life and Letters of Vice Admiral Lord Collingwood* (London, 1968)

Weber, R. E. J. 'The Introduction of the Single Line Ahead as a Battle Formation by the Dutch 1665-6', *MM*, 73 (1987), pp. 5–20

Weigley, R. F. *The Age of Battles: The Quest for Decisive Warfare from Breitenfeld to Waterloo* (Bloomington, 1991)

West, J. *Gunpowder, Government, and War in the Mid-Eighteenth Century* (Woodbridge, 1991)

Wheeler, D. A. 'The Influence of the Weather During the Camperdown Campaign of 1797', *MM*, 77 (1991), pp. 47–54

White, C. *1797: Nelson's Year of Destiny* (Stroud, 1998)

White, T. *Naval Researches; or, a Candid Inquiry into the Conduct of Admirals Byron, Graves, Hood, and Rodney, in the Actions Off Grenada, Chesapeake, St. Christopher's, and of the Ninth and Twelfth of April, 1782: Being a Refutation of the Plans and Statements of Mr. Clerk, Rear Admiral Ekins and Others* (London, 1830)

White, W. H. *A Manual of Naval Architecture for the Use of Officers of the Royal Navy, Officers of the Mercantile Marine, Yachtsmen, Shipowners and Shipbuilders* (London, 1900)

Williams, G. *The Prize of All the Oceans* (London, 1999)

Willis, S. B. A. 'Fleet Performance and Capability in the Eighteenth Century Royal Navy', *War in History*, 11 (2004), pp. 373–92

—— 'The High Life: Topmen in the Age of Sail', *MM*, 90 (2004), pp. 152–66

—— 'The Capability of Sailing Warships, Part 1: Windward Performance', *Northern Mariner*, 13/4 (2004), pp. 29–39

—— 'The Capability of Sailing Warships, Part 2: Manœuvrability', *Northern Mariner*, 14/3 (2005), pp. 57–68

Wilson, T. *Flags at Sea* (London, 1986)

Index

Entries in bold type refer to an illustration on that page.